Perennial Gardens for Texas

In Memory Of

Adele Wilson

2000

Given By

Sonora Women's Club

© DEMCO, INC.—Archive Safe

Perennial Gardens *for* Texas

Julie Ryan

 University of Texas Press, Austin

Frontispiece: The old-fashioned garden of the San Antonio Botanical Center, as it appeared soon after the Center's opening, overflowing with mealy blue sage, lythrum, rose mallows, and annuals such as snapdragons and begonias. The herb garden appears in middle ground.

Second paperback printing, 2002

Requests for permission to reproduce material from this work should be sent to Permissions, University of Texas Press, Box 7819, Austin, TX 78713-7819.

♾ The paper used in this publication meets the minimum requirements of American National Standard for Information Sciences—Permanence of Paper for Printed Library Materials, ANSI Z39.48-1984.

Library of Congress Cataloging-in-Publication Data

Ryan, Julie, date
    Perennial gardens for Texas / by Julie Ryan — 1st ed.
        p.   cm.
    Includes bibliographical references and index.
    ISBN 0-292-78106-7 (cloth : alk. paper)
    ISBN 0-292-77089-8 (pbk : alk. paper)
    1. Perennials—Texas.   2. Gardens—Texas.   I. Title.
SB434.R93   1998
635.9′32′09764—dc21   97-4692

To the benevolent Power that sparks new life in buried seeds and human hearts alike, and to those who nourish both by tending gardens.

৯৯ Contents

❧ Part Three. Plants and Planting

✧ Part Four. Plant Charts

✺ Maps

✺ Tables

𝓟 Preface

As you drive through any little Texas town, look hard enough and you will find a flower garden. Its design may seem haphazard, and the plants may be whatever the nursery had in stock or the neighbors had to share. It will contain the flowers that "do" with a minimum of fuss, either annuals newly seeded each season or perennials that regrow faithfully year after year. Some of the perennials may have grown there for twenty years, for a gardener who seasons the soil to their liking, gives them just the right amount of water, and applies a simple remedy to quell the occasional pest or disease. Some may have survived the demise of the gardener and the collapse of the house, continuing to push their blooms out through a tangle of weeds in spite of no care at all. Such flowers are the subject of this book, along with the hardy bulbs, foliage plants, perennial grasses, and old-fashioned roses that keep on keeping on.

Not only old-time favorites are included here, but also myriad other plants. There are recent hybrids that are true improvements on the old garden varieties. Southern and southwestern native plants, the subjects of my first book, appear as well, including some new to the nursery trade and a few worthy ones still awaiting commercial introduction. There are also exotic plants from comparable climates of the world that our old-time gardeners knew well and others they would have grown if they had only known about them: lilies from South America, daffodils from Spain, flowering herbs from Greece. Surprisingly, books and journals of the past and conversations with elderly gardeners suggest that more plant varieties were widely known fifty years ago than the typical American homeowner with a flower bed has heard of today. Conversely, some English gardeners grew and appreciated our native plants before we did ourselves. Exotic specimens proven in their own native climates, similar to our own and as difficult, continue to make their way into the American market.

Here, then, is a selection of perennial flowers and their garden companions, chosen during eight years of gardening and study with gardeners, nurserypeople, and horticulturists from all over Texas and parts of Louisiana, as well as library research and correspondence with gardeners elsewhere. My purposes in writing are several:

First, I want to present the practical benefits and personal joys of gardening with perennials to those not yet in the know. From a practical standpoint, flower gardens in general are a boon in tough economic times. They brighten one's surroundings and boost the spirit—inexpensively. While the economic downturn of the 1980s reduced nursery sales in general, sales of blooming plants flourished. This may be because flowers in the landscape give surprising pleasure for a minimum investment, when a major landscape renovation or home remodeling eludes the budget. And perennials prolong that investment's dividends over successive years. They generally require much less labor and expense in successive seasons than annuals: dividing, at most, not clearing beds, cultivating, and replanting. And they repay the labor generously, by multiplying. They can enable a flower collection to spread from one bed to many, and to the gardens of neighbors, within a few years.

Gardening with perennials offers two additional special pleasures. One is the satisfaction of observing and participating in their yearly growth cycle, from earth-hidden root to leaf and flower and back again. The other is the beauty unfolded by their year-after-year development. Perennial plantings mature and interweave at the hands of nature, the gardener, and time into forms more beautiful and surprising than a season's growth of annuals, however pretty, can ever give.

This book is also intended to aid southern and southwestern gardeners frustrated by northeastern and West Coast publications and plant sources. Until recently, perennials suited to Texas and similar regions in other states had been given short shrift. Many books on perennials accurately reflect the best plants and proper care for gardens in New England—and California—and England! Most present ambiguities and inaccuracies in regard to Texas and the similar regions of New Mexico, Oklahoma, and the rest of the Lower and Middle South, however. Mail-order catalogs omit heat-resistant plants and label plants "hardy" that a month of summer here would shrivel. The demands of this part of the country are special. Plants must be conditioned to drought, extreme heat, and alternations of heat and cold that seemingly change seasons in an instant. They and their gardeners must withstand the metabolic stresses of summer heat that doesn't let up even at night. Gulf Coast dwellers deal with a narrower, if still high, temperature range, it is true, but they are plagued equally by difficult soils and by the special problems of high humidity. To date, neither garden books nor suppliers present the wide range of plants suited to these conditions.

Another new tool is offered here: basic knowledge of the vegetational regions of the near-Southwest and the South, and of the conditions that determine which plants thrive there. Knowing something of the local soil, climate, and characteristic native plant communities not only makes home more one's own, it helps one garden and experiment more intelligently. This book presents Texas regions as models and describes their conditions in sufficient detail to

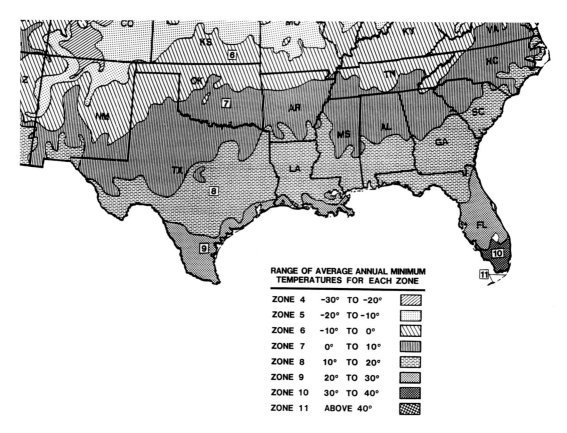

RANGE OF AVERAGE ANNUAL MINIMUM TEMPERATURES FOR EACH ZONE		
ZONE 4	-30° TO -20°	
ZONE 5	-20° TO -10°	
ZONE 6	-10° TO 0°	
ZONE 7	0° TO 10°	
ZONE 8	10° TO 20°	
ZONE 9	20° TO 30°	
ZONE 10	30° TO 40°	
ZONE 11	ABOVE 40°	

Map 1. USDA hardiness zones for the South and near-Southwest. From USDA Plant Hardiness Zone Map, issued January 1990. United States Department of Agriculture, Agricultural Research Service, Miscellaneous Publication Number 1475.

provide a basis for comparison to similar regions elsewhere. Gardeners in eastern New Mexico, Oklahoma, Arkansas, Louisiana, Mississippi, Alabama, Georgia, Florida, and the Carolinas, as well as Texas, should find it helpful.

Perennials presented in this book include both herbaceous perennials, which die back seasonally and then regrow from the roots, and ones with persistent woody lower stems. Some perennials need to be dug up, divided, and replanted after a year or more to thrive. Others live undisturbed for several years, even a human lifetime. A few biennials, which generally grow to blooming size the first season and flower and decline the second, are also included. As you may know, annuals, by contrast, sprout, bloom,

set seed, and die in one year. Reseeding annuals appropriate to perennial gardens are listed, as well.

Charming and vigorous antique roses, invaluable for their contribution to the flower garden as shrubs, climbers, and trailers, are also discussed here. So are complementary small ornamental trees and flowering and evergreen shrubs.

In the pages ahead, Part One, "Gardens," gives the broad outlines of the perennial garden tradition, notes influences in Texas, and presents a sampler of different kinds of perennial gardens, from rock gardens to wildflower gardens to shade gardens, picturing colorful and widely different examples from all across the state.

Part Two, "Regions," introduces the reader to the major ecological regions of Texas and important climatic influences. Each region is both described and pictured in photos of wilderness and of characteristic gardens, grand and small. The gardeners' comments on culture are included when possible. By the end of Part Two, the reader will have glimpsed some thirty different Texas gardens, from desert to bayou.

Part Three, "Plants and Planting," presents more than three hundred perennials suited to the regions of Texas and related states. The plants featured are by no means all of the good ones for the regions considered. They are a selection of the most reliable and available, those slightly more tricky or rare for gardeners who want a challenge, and a few obscure ones that have been so fabulous for one ecstatic gardener that the rest of the world should hear. All are available, at least by mail order. Most are plants that thrive in several regions and are used enthusiastically by many knowledgeable gardeners. Suppositions have been weeded out to the best of my ability; if a plant is recommended for a region, it is because at least one reliable person living there has grown it and reported on it. Not all plants have been tried in all regions.

Flowers about which there is already extensive published information, such as chrysanthemums and dahlias, are not included in this book. A few plants are excluded in favor of more versatile ones; standard cannas and gladioli, awkward in many garden situations, are examples. (With space for a limited number of plants, those included are attractive for general garden use.)

Part Four includes charts that provide easy reference to the plant descriptions in Part Three.

In the past thirty years, we had almost forgotten the gardens that our grandparents tended. Air-conditioning drew us indoors. The demands of two careers left most families seemingly without leisure. The all-green lawns and shrubscapes of the 1950s lingered on. These circumstances did not banish our recollections or stifle our imaginations, however, nor

our desire for color, charm, and fragrance in the home landscape. Now homeowners and apartment dwellers seek out plants and garden designs with just those qualities. Commercial designers are rejecting the formula of lawns, clipped evergreen shrubs, and massed annuals in favor of plantings that include perennials for the casual freedom or formal opulence they can bring to corporate landscapes. Interest in gardening, edible and ornamental, has grown, as well; it is now Americans' leading leisure-time activity. The more mechanized, noisy, and hectic life becomes, the more we seek peace in the place emblematic of both life's beginnings and its perfection: the garden.

This book was written to be a guide to such gardeners, to awaken them to new possibilities. Gardens as vivid and gorgeous as any in England or France can thrive here. They must simply be achieved with different plants, and they will reflect the region's special character.

The gardeners from whom I learned, including those who kindly shared the featured gardens, are old-timers. Some are young in age but have garnered the garden lore of their parents and grandparents and have themselves gardened for twenty years or more. Others first put spade to soil a half-century or more ago. I owe a special debt to my own grandmothers, who made gardens thrive in the dust storms, droughts, and blue northers of West Texas. Many gardeners who helped me in this effort had just such a mama, aunt, or granddad at whose knee their interest began. All confirmed my presentiment that gardeners include a disproportionate number of nice people to know, and that gardening naturally improves one's patience, health, hopefulness, and delight in life.

A garden is a collection of surprise packages. One never knows which will open next, and every season is different. It is hoped that this book will be the first gift in a series of wonderful surprises discovered in the perennial garden: your own garden, in your locale, with plants and techniques especially suited.

৪ Acknowledgments

My deep respect and gratitude go to the late Carroll Abbott, Lynn Lowrey, and Benny Simpson, and to Barton Warnock and Geoffrey Stanford, whose special knowledge and enthusiasm showed me the green world I had always loved in a new light and who encouraged me to learn more and to write.

I would also like to thank my friend, Dr. Althea Romaine Welch, who midwifed this project. Her help compiling the research and her suggested revisions, continued encouragement, and support made me a better writer and this a better book.

I am especially grateful to the following for sharing their gardens and information. They participated in detailed exchanges of data on the adaptation, growth, and care of perennial plants in Texas and Louisiana during a four-year survey.

Raydon Alexander, Milberger Nursery, San Antonio
Cleo Barnwell, Shreveport, La.
Bob Wilson, Nicholson-Hardie Nursery, Dallas
Thaddeus M. Howard, D.V.M., San Antonio
Bob Brackman, Dallas Arboretum and Botanical Gardens
David Christensen, David's and Royston Bulb Co., Gardena, Ca.
Minnie Colquitt, Shreveport, La.
Patty Leslie Pasztor, independent ethnobotanist, San Antonio
Paul Cox, San Antonio Botanical Center
Bette Edmundsen, Hill Country Nursery, Fort Davis
John Fairey, Yucca-Do Nursery, Waller
Carl Schoenfeld, Yucca-Do Nursery, Waller
Peggy Hammel, Peggy Hammel's Garden, Euless
Margaret Kane, The Kane Patch, San Antonio
Steve Lowe, San Antonio Zoo
Eric Lautzenheiser, San Antonio Botanical Center
Michael Shoup, Antique Rose Emporium, Independence
Liz Druitt, Peaceable Kingdom School, Washington, Texas
Barton H. Warnock, Ph.D., Alpine
Glyn Whiddon, Stuart Place Nursery, Harlingen

Celia Jones, Sisters' Bulb Farm, Gibsland, La.
Pamela Puryear, Navasota
Rosa Finsley, Kings Creek Landscaping, Dallas
Logan Calhoun, Kings Creek Landscaping, Dallas
Burr Williams, Sibley Learning Center, Midland
Doug Fuhrman, Corpus Christi
Morris Clint, Palm Garden Nursery, Brownsville
Jack and Mary Scott, Quinto Pintada, Alpine
Marihelen Kamp, Ph.D., Department of Plant and
    Soil Science, Texas Tech University, Lubbock
Joe Woodard, Dallas Historical Rose Society
Helen Jarman, Department of Parks, Lubbock
Russell Weber, Austin
Esther Procter, Procter's Plantland, Weatherford
Bob Lanham, Lanham Nursery, Midland
Connie Patterson, Love and Son Nursery, Amarillo
John White, Texas Agricultural Extension Service,
    El Paso
Greg Grant, Texas Agricultural Extension Service,
    San Antonio
Nancy Brillos, City of San Antonio Parks and
    Recreation Department
John Dodd, Dodd's Family Tree, Fredericksburg
James Taylor, Wolfe Nursery, Lubbock
Jo N. Evans, Haphazard Plantation, Frogmore, La.

Many of the above-named individuals also gra-
ciously permitted photography of their gardens.
These are identified as they appear herein.

    And thanks to the following for welcoming me
into their nurseries, gardens, and, in some cases,
their homes.

Herb Durand, Lowrey Nursery, Houston
Alice Staub, Houston
Marie C. Sullivan, Houston
Lynn Lowrey, Lowrey Nursery, Houston
Mitzi Van Sant, Austin
Denny Miller, Chihuahuan Desert Research
    Institute, Alpine
Ted Turner, Turner's Gardenland, Corpus Christi
Doug Williams, Houston Arboretum
John Carpenter, Native Plant Society of Texas,
    Alpine
Sue Gardner, Ph.D., Corpus Christi Botanical
    Center
Ying Doon Moi, San Antonio Botanical Center
Kirby Kendrick, Santa Fe
Will Fleming, Tomball
James David, Gardens, Austin
Father Robert Williams, Holy Name of Mary Old
    Catholic Church, Austin
Ralph Pincus, North Haven Gardens, Dallas
Rick Archie, Fort Worth
Willis E. Gentry, Sr., Willis E. Gentry, Jr., and
    George Gentry, Gentry's Garden Centers, Laredo

To those who read and critiqued parts of the
manuscript:

Thaddeus M. Howard, San Antonio
Pam Puryear, Heritage Rose Society
Joe Woodard, Dallas Historical Rose Society
Arnold Davis, Native Prairies Association of Texas
Logan Calhoun, Kings Creek Landscaping, Dallas
Greg Grant, Texas Agricultural Extension Service,
    San Antonio

For their hospitality and helpful critique of the manuscript, recognition is due Katie Ferguson of Lowrey Nursery, Houston, and Duncan Alford of Lambert Landscape Company, now deceased.

I would also like to thank:

The Native Plant Society of Texas.
My early teachers of English, French, and writing, especially the late Mrs. Ivy F. Blair of Dallas and Zulfikar Ghose, professor of literature at the University of Texas at Austin and kind advisor in my early writing efforts.
I owe a great debt to my grandmothers, who gardened, and to my mother, who first put a book in front of me.

I am most thankful also to the following:

Joanna Hitchcock, John Kyle, Theresa May, Shannon Davies, Carolyn Cates Wylie, and the staff of the University of Texas Press who participated in this book;
Charles Beard, Brenda Robinson, Jean Robillard, Robert Smith of Paul Talley Photography, photographers Todd Johnson and Robert Goodman, Suzanne McCotter, James Ryan, and other friends and family members who helped in the final details of manuscript and photography completion;
and my late friend, Linda Lunsford, who encouraged me and many other writers and artists.

PART ONE

Gardens

Perennial border for a 1960s "ranch" style house. Former home of Bob Wilson and Ray Hapes, Dallas.

In Search of Regional Gardens

Il faut cultiver notre jardin.
(We must cultivate our garden.)

—*Voltaire*

No one dreams the gardens to be found in Texas without seeing them firsthand. In 1986, Texas' sesquicentennial, I began traveling the state in search of wonderful perennial gardens and attractive perennials that thrive in our conditions. Flower gardens were enjoying a revival, but for perennials, especially, plants and information useful here were in short supply. Individuals and city governments wanted regionally hardy, water- and fertilizer-conserving landscapes. Native plants had been welcomed as the solution, with enthusiasm and success. Indigenous plants such as those in *Landscaping with Native Texas Plants* (Wasowski and Ryan) are indeed thrifty and practical, colorful and charming. They are spirit and substance of our scant remaining wilderness and living mementos of the land as our forebears knew it. As such, they are an irreplaceable biological and cultural resource. And they make gardens that are truly expressive of regional character in an America of indistinguishable shopping strips. In addition, they provide an escape from the limited palette of "standard landscape materials." Even so, native plants do not display the entire range of forms, colors, and textures—nor in some cases the well-mannered behavior—that the plant world offers gardens. Putting regional pride aside, many exotic plants are as Southwest-hardy and thrifty as those native here. Most experienced gardeners combine any and all plants that suit the conditions on their land, the chosen type of garden, and the amount of effort they intend to expend. Not all Texas native plants adapt to the well-watered, fertile conditions necessary for many other desirable plants. A decade ago, it seemed to me that a far wider range of choices was available for regionally sensitive and sensible gardens, including native and introduced plants, old and new varieties.

I hoped to find not only new plants but also new styles of gardens. The landscape seemed to be held hostage by a formula adopted in the 1950s. Landscapes remained like fifties architecture, simple, spare, and unadorned. Large expanses of mowed lawn and massed evergreen shrubbery were the rule. This was the final development of an earlier tradition; it was the "landscape style" originated in eighteenth-century England, written small. There, and in American examples like New York's Central Park, ornamental gardens were abandoned in favor of grassy and wooded terrain sculpted and planted to resemble idealized wilderness. Sweeping vistas were its focal points, and only a bridge or gazebo told it was the work of human hands. The dominance of lawns, trees, and shrubs was what translated from the English landscape style to the small homesites of twentieth-century America. It became a formula applied unquestioningly, with only the mowing and trimming preserved and none of the wild,

country-like vistas of the original English vision. By the 1980s, American homeowners were eager to enjoy the color, ornament, and surprise of other styles, periods, and places.

My search was richly rewarded. I found not only gardens of perennials, but also gardens of cacti, tropicals, bog plants, beach plants, roses, and flowering shrubs. Despite Texas' harsh climates and difficult soils, gardens could be found in every locale. Several especially large and fine gardens are described at length herein, along with more than a score of equally delightful small gardens from the Trans-Pecos desert to the moist Piney Woods.

Mealy blue sage, white allium, and yellow-green clouds of dill survive in a neglected garden in the little town of Cranfills Gap.

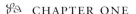

CHAPTER ONE

Cottage Gardens and Perennial Borders: A Historical Sketch

To devise these living pictures from simple well-known flowers seems to me to be the best thing . . . simple and modest, bold and gorgeous . . . pictures of living beauty.

—*Gertrude Jekyll*

Cottage gardens and perennial borders have been much touted in popular magazines in recent years. The profuse bloom, variety, and casual arrangement of cottage gardens are very appealing. Their scale is also well suited to small modern homesites. In addition, cottage gardens that are properly prepared and planted require surprisingly little maintenance. Classic perennial borders, for their part, have been considered the highest expression of the art of gardening. The design principles embodied in the grand borders of the great English gardens can also be applied to dazzling effect in gardens of simple plan and small dimensions.

Several gardens that appear in the pages to follow are interpretations of the cottage garden as it originated in England. However, the cottage garden in its simplest form was a universal of human society. Whether surrounding a Tudor cottage or a grass hut, primitive home gardens of food crops and herbs for medicinal, magical, and culinary purposes existed in virtually every agricultural society. The floral beauty of cottage plants in these early gardens was incidental to their practical and ritual uses. Commoners found greengrocer, pharmacy, and toiletry shop in the plants outside the cottage door.

In England the cottage garden can be traced from its nascence as the mainstay of the small tenant farmers of the late fourteenth and the fifteenth centuries. Their economic status had been elevated from that of landless serfs to free cottagers. This change was a result of the labor shortage and housing surplus that followed the bubonic plague or Black Death. Cottagers kept bees and grew herbs and vegetables, as well as fruits and berries from the woods and hedgerows, for food, flavoring, and medicine. As the general populace rose above bare subsistence in the sixteenth and seventeenth centuries, they nevertheless kept to these old ways of gardening.

During the 1500s, purely ornamental plants and plantings began to appear in English cottage gardens. A note of formality entered with the "knot" garden, made of dwarf shrubs, herbs, and flowers planted and clipped in intricate intertwining designs. An influx of exotic plants from the Near East and, in the seventeenth century, from the New World, further enriched cottage gardens. These remained the gardens of the commoners, nonetheless; the nobility's tastes were less constant. During the Restoration, the French *parterre* style became the rage. Many knot gardens of the Renaissance were dug up and replaced with patterns of clipped box-wood, lavender, or santolina, filled with flowers and colored pebbles or glass. This simulated "embroidery on the ground," or *broderie par terre*, became known simply as *parterre*.

Destruction of traditional gardens continued in the Victorian era, when "bedding out" was the height of fashion. (This term refers not to sleeping in the open air, but rather to the setting out of greenhouse-grown small flowering and foliage plants in ornate patterns reminiscent of Oriental carpets.) All the while, the old cottage style was preserved in the gardens of the poor, country people and cottage artisans.

The English cottage garden of the nineteenth century was characterized by mingled plantings of ornamentals, herbs, vines, and fruit trees arranged

This vegetable patch glows with dill in spring flower and pink native Texas phlox. Garden of Julie and W. J. Grichar, Bremond.

A rose-covered cottage overlooks foundation plantings of pink oxalis and fragrant stock and an island bed of native columbine and pansies. Former home of Mitzi Van Sant and Lance Bertelsen, Austin.

informally. There was no lawn. Definition was given to the green and flowery profusion by paths or walkways from gate to door and by a surrounding wall or fence. Potted plants, trellises, and small stone or bricked areas for outdoor seating were common features.

Starting late in the last century, the cottage garden was revived and reinterpreted as an artistic garden style. This was a reaction to the highly artificial gardens then in vogue, increasing urbanization, and, as venerable English gardener Roy Genders puts it, "rapidly growing industrial ugliness."

This interpretation of the English cottage garden as a conscious style came at the hands of garden innovators of the time, of whom the artist Gertrude Jekyll is considered to have been the most influential. She at once honored the early cottage gardens and accommodated the landscape needs of contemporary cottagers. The new cottage style was "a romanticized concept . . . more closely related to a reduced version of the herbaceous border of a big estate than the truly traditional 'cottage' garden," writes English author and naturalist John Feltwell. Jekyll has many successors in the cottage tradition. Margery Fish, whose famous cottage garden is at East Lambrook

Manor in Somerset, brought an emphasis on individual plants, rather than the large drifts and complex color schemes of Jekyll's gardens. Penelope Hobhouse and Rosemary Verey continue to apply painterly color theory to gardens, as Jekyll first did.

Miss Jekyll's pivotal role in garden design transformed more than cottage gardens. She shrugged aside the previous conventions of the formal, evergreen Italianate garden, the French *parterre*, and the sometimes hideous Victorian "bedding out." She is viewed as having synthesized, and provided a design theory for, the major innovations of her time. In her own work, she accepted colleague William Robinson's broad lawns and "wild gardens" of woods and waters planted with exotic plants—but she resisted the appeals of his enthusiasts that gardens should be abolished altogether in favor of such contrived "wilderness." In designing ornamental borders, she did not stick with the earlier, purist style of herbaceous border composed entirely of perennials, as espoused by a predecessor, Mr. Shirley Hibberd. Rather, she developed this stricter style of perennial border into the mixed border of perennials, foliage plants, shrubs, annuals, and bulbs, usually backed by large evergreen shrubs.

Texas extension horticulturist William C. Welch, a proponent of traditional garden plants and styles, has described the perennial border as "just a strip of the cottage garden." The border does offer profusion and variety similar to that of a cottage garden and also many of the same plants, but they are arranged according to a far more ordered plan. The border is not merely an elongated bed full of randomly planted perennials and complementary plants. Classic perennial borders were painstakingly designed according to height, form, hue, and bloom times, with definite color schemes. Thus is provided a changing array of color and form, with some new beauty every week. Foliage color and texture complement bloom and add interest in themselves. Flowers offer shapes from spikes to sprays to heavy, nodding clusters.

In making borders, Gertrude Jekyll also employed sophisticated color theory developed in her years as a painter. Her gardens played on the responses of the human eye to color. In the original Jekyll gardens, each border started with dark and gray foliage with the flowers in primarily blue and gray-blue, accented by white, pale yellows, and pale pinks. Next were strong yellows, and then oranges and reds. The color continuum then reprised the golds, yellows, and pastels, ending this time with purples and lilacs rather than blues. This arrangement made each planting accentuate the color of the adjoining one, in the same way that staring at red lettering will cause a green after-image when the eyes are closed. Focusing on the blues at one end of the border, for example, creates a yellow after-image that intensifies the nearby yellows, to dazzling effect. (As the Amelia Lay Hodges Garden at the Dallas Arboretum matures, visitors have an opportunity to experience firsthand the effects of Jekyll's techniques, employed in this 1989 garden.)

As created by Gertrude Jekyll, the perennial border is an art form as plastic, subtle in design, and sophisticated in color scheme as any other visual art. The techniques that make such gardens superb are not merely of historic interest; they can be employed in much simpler plantings today.

Miss Jekyll's gardens, paired with the architecture of her collaborator, Sir Edward Lutyens, created a rich heritage for England and brought new richness, diversity, and charm to the gardening world. In recent years, a new interest in Jekyll's legacy has arisen in the United States. However, Texas examples of cottage gardens, perennial borders, and "wild gardens" draw on diverse sources besides our English heritage.

Gardens in the Southwest betray a strong Hispanic influence, dating back to the gardens of the early Spanish missions. The patio, derived from the Moorish courtyards of the eighth century during the Moors' domination of Spain, is one element transmitted here by the Spanish. It became a given of southwestern homesites.

Long before European settlement here, in Mexico and Central America the native peoples made dooryard gardens of squashes, corn, beans, other vegetables and grains, and medicinal herbs. In South Texas, one still catches glimpses of colorful, crazy-quilt yards where hibiscus, gourds, peppers, zinnias, coral vine, tomatoes, corn, and beans mingle freely over bare, dry soil. Perhaps they give a glimmer of cottage traditions of our Indian and Hispanic forebears—an intriguing subject for further exploration.

German settlers of Central Texas made cottage-style gardens of irises, herbs, roses, annuals, and perennials, brightly colored and neat as pins. Such plants grow today on the grounds of the Pioneer Museum in Fredericksburg, surrounding a reconstructed house and outbuildings of the mid-1800s, and at numerous private homes.

Another garden style seems unique to the southern United States, although its equivalent probably exists in other hot, dry parts of the globe. Along a sandy riverbottom northeast of Independence, Texas, I found a garden probably more typical of early Texas gardens than any of the others I saw: a "swept yard." From her 1915 frame cottage,

Bright annuals fill a crescent bed in front of the post office at Round Top.

perfectly adapted to nature as nature is manifested here. There were no shrubs against the house to harbor snakes. The plants that grew survived on rainfall; conveniences such as rubber garden hoses and sprinkler heads, much less irrigation systems, did not exist here during this garden's first thirty years. Water and leisure were too scarce for such nonsense as hauling water for a posy.

Many people aged fifty or older with whom I have talked remember such gardens from childhood. Black and white folk alike kept swept yards. My father recalled them from Central Texas, around Tracy and Rockdale. Gardeners in areas as diverse as the Piney Woods and the Rolling Plains insist that the swept yard was more typical of early Texas gardens than profusely planted, European-style plots. These Raydon Alexander of San Antonio recalls as fashionable luxuries of the well-to-do, modeled on garden plans purchased from traveling garden designers and made with mail-order plants. "Ordinary people's" gardens were of annuals such as larkspur, poppies, zinnias, cornflower, globe amaranth, celosia, cosmos, and amaranthus, which they sometimes planted over bearded iris for color after iris time, as Mr. Alexander's mother did. Or they were swept yards, like this one.

One wonders, thinking back on old-timers' talk of "chopping cotton," if the days spent stooped over the rows with a hoe made householders unable to abide the sight of a weed in their own tidy yards, and so they chopped at home when they weren't chopping for pay. Mrs. Breedlove lived into her nineties before laying down her hoe. With its minimal pattern and austere ground, her yard was curiously modernistic, almost abstract. It was also a garden that declared its gardener to be both thrifty and diligent, and no doubt about it.

Addie Breedlove looked out on a meticulously clean, almost severe landscape. There was no lawn and not a stray weed. Here was a rosebush, there a flower, there a bulb, as carefully placed as the knots in a knot-tied afghan. Every weed was pulled, and the sandy ground was swept with a broom, as one would sweep a room. Along the fence and spotted around the yard were an ancient fig, a pear, and a crape myrtle. In spring and early summer, verbenas, 'Seven Sisters' rose, amaryllis, and crinum lilies bloomed. A boxwood had been carved into a topiary.

Mrs. Breedlove's mother lived in this house before her and kept the yard in the same way. It was

A young pear tree stands among red Gregg's salvia, pink verbena, nierembergia, irises, and Shasta daisies. Daisies, blue salvia, and rose 'Louis Philippe' line the back porch of the reconstructed C. C. Hairston house at the Antique Rose Emporium, Independence.

A Garden Sampler

A garden is so much an individual affair—it should show . . . distinctly the idiosyncrasy of its owner . . .

—Reginald Blomfield

Our foremothers once displayed their skill at needlework in decorative samplers of every different stitch. In similar fashion, this chapter presents Texas gardens in a variety of styles.

A Cottage Garden

Michael Shoup's garden at the Antique Rose Emporium, in the Blacklands town of Independence, pays nostalgic homage to days gone by. Its centerpiece is a stone cottage reconstructed from the remains of the C. C. Hairston home, built during the days of the Republic of Texas. Shoup would be the first to admit that the garden is probably more lush than those our snake-wary, water-sparing forebears grew. It represents Texas gardens as they might have been, with water and leisure enough—our heritage viewed through the rosy lens of nostalgia for a "simpler" time. However much idealized Shoup's garden is as a historical representation, it is an example of bountiful bloom in a small space that is readily applicable to small modern homesites.

The garden is in the style of a traditional English cottage garden. Heaps of flowers, intermingled in an apparently random fashion, are given definition and form by the straight lines of fences and paths. Although the style is English, the content is Texan. Most of the plants are varieties grown in Texas in the mid-1800s; one finds no portulaca or 'Grape Cooler' periwinkle here. Old-fashioned roses, hollyhocks, and spicy pinks hold sway. Some of the flowers are native Texas plants, such as Hinckley's columbine and "standing cypress" (*Ipomopsis rubra*). Others, such as iris and biennial foxglove, are good, old-time garden plants. Flowers tumble from fence-top to foot level, planted in clusters and drifts for bloom ten months of the year.

The garden kicks off to a sparkling start in late March and early April, with columbines, pinks, foxgloves, mealy blue sage, penstemon, bearded iris, and heaps of roses along the fence and twining over the front gate. In mid-spring, the blue sage is joined by coreopsis, standing cypress, a collection of Gregg's salvias, petunias, and scattered rose blooms. By late summer, the ruellia or "Mexican petunia" has put up its dark green leaves and blue-violet trumpets. Later still, the shrubby cuphea called "cigar plant" attracts hummingbirds with red-shaded orange tubular flowers, and *Salvia leucantha* and Maximilian sunflower paint the skies with towers of amethyst and gold. Cool fall weather brings the roses into a second flush of bloom, on shrubs now double their spring size. In winter, the leaf rosettes of foxglove and coneflowers, green yarrow fronds, and pale fountains of dried ornamental grasses remain. The garden's brief two-month rest is broken in March, when it bursts into bloom again.

"We started the garden in the fall of 1985," Shoup recalls. "Many people helped." It was intended as a test garden and display space for plants Shoup was introducing into his business, Containerized Plants. Previously, the company had grown standard landscape plants for wholesale to landscape and retail nursery companies. The contagious enthusiasm for native plants of his propagator, Tommy Adams, led Shoup to include some natives in the company's offerings. Friends Pamela Puryear and Bill Welch,

dedicated rose collectors, encouraged Mike's interest in old roses. Puryear had been collecting cuttings from old-time roses found in ditches, abandoned homesites, and old cemeteries for some years. "She's really the original instigator of interest in old garden roses in Texas," says Shoup. When Shoup grew the first heritage rose he collected, rampantly growing yellow 'Mermaid,' he was hooked. He reflected that these "found" roses had survived for years all over Texas without benefit of human care and reckoned that their hardiness was just what contemporary homeowners would like. Shoup paraphrases the decision that led him and Welch into the old-rose business as "Let's fool with them and see what happens." Their brief partnership later gave way to the demands of Welch's teaching career, but the retail Antique Rose Emporium was launched.

A year after the first Antique Rose Emporium catalog was mailed, the garden was begun—an effort to show what could be done with this assortment of Texas-tough, old-time plants.

Architectural reclamation came first. Of the two-story stone house that had stood on the property, only the kitchen remained. The rest of the structure had been scavenged for stone in the 1950s. The

Detail of the cottage garden, reconstructed portion of C. C. Hairston house at the Antique Rose Emporium, Independence.

Rose 'Cramoisi Supérieur,' pale pink dianthus, purple verbena, magenta pinks, red dwarf carnations, foxgloves, and pink-and-rose pinks line a path. Antique Rose Emporium.

kitchen's porches and roof had long since caved in. The site was overgrown with invading hackberry trees. Shoup had the trees bulldozed and the land leveled. He sought the services of Gordon Echols, a restoration architect at Texas A&M University, to oversee the renovation. Designs for new porches in period style, trellises, and picket fences were drawn up. The fence pickets were made by hand to an old pattern and painted with a special finish that simulated natural weathering. Garden plans for the first borders, about a fifth of the present plantings, were drawn by Welch and Nancy Volkman. Then the garden-making began.

"First we fenced it in. Then we tilled the soil and added pine-bark mulch. This is black loam with plenty of limestone," Shoup notes. Rock walks were laid encircling the house and on a central axis from front and back doors.

"Then we started plugging in plants," says Shoup. "Typical of a cottage garden, we just put things where they looked right." They clumped the flowers together, grouping tall ones in the back and shorter ones in the front. The roses selected are proper for the house's period, such as 'Archduke Charles,' which dates to 1843.

"We collected plants and put them in the garden," Shoup recounts. "The magenta, double red, and pink-and-maroon dianthuses were collected from old gardens."

In addition to the cottage garden, rose arbors, an old corncrib, and a converted barn were added to the property in 1985. In 1987, a perennial border was

Magenta dianthus, gladioli, foxglove, Shasta daisies, bearded irises, and an old hand plow fill a fence corner at the Antique Rose Emporium.

planted outside the west fence of the cottage garden and also two island beds in front of the cottage, miniatures of the surrounding garden. That fall, a new rose pergola was added, as well as an iris bed along the east fence. In the spring of 1988, ground was broken for an herb garden in the back yard, and picnic tables and benches were set up for visitors.

The cottage now sits swallowed by roses and other flowers, with more roses trellised on its east wall and over the gate. Herbs grow behind, and flower beds with room for tall grasses and large, clump-forming perennials flank the side fences. The pergola frames the property's eastern edge. It's an extravaganza in the cool of spring and fall.

"This was not so much an attempt to mimic old Texas styles of gardening as it was to use plants of the era," says Shoup. "This cottage garden is more elaborate than what people did then, more English-style, but with Texas plants. It is far more work than any pioneer would put into a non-economic crop."

But it demands surprisingly less work than many contemporary homeowners put into their lawns and modern rosebushes. Shoup estimates that he and then-manager of the Emporium, Liz Druitt, put in about three or four hours every two weeks, weeding.

Summer watering, now that the plants are well established, is a weekly deep soaking with a lawn sprinkler. Fertilizing, a half-hour task, is done quarterly. Shoup recommends composted manure, which is combined with pine bark to mulch the garden. "This promotes disease-resistance, vigor, and color," says Shoup. The mulch is supplemented in spring and fall with a commercial fertilizer with sulfur and a 13-13-13 nitrogen, phosphorus, and potassium ratio. Although Shoup dislikes chemical pesticides and fungicides, he concedes that their use is necessary to keep the masses of roses looking their best on display. "The health of these old roses is not harmed by the insects, but their foliage and flower color are affected," he says. "In spring we spray with Malathion to control thrips and aphids. We spray with fungicides only when mildew is a severe problem and makes the bushes really ugly. Although the mildew won't hurt their health, it takes a couple of sprayings in spring and fall to keep the plants attractive."

The roses are pruned lightly with hedge shears for good shrub form, rather than radically, eliminating weaker canes, as is done with Hybrid Tea roses.

"With old roses, you just prepare the soil and

plant the plant—it's no more care than a typical landscape shrub like pittosporum," Shoup comments. "We use roses as ground covers, pillars, climbers, cascading shrubs—the diversity of form is infinite. They are valuable for the landscape uses of the plant, not just for the blooms."

"What we are trying to show," he says with a smile, "is that Texas has the plants to grow a garden as beautiful as in France or England—a garden that will take the abuse of this harsh environment." Looking at the blooms billowing around Shoup's 150-year-old cottage, the visitor must concede that blue northers and three-month droughts seem a long way off, and Texas doesn't appear harsh at all.

More Cottage Gardens

PRAIRIE STYLE

The garden in front of the prairie bungalow might have been put together by a lively granny with an adventurous color sense and an uncommon knowledge of plants from Europe, Asia, and the wilds of Texas and Mexico. In fact, it is the work of Rosa Finsley and Logan Calhoun, landscape architects of a different persuasion. Cottage gardens, native plants, rock-strewn country ponds, and old homeplaces are among their favorite things.

Flower borders ring the tiny, raised lawn of this house in a not-yet-gentrified area of old East Dallas.

Around a prairie bungalow grows a garden worthy of a world-traveling granny. From foot of path: wild primroses not yet in bloom, a dwarf pomegranate, 'Huntington Beach' rosemary, yellow pompom mums, bearded iris, and white Gregg's salvia. On the right, blue fall aster weaves among the silvery leaves of native Texas cenizo. Former studio of King's Creek Landscaping, Dallas.

The grass is parted by a stone walk and steps that lead from the street to the broad, shaded front porch. The blue-gray of 'Koster' variety Colorado blue spruce offsets the garden's many greens. In the border, forest-green mugo pine contrasts with 'Petite Pink Scotch' rose and the dainty Polyantha rose 'Cecile Brunner.' 'Huntington Beach' rosemary blooms blue-violet most of the season, and wild asters put on a show in fall, mingling their dime-size lavender-blue blooms with the silver-gray of native cenizo, or Texas sage. Creeping thyme fills in between the stones of the steps and walk. Shrubby perennials like pavonia and Gregg's salvias in several colors mound softly. Bearded irises punctuate the border's upper edge. Even the curb is overrun by spreading flowers; chicory and evening primrose poke up between the sidewalk slabs.

On the yard's south edge, the border is surmounted by a screen of small trees: Texas pistachio, Mexican redbud, and Mexican walnut. An American beautyberry shrub, with its mulberry-colored fruit, and a flowering Turk's cap nestle along the driveway's side, in the narrow understory below the trees.

The brimful, busy little garden laps against the high front porch. Dwarf peaches in pots flank the steps, and leisure is offered by a porch swing and wooden Adirondack chairs.

One wonders how it is that the designers who work inside confine themselves to telephone and drawing board, with this inviting porch and garden just outside the door. Prompting the desire to stop and linger must be one of the hallmarks of a good garden.

URBANE

The cottage style is restated in contemporary terms in a University Park garden a few miles from downtown Dallas. The stone house, designed of brown stone and red tile by 1930s architect Charles Dilbeck, is now painted white, which gives a Spanish Mission feeling. Visible from all sides as the garden is on its corner lot, its plantings must offer greenery and color year-round. Bulbs, perennials, and roses bloom against hollies and multicolored junipers. Unlike a traditional cottage plot, the garden has no fence,

A cottage garden in urban confines graces its small space from fence to fence. Red azaleas, red and yellow tulips, and dark blue pansies blanket beds beneath yellow Lady Banks roses in full bloom. Kirby Anderson home, Dallas.

The garden of a Victorian home overflows with roses including 'Archduke Charles,' as well as petunias, double portulaca, a tree hibiscus, and pink rain lilies. Former home of Bob Wilson and Ray Hapes, Dallas.

and the planting area is asymmetrical and broken up into many small spaces. Local landscaper Carl Neels designed and planted the garden, and then-owner Kirby Anderson maintained and improved upon it. She spent as much time working in the garden as the demands of a business and mothering three children allowed.

The garden contained 'Sherwood Red' azaleas, Hybrid Tea roses, coreopsis, Shasta daisies, agapanthus, hardy blue asters, ageratum, verbenas, black-eyed Susans, and 'Lady Banks' roses. Tulips, pansies, and begonias were added in season. Hydrangeas filled a north window planter and trailing lantana another one. Kirby met the challenge of her garden's high visibility by cutting back the perennials when they were out of bloom and interplanting seasonal annuals.

The cheerful, welcoming spirit of the garden was well expressed in the wide-open patio door and a small plaque on the low patio wall that read, "God first created a garden."

BEYOND VICTORIAN

A riotous little cottage garden, complete with Victorian cottage, came to my notice one year at summer's end. It stood along a shortcut across the north side of downtown Dallas, looking admirably flush for August.

Bob Wilson and Ray Hapes owned the Victorian cottage in the old State-Thomas neighborhood. The area had been an upper-middle-class Jewish community in the 1800s, then a freed slaves' town, and finally a mixture of restored houses and empty lots cleared and left bare by failed real estate speculators. When Wilson and Hapes moved, they packed the garden flowers along with the furniture and moved them, too. Although the ranch-style house they later shared in North Dallas bore no resemblance to the Cottage on Thomas Avenue, the gardens were rather similar. Both were inspired by gardens that Bob recalls from his childhood, not in England but in West Texas.

The cottage stood in the middle of an un-Victorian tumble of flowers: old-timey roses, black-eyed Susans, hybrid crinum lilies, pinks, verbenas, daylilies, Texas and Mexican zephyr lilies, and a hibiscus trained into a tiny tree. The small lot was lined with rosebushes on the fences, with lythrum, mallows, and roses in the semi-shady back yard, and in the front, no lawn, just flowers.

"You know, a flower garden is really less trouble

to keep in summer than a lawn," says Bob. "Keeping the grass in tip-top green condition takes watering every day. The flowers and roses can go three or four days, even when temperatures are above 100° every day. Once they're well grown, the shade they cast cools their roots and discourages weeds."

The much larger landscape of their more recent home was bordered with colorful mixed beds of perennials, roses, and annuals. The flowery front yard that had once existed at the old house was replaced with a carpet of St. Augustine grass. It didn't look like the same place. It wasn't.

Perennial Borders
FOR A RANCH-STYLE HOUSE

Bob Wilson and Ray Hapes' second house fell a few periods later than their first one, in both domestic architecture and garden design. The first home was a Victorian cottage set in a nineteenth-century-style cottage garden. The later home was a 1950s "ranch," surrounded by mixed perennial plantings. Wilson and Hapes subdued the house's salmon-painted trim and wrought-iron porch details with a coat of dark gray-green and ignored its era in creating classic ornamental borders.

As time passed, the garden more and more resembled high flowery walls rising around a deep green carpet. The 20-foot-tall arborvitae that rimmed the lot across the street created a forest-green backdrop for views of Hapes and Wilson's handiwork. Flower borders encircled the 100-by-160-foot corner lot in a double ring, the inner one around the house wall and the outer one at the property line. The outer border framed the property with tall, mostly old-fashioned roses, irises, crinum lilies, salvias, and other perennials, and annuals down to ankle-high lazy daisy. Native plants mingled with old garden favorites.

Since early 1987, when the border's roses went in, they reached diameters of 6 feet; their maximum height was attained each fall, after February pruning and a season's new growth. Ray cherished such antique varieties as 'Louis Philippe' and 'Cramoisi Supérieur,' both Chinas; 'Lady Hillingdon,' a beautiful apricot Tea rose; and pert little 'La Marne,' a Polyantha whose pink flowers bloom en masse. "'La Marne' fades beige," says Ray. "It's what you call 'clean.' The flowers are not unsightly when they die, which is a good thing, because they're too profuse to remove every day." He has no particular liking for modern Hybrid Teas, Ray says; "the

Yellow pansies, blue thrift, an unnamed Louisiana iris seedling, and silvery curry plant flank one side of the walkway of Bob Wilson and Ray Hapes' garden. As time passes, the garden increasingly resembles flowery walls surrounding a deep green carpet. The large coral and apricot shrub rose at right rear is 'Mutabilis.'

A corner border frames the house with yellow pansies, red English rose 'The Squire,' Penstemon tenuis, *and blue thrift. At left rear, rose 'Penelope' froths with white blooms. Former home of Bob Wilson and Ray Hapes.*

flowers are so oversize and gaudy, compared to the soft colors and masses of flowers on the old roses."

Ornamental trees of the Deep South had their place in the garden, too. Fragrant white *Gordonia* and dwarf magnolia accented the flower border. There was a flowering quince, planted when the house was built, that had reached roof-high.

Mallows in the garden included a pale pink halberd-leaf mallow (*Hibiscus militaris*) and a "Texas star" hibiscus (*H. coccineus*), as well as the giant *H. moscheutos* hybrid 'Mallow Marvels.' Ray's inherited amarcrinums, large scented lilies with a pink tinge from their amaryllis parent and the ever-green foliage of crinums, were quite beautiful. One of Bob's prizes was a large-flowered, honey-scented pink-and-white verbena called 'Pink Parfait,' shared

with him by a nurseryman friend who was given it by an elderly lady in East Texas.

The gardeners reveled in unusual combinations, such as Texas white prickly poppy, lythrum, and crinum lily. Or the ancient "changeable rose," *Rosa chinensis* 'Mutabilis,' coreopsis, and iris. "Look," says Bob, "Aggie cotton." The purple-leaved cotton plant has rose-colored hibiscus-like blooms hidden under the leaves and, in September, a cotton boll was forming.

Along the east, street-side fence, roses and giant 'Mallow Marvels' formed a man-high background for shorter flowers. Leaving the back yard, one passed between the fence planting and a bed of fragrant large-flowered Hybrid Tea roses. The gate was clustered with native pink coneflowers, lythrum,

Thrift, irises, woadwaxon, and rose 'Red Jacket.' Former home of Bob Wilson and Ray Hapes.

Bob's one wish was that he had room to make the beds a little wider—12 feet instead of 6 to 8, maybe. "I could get away from this 'bouquet' effect of a few of one kind of plant with small groups of others, and into planting larger areas of each thing," he said.

As for garden chores, "there's rarely a feeling of 'Oh gosh, I'm behind!' It is a free-form garden, so maintenance is not that pressing. The plants have grown up so thick and tall that they shade their own roots and shade out the weeds. I'll probably get more involved in adding in annual color next season, but you know, the people who drive by and tell us they love the garden don't seem to have missed the annuals we left out this summer."

Bob has gardened as long as he can remember. Lowlanders who consider the High Plains of West Texas a flat, sandy waste may find the gardening tradition of Bob's family a surprise. Also surprising at first mention are the many flowers that thrive in West Texas' severe wind, cold, and heat but decline in milder, more humid climates.

"Ever since I can remember, there were flowers—at my mother's and my grandmother's, out around Lubbock, where I grew up. My dad was a cattle rancher. We lived several different places, and my mom had a garden at every one. With that well-drained soil and the cool nights, there's never a problem with things rotting like they do here. Dianthus, for example. She had dahlias, gladioli, globe amaranths, just a mix of flowers. Out on the ranch, there were irises, daisies, pussy willows. In the fifth grade, my mother let me dig my own flower bed. There was a bunkhouse with a screened-in porch, and that was my greenhouse. That's where I learned my style of gardening, with lots of different flowers together."

Gardens are still Bob's personal retreat. He calls the Dallas garden his "happy-hour spot." "The best time to go out is after dinner, just for a stroll to enjoy the serenity for an hour or two."

and profuse pink-and-rose blooms of 'Betty Prior,' an early Floribunda rose. The edge of the bed dripped with white and pink rain lilies, blue nierembergia, and thrift.

On the garden's opposite side, the bed adjoining the neighbors' yard was a test area. "I use my gardens to learn by," said Bob. At the time, the bed was full of old single-flowered roses, such as 'Frensham' and 'White Wings.' "I know that if I were doing this just as an ornamental landscape I would use far fewer plant varieties," he said. "But I have a few of everything so that I can see how they do."

The raised beds were built by digging down 2 inches, poisoning the Bermuda grass, and laying an edging of railroad ties, which was filled with a mixture of soil and pine-bark mulch. Occasional herbicide application to the Bermuda just outside the ties kept the grass from invading. The soil was heavy but fertile to start with. Judging from horseshoes discovered while they were digging, the gardeners concluded that the lot was previously the grounds of a horse stable.

In late summer twilight, Texas bluebell and the warm colors of dwarf cannas, marigolds, orange cosmos, and rudbeckia 'Golden Glow' shine from Margaret Kane's San Antonio garden.

IN THE KANE PATCH

Margaret Kane lives in the toe-tip of Texas' heavy blackland soil belt, where it tapers out in San Antonio. Her garden, familiarly known as "the Kane Patch," contains native Texas plants, old garden flowers, dwarf and pastel cannas, tropical gingers, vines, shrubs, and foliage plants. Many San Antonians garden in limestone and caliche, but Mrs. Kane's garden is firmly rooted in gumbo clay. Her family, of English ancestry, moved to Texas from Mexico in 1919. She and her husband have lived in the same house since the 1930s, as the city has grown up around them. In the beginning, they were on the edge of town.

Mrs. Kane is a serious gardener who records her horticultural trials for the benefit of her peers. Many horticulturists consider her an expert on perennials and native Texas plants. She maintains a computerized list of all the plants in her garden by botanical names, noting their winter-hardiness, and another list of plants she would like to try. Many supposedly tender varieties have survived lows of 9° F in her garden. She has traveled the nation searching for plants, swapping with gardeners from Oregon, Washington, California, Louisiana, and Virginia. In Wisley, England, the American native *Zephyranthes* lilies in the National Trust garden are a gift from Mrs. Kane.

A perennial border of plants of yellow, gold, orange, red, and blue hues lines the eastern edge of the property. There are Indian blankets, Texas bluebells, 'Golden Glow' rudbeckias, native *Rudbeckia hirta*, heliopsis, and chicory, to name only a few, and her favorite montbretia, flame-red 'Lucifer.' Orange-and-yellow hummingbird bush, *Cuphea micropetala*, starts blooming in August and continues until frost. *Penstemon baccharifolius*, the little coral rock penstemon, performs equally well. There is yellow Mexican mint marigold, *Tagetes lucida*. The old-fashioned crinum lily 'Ellen Bosanquet' opens its rose-red trumpets in early summer. Native scarlet *Salvia coccinea* adds a touch of clear scarlet. White *Penstemon digitalis*, Mrs. Kane says, is remarkable for its ability to withstand submersion in water for several days after a heavy rain.

The house front is draped with pink-flowering coral vine, or queen's wreath. Along the side street, the back yard is bordered by a collection of rose mallows in every color, including yellow *Hibiscus rockii* and Duffy's mallow, the offspring of native *H. coccineus* and the hybrid 'Mallow Marvels.' In the back yard, pecan trees shade the St. Augustine lawn and flowers throng the borders. In the east border,

Gloriosa lily and white spiderwort bloom in a semi-shady corner of Mrs. Kane's back yard.

sprinkler to run through and the dasher of an ice-cream churn to lick before the afternoon was over.

Another remarkable thing about Mrs. Gamblin's garden was the way that all the energy she had poured into it over thirty years seemed to be returning to her, late in life when her accustomed vigor was slowed by the effects of age and illness.

It was an ordinary-sized back yard made to seem larger by the massive pecan boughs spreading overhead and the tall borders of flowers that covered the fences in foliage and bobbed among the rows in the vegetable patch. You couldn't take in the entire garden in one glance. There was a lot to look at, corners to wander to, and nooks to linger in.

In summer, the pecan tree shaded a large island bed of common rose and pink garden impatiens and magenta *Impatiens balsamina*, the old-fashioned touch-me-not. The cold-tender flowers had reseeded themselves there in the shade for twelve or fifteen years. White caladiums and the delicate foliage of columbine, past bloom, mingled beside them, and thick St. Augustine grass lapped from the island to the flower borders and patio.

In a rear fence corner, tall butterfly gingers screened the neighbors' yard. Raised timber-edged beds overflowed with blue forget-me-nots, tall crayon-gold cosmos, pink summer phlox, and pale,

tropical gingers bloom, root-hardy to 16° F. Gloriosa lily twines next to widow's-tears (*Tradescantia* spp.). Violet annual torenia blankets their feet. Over the garden shed, a fifty-year-old 'Madame Galen' trumpet vine climbs, trained into a graceful tree form with a trunk as thick as a man's arm.

In the west border, hostas and tender tropical foliage plants grow, submerged in pots that will be removed in winter for frost protection. Now, they are top-dressed with soil and look like a permanent planting. Among the green and silver leaves, native columbine blooms and variegated ivy twines.

Shade Gardens
A HOMEY BACK YARD GARDEN

For one who knew the delights of a Southern childhood, a visit to the San Antonio garden of the late Cora Gamblin was a step back in time—to summer in back yards shaded by big oak or pecan trees, with okra and tomatoes to pick and the hard-flying seedpods of touch-me-not flowers for aerial battles. When I visited Mrs. Gamblin, I was an adult and she a new acquaintance, hardly kin, but her garden had the feeling of home, as if there would be a lawn

Red and pink rose mallows with yellow Hibiscus rockii. *Garden of Jack and the late Cora Gamblin, San Antonio.*

A pecan tree shades a large island bed of common garden impatiens and Impatiens balsamina, *one of the flowers known as touch-me-not. Garden of Jack and Cora Gamblin.*

velvety salmon cockscomb. After wandering through rows of corn and tomatoes, one came upon the back fence, covered thickly in subtropical herbaceous plants where another gardener might have prosaically planted shrubs. Red-flowered clerodendrum and bush morning glory, *Ipomoea fistulosa*, stood 7 feet high, with four o'clocks and more magenta-pink phlox massed at their feet. Plants by the quaint names of Cashmere bouquet and French hollyhock had escaped through the back fence to bloom in the alley.

The limestone patio was bordered by a low bank of tropical gingers, set close for patio-sitters to admire their pastel, curiously shaped blooms. Around the west side of the house in a place below the kitchen windows that many homeowners would

ignore, Mrs. Gamblin had massed man-high mallows, *Hibiscus moscheutos*, both red and white with a rose eye, and yellow-flowering *H. rockii*.

Mrs. Gamblin and Margaret Kane were long-time friends who shared a love of gardening while amiably disagreeing in their color preferences. Mrs. Gamblin favored tender pinks and mauves, colors Mrs. Kane does not allow in her garden of bracing yellows, golds, oranges, and true blues. In their long friendship they shared seed, seedlings, and plant lore.

This shady, sheltering refuge had grown from a bare, flat lot with "heavy, black clay you wouldn't have thought you could garden in," as Mrs. Gamblin recalled it. Over the years, it had become a gathering place for friends and neighbors. In summers late in her life, Mrs. Gamblin gardened only until nine or

Two colors of Salvia greggii, *cenizo, soft-leaf yucca, and willow. Austin.*

Ancient, massive live oaks and St. Augustine lawns are two of Austin's most characteristic and satisfying landscape features. On the shady grounds of an Austin estate, they are ringed, not with the customary hedges of pittosporum or Indian hawthorn, but with borders of Texas mountain laurel, Gregg's salvias in pink, wine, and salmon, and old-fashioned altheas and daylilies—a colorful and drought-resistant mixture. These native plants and old garden cultivars make the shrub borders, woodland trails, and water gardens here Texas-tough.

The mixed border wraps around the main lawn and opens onto a shaded pathway. In summer, bright pink garden phlox mark the entrance, but one stepstone down the path, white-leaved and white-blooming plants take over. This is the moon garden, designed especially for viewing at night. From the vantage point at the beginning of the path, one looks down a corridor of white-flowering small trees, shrubs, and flowers at the moonlike, disc-shaped statuary at the end. Walking the path, one is enclosed by trees that arch overhead and low, creeping flowers at pathside. In spring, white narcissi, pinks, thrift, and iberis crowd close, shaded by Texas whitebud and flowering plums. In summer, white crape myrtles, variegated hydrangeas, and caladiums carry the theme.

Just east of the main lawn, a dry slope overlooks a water garden, shaded by willows and pecans. Gray Texas sage, or cenizo, combines with soft-leaf yucca. Bronze fish by Sirio Tofanari, described as the foremost twentieth-century Italian sculptor of *animalerie*, surmount a limestone ledge. Old single daylilies and peach-pink 'Margo Koster' roses add color. With natives and hardy garden plants, the homeowners have found a way to achieve the full, rich-textured quality of an English garden through Austin's long, hot, paradoxically humid but often rainless growing season.

ten in the morning, to avoid the overpowering heat. In the cool of the evening, she and her husband enjoyed their oasis. "The gardening I've put in all these years has paid off," she said, in her seventies. "Now, just when I'm feeling like slowing down and taking it easier, all I have to do is water and weed a little. The garden seems to just about take care of itself."

In the shade of willows and pecans, a dry slope clad with gray cenizo and soft-leaf yucca overlooks a water garden. Austin.

Gardens of Native Plants
A NATIVE HILLSIDE GARDEN

The house that was Frankie Clark's Austin home sits where the foothills of the Edwards Plateau begin. This is the verge of the tumbled Hill Country that is the heart of Texas, geographically and, for many, sentimentally. The house perches below the crest of a sloping lot in the limestone hills of the city's west side. A long arroyo-like finger of wilderness lies behind and below it where deer browse.

In making their landscape, the Clarks refrained from the laborious and nonsensical—but all too common—course of removing boulders and hauling in soil for a conventional lawn and shrubs. Instead, Frankie and local landscape architect Stan Powers improved on nature as it is found there without battling it.

Trailing wildflowers and ground covers blanket the rough ground with greenery and bloom, and striking, strong-textured native shrubs and perennials define the space and add seasonal interest. The planted landscape blends into the wild one so naturally as to make Central Texas' semi-arid hills seem gardenlike—and give the actual garden that sense of escape that we seek in wilderness.

Guests round a limestone wall crowded with softly mounded gray and green santolinas and enter the front garden among clumps of native flowers and shrubs. A massive silver-gray cenizo stands out against evergreen yaupon holly at one side of the property, and on the other side red yucca and *agarita*, or threeleaf barberry, grace a clearing. There are pink pavonia, orange-flowering hummingbird bush (*Anisacanthus quadrifidus* var. *wrightii*), and pale salmon-pink *Salvia coccinea*. The less cold-hardy nature of this pink form of *S. coccinea*, compared to the common scarlet form, seems a small price to pay for its delicate, barely pink hue. The path steps past these among pink *Verbena* 'Elegans,' mingled with

Pink verbena, mealy blue sage, pavonia, and native acanthus color this rocky Hill Country garden. Former home of Frankie Clark, Austin.

Wormwood, acacias, santolina, Mexican oregano, and scarlet, white, and red salvias surround a naturalistic rock pond on Sue Pittman's "art ranch" near Burton.

Asian jasmine to cover the ground. Clumps of strawberries are tucked between the ground covers, high on the hill in shade. Scarlet *Salvia coccinea* and mealy blue sage dot the landscape's lower elevation, where the path crosses a wooden bridge over a small, half-hidden pond to the house's front deck.

This is a low-maintenance landscape. The ground covers mask a drip irrigation system. Now that they have grown in and the other plants have matured, weeding is minimal, and spot-watering by hand is rarely necessary.

By selecting heat-hardy native and well-adapted plants, Powers and Clark achieved almost season-long bloom. Varied foliage hues and winter berries provide year-round interest. The landscape echoes and emphasizes the natural environment from which it springs, and invites a casual, relaxed approach to life that locals can tell you is the Austin way.

A NATIVE ROCK GARDEN

Sue Pittman's ranch near Burton is in the East Cross Timbers of Texas, a 300-mile-long strip of sandy soil whose only other constant in its long stretch is the presence of post oak trees. Sue's place might be called an "art ranch." In its woods and dells she has carved niches for sculptures and environmental art by contemporary Texas artists.

In my opinion, the ranch's horticultural high point is a rock garden. The design and original plantings were done by Tomball, Texas, landscape designer Will Fleming. He brought in tons of earth and rock to build up rugged mounds. Ponds were built and an array of drought-tolerant, heat-hardy native flora planted. There are Mexican oregano, salvias, acacias, feathery gray *Dalea greggii*, and artemisia, to name only a few. From 1986 to 1988, subsequent gardeners added garden perennials like woolly lamb's-ears (*Stachys byzantina*), monarda, and lavender. The result is tough, colorful, and rustic—a very Texan sort of rock garden.

Dusty miller, red-and-gold daylilies, and 'Coronation Gold' yarrow contrast silver, green, and gold against a background of (from left) pink snapdragons, three colors of salvia, cosmos, mixed dwarf snapdragons, and daisies. San Antonio Botanical Center.

An Old-fashioned Garden

The old-fashioned garden at the San Antonio Botanical Center is the work of many hands. It is not a representation of a particular period garden style, but rather an old-time mixture of simple garden flowers. The plants, mostly perennials, include old garden varieties, modern cultivars, and natives of Texas, New Mexico, and Mexico. Everyone on the staff of the 33-acre public garden takes an interest in this garden, and rarely does a visitor come to the grounds without strolling through. The garden stands halfway up a hill in the shade of a pink-flowering chitalpa tree, looking westward over the city. Behind it, a quaint observation tower—now decapitated and much mourned—formerly topped the hill to the east. The futuristic glass peaks of the Lucille Halsell Conservatory jut into the sky. In the garden, limestone-bordered paths wind among a changing display of perennials and bright annuals. Any single bed of it would fit comfortably beside a private home.

The garden's plan is in the shape of a butterfly. A small, lozenge-shaped bed forms the butterfly's body. To the east and west are its wings. Long, narrow borders to the west and north and triangular beds on the east frame the garden and provide space for tall flowers and seasonal annuals. On the south are beds of herbs and a rock garden of plants of arid West Texas and Mexico.

In mid-spring, the butterfly garden is a wave of flowers of varied heights and hues ranging from iris purples, blues, and white, blue and white native salvias, and silvery dusty miller to red verbena, golden daylilies, the oranges and yellows of cosmos and coreopsis, and the confetti hues of hybrids of wild Texas *Phlox drummondii*. On the drier, uphill wing of the garden, sky-blue fall salvia, justicia, and hummingbird bush await their time to bloom. Veronica and red-hot poker (*Kniphofia*) make their appearance. Near the chitalpa tree, there are drifts of red Gregg's salvia and white daisies just ending their season. A wall of tall, salmon-pink snapdragons stands guard in the north border, and perennial sweet peas drape the gate that leads into the rose garden. In fall, velvety annual ruby-red cockscomb and lemon marigolds frame the perennial garden on the east. Then the garden will glow with the golds, burnt oranges, and violet of Mexican mint marigold (*Tagetes lucida*), cuphea, castor bean, and *Salvia leucantha*.

The garden was indicated in the original design for the Botanical Center grounds drawn by local landscape architect Jim Keeter. Keeter's plans located the Center's ornamental areas and dictated the shapes of the beds. In 1980, the gardens were opened to the public. Don Pylant, who was assigned to the garden during 1980 and 1981, says, "Back then, our hardiest perennial was nutgrass." At first, the garden was bedded out seasonally, mostly with annuals. Pylant says that the intention behind making the garden a mixed perennial-annual planting was primarily aesthetic. "People like to see variety," he says. "How long can you spend looking at 100 square feet of marigolds?"

Another improvement needed in the garden from its caretakers' viewpoint was erosion control. It was one large, sloping area with no paths or retaining walls. "Every time it rained," says Pylant, "we had to go down to the rose gardens to find most of the flower beds. The soil just washed away." The uninterrupted planting area also left no standing room from which the plants could be reached for maintenance.

Pylant and Paul Cox, then Center horticulture supervisor, made the early improvements in the garden. They dug out the nutgrass and applied Vapam to kill what was left. Terraces were built.

Sweet peas, tall pink snapdragons, salvias, cornflowers, cosmos, and campanulas mingle, as vivid as an old-fashioned crazy quilt. San Antonio Botanical Center.

Top: The east "wing" of the butterfly-shaped garden holds zinnias, rudbeckia 'Goldsturm,' pink phlox, lythrum, and purple-leaved perilla. San Antonio Botanical Center.

Bottom: The highlight of the desert rock garden is a Manfreda *in bloom. San Antonio Botanical Center.*

"The rock work was an after-work project," Pylant smiles wryly. "We finally finished it with the help of a city crew."

Within two or three years, Center staff had started mixing custom soils for the garden. The beds had originally been dug 1–2 feet deep. Beneath the cultivated layer was hard-packed black clay. The lower, wet area was back-filled with well-drained soil. In the higher, dry areas, plenty of humus was added. These soil improvements brought the topography of the garden to its present contours. The plantings continue to evolve.

The introduction of perennials was undertaken by Center gardener Ying Doon Moy. Paul Cox continued to draw up planting plans, and Moy and other gardeners installed the plants. Because of supply problems, "every day the plan changed," says Moy. Plants specified were often unavailable from the city greenhouse, so the gardeners had to use what they could get. Construction of a greenhouse at the Botanical Center eventually relieved this problem.

As an experiment, lythrum was planted in the damp, oblong border at the bottom of the site. It soon reached 6 feet in height, looking like gigantic pink flames from the overlooking hilltop. In 1987, the hybrid chitalpa tree was added, for shade in the central bed. Cross-bred from the white-blooming Deep South catalpa tree and pink-flowering desert willow (*Chilopsis linearis*), chitalpa is a long-blooming, slender-leaved tree that provides light shade ideal for garden flowers. The peanut-shaped bed at the tree's feet was intended for a close-inspection bed of dainty flowers. Pylant's and Cox's early designs included tall plants around the perimeter of the garden so that visitors would have to walk inside to see more.

Asked who tends the garden, the gardeners used to reply, "Mr. Moy, Nancy, and the mockingbirds." Nancy Brillos brought cottage-gardening experience and an interest in color planning to the garden. She has since left to become manager of the city Parks Department greenhouses. "It's a group effort," she says of the garden. "Everyone likes to see different things." Moy loves knock-your-socks-off color; Brillos preferred softly blended color schemes. During her stint there, the two worked together to keep the garden in peak condition. Fertilizing is one chore. "What kind we get, we use," Moy put it. In fall and spring, a slow-release, sulfur-coated urea lawn fertilizer, 15-5-10 ratio, is used, for economy's sake. In early spring, Nancy applied a 20-20-20 soluble fertilizer every ten days, to promote bloom. Her daily care routine for the 5,000-square-foot garden took three hours a day in spring. The rest of the growing season, watering and weeding take an hour a day. "There's a lot of weeding," she says. Root division is a project she had hoped to get started, because many of the plants had been in the ground undisturbed for three years. The salvias, iris, and cuphea particularly needed division to encourage better growth and make room for more. Very few of the plants stay green in the winter. Moy would like to see an evergreen hedge planted on the north side to protect the garden from winter cold that is more severe in this natural cold sink than farther up the hill.

"It's design by committee," Brillos sums up the evolution of the garden. "We're used to getting lots of comment." Perhaps the two-cents'-worth that coworkers and visitors are all eager to put in is a measure of how dearly this old-fashioned garden is loved. Everyone considers it a little bit his or her own.

Top: Red garden verbena, lythrum, lemon marigolds, and pink phlox spill over a limestone bed. San Antonio Botanical Center.

Bottom: One tiny area of a raised bed is crowded with green sedum, nierembergia, rock penstemon, and tender evolvulus 'Blue Daze.' San Antonio Botanical Center.

Regions

Longspur columbine, Big Bend.

Regionally Speaking

. . . dirty fingernails are not the only requirement for growing plants. The gardener must be willing to study as well as to dig. He must know the part of the world a plant comes from and under what conditions it grows naturally before he can establish it in his own garden.

—Elizabeth Lawrence

Texas contains within itself the climates of the Deep South, the Great Plains, and the vast Chihuahuan Desert of Mexico in one immense, contradictory package. This diversity is complicated by the irregular descents of cooler Canadian weather from the northwest—the "blue northers" that bring sudden and astonishing temperature drops. Texas' roller-coaster alternation of freezes and thaws can be harder on plant life than the unbroken severe freezes of more northern states. In the warmer months, the Canadian airstream often collides with warm, moist air from the Gulf of Mexico, producing thunderstorms and occasionally tornadoes.

Conditions in different parts of Texas also exist in New Mexico, Oklahoma, Arkansas, Mississippi, and on across the South to North Carolina. Residents there will recognize in Texas' Upper Gulf Coast and Piney Woods similarities to the Lower South, in Texas' Lower Rio Grande Valley the near-frostless climate of central Florida, and in Texas' Trans-Pecos the searing northern reaches of the Chihuahuan Desert that also extends into New Mexico.

There is hardly another part of the United States with natural conditions as varied as those of Texas. The moist pine-hardwoods forests of East Texas get as much rain annually as Miami does. Texas' western tip, some 700 miles away, is desert, with rainfall similar to that in Phoenix. North to south, Texas spans 860 miles, from the Panhandle with its dust storms and blue northers to the palm- and bougainvillea-splendored Lower Rio Grande Valley.

The major ecological regions of the state have been delineated in various ways by other writers, landscape architects, and naturalists. The eight regions in this book (see Map 5, at the end of this chapter) are based on ten in Frank W. Gould's map "Vegetational Areas of Texas" from his work *Texas Plants: A Checklist and Ecological Summary,* published by the Texas Agricultural Extension Service.

From a gardener's point of view, matters must, of course, be diced even more finely to speak to his or her practical concerns. Within each region exist numerous types of ecosystems, or plant and animal communities interdependent with climate and soil. Within each

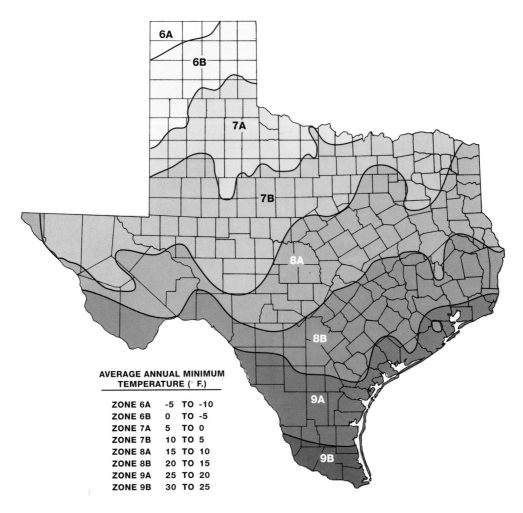

Map 2. USDA hardiness zones for Texas. From USDA Plant Hardiness Zone Map, issued January 1990. United States Department of Agriculture, Agricultural Research Service, Miscellaneous Publication Number 1475.

locality, even within one site, microclimates may exist that are drier or more humid, more acid or more alkaline, hotter or cooler than the larger system of which they are a part. These are factors with which field scientists and gardeners alike become familiar as they go about their work.

Despite these fine points, the basic regional picture, while very general, is a place to start. It enables one to begin to make sense of one's own garden in terms that can be related to the experi-ences of others as far afield as one cares to go. Worldwide climate zones have been mapped, maps that can show us our counterparts in other conti-nents. This greatly enlarges the range of plant materials we may try.

Readers outside Texas can learn from the region descriptions herein which Texas region is most like their own and what information is needed to form an accurate description of their own region. Toward this end, local publications, state and county

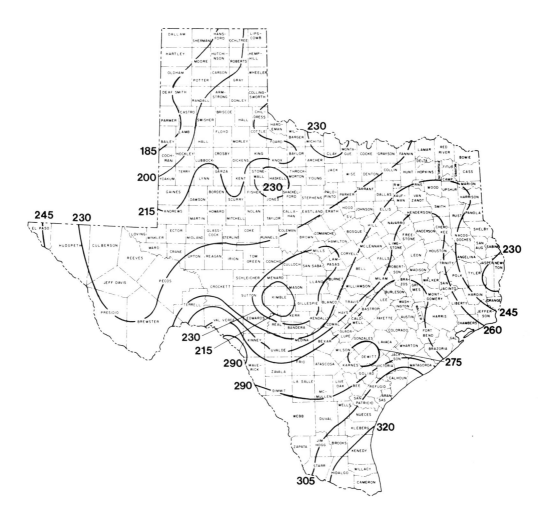

Map 3. Mean length of frost-free period (in days). Adapted from Griffiths and Orton (1968). From Checklist of the Vascular Plants of Texas, *by S. L. Hatch, K. N. Gandhi, and L. E. Brown. 1990. Published by Texas Agricultural Experiment Station, Texas A&M University, College Station. MP-1655.*

extension agents, and nursery horticulturists can be helpful. Learning the particulars of the specific site, such as rainfall; pH of soil and water; and soil fertility, mineral content, and structure, comes next. Here again, local specialists can help, including university and commercial soil-testing labs. Gardeners thus informed will be able to make best use of the charts and descriptions in the Plants and Planting section of this book to find the plants most likely to thrive in their gardens. Not only gardeners

in other states, but Texans as well should seek out more specific local information on average annual minimum temperatures, first and last frost dates, and other climatic conditions.

Map 2 shows the USDA hardiness zones for Texas. The USDA zone designation for each area indicates the average minimum temperature, a significant factor in plant survival. Cold-hardiness of plants is commonly given in books and on nursery tags in these zone ratings; if a plant is said to be

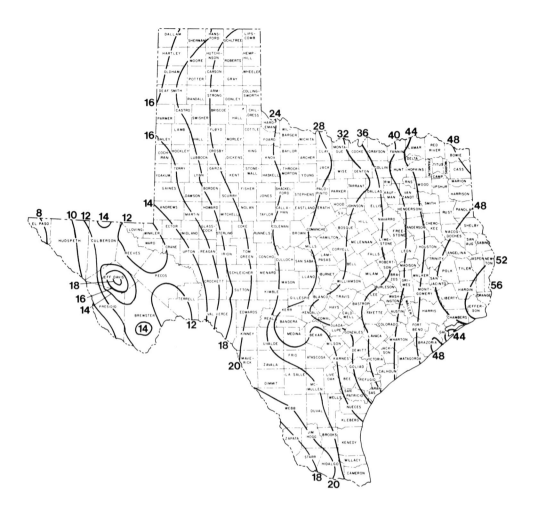

Map 4. Mean annual total precipitation in Texas (in inches). Adapted from Griffiths and Orton (1968). From Checklist of the Vascular Plants of Texas, *by S. L. Hatch, K. N. Gandhi, and L. E. Brown. 1990. Published by Texas Agricultural Experiment Station, Texas A&M University, College Station. MP-1655.*

"hardy to Zone 8," that means it can withstand the average minimum temperatures of Zone 8 (10–20° F). This is unfortunately the only universally used designation of plant hardiness, despite the fact that other factors are important, especially in the South and Southwest. In order to choose plants that will succeed in your garden, you must select ones whose other needs are also matched by local conditions: the average *maximum* temperature; light intensity (sunlight is stronger the further south one

goes and the lower the humidity); humidity; soil type; and rainfall or available irrigation. Maps 3 and 4 indicate major climate determinants other than minimum temperature.

The term "hardy" in northeastern garden books is really shorthand for "cold-hardy," because cold is the survival issue in the North. It says nothing about heat tolerance. A plant cold-hardy to Zone 4 (average minimum temperature -20 to -30° F) may die in Zone 9, where winter cold rarely falls below

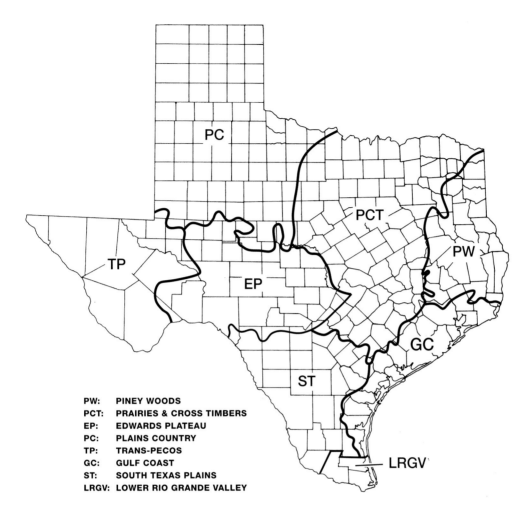

PW: PINEY WOODS
PCT: PRAIRIES & CROSS TIMBERS
EP: EDWARDS PLATEAU
PC: PLAINS COUNTRY
TP: TRANS-PECOS
GC: GULF COAST
ST: SOUTH TEXAS PLAINS
LRGV: LOWER RIO GRANDE VALLEY

Map 5. Vegetational areas of Texas. Modified from a map by Frank W. Gould, in Texas Plants: A Checklist and Ecological Summary, *1969. Published by Texas Agricultural Experiment Station, Texas A&M University, College Station. MP-581 Revised.*

20° F. Its demise will be not from winter cold, but from summer heat. A zone map that combines maximum *and* minimum temperature ranges, along with other critical factors, has yet to be devised. In this book, the term "heat-hardy" also appears, to indicate viability in prolonged, extreme heat.

The recommendations of many gardening experts presuppose neutral to slightly acid water and that fertile, friable commodity known as "good garden soil." This is a mistaken assumption in much of Texas.

Soil can always be improved, but the alkalinity that predominates in most of Texas is hard to conquer; alkaline water counteracts the effects of acidifying fertilizers. It is more sensible to use plants that don't require an artificially created habitat. Plants, after all, have developed in response to the given conditions of water, soil, and weather in their native locales. This book relates perennial flowering and foliage plants to regional conditions in a way that should make garden experimentation more successful.

The Clymer Prairie, a virgin haymeadow preserved by efforts of the Texas Nature Conservancy, is a sea of purple horsemint, basketflower, and the starburst foliage of Maximilian sunflower.

The Prairies and Cross Timbers

Europeans are often reminded of the resemblance of this scene to that of the extensive parks of noblemen in the Old World; . . . the lawn, the avenue, the grove, the copse, which are there produced by art, are here produced by nature.

—*James Hall (1841)*

If the region that contains the prairies and timber belts of North Central Texas were fully named, it would be called the Post Oak Savannah, Blackland Prairie, East and West Cross Timbers, and Grand and North Central Prairies Region—a mouthful. All these distinct ecological areas are considered as one region because of their common prairie heritage and similar weather. For convenience, Prairies and Cross Timbers is a good shorthand. (Of course, other prairies also prevailed westward through the High Plains in West Texas.) Today only small tracts survive in the native condition characterized by these regions' names. But even though the tallgrass prairie and the Cross Timbers, for example, are mostly obliterated, the soil, water, and weather conditions that fostered them remain. They run in what are more or less long, beltlike zones that roughly parallel the Gulf Coast, starting just inland from the coastal counties. As one moves from east to west across the region, soils vary widely, elevation rises, and annual rainfall decreases from 42 inches to as little as 25.

The region's most productive land, the Blackland Prairie, contains the fewest remaining parcels of land in prime original condition. To see it now, one would never guess that this was the 12-million-acre southern range of the great North American Tallgrass Prairie. Today, tallgrass prairie is the rarest kind of American wilderness, and Texas has the largest unprotected acreage of it. Its preservation is a priority for groups like The Nature Conservancy and the state's Texas Natural Heritage Program. Cropland and gardens abound in what was the Blackland Prairie, from McKinney south to the black soils' toe-tip in San Antonio. So, of course, do airports, pavement, and buildings.

Horticultural practices are specific to each of these subregions, as might be expected. Here, as elsewhere, critical factors include average minimum and maximum temperatures, length of growing season, soil structure, soil and water pH, and moisture. The shorter frost-free period and more severe cold of the northern half or third of the region as a whole is a limiting factor for many plants, such as *Salvia leucantha,* for example. This violet-and-white salvia generally winters over in the Blacklands and shortgrass prairie regions from San Antonio north and east to Austin and Bryan but is not reliably cold-hardy farther north than, say, Corsicana.

Soils vary widely. There are acid sands and sandy loams in the Post Oak Savannah and dark, calcareous clays in the Blacklands and Grand Prairies. The North Central Prairies have neutral-to-acid, sometimes stony soils. Many plants commonly grown are soil-specific, adapted either to well-drained, sandy soil or to moisture-retentive, clay-bearing soils. In their natural state, the dense, heavy clays of the Blacklands, although fertile and water-retaining, are too restrictive of air, water, and root passage for many plants. When unimproved, they are also difficult to work. However, added organic matter greatly improves soil structure and widens the range of usable plants. The sandy soils are friable and quick-draining but may be low in organic matter and nutrients.

Precipitation is generally heaviest in spring. As natives often say, "We get plenty of rain here. Thing is, we get it all in two days." As for relative rainfall, past Fort Worth ("where the West begins"), the drier land supports vegetation more like that of West Texas. Dry gardens also harmonize better visually with the surrounding terrain. For reliable information on local conditions, extension agents and local nurserypeople are the best sources. The average minimum temperature range is 10 to 0° F. Summer

high temperatures in the high nineties and low hundreds are typical. Altitudes range from 300 to 800 feet above sea level.

An Artist's Garden

A magical garden lies in a wooded stretch of Texas' Post Oak Savannah that is called Pine Island. Here, midway between Houston and Bryan, pine trees grow in slightly acid, mostly sandy land—a seeming fragment of the East Texas Piney Woods, separated from it by some 60 miles. There is more to the garden's tranquil and even haunting mood than its curious locale, however. On spring mornings when the mist drifts in from the Gulf some 70 miles away and rises among the woods and flowers, nature and art play here in an intriguing way.

Wilderness temporarily regained full sway when farming here was abandoned, and lingers in the abundant native vegetation. The countervailing influence of art is wielded by artist and design professor John Fairey, who chose this as his home in 1972.

The entrance drive, which at first glance resembles a forest trail, disappears from view around a bend. Following it, the visitor emerges into a scene half-hidden by woods at once wild and artful. These are native trees, but they stand banked thigh-deep in yaupon hollies and macrantha azaleas, grown together and carefully clipped into flowing, cloud-like forms. A raised wooden walkway juts out from the house. Beyond it in the north garden appear the starry white flowers and slender limbs of a small gordonia tree, growing as it would in a forest clearing in the East Texas wilds. Elsewhere in the garden, naturally columnar fastigiate yaupon trees formally punctuate the end of a path, like paired columns. There is a wandering creek, its banks crowded by native shrubs and irises—and there are sweeping expanses of mowed green lawn.

Such contrasts characterize the garden's indefinable feel. Several elements seem to contribute. Long

Carefully sheared yaupon hollies and pale blush Azalea satsuki *'Koryu'* mark the entrance to a woodland garden of Texas' Post Oak Savannah. Garden of John Fairey, Waller County.

The morning mist creeps in from the Gulf some hundred miles away and wraps the garden in mystery. Pictured are pink coneflowers, daylilies 'Ethel Shepard' and 'Orange Bowl,' 'Sulphur Queen' yarrow, and at far right, agapanthus.

fingers of woods extend over neighboring hills into the land. The spirit of wilderness has been preserved by making only the most deliberate changes in the native growth. Flowing masses of shrubbery and solitary sculptural plants are counterposed. Two characteristics rarely seen outside the Japanese garden tradition appear. The setting of a single form against a simple setting invites the eye to linger and discover subtle qualities that might otherwise have gone unnoticed. And the natural world is reverently reflected in plantings that emulate nature's own forms and relationships.

In 1972, John Fairey, then an abstract expression-ist painter, changed his Houston studio for this 7-acre piece of ground in the country. A professor of design in the college of architecture at Texas A&M University, he found a new challenge and inspiration in the barbed-wire-tangled land with its falling-down farmhouse. At his hands, the disarray gradually gave way, transformed into the landscape garden that has become his life work.

As well as a place of beauty and a personal refuge, it is a preserve of native Texas plants and plants from counterpart climates worldwide.

The indigenous plant collection here surpasses that of some botanical gardens in the state. Exotic specimens represent China, Japan, Korea, Taiwan, New Zealand, and Australia—any region with a climate similar to Texas'. The garden includes Australian violets, tiger lilies from Japan, salvias from Iran and the Himalayas, and blooming shrubs and trees from the American Deep South. Mr. Fairey has collected plants in Mexico with respected Texas horticulturist Lynn Lowrey and invested in expeditions of British plant-finders. The more than 2,000 varieties of flowers, shrubs, and trees have been listed for use in an exchange program with the North Carolina State University Arboretum, the Botanical Garden of the University of British Columbia, and the State Botanical Garden of Georgia. There are more than 30 oak species, 70 magnolia species, and 175 varieties of azaleas.

How the design melds the garden's horticultural array into a visually pleasing whole is a story in itself.

Evergreen shrubs, massed in long rounded banks, serve as the backbone of the garden. "I try to define an area with shrubbery to house a special perennial," Fairey explains. "The azaleas and yaupons allow me to assemble specimen plants in a varied collection, without it looking spotty. The leaf texture of the evergreen shrubs unifies the plan." These azaleas are not the well-known 'Sherwood Red' and 'Hino Crimson' that put on displays of solid bloom in spring, but rather the less commonly used macrantha azalea, *Rhododendron macranthum* (*R. indicum*). Disease-resistant and sun-tolerant, this ancient satsuki has been in cultivation in Japan for four or five hundred years, says Fairey. Its salmon flowers appear not in a flush, but scattered, a more subtle show. Bloom is heaviest in May and June and again in October and November. In some areas of the garden, yaupon hollies echo the azaleas' dark green color and fine leaf texture. Nestled against this background are bulbs and perennials including daylilies, salvias, penstemons, cupheas, a half-dozen types of lily, coneflowers, yarrows, terrestrial orchids, and four species of iris.

Growing conditions are similar to those in East Texas.

The project began as a woodland garden in the dappled shade of large hardwood trees. It is divided almost in half by a constantly flowing creek. Beds and paths were developed first, in a layout that breaks the flow of water across the land, which is the watershed for the surrounding area. "The beds were designed to be viewed from the windows of the house," says Fairey. "I laid their outlines with a garden hose and went up in the trees to check them before planting." There was a rough color plan to guide selection of the azalea varieties and to help keep in mind the seasons of perennial bloom.

Azalea plantings stream out from the rear of the house, lengthwise down the property. One azalea bank loosely parallels the property's south fence. It skirts an island perennial bed and branches along woodland paths that lead westward under the shade of large trees. Another azalea bank lies about 30 feet further inside the property. Azaleas are also massed

Scarlet buckeye and Iris pseudacorus *bloom on the creek bank. Garden of John Fairey.*

Sweetly scented deciduous azaleas glow saffron in the garden on the north side of John Fairey's converted farmhouse.

north of the house, creating niches for tiger lilies, daylilies, clematis, and numerous other perennials, in view of the kitchen windows. On the house's east side, a small lawn laps against a gallery overlooked by the kitchen and by the bridgelike entry deck. Azaleas bound this lawn and form a backdrop for mahonias, foxgloves, and specimen azaleas of smaller varieties.

Sandstone and native brown rock from the Hondo, Texas, area edge the paths and form risers for steps that descend the gradually sloping grounds. Pinkish iron ore fragments and sand, quick to shed water in this high-rainfall area, form the paths

themselves. It is an attractive surface. Another important characteristic, Fairey says, is that it doesn't crunch underfoot when you're sneaking up on marauding armadillos.

Change has been continual. Renovation of the original farmhouse was completed in 1973. The azaleas were moved in 1980 to make room for construction of an addition. When it was completed in 1982, refinement of the garden was begun, only to have a tornado revise the plan in 1983. It uprooted fifteen large trees and changed the shaded garden to one in which new azaleas have to be laboriously tented with shade-cloth until they are established.

The influx of sunlight prompted the inclusion of more perennials, in both the south and north gardens. Now, young trees planted in the early 1970s are beginning to form a new canopy.

His artist's eye holds Fairey's collector's urge in check. His real loves among his plants are those that are unusual and striking in themselves and also contribute to the overall effect of the garden. *Salvia forskahlei,* an acquisition native to Iran, is a favorite. It combines large, bold evergreen foliage and blue-and-white flowers that seem not to stop coming. "It bloomed from May to July," says Fairey. "I just cut it back in August, and it will bloom again. Many things are pretty for three weeks or a month, and that's it. This is really special."

Fairey's assistant Carl Schoenfeld, who has worked with him in the garden since 1983, favors *Salvia moorcroftiana* from the Himalayas. "We're really surprised and pleased that a Himalayan mountain plant blooms all spring here," he says.

An assortment of small annual cupheas wins Fairey's approval for their vigorous reseeding. A hot-pink-and-lavender specimen from Concan, Texas, a purple-black native cuphea, and the familiar tropical "Mexican heather" bloom all summer and, despite their cold-tenderness, come back en masse from seed. Half of a plant of tropical cuphea lived through the winter and reseeded an area 3 by 4 feet the next spring. *Salvia regla,* the Davis Mountains shrub sage, is another favorite for its scarlet blooms over a long season in this Zone 9a locale.

Fairey collects clematis, as well. Native *Clematis texensis* with its red, pitcher-shaped pendant flowers, European hybrids, and volunteer seedlings all have places in the garden. One accidental hybrid bears white flowers as large as salad plates.

Flowers are grouped in sometimes bold color combinations. "Right now we have pink Carolina rose, orange milkweed, and lilac Mexican heather blooming together," he says. "Everyone groans, 'Ugh—purple, orange, and pink!' but the colors are just the right shades and really quite beautiful together."

Soils for Fairey's shrub and flower beds are made by recipe. All the beds are dug down 2 feet. For perennials in porous soil, coarse sand and ground pine bark are dug in. The sand, soil, and bark are mixed at a 1:1:2 ratio. Clay soil is removed completely and replaced with the sand and bark mix. The mixture also contains amendments as numerous as cake makings: fretted trace minerals, Dursban, dolomite lime, a small amount of blood meal and cottonseed meal for a slow release of nitrogen. Fairey mixes these with a shovel, a wheelbarrow, and a coffee can on the parking area on the northeast side of the house, where a wood chipper is permanently located.

Many visitors say they discern a Japanese quality in Fairey's garden. Leafing through Japanese garden books after the garden was in its present form, he discovered that many of its features, such as the stepstones and mounted stone reliefs, resemble details in Japanese architecture. One Japanese device that he found his garden shares is "the creation of a feeling of a larger space in a series of small spaces." Harmonious blending with the surrounding natural environment is another common characteristic. The gardens, rather than being treated as decoration, emphasize the land's contours. They create naturalistic settings for specimen plants of especially striking texture and bloom. "There's a difference between gardening and just planting plants. You have to think twenty years ahead and all the way in between," he says.

Four-dimensional creations surround him now with color, life, and change. There is always an element of unpredictability. "I would never go back to painting again," he says. "It's so two-dimensional." He has found a medium that combines and transcends both fine art and horticulture. "I began the garden, and it crowded out the paintings," he says.

Above Cibolo Creek, yucca-studded limestone terraces characterize the Edwards Plateau.

CHAPTER FOUR

The Edwards Plateau

On attaining the eminence we were at once on a rocky plateau from which we could view in every direction hilltops piercing one above another . . . till they were closed from view behind the blue veil of distance.

—*J. W. Benedict*

The Edwards Plateau is that stony tableland "deep in the heart of Texas." On the east and south, it breaks up into the picturesque canyons of the Hill Country and then declines to the plains below. It blends into the southern Plains Country and the Trans-Pecos on the north and west. There are glorious wildflowers and peach and pecan orchards. The soil is thin and the water scarce, but there are some charming gardens that easily surmount these challenges.

The altitude ranges from 1,000 to over 3,000 feet. The hump-backed granite hills deep in the Hill Country look like Greece without the Mediterranean. The soil here is a thin layer over limestone or caliche in most parts and over granite in the central portion. It is well-drained and usually alkaline. The land is used primarily as livestock range. Rainfall ranges from 33 inches in the east to 15 inches in the west, peaking in May and June and in September. Drought is frequent.

The climate is no problem when well-adapted plants, indigenous or exotic, are used. In Fredericksburg, the Pioneer Museum surrounds an early homeplace with a garden of plants common in the early part of the century: 'Kwanso' daylilies, coreopsis, coneflowers, lantana. Nearby, the historic Erik Von Handoken home overlooks a garden of roses and bearded irises, planted row-fashion like corn or beans. Gardens of annuals such as larkspur and corn poppies are more common than perennial plantings.

Parts of both Austin and San Antonio lie on the edge of the Edwards Plateau. There, gardeners tackle the challenge of maintaining well-groomed city landscapes in semi-arid circumstances.

In the side yard of an early Fredericksburg homeplace, red and yellow roses and bearded irises brightly contrast with the silvery sides of an old shed.

San Antonio Borders

Raydon Alexander grows an English-style mixed border on San Antonio's north side, as a display garden for the nursery-landscape company with which he is associated. The garden is also the highly personal expression of a world traveler and avid horticulturist. Variously textured and colored conifers and broadleaf evergreens are combined in traditional English fashion to add substance and year-round interest to the garden. One flowering display succeeds another during the ten-month growing season. A surprising wealth of plant varieties thrive in a 10-by-30-foot border and three 10-by-10-foot raised island beds.

In spring there are drifts of fuchsia-pink Louisi-ana phlox mixed with golden alyssum, or basket-of-gold (*Aurinia saxatilis*). Through these mats of color grow clumps of small-flowered narcissi such as 'Cragford,' 'Actaea,' and 'Cheerfulness.' The sharp pink of the phlox, clear yellows of the alyssum and narcissi, and sage greens of iris leaves and striped oat grass make vibrant harmony. Lamb's-ears, golden marjoram, and *Nepeta mussinii,* Ray's favorite of the showy flowering catmints, mingle in the garden's foreground.

Later various salvias appear, from small *Salvia* × *superba* and meadow clary (*S. sclarea*) to tall Pitcher's sage and deep violet 'Indigo Spires.' Tall pink and white border phlox, yarrow, scabiosa, coreopsis, and balloon flower (*Platycodon grandiflorus*) also fill the mid-ground. Behind them, large-flowered clematis appear, clambering over the shrubs. Here also are tall rudbeckias, helianthuses, lilies, and old roses, as well as David Austin's new "English roses" of mixed antique- and modern-rose parentage. Scattered through the border bloom clumps of early, mid-, and late-season iris, including heat-tolerant arilbred hybrids. Golden yuccas are used as large foliage accents. Rosemary, lavender, and various thymes add a Mediterranean touch.

In fall, added color comes from asters, boltonias, goldenrod, eupatorium, and bulbs such as oxblood lily, lycoris, and small but beautiful sternbergias and autumn crocus. Tiny wild cyclamens, *Cyclamen coum* and *C. hederaceae,* regrow each year, described by Ray as "a special delight," even though the small flowers are often lost among their larger neighbors.

Temporary color is often used to mask dormant perennials. Favorite annuals and biennials for this purpose are Shirley poppies, cosmos, campanulas, foxgloves, and baby blue-eyes, or *Phacelia.*

Ray observes that most San Antonians who want garden color in their landscapes simply add a strip of annuals. Perennial-growing seems to be in its infancy here. Doing it successfully depends on selecting plants that meet the demands of trying local conditions. However, Ray has discovered that far more plants can thrive here than the public "is generally led to believe." One obstacle in public acceptance of perennials has been the identification of "perennials" with traditional northern varieties that either don't perform well here or don't survive at all. The metabolisms of many simply cannot withstand San Antonio's ten-month growing season and around-the-clock summer heat. Others bloom too briefly to be of much use in a season this long. Another obstacle is the public's expectation of nonstop mass bloom like that of annuals, without knowledge of the planning and ongoing mainte-nance necessary to orchestrate and encourage such a display from an assortment of perennials. The popularity of perennials, Ray believes, will grow as information is spread and such misconceptions are dispelled.

There are many ins and outs to gardening in the San Antonio area. The soil profile is complex, and the weather capricious. Ray points out the dividing line between the Blacklands and the Edwards Plateau, Interstate Highway 35. "The Blacklands side, on the east, is fertile, deep clay. On this west

Louisiana phlox, basket-of-gold, and tazetta narcissi bloom in April in Raydon Alexander's display garden. Milberger Nursery, San Antonio.

Raydon Alexander's Japanese garden was marked by a traditional decorative post with the inscription "A flower blooming out of a rock . . ."—a fitting description for the adjoining Edwards Plateau. Milberger Nursery.

side, there's limestone and flint with pockets of very mineral-rich soil." Winters here alternate between only a week of freezing weather and two to three weeks, from Zone 9 to Zone 8b conditions. "There's no consistent pattern to the rainfall," Ray says. "People make the mistake of not watering in winter, and they lose plants." There have been summers when water was rationed in San Antonio, so drought-resistant plants are recommended.

For perennial beds, Ray counters the shallowness of the soil by digging 2 feet deep, if he doesn't hit solid rock, or by building the bed up a foot with a retaining wall of landscape timbers. The bed is then backfilled with a commercial soil mix. To increase fertility, he adds superphosphate, muriate of potash, and nitrogen in the form of ammonium sulfate or bone or blood meal.

Alexander grew up gardening in San Antonio and later worked in England and Europe for some years, including a stint as an estate gardener in Greece. This position drew on his knowledge of English gardens and his Texas background in dry-country gardening. It sent him home with a wealth of Mediterranean plant lore applicable here, which he put to use in Marin County, California, before settling again in San Antonio.

He experiments continually with new plants and has discovered far more Texas-hardy ones than are commonly known. He has succeeded with peonies by selecting only the earliest varieties and has re-bloomed tulips for years by planting them in well-drained beds that are left dry in summer.

For years, plantspeople all over Texas have pondered the true identity of a small-flowered blue aster that flowers profusely in fall. "Hardy blue aster," *Aster amellus* (an Italian species), and *A. × frikartii* are among the various monikers that have been applied to it. One of Ray's test beds has been devoted almost entirely to growing varieties of *Aster oblongifolius* to determine its relation to the ubiquitous but nameless flower. Some of the *A. oblongifolius* varieties from Tennessee proved to be identical.

Further confirmation has come from a specialist in the genus, the curator of the Herbarium of the University of Illinois at Urbana-Champaign, that this aster is indeed *Aster oblongifolius* var. *angustatus*. This aster appears to be native to southern Tennessee, and it is related to the less-showy variety *rigidulus* that grows in North Texas.

Ray has found many traditional garden flowers to thrive in San Antonio, such as crinums and amaryllis, as well as flowers rarely grown here: Japanese anemones, rubrum lilies, and foxglove (*Digitalis purpurea*). "Society garlic," a relative of the alliums, is the only one of its kin that he finds does well, a pleasant exception to his rule: "Generally, with alliums, I have the best luck with the ugliest."

Ray's garden at Milberger Nursery is a sequel to larger plantings removed to make space for road-widening. These were a 60-foot ornamental border composed of three perennial beds and a small Japanese garden. The Japanese garden was instructive for its examples of Texas-hardy counterparts of traditional Japanese plants. It included pink *Prunus blireana*, which he considers the showiest flowering plum, flowering quince, barberry, ferns, hollies, shaped boxwood, and a mosslike mat of tiny-leafed creeping *Veronica repens*.

A wooden post that stood in the Japanese garden now leans in a corner of Ray's office. The inscription in Japanese characters is translated: "A flower blooming out of a rock, that is *yugen*." Ray interprets *yugen*, this special quality toward which Japanese gardens strive, as a paradox: "the ephemeral and beautiful coming out of the severe and permanent." The phrase evokes the wildflowers that sprout on the rocky Edwards Plateau. It also captures the task of gardeners in this severe but beautiful land.

Plowed red ground, stretching as far as the eye can see, is a familiar sight in the High Plains. Brick ranch houses hide behind windbreaks of native junipers, tall Italian cypresses, and fat arborvitae, *like quail sheltering in a fence corner.*

The Plains Country

Here, for the first time, we saw what one might call an ocean prairie, so smooth, level, and boundless does it appear. It is covered with a carpet of closely cropped buffalo-grass, and no other green thing is to be seen.

—A. W. Whipple (1856)

The High Plains can appear deceptively barren: flat, red land as far as the eye can see. Virtually none of the original prairie survives. But irrigation sparks life in the rich red-brown topsoil laid down by the prevailing winds over millennia; cotton, grain, and many temperate-zone flowers thrive. Spring rainfall fills the roadsides and fencerows with wildflowers.

Two images capture the land above the Cap Rock for me. The first is plowed red ground, stretching in all directions to meet the wide sky. The second is a brick ranch house with its cluster of outbuildings, hunkered down in the middle of its fields inside a rectangle of evergreen hedges. Like a quail sheltering in a fence corner, the house hides behind windbreaks of native junipers, tall Italian cypresses pointing skinny fingers at the sky, or fat arborvitae as big as houses themselves. These are the protectors that enable lawns to grow and flowers to bloom, despite the wind, and that keep the dust storms' heavier drifts on the *outside* of the window sills.

The High Plains and Rolling Plains of Texas are part of the Great Plains of the central United States. They are clearly divided by the Cap Rock Escarpment, a clifflike break that separates the rolling land below from the high, flat plains above. Elevation ranges from 800 to 3,000 feet on the Rolling Plains and 3,000 to 4,500 feet on the High Plains. The High Plains are the Llano Estacado, or Staked Plain, of early Spanish explorers. The Red Rolling Plains lie between them and the North Central Prairies. "South Plains" is the name by which the nineteen southern counties of the High Plains are commonly identified. The Panhandle is the northernmost, Zone 6, portion of the state that juts into Oklahoma. In this work, "Southern Plains Country" is used to refer to both the commonly called South Plains and the adjacent Red Rolling Plains.

Rainfall ranges from 26 inches in the east to 14 inches in the west, with highs in spring and fall. Soils include sands and clays, neutral to quite basic. Extreme mineral deficiencies and low organic content occur in many areas. High winds, sudden temperature drops, and frequent drought are characteristic of this area. Irrigation from wells that plumb the deep subterranean Ogallala Aquifer has enabled this dry, windswept area to become a leader in agricultural production, of cotton, in particular.

In June 1986, after an unseasonably wet May, the little High Plains town of Lamesa had flowers on every alley and street corner: obedient plant, evening primrose, Indian blanket, feathery red standing cypress, and purple, sand-hugging tansy aster. An electrifying bed of hot pink sand verbena and deep purple *Verbena rigida* brightened a service station. Late summer brought bristly magenta gomphrena "bachelor buttons," orange-and-yellow lantana, cosmos in every shade of pink and orange, and tropical queen's wreath vine dangling its silvery white and pink lockets. Fall on the High Plains recalls mounds of hardy blue aster, marigolds running riot in the alleys, and a small stucco house in Lubbock, its entire front yard filled with nothing but tall golden Maximilian sunflowers and sand.

The Plains are good garden country, despite their epic weather. "The weather phenomena of the Panhandle may be described under five types of occurrence," writes Fred Rathjen in the *Southwestern Historical Quarterly*. "The thunder storm, hail, the norther, the blizzard, and the dust storm." The average winter low temperature in the twenty counties of the Panhandle is between -10 and 0° F, a Zone 6 range; in the southern portion of the High Plains (the "South Plains") and the adjacent Red Rolling Plains, Zone 7 winter lows of between 0 and 10° F prevail. The average summer temperatures are a 97° high and a 74° low.

The standbys of High Plains gardens are annuals, Hybrid Tea roses, chrysanthemums, and bearded irises. This is not because other perennials won't grow there; they simply seem to have been outnum-bered. This evidently began happening in the 1950s. Some nurserypeople theorize that the development of large growers in California and Texas after World War II made the small-scale growing previously done by local nurseries a losing proposition. Annuals, for unknown reason, became the "color" product on which the new large growers in the Plains Country concentrated. Now a new, adventuresome crop of nursery operators is responding to a restive public by producing a retail selection of natives and perennials that is reportedly wider than has ever been available here before.

Helen Jarman of Lubbock maintains the city's public plantings. Since 1983, her department has tried perennials grown from seed from three national seed companies. So far, a few well-known species are in use. The city's Buddy Holly memorial is surrounded with Shasta daisy 'Little Miss Muffet' that blooms until frost, Jarman reports. Texas bluebells, perennial gaillardia, physostegia, yarrow, and lantana have all done well; the yarrow has regrown for three years. Dusty miller has proven to be a good source of silver-white foliage. Reblooming varieties of bearded iris have given the expected repeat performance in fall. Daylilies have proven reliable, as well.

On the southern edge of the Plains in Midland, Bob Lanham has conducted his own perennial trials since 1986. Friend and fellow nurseryman Burr Williams says, "Bob's real high behind perennials! He had a 50-by-30-foot area full of liners, selling them just so people would try them and come back and tell him how they did. You could see stuff over there you'd *never* seen before." The stock included California-grown liner, or seedling, plants as well as plants grown from seeds and cuttings collected from the wild and from the gardens of obliging gardeners. "When we saw a nice garden, we'd just stop and go up to the door and ask them to tell us about it," says Lanham. He adds that almost all of the older gardeners were ready to share samples. After two years' experience growing the new selections, Lanham reports one successful garden plant from the California source: *Evolvulus* 'Blue Daze' (a tender perennial used as an annual north of Zone 9b). Seven Texas natives and old-fashioned perennials turned out to be excellent garden plants: pink evening primrose, sand verbena, blue flax, scarlet sage, Texas bluebell, and two ruellias. Lanham feels there is a definite market for his winners, because "so many people are tired of planting annuals again and again."

Burr Williams specializes in native plants. His Gone Native nursery and landscape company provided hardy landscapes to many Midland home-owners. Then he got busy teaching schoolchildren about plants at the Sibley Learning Center in town and cut back landscape operations. His business now concentrates on growing and retail sales and leaves the landscape design and installation to others. "The nature center," as it is known, is a private institution that Burr helped found. His interest in native plants is both passionate and practical. "Many popular garden plants just won't make it here," he says. "Not only is our soil salty and alkaline; so is the water. People who buy acid-loving shrubs like azaleas find that they die in one season."

People who can recall Plains gardens kept by their parents or grandparents confirm the wide variety of garden plants that are adaptable there. Dallas horticulturist Bob Wilson recalls the Lubbock garden of his grandmother, Mrs. Albert A. Roberts. "She had tons of bearded iris, tons of daylilies, daisies, sweet William, and lythrum. She grew dahlias and gladioli that she replanted every year. Moss roses (portulaca) and dwarf bachelor buttons (gomphrena) made ground covers. There were these tiny garden pinks—I don't know what they were—little lacy dianthus that looked like the 'Wee Willie' *Dianthus chinensis* that we have now."

In 1951, Mrs. Roberts' home was completed, and the back yard was fenced 6 feet high with cinder blocks, Bob recounts. "The flower beds are about 6 feet wide and go all the way around the yard. Inside the fence is the flower border and inside of that, a sidewalk. Inside the sidewalk is Bermuda-grass lawn.

You could walk around on the sidewalk to look at the plants. It was really nice." The garden is still nice, he says, despite the fact that, in her eighties, his grandmother is not able to keep it in quite the gorgeous condition he remembers from his childhood.

"It's a lot easier to mix plants with different moisture needs out there," Wilson comments. "My grandmother's beds had that little 'Buddy' gomphrena scattered all through them as ground cover, even sticking in and around the bearded iris. She actually waters her bearded irises once a week along with the other plants, even in summer, and it doesn't hurt because the sand just drains it away. If I did that in Dallas, the iris would rot." Rot-prone dianthus, campanula, and gypsophila do better there than just about anywhere else in the state, for the same reason.

Alternating warm spells and freezes can do damage, but most gardeners here take winter seriously enough to protect their gardens early on. High winds are countered by placing plants on sheltered exposures and by staking. Favorable factors for High Plains gardens are high evaporation rates, well-drained soil, and cool night-time temperatures. All three mitigate against root rot and mildew, common problems in areas with higher humidity and/or heavy soils. In addition, the comparatively lower night-time temperatures slow the metabolic rates of plants. This may enable plants of more northerly regions that don't normally survive in the eastern two-thirds of the state to thrive here. The nightly cooling and comparatively shorter growing season may be sufficient to protect them from the nonstop growth that commonly causes their early death in southern climates.

I recall a back-yard garden in Lamesa that had Turk's cap, red garden verbenas, Shasta daisies, orange-and-red lantana, annual cosmos, asparagus fern, garlic, an apricot tree, and, I am sure, many other flowers that I have forgotten. My paternal grandmother may have grown those flowers because she knew them from her Rose Hill, Mississippi, home. Most of these are still common today. The trick with many other old garden varieties is finding

Top: Salvia coccinea *and purple coneflowers made dusky by the half-shade fill a corner of Ed and Margaret Kennedy's garden in Midland.*

Bottom: Cacti, yucca, and a squash vine in pots cluster by the Kennedy swimming pool.

Barrel cactus, cutleaf daisy, and star grass. Kennedy garden.

them in a nursery or mail-order catalog or in the garden of a gardener who will share. As more landscapers and gardeners plant perennials, both old-fashioned and new-found varieties, and more nurseries discover that they can be profitable, the supply is bound to grow.

Four Native Gardens in Midland

The home of Burr Williams' clients Ed and Margaret Kennedy belies the notion that native plant-scapes are all "wild garden" meadows or thickets. The front yard of their modern home is "about the most traditional thing she has," he says. It is lined with contrasting banks of evergreen and "evergray" foliage: dwarf yaupon, cenizo, and liriope. Spiky yucca and billows of tansy aster add contrast and color. The home's north border has a background of native acacias and small live oaks, pruned into standards. Their feet are covered in drifts of perennial gaillardia and candytuft. There's ocotillo, or "coachwhip," too. The most used part of this home's landscape is the walled pool and patio area. The rigors of reflected heat and firecracker-hot summers are bested by masses of potted cacti and succulents in an array of colors. The small, semi-shaded green space nearby contains perennials and a small patch of lawn. There are *Verbena rigida, Zinnia grandiflora,* and yucca. A variety of purple coneflower puts out dusty-rose daisies. Blue-violet native Texas bluebells or prairie gentians mix with native foliage plants and a rose-red penstemon tentatively identified as *Penstemon campanulatus* 'Garnet,' propagated from trial specimens given Williams by Huntington Gardens in Pasadena, California. Mrs. Kennedy is an avid gardener, and she continues to add to and meticulously maintain the plantings Burr designed.

John and Marian Kimberly's front lawn is framed by a Burr Williams perennial border that could be found only in the Southwest. It contains none of the commonly recognized perennials grown in northern U.S. and English gardens. Instead of a hedge of holly or yew, Chisos rosewood (*Vaquelinia angustifolia*) forms an evergreen background. There are salmon, pink, white, and red Gregg's salvias. *Tecoma stans,* or yellowbells, a shrubby tropical plant that winters over in the southern third of the state, provides feathery foliage and clusters of lemon-yellow tubular flowers. Red yucca, *Hesperaloe parviflora,* sends up its arching stalks of coral flowers.

Another attractive Williams landscape surrounds the home of Robert and Dede Plank. The front garden is adrift with flowers and blooming shrubs: red *Salvia greggii,* orange *Anisacanthus quadrifidus* var. *wrightii* or hummingbird bush, and soft-fronded *Mimosa depocarpa* with its pink bottlebrush blooms. The ground is blanketed by pink evening primrose, yellow wild daisies, and white spectacle

pod, also called colloquially "jackass clover." A big golden leadball tree, *Leucana retusa,* shades the house front. Native plantings surround the house and fill a courtyard garden as well.

Burr's own home betrays the plight of the nurseryman: a landscape gone wild (as well as native) with healthy flowers. Blue flax, *Linum lewisii,* mingles with the grass. Red Gregg's salvia, American germander, and daylilies have grown into a thicket in the thin shade of mesquite trees. Red Turk's cap blooms luxuriantly on a shady side of the house. Perennial angel's trumpet, *Datura wrightii,* opens its gleaming white blooms from night-time until late the next morning. This member of the nightshade family is extremely poisonous; those who

An assortment of salvias, Tecoma stans, *and red yucca border the lawn of John and Marian Kimberly in Midland.*

Shaded by a golden leadball tree, Leucana retusa, *the garden of Robert and Dede Plank billows with red salvia, hummingbird bush, pink showy primrose, yellow wild daisies, and spectacle pod. The pink bottlebrush blooms in the foreground are* Mimosa depocarpa. *Midland.*

Night-blooming Datura wrightii, *a perennial, gathers dew in Burr Williams' Midland garden.*

grow it are advised not to pick its flowers or ingest any part of the plant.

The Turk's cap relates to another of Burr's interests: the old-time flowers that were brought into West Texas by pioneers and birds and spread by neighborly swapping—and birds. Turk's cap is one he says nurseries didn't sell until recently. It's "always been there," like ruellia, or Mexican petunia, and a lavender perennial aster with no authoritative identification by anyone that seems to grow all over the state. Burr calls it "New England aster," although it may prove to be the same as the San Antonio aster identified as *Aster oblongifolius.* Burr praises Bob Lanham's efforts at bringing such old garden flowers back into the local trade.

American germander, red Gregg's salvia, and daylilies mingle in the thin shade of mesquite trees in Burr Williams' garden-gone-wild.

Longspur columbine blooms below a waterfall at the foot of the Chisos Mountains in Texas' Big Bend.

CHAPTER SIX

The Trans-Pecos

[At Antelope Spring] the plateau, smooth and sterile, with rushes and waterpits in the foreground, and the rocky peak . . . in the background, formed a most characteristic desert scene . . .

—*Julius Froebel (1859)*

It seems presumptuous to ask for the austere grandeur of the deserts and mountains of the Trans-Pecos area of Texas—and gardens, too. The vast, tumbled landscape of this westernmost region of the state holds everything from baking alkali flats to conifer-capped mountains. But, being human, many of us want oases of greenery and flowers around our homes, even in the desert. Here, the great Chihuahuan Desert of Mexico extends into the United States. Altitudes range from 2,500 to 8,800 feet. Average annual rainfall in most of this region is less than 14 inches, although it increases slightly at higher elevations. The high rainfall months are usually July and August. Most of the native vegetation is so well adapted to drought that it blooms when the rains come, whenever that may be.

The primary geological formations in much of the region are mountains and intervening *bolsones*—basins with no outlet that simply collect the drainage of the mountains until it evaporates, leaving all of its accumulated minerals behind. Gardens are not easily created in the portion of the Trans-Pecos where creosote bushes, grasses, and cacti dominate. The soil is often salty and mineral-laden, sometimes as hard as concrete. The limestone areas, such as the Glass Mountains, are also rugged and alkaline. However, they bear diverse flora. The igneous, or volcanic, areas, such as the Davis Mountains, contain more gardenly iron-rich acid soils and deep underground reservoirs of fresh water. Even in the desert flats of the Rio Grande Plains, people grow native and adapted flowers and flowering shrubs.

The wilderness areas of the Trans-Pecos are better known than the gardens. In the Black Gap Wildlife Management Area, one finds Havard's bluebonnets 18 inches tall and the soft pink blooms of

A ten-acre garden of native Trans-Pecos shrubs is the pet project of Dr. Barton H. Warnock, professor emeritus of Sul Ross University. The land is part of the immense Iron Mountain Ranch, named for the one igneous peak of the Glass Mountain range, seen in the distance. Photo copyright © 1986 by Barton H. Warnock.

tamarisk, or "salt cedar," as it is called. Wild relations of the garden four o'clock cling to the sand, globe mallows bloom, and white spires of *Polygala alba* shine in the sun. Wild burros roam the canyon walls. Rattlesnakes sunbathe in rocky crevices. In the Chisos Basin, the heart of Big Bend National Park, lovely madrone trees with their pink inner bark flower, and deer browse around the campsite.

The domesticated side of the Trans-Pecos has its surprises, too. One is a proper English garden at a stone motel court in the town of Fort Davis. The British proprietor, Mr. Malcolm Tweedy, tends a velvety green lawn circled with evergreen hedges and a border of daisies, miniature gladioli, pinks, roses, and a score of other flowers. The scene is completed by his terrier, which has made a dogtrot in the cool shade under the overhanging flowers at the edge of the border.

In Alpine, one sees growing in front yards the South African perennial *Kniphofia uvaria*, or red-hot poker, strictly a florist plant to denizens of hot, wet places. One unusually damp May, the highway from Alpine east to Marathon was lined with Engelmann's daisies, false honeysuckle, wild primroses, pink woolly paintbrush, cassia, and scores of other wildflowers. The private garden created by Barton H. Warnock on the Iron Mountain Ranch near Marathon was a botanist's delight. In the mountains south of Alpine, I visited one of the most beautiful gardens I saw, Jack and Mary Scott's Quinta Pintada, which concludes this chapter.

Glass Mountains Shrub Garden

Barton Warnock has made the plant life of his Trans-Pecos home a life's work. His three field guides for the region are its botanical bible. Of the public and private gardens he has developed there, his pet project is a 10-acre shrub garden in the shadow of the Glass Mountains, on the vast ranch of William B. Blakemore II. When I saw it, Dr. Warnock had not gotten around to weeding yet, and therefore uninvited wildflowers were in full bloom.

The Glass Mountains are limestone formations as old as the Appalachians. Their name is a translation of the Spanish Sierra del Vidrio, believed to have been given for the glassy sparkle seen in the limestone escarpment from a distance. The basin it surrounds is considered a geological window, where the rock and earth strata of many different ages are buckled up and eroded away so that all are exposed in one comparatively small range. Blakemore's ranch contains Iron Mountain, the only igneous rock in the Glass range, and a large tract of the basin land that was formed over millennia of erosion and outwash from the mountains. Warnock was invited by Blakemore to use the ranch for field studies intended to crystallize the botanist's thirty years of teaching and study and enable him to record his plant lore in written form. Blakemore generously provided vehicles and his workers' help and eventually set aside land for the specimen garden.

The garden is outlined in white limestone rocks. Native trees mark the perimeter and spaces throughout the garden: madrone, willow, walnut, Texas pistachio, Parkinsonia or retama, Texas ash, soap-

tree, and a local variety of bigtooth maple. There are colorful flowering desert willows, redbuds, and plums. At one end of the plot there is a fruit orchard, and grapes grow in a fencerow and on a wooden geodesic framework. A 6-foot hail fence keeps out rabbits and snakes. Ten-foot-tall magueys, *Agave havardiana,* stand sentinel at one edge of the garden.

The garden is intended to display flowering woody perennials and shrubs, surrounded by clear ground. On the June day we are looking at it, the spring rains have spawned wildflowers everywhere. Knowing that he is in the company of a hopeless wildflower lover, Warnock can't resist gibing, "Now, this garden will look a lot better when I get all the weeds out of it."

Showy coral-red muskflower, a member of the four o'clock family, delights the eye and repels the nose. Its musky smell, resembling the odor of old meat, earned it the name "devil's bouquet." It is only one of many four o'clocks that live in the Trans-Pecos. Mounds of clear yellow *Zinnia grandiflora* crop up among the rock borders and the larger plants. This is one desert plant that is used successfully in Edwards Plateau and South Texas gardens; the San Antonio Garden Club plants a striking combination of it and lavender asters.

Cassia roemeriana forms foot-high mounds of inch-wide, golden-yellow blooms. Home gardeners

Mexican oregano, Poliomintha longiflora, *on Iron Mountain Ranch.*

Pavonia, or rock rose. Iron Mountain Ranch.

are familiar with its cousin *C. alata,* a tropical senna called "candlestick tree" that grows man-high in a season and dies out in winter.

A low, mat-forming ground cover that some native plantspeople think should be developed as a landscape plant blankets the ground here and there. It is *Dyschoriste decumbens,* with lavender flowers and small, fleshy leaves that form a resilient mat, even in prolonged drought. There are also plenty of globe mallows, purple-blooming snakeweed or *Dyschoriste linearis,* and showy *Bouvardia ternifolia,* the "firecracker bush," with bright red tubular flowers.

Long-blooming woody perennials make an important contribution to the garden. *Poliomintha longiflora,* or Mexican oregano, is covered with blooms after the recent rains. There are mounds of soft green pavonia, with its small, round pink hibiscus-type blooms. These Texas natives are both available in the commercial nursery trade. Bird-of-paradise, *Caesalpinia gilliesii,* is an open, airy shrub with yellow flower clusters set off by long red filament-like stamens. Many little houses in nearby Alpine are surrounded by these showy plants, growing wild.

Desert Garden at Lajitas

The Barton Warnock Environmental Education Center at Lajitas is 100 miles further south, 1,700 feet lower, and even drier than Iron Mountain. It is only a few miles from the Rio Grande. Warnock writes of the Rio Grande Plains area as "thousands of acres of creosote bush *Larrea divaricata* mixed

Cacti and ocotillo mark the trail head of the Lajitas Museum and Desert Garden, a stone's throw from the Rio Grande. It is now part of the Texas Parks and Wildlife system.

with varying amounts of other shrubs including ocotillo, Spanish dagger or Torrey yucca . . . and Gregg's catclaw *Acacia greggii.*" He drew the original plans for the museum buildings, patio, and garden. Houston businessman Walter Mischer raised funds to purchase 99 acres of land adjacent to his remote Lajitas resort village, where an old cavalry post used to stand. El Pasoan Ray Duncan became the director and planted the garden, which now receives visitors from all over the world. Most of the museum's acreage is kept in wild condition as a nature preserve, but several acres have been developed into an ornamental garden of beds bordered with native rock and filled with cacti, desert perennials, grasses, and shrubs.

Although the display garden is no longer maintained in the same form, a look at the plants and their care is informative for the region's gardeners and other desert-lovers.

Duncan considered the cultural practices employed at the Warnock Center unusual. "In most desert gardens, they change the soil," he said. "When Dr. Warnock first planned the garden, his idea was to see what would grow in the existing soil, by improving only the moisture level." According to Duncan, this is a "new" desert that dates back to a climate change that occurred only about twenty thousand years ago. The archaeological evidence of those damper days indicates that higher elevations, over 4,000 feet, bore conifers, and the lower elevations of 2,000 to 2,400 feet were blanketed with pinyon pines and oaks. Duncan reintroduced similar strains of hard-woods along the outer borders of the garden with success. "You'd be surprised what will grow here, with water," he said.

The stiff, spiny stems of ocotillo, or coachwhip, arch over the garden path behind the museum building. This remarkable plant puts out thick clustering leaves when it rains and drops them when drought forces it to conserve moisture. In early spring, clusters of brilliant orange-red flowers tip the branches. Another drought-defying plant, the prickly pear, appears here in pink-fleshed varieties,

Showy primrose at Lajitas.

as well as green. The bristles on the dusty rose pads are rose-colored, too. Beds of showy flowering cacti are top-dressed with black rock to set off their mounded, bristly forms. Many cactus species fill the Desert Garden collection. One is pencil-stemmed Christmas cactus, or tasajillo, covered with inch-long red fruits in winter.

Pink showy primrose (*Oenothera speciosa*) shows its hardiness here, blooming in a rock bed in full sun. Again, wild yellow *Zinnia grandiflora* makes cheery little ankle-high mounds of yellow flowers and airy foliage. There are many salvias or sages. Honey-scented scarlet gaura, *Gaura coccinea,* crops up here and there, deceptively delicate in appearance. A perennial rock bed became a grass garden by

A garden of desert perennials and volunteer grasses at the Lajitas Desert Garden.

happenstance, and the feathery grasses were so attractive that Duncan let them stay, mingled with the flowers.

A striking and unusual member of the rose family mounds by an irrigated pond in the center of the garden. It is *Fallugia paradoxa,* Apache plume. The 4–6-foot-tall shrub bears single, white wild-rose blooms. The fruits trail feathery plumes that give the plant an ethereal, feathery appearance, sheer and white as a cloud in the sunlight. It may be seen on fencerows through the arid parts of the state.

Observations that Duncan and Warnock have made about gardening in the Rio Grande Plains could be useful to other desert gardeners. The soil has been improved simply by drip irrigation. The water has slowly leached out much of the accumu-lated salts and minerals that make Trans-Pecos soils difficult for most plants. The slow dripping gradually penetrates soil that is not normally permeated by rainfall, improving the soil structure. "This was an inland sea," explained Duncan. "The clay soil of what was the old ocean floor is so tight that water had never permeated it. The only place where water naturally permeates the soil here is on bluffs and creek washes, where more porous soil layers are exposed by erosion. There you can see a heavy concentration of plants, because of the moisture." The channels that the water makes through the soil also improve its aeration and make soil looser and easier for plant roots to penetrate. In the museum courtyard, where the pitched roof directs the rainfall, plants grow larger and faster.

This desert garden shows that, wherever one is, a garden can be made with available plants. Plants adapted to the region, planted to harmonize with the surrounding terrain, erase the garden's boundaries. They present the region's beauties, concentrated and heightened. By echoing the subtler beauties of the wild surroundings, they open our eyes to them. After spending time in a native garden, one notices anew the same plants in meadows, woods, and fencerows, places that are sometimes their only refuge, and sees the region in a new way.

These two gardens and short region description represent only a fraction of the diversity of the Trans-Pecos. The Davis Mountains, the Guadalupes, and the varied habitats of the Chisos Mountains of Big Bend National Park, as well as the desert basins, all have their own distinctive plant and animal communities. The irreplaceable small remnants of nature in pristine form deserve preservation for their own sake. They also may offer society unknown practical benefits, including more plants likely to adapt to garden culture than have yet been tried. Paradoxically, here as elsewhere, many plants accepted into the nursery trade are threatened in the ever-shrinking wild, by expanding development and agriculture, and by irresponsible private collecting and commercial poaching.

A Desert Mountain Garden

Mary Scott of Alpine, out in Texas' Big Bend country, calls herself "a thorough desert rat." "I've always lived in desert country," she says, "and that's about all I know anything about." In 1980, she and her husband, Jack, built their home in the Davis Mountains just south of Alpine. Retired, they travel, photograph nature, and explore the neighboring wilderness. Around their home, common garden flowers mingle with native plants, some collected in the wild and some purchased from a nearby botanical garden. "La Quinta Pintada," Jack has dubbed it: "quinta" as the fifth-mile rest station of the early Spanish travelers was called and "pintada," painted or colored, for Mary's flowers and drawings.

A rock garden curves around the Scotts' house. Close by, specimen native shrubs, agave, and cacti add height and interest to the landscape, which blends gently into the surrounding rangeland. In the distance loom the mountains. "Our 'lawn' is range grass," says Mary, "and it goes pretty well unattended until the fall, when Jack mows it to eliminate the fire hazard." The property also contains Jack's pecan and fruit groves.

A native of El Paso, Mary had "always" grown familiar garden flowers: daisies, petunias, zinnias, pansies, stock, and snapdragons. "Since starting a yard in Alpine in 1981, I have leaned almost entirely toward the Chihuahuan Desert types and the

Oxalis, elderberry, red petunias, yellow marigolds, Gregg's salvia, and red and yellow nasturtium border the terrace of Jack and Mary Scott's home near Alpine. The mountain they dubbed "Sleeping Baboon" looms on the horizon.

Petunias, penstemon, marigold, and gray-leaved native salvia. Scott garden.

conservation of water," she writes. She attributes the growth of this interest to the nearby Chihuahuan Desert Research Institute, which maintains a large public desert garden of indigenous plants, as well as conducting and disseminating research on the region. Now Mary's pansies and petunias find a home in big wooden planters on the brick patio, and plants endemic to the Trans-Pecos, such as red Davis Mountain sage (*Salvia regla*) and shoulder-high Havard's penstemon, fill the rock garden. This makes sense in country where rainfall is often less than 12 inches per year and drought sometimes lasts all summer. When rain does fall, the rangeland flowers.

The Scotts' home sits on a slope. Averse to cutting into the hillside to create a level site, the builder made a level platform of stable washed sand to support the house foundation. At its northwest corner, the house is at ground level, and on the opposite side, it sits above grade on the sand bank. A brick terrace wraps around the north and east sides, bordered by Mary's rock garden. The curb and foundation for the flower beds were built at the same time as the house. Soil from nearby, mounded up against the terrace foundation, forms the beds. Their gray rock surface was Mary's project. "I gathered it off the land," she says. "It took a couple of years, adding to it bit by bit. I'm not one of those people who can haul rock day in and day out. Then, of course," she chuckles, "I had a Cactus and Succulent Society meeting coming up, so I worked real hard to finish in time." The rock mulch suppresses weeds and conserves moisture, as would an organic mulch.

The "plain old mountain soil" that forms the

beds requires amendment with peat moss and fertilizer at planting time. "Very hard and dry," Mary describes it. "What we need most of all is compost. The nutrients are all washed out of the soil. I make compost, get manure, and fertilize a little with chemicals. The chemical fertilizer I use as little as possible because it doesn't build the soil, it just feeds the plant roots a little." Occasionally she and Jack make a trip to the cattle barns at nearby Sul Ross University to haul manure, which they compost before applying it to the beds.

Mary gardens for several days at a stretch in the spring, when there are lots of new plants to get into the ground. "When I get what I want *mostly* done— I never get through—then I lay off a while and just water it." Watering is done by hand, with a garden hose. She enjoys the exercise. "When I don't do anything, I feel stiff at the end of the day. It's keeping you healthier, just getting out and growing your bones in all directions."

Before she retired, Mary was a draftsperson with the El Paso electric utility company. She drew the house plans herself. Her eye for line and form shows in the organized but informal massing of flowers around her home. She shared this artistic ability with her brother, the late Elliott Means. "He was a fine Western artist," she says. "During the thirties, he spent most of his time in New York, doing magazine illustration to earn a living." His career established, Means returned to the West to paint his favorite subjects. His work is prominently displayed on the walls of La Quinta Pintada.

Mary's love of gardening began in childhood, when she visited her grandmother in Mexia, Texas. "That was a long time ago," says Mary. "My grandmother grew roses, all kinds of geraniums, all the old garden flowers. She was the only one in town with a greenhouse—it was a tiny one. When spring came and it was time for high school graduation, my grandmother furnished all the girls their bouquets."

The flowers on which Mary Scott lavishes the love learned long ago would make bold and amazing bouquets—spiky and towering. Instead, she and Jack share them with the hawks, the coyotes, an occasional visitor, and the desert skies.

A volunteer netleaf hackberry shades Mexican poppies, petunias, and coral Penstemon barbatus *var.* torreyi. *Gray sedum grow in the rock crevices. Scott garden.*

Pines and quiet ponds characterize the Piney Woods. This scene is from the homeplace of Mr. Parsons, near Jasper.

CHAPTER SEVEN

The Piney Woods

*This [Jasper County] may be
regarded as a heavily-timbered
country, there being little prairie
within its limits . . . On the banks
of the water-courses is to be found
a very heavy growth of magnolia,
beech, walnut, and a variety of oak
timber; but the majority of the
uplands are covered with pine . . .
In the southwest corner of this
county is a region . . . known as
the thickety country . . .*

—J. de Córdova (1849)

The Piney Woods, also called simply East Texas, are Texas' portion of the Deep South. They are the southwestern tip of the great American pine-hardwood forest that extends east to Florida and northeast to Virginia. The prevalent forests are dotted with swamps and with cultivated and pasture land. Ecologically speaking, the Piney Woods are part of the southeastern United States.

Annual rainfall averages from 40 to more than 50 inches, distributed fairly evenly throughout the year. The sands and sandy loams that comprise Piney Woods soils are usually acid (pH 6.5 or less). Surprisingly, drought can occur in this comparatively well-watered region, even when drier parts of the adjoining Blacklands and Gulf Coast remain unaffected. This is because the sandy soils drain more rapidly than the clay soils of those regions. The Piney Woods' ground elevation is 200 to 500 feet above sea level.

Plants well adapted here are those that do well through the Lower and Middle South, a selection distinct from those that thrive in the calcareous and/or alkaline soils in most of the rest of Texas and the Southwest. This region resembles the Piedmont of the Carolinas.

The high, thin shade of conifers and the friable, acid soil nurture understory plants typical of the southeastern pine-hardwood forests. This is the natural home of wild azaleas and flowering trees such as magnolia, gordonia, and halesia, or silverbells. Yaupon holly and deciduous possumhaw holly are common. The old, simple narcissus species and varieties, some with names that must have traveled with them from England, like 'Sir Watkin' and 'Queen Anne,' are widely naturalized here. One finds "water chinquapin," the native Texas lotus; halberd-leaf hibiscus; oakleaf hydrangea; Carolina lily; bird's-foot violet; and wild irises. Obviously, this region's climate and plant communities make it unlike anywhere else in Texas.

A Woodland Garden in Longview

Imagination at play with nature animates the shady acreage of A. C. and Janice Upright, near Longview. Gardener and artisan David Romero of nearby Hallsville once spent two days a week with them, garden-making. The Uprights gave Romero free rein to unite elements from the surrounding land and faraway, objects found and fabricated, in a landscape that is colorful and full of surprise.

From first glance, the Uprights found their 50 acres of woods, fields, and a ravine sloping to a cow pond peaceful and pleasant. The veteran floral designers felt it needed something more, though.

Something much more, as it has turned out. In 1983 they enlisted Romero to effect a transformation that was still going on five years later.

The surrounding woods and scattered native cedars, redbuds, dogwoods, and privets were kept; wild ferns and mosses were moved to transform the old ravine. Yaupon, azaleas, and bridal wreath contribute to the garden's foundation. "In very early spring, it's a fairyland," says A. C. "All that white is just wonderful."

The garden is unified by the kaleidoscopic geometry of hand-laid brick, set to patterns only in

A water garden is shaded by a giant topiary swan trained by garden artisan David Romero. Home of A. C. and Janice Upright, Longview. Photo © 1987 by Robert L. Goodman, Jr.

Upright garden.

Romero's mind's eye. Brick walks descend from the home's rear terrace. They skirt an upper lawn and pass downhill, past a series of pathside gardens shaded by high trees. The north walk pauses first at a small Oriental water garden shaded by a giant topiary swan that Romero carved from an ancient privet. Through an arch, the wooded lower slope descends to a waterside terrace.

The broad brick steps that descend the garden's south side are flanked by blooming perennials or potted color, depending on the season. Side paths explore forest nooks, one holding a homemade St. Francis shrine. European, Asian, and folk mementos preside in other garden spots.

Perennials find a place among bromeliads, tropicals, water plants, topiaries, flowering shrubs, and native trees. These include blue ajuga, river ferns, native pink coneflowers, and tender species like ageratum, geraniums, and caladiums. Color is continued almost year-round with annual flowers and tropical plants. In winter, many of the tender plants, like the geraniums, are dug up and trenched for frost protection until the following spring.

Everywhere there is contrast, between naturalistic and Oriental garden styles, green woods and exuberant Latin color, statuary and whimsical topiaries. This eclectic mix may derive from Romero's dual cultural heritage or from the influences of the Uprights' adventuresome floral and decorative trade. It is the unique personal expression of a special collaboration. In this series of small gardens-within-a-garden, every view has something different to delight, inspire, or amuse.

The Piney Woods 75

Dunes on the inland side of Padre Island are covered with wild grasses and a solitary sunflower.

CHAPTER EIGHT

The Gulf Coast

In the Gulf Coast area, as in many places, some of the most interesting plant life is in the ditches and the fencerows. *Kosteletzkya* mallows grow knee-deep in salty ditch water, their 6-foot stalks of small, pale pink hibiscus blooms swaying gently in the breeze. Along the highway north of Angleton, wild pasture rose, *Rosa bracteata,* covers the barbed wire fences, beautiful except in the eyes of farmers bedeviled by it. The shiny dark green leaves set off white flowers centered with nests of fuzzy golden stamens. On the coastal dunes grow beautiful plants that will almost certainly die if you try to take them home to plant them—and others, like the pretty sea oats often used in dried arrangements, whose relative, northern sea oats, does well all the way into North Texas and is available commercially.

The Gulf Coast of Texas combines marshy areas and dunes near the shoreline with low-lying inland grasslands that support ranching and farming. On the Upper Gulf Coast, rainfall varies from 50 inches in the east to 35 inches in the west, distributed fairly evenly throughout the year. The growing season is about 310 days. On the Lower Gulf Coast, southwest of Port Lavaca, annual rainfall is usually less than 30 inches. The growing season there lasts 335 days or more. Humidity and warm temperatures are the rule.

Soils of the Gulf Coast are generally acid, varying in structure from sands, sandy loams, and clays in the marshes to heavier clays and clay loams in the prairies. Climatic conditions of the Upper Gulf are similar to those across the entire Gulf Coast of the United States. In gardens, scores of semi-tropical plants join the natives, and moisture-loving ferns and flowers abound.

The Upper Gulf Coast

The Upper Gulf Coast offers the private and public gardens of Houston, both elaborate and casual, manicured and half-wild. On the elaborate, European end of the scale, there is Bayou Bend, the estate of the late Ima Hogg, now a public garden. The Houston Arboretum and Armand Bayou Nature Center offer wilderness and wild gardens in, respectively, woodland and coastal settings. Mercer Arboretum presents varied gardens, plant collections, and woodland trails.

Home gardens in Houston range from magnificent to modest. There are bog gardens, woodland gardens, and native shrubberies. An attractive courtyard garden in the University of Houston area is lined with beds of cast-iron plant, crocosmia, Shasta daisies, maidenhair fern, and liriope. The home of Marie Sullivan sported a front walk lined with tall, lavender-flowered "society garlic" and back yard beds of daylilies, mallows, rudbeckias, and daisies. The native Texas plantscapes of plantsman Lynn Lowrey are well known for the feeling of woods and wilds they bring to mid-city. Nursery owner Katy Ferguson, a Lowrey protégée, also worked in this vein; among her residential landscapes are a native iris garden and a native mixed border on the grounds of the Houston Garden Club.

AN ENGLISH GARDEN IN HOUSTON

A garden that captures the English garden style in Gulf Coast terms is that of Alice Staub in River Oaks. Alice planted gardens for friends who liked hers and eventually found herself in the garden-making business. In these pages, Alice's garden is shown in early spring and in midsummer. Flowering trees, softly colored Hybrid Tea and Floribunda roses, native perennials, bulbs, and tropical gingers all grow there.

The house is screened from the street by tall, moss-draped trees that shade a narrow border of grasses, perennials, bulbs, and roses. There are silvery grass, Louisiana irises, daffodils, Gulf Coast penstemon, stokesia, old-fashioned amaryllis (*Hippeastrum gracilis*), and other flowers. Old-fashioned rose 'La Marne' and modern 'Iceberg' crowd the border's end, where a wrought-iron arch festooned with variegated potato vine marks the entrance to the private portion of the garden.

Here, the garden is most English, with its smooth lawn bounded by rose and flower borders and its

The home of Alice Staub, which she calls "a big cottage," is adorned with trellised roses: a yellow one and 'Dortmund,' not in bloom here. A brick walk angles to the garden's back corner, crowded by Choisya *on one side and roses and perennials on the other. Houston.*

various features: paths, a background of tall evergreen shrubs, a garden hut (made by masking an old garage with bamboo mats), and the house itself, a large cottage. Dallas gardeners exclaim over all the shades of green in Alice's garden. Not only the humid Gulf air and abundant rainfall, but also her careful selection of foliages is responsible.

The house, which Alice calls "a big cottage," shelters a brick patio with tropical frangipani and a border of roses. A yellow rose and Carolina jessamine climb lattice screens; 'Dortmund' rose frames an east window. A brick walk angles toward the garden's back corner. It is crowded by choisya on one side and roses and perennials on the other. The lawn is framed by borders: one of seasonal perennials,

At the end of Alice's front border, roses including modern 'Iceberg' and old-fashioned 'La Marne' crowd an arch festooned with variegated potato vine.

In the private side yard, the garden is most English, with its smooth lawn bounded by rose and flower borders and its various features: paths, a background of tall evergreen shrubbery, and a garden hut. Alice Staub's garden.

Hedychium × kewensis *against a background of evergreen shrubs in Alice Staub's garden.*

including native plants, one of roses and gingers, and the third exclusively of roses. In the perennial bed, ferns, verbenas, lantana, and Louisiana irises mingle with New England lythrum and native Texas flame acanthus and Gregg's salvia. A clerodendrum stands sentinel like a red candelabrum. Biennial French hollyhock and impatiens appear, also.

Drainage can be a problem in such a low-lying, flat site. The slight elevation of the flower beds helps this. Soils in the region are generally acid and vary in structure from sands to sandy loams and clays. The acidity of the soil in some areas here makes growing roses easier than in many other locales. Ample rainfall of up to 50 inches a year is a boon, although the combination of heavy rainfall and high humidity encourages fungal infections and root rot.

Like most gardeners, Alice insists that her garden isn't as good as it would be earlier in the season or if she spent less time gardening for others. But when pressed, she concedes that she, like most of us, never has the time she thinks a garden deserves. She feels that visitors will expect a lavish, springlike display of "color," not the shifting bloom of other seasons that satisfies the gardener. It's good to know that a sketchily tended garden can look this wonderful and that every season doesn't have to rival spring.

A surprising example of good gardening is in Angleton. An excellent mixed border adorns the front of a bank. Pines, hollies, junipers, and variegated privet are combined with crape myrtles, native yucca, tropical hibiscus, and blooming annuals like portulaca. The same design could be accomplished with perennials. In cold-winter regions, one would substitute hardy mallows for the tropical hibiscus and low, summer-blooming, heat-hardy perennials like lantana and prairie verbena for the portulaca.

The Lower Gulf Coast

The Lower Gulf Coast, down the coast from Port Lavaca, represents the other extreme from Houston in Texas coastal conditions. The Upper Gulf Coast visibly gives way to the Lower where the hardwoods give way to scrub.

Further south, Corpus Christi stands at the ecological crossroads of the Gulf Coast and South Texas. The people who live here occupy the narrow zone between the Gulf of Mexico and the arid South Texas brush country. They are shore dwellers with dry range at their backs.

The lush, wildlife-filled wilderness into which the early settlers came is now forever altered. It diminishes daily, the fragile sand dunes savaged by off-road vehicles and condominium development.

Present-day residents of Corpus enjoy balmy sea breezes and a long warm season, balanced by the vicissitudes of blistering sun, salty wind, occasional sudden freezes, and drought. The town is a microcosm of three climates: the seaward and inland faces of the coast and the brush country. Padre Island and the bay shore as far as a few blocks inland are classic acid-soil, windblown, salt-sprayed beach property. A clay-soil area lies inland from the beach lands. Further inland, the west side of town abuts the King Ranch, South Texas' best-known expanse of dry rangeland. Those who garden in any of these locales have their work cut out for them. They meet the challenge with heat-hardy perennials and shrubs, both natives and tropicals.

Sabal palms grace Ocean Drive, and soft-hued oleanders and brilliant bougainvilleas grow all over town. Many tropical plants almost take care of

This mixed border in front of a bank in Angleton is composed of pines, hollies, junipers, variegated privet, native yucca, crape myrtles, tropical hibiscus, and blooming annuals. The same effect could be accomplished with hardy mallows and low perennials such as lantana and prairie verbena.

This Lower Gulf Coast garden is modeled after public gardens in Mexico, walled and shaded, with winding paths. A rooftop deck draped with pink queen's wreath overlooks the patio and surrounding pots and raised beds of cacti, cycads, and tropical and South Texas native plants. Home of Sue and David Gardner, Corpus Christi.

themselves in this climate where annual low temperatures rarely fall below 20–25° F and an average of 335 days can be expected to be frost-free. Rainfall averages 25 to 28 inches per year. Inland conditions are sufficiently arid for cacti and cycads, while the beach climate is mild and moist enough for such tropical vines and flowers as tolerate salt. Heat-loving annuals perform beautifully, and palm trees survive all but very unusual winters. Many tender perennials grown only as annuals further north thrive year-round here. Heat-loving, drought-tolerant perennials popular elsewhere would make wonderful additions to the tropicals that are habitually grown here.

A MEXICAN-STYLE WALLED GARDEN

Corpus resident Sue Gardner had a large garden of her own—and the beginnings of a garden for the whole city. A doctorate in botany, earned amid the demands of child rearing and 250-mile commutes to Texas A&M University, prepared her to direct the new Corpus Christi Botanical Gardens. The gardens are the product of a local botanical society organized by the Gardners and several friends and now enthusiastically supported by the community. The 235-acre grounds combine unspoiled chaparral characteristic of South Texas and wetlands, as well as gardens of tropical and old-fashioned flowers. When the gardens are completed, they will include palms, shrubs, roses, desert plants, trees, and orchids. Protected courtyard gardens of tropicals and exotics will nestle among Spanish Colonial–influenced structures.

Sue and David Gardner's home garden was as interesting as the Botanical Gardens promise to be. They modeled it after their favorite public gardens in Mexico: walled and shaded, crisscrossed with winding paths for strolling. Mounded beds contain collections of cacti, cycads, tropicals, and South Texas native plants. "Wild olive" trees (*Cordia bossieri*) flower, and palms bend overhead. The mood was very tropical and, in the shadier corners, mysterious. Pre-Columbian carved stone statues of gods, jaguars, and frogs emphasized the Mexican flavor. A tiled swimming pool provided a note of coolness in the brilliant sunlight. Stairs mounted to a deck on the roof of this rambling contemporary home, from which one looked over a tangle of pink-flowering queen's wreath onto the garden. There was a greenhouse of tropicals such as heliconia and strelitzia, or bird-of-paradise, and a hidden garden in a far corner shaded by a bamboo lattice.

A BEACH GARDEN IN CORPUS CHRISTI

A contrasting example of Lower Gulf gardens is a landscape designed by Elaine and Ted Turner. This oasis is in South Corpus Christi, on the Cayo del Oso, a shallow inland salt lagoon, until 1987 the Turners' home. Less than 30 inches of rain falls here in a year, and gardeners must deal with strong, salt-laden winds and somewhat alkaline soils. The growing season averages eighty days longer than that of Houston, and the temperature range is hotter by 5° F.

The landscape is a casual, colorful environment that reflected the Turners' relaxed way of life, a nurseryman's dream: color with almost no care.

Ted Turner owns both a retail nursery and a wholesale business that provides the nursery trade with dwarf pittosporum and oleander varieties he has patented. The best-known of the oleanders are 'Shari D,' named for his daughter, and 'Carnival.' A large cream-colored 'Shari D' leaned over the front door of the Turners' former home, and other oleander varieties lined the path that led downhill to

Pre-Columbian carved figures of gods, jaguars, and frogs emphasize the garden's Mexican flavor. Gardner home.

Stairs ascend to an upper deck, past oleander, giant ophiopogon, and pittosporum. Turner home, Corpus Christi.

the back garden and the Oso. The Turners' front yard was a lawnless garden of palms, pittosporums, oleanders, and birds-of-paradise (strelitzia) surfaced with bark mulch rather than grass. White periwinkles and red dianthus dotted a bed along one property line and grew in the shade of a palm. Giant liriope was used for accent.

In back, green wedelia, a tough, flowering ground cover, draped the rocky slope that drops down to the Oso. Native to the American tropics, wedelia is dotted with yellow daisylike blooms throughout the over-ten-month growing season. 'Madame Galen' trumpet vine covered a fence, and paths curved around the corners of the house past blooming tropical jatropha, dwarf pittosporum, and palms. Large oleanders and standard pittosporums lined the house wall, with colorful crotons heightening the effect. Pots of petunias and other annuals brightened a large wooden deck. A wooden bridge connected the deck to a thatch-roofed gazebo set on stilts in the edge of the Oso—ideal for sunset-watching or early morning coffee or an ocean fort for grandchildren.

Ted Turner began gardening as a child, with his mother. They gardened wherever they lived, as his father's oil drilling work took the family around the region. He knows garden culture in Corpus' Padre Island, its coastal plains, and its brush country area, more characteristic of inland South Texas than the coast. "The island is sand, on the acid side. Elsewhere the soil is mostly black gumbo clay. It's on the alkaline side—gardenias won't grow here." To acidify the soil, Turner uses aluminum sulfate for quick results and slower-acting soil sulfur for the long term. The pH of the water is mostly neutral. Two special problems for gardeners here are the salt and the wind. "Plants turn white as far as 15 blocks from the shore, from the salty wind," he says. "Rainfall washes it away." Turner finds that drip irrigation systems are effective in leaching the excess salt from the soil, but overhead watering is necessary to rinse salt off the plants, either by hand, with sprinklers, or with an irrigation system with pop-up sprinkler heads. The wind here can "worry a plant to death. It can kill the crown of a palm tree," he says. March, April, and May are the windiest months. To protect low-growing flowers and foliage plants, Turner positions large shrubs as windbreaks. Proper fertilizing enables plants to withstand the wind better. Turner applies a balanced fertilizer four times a year; in saltwater areas, up to six annual feedings are recommended.

Christi Foote's blackland garden on the inland side of Corpus Christi grows Hybrid Tea roses and pink verbena.

A TRADITIONAL GARDEN

Amid all this horticultural variety, another Corpus Christi gardener keeps a traditional landscape of lawns, shrubbery, roses, and perennials appropriate to the climate.

Christie Foote lives in town, on the median clay between the island and the brush country. Hers is a small frame house surrounded by St. Augustine lawns and flower borders. The side entrance of her home is attractively planted with crape myrtles, tropical jatropha, *Lantana camara* hybrids, and evolvulus. An old tree stump in the shady yard is filled with blue tropical plumbago. The back yard is her park. In the shade of a tree, begonias and Gerber daisies mingle with tropical foliage plants around a smiling stone cherub. The island bed that bisects the lawn contains Hybrid Tea roses, Shasta daisies, and pink verbenas. The fence line is planted with evergreen shrubs, plumbago, and other perennials.

Mrs. Foote follows much the same cultural practices as do gardeners with similar gardens in North and West Texas. The beds were composted well when they were first dug. Compost is applied again in fall and spring, improving not only the fertility but also the drainage and aeration of the heavy clay soil. Applications of soil sulfur help moderate its mild alkalinity. Mulch deters weeds and frost damage, and conserves moisture. Over the years, the garden has reached a healthy condition maintained by regular, but not intensive, care.

Modest amenities, like a picnic area, lawn chairs, and a birdbath, define functional areas of the garden and give it proportion and focus. A weathered frame garage across the neighbor's fence is homely but homey, like an old barn.

Mrs. Foote says that, in her eighties, she must have help mowing and hauling compost. She does the rest of the work herself, in early morning before the heat drives her indoors. She says that, despite the inevitable losses of loved ones and physical strength that come with advanced age, the garden keeps her happy and healthy.

Yucca in bloom, with lantana and cholla in background, mingled with native short grasses typify the South Texas "brush country." San Antonio Botanical Center. Photo © 1998 Todd Johnson.

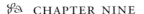

CHAPTER NINE

The South Texas Plains

. . . the Rio Grande Plain, except for a few large, well-known clearings,
is the Brush Country, the land of thorns.

—*Richard Phelan*

The brush country "begins where the marshland ends," as naturalist
Eric Lautzenheiser puts it—only a few miles inland from the coast.
A short drive from the beach, one finds mesquite brush and prickly
pears. Their domain spans the south-central fifth of the state, south
of an imaginary line that runs from Victoria, which is about 85
miles north-northeast of Corpus Christi, westward through south
San Antonio to Del Rio.

The South Texas Plains are level to rolling brushlands, hot and
arid. The altitude ranges from sea level to 1,000 feet. Temperatures
well above 100° F are commonplace in summer. Average annual
rainfall ranges from 30 inches in the east to 15 inches in the west.
Occasionally there are devastating droughts. Peak rainfall is in May
and June, with a minor peak in September. January and February
are usually dry. Soils range from very basic to slightly acid and
include clays and sandy loams. There are great differences in soil
drainage and absorption. Livestock range is the prevailing agricultural use of the land. Mesquite chaparral prevails.

Laredo Gardens

In the city of Laredo on the Texas-Mexico border, gardeners have
a wide range of plants to choose among: heat-hardy perennials,
tropicals, and plants native to the region. "The criterion for what
we use is what lives through July and August," says Gladys Keene,
a north-side homeowner.

The garden of Willis and Guadalupe Gentry, longtime nurserypeople, reflects the abundance of usable flora and lifelong enthusiasm for plants. The family's fenced back yard is taken up mostly by
a swimming pool and a covered terrace. The 65-by-35-foot area

*Vines and palms
half hide a gazebo
in the lush Laredo
garden of Guadalupe
and Willis Gentry.
Ruellia, lantana,
and bougainvillea
provide color in
November.*

between the back fence and the pool is luxuriant with plants. Raised beds and terraces are filled with perhaps fifty varieties of trees, vines, shrubs, and perennials. A wooden kiosk that once held a sales counter at the family nursery is now transformed into a garden hut, swathed with bougainvillea and other tropical vines. Tropical plumbago, Mexican petunia, and spiderwort make a large bank of mixed purples and blues. "They come up like weeds here," says Mr. Gentry. He reworks the beds each January or February and cuts back the plants to keep them in bounds. Lantana gets cut down to a stub twice in the summer because it grows so large here. Daffodils grown in raised beds, a large-cupped 'King Alfred' type and an orange-and-cream Tazetta, have come

back for four years. Orange lantana spills along the garden's edge. Bloodflower (*Asclepias curassavica*) and peach bougainvillea in pots spread long flowering branches. Potted flowers carry the display onto the pool's paved borders.

The garden is fertilized once a year with a specially formulated low-ammonia, balanced fertilizer produced by the Gentry nursery. In the summer, Willis Gentry waters twice a week.

A native San Antonian, Mr. Gentry moved to South Texas to begin his own company after fifteen years in the wholesale nursery business. He has lived there twenty years, and his horticultural curiosity has never abated. "The whole time that I've lived here, I've kept growing more and more plants from

The showpiece of the Laredo garden of Willis Gentry, Jr., is a 100-foot border of small trees, flowering shrubs, and cascades of lantanas and verbenas that bloom even in summer's worst heat.

Mexico and tropicals," he says. "Now that I've visited Canada and Alaska, I can't wait to try to grow some of those plants here."

Willis Gentry, Jr., is a landscape architect. The showpiece of his home landscape is a 100-foot streetside border against the 8-foot wall that surrounds his back yard. The native soil is mounded up and terraced with rock. Small trees, flowering shrubs, and cascades of lantanas and verbenas make billows of color that withstand the summer heat. Trailing and shrub-form bougainvilleas, wild olive tree (*Cordia bossieri*), crape myrtle, and cenizo are just a few of the large plants. There are also barberry, *Lantana horrida,* iceplant, moss rose, and trailing lavender lantana. After just eighteen months in the ground, the planting is full and mature. Slow-release, balanced fertilizer tablets are applied once a year. It's the bountiful effect of an English garden, created with Texas-tough plants.

Ann Neel is a gardener's gardener. "I just try one of everything," she says. Her large back yard contains a lawn lined with bulbs and perennials, a vegetable patch with row plantings, and, in a corner, a small water garden.

From her experiments with bulbs, she finds that Dutch iris, red spider lily, white hymenocallis, amaryllis, society garlic, and Easter lily (*Lilium longiflorum*) thrive. Agapanthus fails. River fern grows in thick masses in the borders. 'Indigo Spires' salvia blooms freely, and Mexican hat blooms all year round. Other successful perennials in Ann's garden are *Verbena tenuisecta,* purple coneflower, Turk's cap, and lantana. *Dianthus deltoides* and a red border carnation do well in summer, despite a continual battle with ants, which eat the roots.

Vines drape Ann's back fence. Confederate jasmine and orange trumpet vine abound, but coral honeysuckle is less enthusiastic. Vines form a backdrop for flowers and shrubs along the fence. A *chile pequín* grown to the size of a small tree catches the eye.

"Some of the soil is sandy and well drained, and some is sticky," Ann says. "You never know what you'll find." She forks up new beds. Garden clippings layered an inch or two deep and let dry first are mixed in, along with peat moss. Drip irrigation waters the borders.

David and Mary Lamar Killam, natives of Laredo, insisted on a Mexican-style house that

Malvaviscus arboreus *var.* mexicanus *in Willis Gentry, Jr.'s garden, Laredo.*

The salmon pink wall of Mary Lamar and David Killam's Laredo home is a foil for native orange and South American purple lantanas, two species of cenizo, ligustrum, crape myrtles, and 'La Marne' rose.

would reflect the region. The salmon-colored stucco and heavy wooden doors and details suggest San Miguel de Allende, not the United States. The garden, Mary Lamar feels, also had to express the relaxed feeling of life along the border. "I didn't want a 'kept' or trimmed look," she says. "The sage bushes are not pruned. I like the garden more natural. Gardeners keep coming by and asking me if I don't want the trailing lantana trimmed back off the sidewalk." The landscape was designed by Jim Keeter of San Antonio, revised from a first plan that Mrs. Killam considered "very San Antonio, with lots of live oaks," to a more colorful South Texas look.

Color harmony is important in the Killams' garden. The peach shade of the house stucco sets up a vibrant contrast with the grays, lavenders, pinks, and greens of the plantings. There are the grays of native cenizos and dalea, the lavender of trailing lantana and hardy blue asters, and the pale blue of tropical plumbago. Indian hawthorn and gray-green lantana provide a green background. 'La Marne' roses pick up the pink tinge of the house. A 'Mutabilis' rose decorates one house corner.

In the Rio Grande Valley, a Harlingen resaca *flows, one of the small tributaries of the Rio Grande that still run.*

The Lower Rio Grande Valley

What grew in the Valley before those assembly-line rows of vegetables? Why, brush, of course—a prickly, hot jungle full of fruits and seeds and cactus apples, swarming with wildlife . . . In the southernmost reaches are tropical plants and animals whose main abode is Mexico. Towns in the Valley are full of trees and vines and flowers.

—Richard Phelan

The Lower Rio Grande Valley is Texas' horn of plenty. Total agricultural sales for the region in 1985 were $393 million. Texas ranks second among the states in agricultural production, and the Valley counties lead the state. Irrigation enables the flat, arid land to produce up to three crops a year. The growing season is ten months long, or even eleven in mild years. The river winds over 800 miles through canyons and desert to arrive at this shallow plain—not a valley at all—in Hidalgo, Willacy, and Cameron counties. The Valley is almost subtropical, with brief, infrequent winter low temperatures of 25 to 30° F. Inland, the terrain is flat, dry, and brushy. At the coast and where the abandoned tributaries of the Rio Grande called *resacas* are irrigated, a tropical lushness prevails. Rainfall averages 20 to 26 inches a year. Stately palm trees, imported by early housing developers, outline roads and housing tracts. Bougainvillea vines and flowering trees abound.

Plants of tropical Mexico, South America, Africa, and Australia run riot in gardens. The flowering plants are shrubs, and the flowering shrubs become trees. Plants North Texans think of as conservatory specimens serve as foundation plantings around Valley homes: sago palm, Mediterranean fan palm, tropical hibiscus. The wax mallows, known in the rest of Texas by shrubby, shade-loving Turk's cap, are represented here by a tree-size form with flowers to match. The Mexican variety of *Malvaviscus arboreus* bears spiral, cake-decoration scarlet or pink blooms 3 inches long that hang at eye level.

The critical test for perennials here is their ability to survive without winter cooling sufficient to induce dormancy. Herbaceous perennials, so often dormant in winter further north, are commonly evergreen here; thus they are denied a rest period when top growth and flowering cease. Many northern perennials cannot sustain the metabolic pace set by the heat and this long growing season, unbroken by sustained frost. The freezes that do occur in the Lower Rio Grande Valley usually last for only a few hours in the early morning, before the rising sun warms the air. Yarrow, daisies,

Malvaviscus arboreus *var.* mexicanus.

mallows, lantanas, ruellias, pavonia, tropical plumbago, salvias, and verbenas are perennials that thrive here. Ones too tender for the humid chill in the northeastern half of Texas fill many gardens: jatropha, coral vine, and *Tecoma stans* are examples.

Palms and Pothos

Stuart Place Nursery in Harlingen, owned by Glyn Whiddon, offers myriad flowering plants unfamiliar to northerners: yellow-blooming, shrubby *Galphimia glauca;* blue-flowered evolvulus ground cover; justicia with its orange-red tubular flowers; Cape jasmine. Along with standard landscape trees and shrubs, the nursery stocks tropicals, heat-hardy perennials and annuals, and native plants.

A visit to the home landscape of Stuart Place clients Weezie and Dial Dunkin would make frost-weary travelers envious. Sago palms flank the front door. Hedges of pink and white hibiscus line the patio, a backdrop for bird-of-paradise (strelitzia), dwarf pittosporum, and wood ferns. The red blooms and green-and-white leaves of variegated hibiscus make a striking accent planting. Gerber daisies brighten semi-shaded spots, and *Lantana montevidensis* and hybrids of *Verbena peruviana* bloom in the sun in large containers. Dunkin, at one time in the nursery trade, designed the land-

scape and brought in Stuart Place for later refinements.

Brownsville's gardens revel in tropical plants. The garden of a local restaurateur is a formal grove, complete with white marble statuary, draped not with English ivy, but with the common pothos ivy that decks many an office filing cabinet in more northerly climates. But here pothos reaches its vigorous tropical phase, climbing to the treetops, with leaves as large as elephant ears and lobed like split-leaf philodendron. Neighbors Jimmy and Lorraine Mayer enjoy a back-yard papaya orchard. Their flower border and orange trees are edged with tender asparagus fern, a hothouse specimen in most of the United States.

Morris Clint of Brownsville sells a wide variety of flowers, bulbs, and roses from a nursery next door to his home. The work of his mother, Katherine L. Clint, and sister, Marcia Clint Wilson, with rain lilies, genera *Zephyranthes* and *Habranthus,* is noted among bulb fanciers. Clint offers *Dietes vegeta,* African iris, an unusual perennial better suited to the Valley than bearded iris. Its beardless, irislike flowers are marked by golden orange and purple eyespots.

Plants North Texans think of as hothouse specimens form foundation plantings in the Valley. Here, white and variegated hibiscus, Strelitzia, *and ferns. Dunkin garden, Harlingen.*

In the tree-filled garden of Lorraine and Jimmy Mayer, asparagus fern covers the feet of a small orange tree. Brownsville.

At the Gladys Porter Zoo in Brownsville, the tender perennial Tecoma stans, *called* esperanza *here, grows tree-size.*

Flowers like Trees

The Gladys Porter Zoo in Brownsville is a botanical delight. Tropicals and South Texas natives are its ornamentals. *Tecoma stans,* or yellowbells, a tender perennial, shades the animals' pens. A knee-high, semi-woody flower in the South Plains, it becomes a multitrunked shrubby tree here, know as "esperanza." *Russelia equisetiformis,* or firecracker plant, makes a striking tall, weeping, pencil-stemmed ground cover, light green with red-orange tubular blooms. Bougainvilleas in every shade drape walls and climb the free-form molded "rock" walls inside the zoo. These are hybrids such as salmon 'Sundown' and wine-red 'Barbara Karst.' Vivid oleander varieties such as cerise-pink 'Calypso' grow at the zoo's entrance.

Many tropical bedding plants grow year-round in the Valley. Shrimp plant (*Justicia brandegeana*), jacobinia, cassia, and copper plant are common in borders. Tropical *Plumbago auriculata*, winter-hardy through Zone 8b, mounds over walls and borders, heaps of palest blue flowers on long, arching green basal stalks.

A Rosy Future

Rose gardeners find a range of problems not encountered outside the Valley. "Roses have to be grafted on a rootstock adapted to the area," says Glyn Whiddon. "It is old garden rose 'Dr. Huey,' not the multiflora stock used by most East Texas

Bougainvillea 'Sundown' on a molded artificial rock wall at the Gladys Porter Zoo.

rose growers." Even with the proper rootstock, roses respond to local conditions with varying success, points out Morris Clint. Yellows bleach in the sunlight and heat. Petals of delicate substance tear in the high winds. The Texas Agricultural Experiment Station at Weslaco is conducting trials of Mexican rootstock for grafted roses. The objective is to find stock suitable for local growing of grafted roses adapted to South Texas.

Clint goes on to say that antique roses, hardier in landscapes, are little known in the Valley. He believes that six or seven old-rose types commonly seen here may have originated in France during Spanish Colonial days. The necessary work to key them to old Southern roses now in circulation has

yet to be done, however. Banksia roses, Noisettes, and Polyanthas that grow well in other subtropical regions are also likely prospects for the Valley.

In the Lower Rio Grande Valley and South Texas, the traditional idea of the perennial garden breaks down. Here where the diverse floras of the tropics, the desert, and the beach all flow together, there's no particular reason to specialize. There are excellent reasons to add more perennials to the plants customarily used here, however, and to draw from the perennial garden style.

Of the flowers grown in these regions, ones more consistently reliable in the entire southern third of the state are included in the Plants and Planting section of this book. A mixed garden style incorporating long-blooming, warm-climate perennials with annuals, tropicals, yuccas, and cacti would have an entirely new richness and interest. Options abound. As Elizabeth Lawrence, the masterly southern gardener, concluded, "I think if I were beginning anew I would lay it (her garden) out in the manner of gardens of Southern France, in a formal pattern of shrubs and flowers and pebbled squares enclosed by walls and shaded by lindens: the sort of garden that is made for hot weather by wise people who adapt to their surroundings." Some of the beautiful effects of classical perennial gardens could find a dazzling, fresh expression with plants uniquely Southwestern and tropical. Cutting gardens and gardens of Mediterranean herbs are naturals here. A Mexican-style walled garden of heat-hardy perennials would be apt. So would a uniquely South Texan mixed border of yuccas, cacti, peppers, desert flowers, perennials wild and gardenly—a melting-pot border of everything striking and hardy here. For those in this region who would like to further develop these possibilities, there is an added enticement in the ample range of native perennials and adapted perennials from similar climates worldwide.

Plants and Planting

Louisiana phlox with tulips.

Plants That "Do" and How to Grow Them

. . . the mystery and intrigue that overwhelms most gardeners— making a plant . . . grow, blossom and bring forth its fruit in an unfriendly atmosphere, complicated with numerous problems.

—Dewey Compton

Plants that "do" and garden-making with them are the subject at hand. Before getting down to such business it is time to reflect, caution, explore garden design, and explain terms.

The reflections (on gardening's pleasures and nature's examples) and cautions (on native plant preservation) follow shortly. Garden styles and themes and basic design are explored in Chapter 11.

Chapter 12 explains the horticultural terms in the plant descriptions and charts that fill the rest of the book. This chapter also serves as an introduction to garden conditions and gardening practices.

Chapters 13 through 17 each present a group of plants. Chapter 18, Techniques, is a basic guide to gardening methods.

This preview of Part Three is provided to direct readers, so that novices may get their feet wet, ponderers may ponder, and avid gardeners may skip the chatter and plunge right in to see if I have managed to come up with any plants that they don't already grow.

Pleasures of Gardening

Gardening, unlike so much in life, is not a contest. It is an experiment, gardener friends point out. "You should tell people that even gardeners who've been at it for years are still just trying this and that to see what works. New gardeners shouldn't get hung up on success and failure—that's not what it's about."

". . . A work of cooperation between [the gardener] and nature," nature photographer Josephine von Miklos calls a garden, "and to this extent he shares in nature's miracle . . ."

"God forbid the garden should ever look exactly the way you want it to," says another, highly artistic landscaper. "Then what would be left?" He cherishes like a perfect day or an unexpected gift those rare times when his design and labor, the soil, the weather, and the mysterious ways of his plants all collaborate in a brief moment of perfection. "The rest of the time, you dig and scheme for those high points," he says.

Others of us may be motivated less by that aesthetic thrill and more by nature's curiosities, the fragrance of flowers, or the pleasurable mild ache and afterglow of a day's digging in the sunshine.

Ecology

Communities of plants of like needs are the rule in the wild. You may have noticed vivid blue, tripetaled spiderwort in shady fencerows with pink oxalis nestled at its feet. In sunny, moist prairies, the blue-violet bells of Texas bluebell sway amid horsemint's pink-purple or green tiered blooms like Chinese pagodas. The same principle of natural communities that is seen in the wild applies in the garden. All the organisms present, not just the plants, take part: insects pollinate plants; plants feed insects and animals; soil organisms recycle debris and nourish new life.

Aesthetically, too, wild plant communities are instructive for the visual variety and harmony they often display and for the balanced arrangements they arrive at simply by each plant seeking out its preferred spot.

Botanical melting-pots are what our flower patches have become in the course of thousands of years of global plant-trading. Plants as diverse as the rose-and-white Lady tulip from Turkey's dry hills and feathery magenta-pink lythrum from wet European roadsides are ours. Growing conditions appropriate to each plant's specific needs are, of course, the key to success. "What's sad is when people mix things that aren't even ecologically compatible," says a nature-wise salesman for a major U.S. grower. "There's no way the plants can thrive, not to mention that they look odd together."

Plant Sources and Preservation

Plant sources and preservation have become critically interrelated. Amid the activity of gardening and the commercial trade, the relation of garden plants to the wider green world is often ignored. This short-sightedness has become a public issue, as natural areas and species have reached critical survival points, while once-accepted horticultural practices and public ignorance contribute to their destruction. Gardeners should be aware that the means by which plants are obtained affect their survival as species and the survival of their natural sites. The charge to gardeners should be, insofar as is possible, to buy only plants and seeds obtained by responsible means.

Ironically, new enthusiasm for native plants in the past two decades has often been destructive to them in the wild. Excessive and destructive commercial collecting has long been a problem in the Middle East and the Mediterranean area. In recent years, local populations of "cactus in Arizona, terrestrial orchids in Michigan, carnivorous plants from the Gulf states, and woodland species from the mountains of North Carolina" have been decimated by unscrupulous commercial dealers, according to the journal of the Perennial Plant Association. In Texas, cactus species of the Trans-Pecos and lady's-slipper orchids in the Piney Woods are two plant groups that have taken much abuse.

In 1989, the well-known W. Atlee Burpee & Company, a major mail-order supplier of seed and plants, stopped collecting for sale in its own operations. Despite the fact that collecting is a woefully inefficient source of viable plants, some suppliers persist. So do private individuals.

As early as 1970, collecting by the public was cited by Texas plantsman Carroll Abbott as the cause of the near-disappearance of "mountain pinks" (*Centaurium beyrichii*) and many other wildflowers that used to blanket state roadsides. Texas naturalists report that publicity of the 1987 rediscovery of a colony of one of the showiest of Texas wildflowers, 3-foot-tall wine-red *Salvia penstemonoides*, thought extinct, was followed by inroads of scavengers who threatened to wipe it out—this despite its being easily grown and germinating in about ten days.

Contrariwise, native plant populations are also threatened by the introduction of garden hybrids to the wild, where they may obliterate natural communities by crowding, interbreeding, and generally changing the natural balance. Texas Natural Heritage Program staff say that uninformed well-wishers often disrupt nature in this way, mistakenly believing that they help conserve wilderness by transplanting garden plants there. Anytime cultivated plants grow near wild populations of the species, dilution of the native gene pool may occur.

Collecting played an important role in the introduction of native plants to commerce in Texas, where there were no significant retail or mail-order sources until the late 1970s. The first plant stock resulted from private collecting by the few enthusiasts persevering enough to observe, tag, and harvest wild seed and plants at the proper time and nurse collected seedlings through transplant shock or deal with the sometimes erratic germination of wild seed. These individual efforts, along with work by universities, experiment stations, and growers, provided today's information on culture as well.

Today, reputable commercial growers and natural scientists alike strongly advise gardeners not to purchase plants or seed of questionable origin and, in general, not to collect plants from the wild. There are few valid reasons to do so. A large number of species adaptable to garden culture are available commercially. Such nursery-grown stock and seed are generally stronger and perform better in cultivation than wildlings. To expend the effort to collect common plants that are now widely available commercially rarely makes sense, given their often weaker performance in the garden and the damage frequently done to wild areas by collecting. As for uncommon plants, casual collection is unjustifiable. "If you take away plants from a rare or uncommon population, you're taking away some of the population's genetic material," explained Patty Leslie, who managed the native areas of the San Antonio Botanical Center and searched for and propagated endangered plants as part of the national program of the Center for Plant Preservation. "Those genes may be important for the colony's survival. Because of the genetic diversity and ability to adapt to change that is lost by removing some of the plants, a minor change in environment may be enough to push that population over the edge" to extinction.

Endangered plants and habitats are protected from collecting and destruction by state and federal law.

There *are* situations in which collecting is appropriate. Effective and responsible collecting requires dedication and self-education, however, and those with only casual interest should not attempt it.

Aspiring collectors must acquaint themselves with endangered species on state and federal lists, available from the Texas Natural Heritage Program of the State Land Office in Austin and similar programs in other states. They must obtain the landowner's permission, and they must learn and practice proper collecting techniques.

Plants in the path of planned development are certainly good candidates for collection; native plant societies often conduct such rescues. Otherwise, collection only of seed, and only of very common plant species in sizable populations, is advised. Not even seed should be taken from populations so small that they can easily be counted. Collection of plants legally designated "rare" or "endangered" is punishable by law. Collection of those recommended for such designation by the scientific community and of uncommon plants is strongly discouraged.

Responsible nursery operators now get parent stock for propagation primarily from previously collected stock at other nurseries and collect from the wild only rarely, if at all, growers say. Container-growing and field-growing of native plants prevail, and even some large trees are container-grown. This not only protects the environment; it produces plants with a far higher survival rate.

There are a few ways to tell if native plants and seed are nursery-propagated or wild-collected. Nurseries that do propagate their native plants themselves generally proudly state this in their catalogs. The New England Wildflower Society's booklet *Nursery Sources of Native Plants and Wildflowers* lists propagated sources of some native species. Phrases in catalogs such as "[name of state] grown" may mean that plants listed are wild-collected. Beware of advertising reading "species" or "wild"; ask the supplier for details. Extremely low prices are suspect. Groups of plants most likely to be collected, because they are difficult or slow and therefore uneconomical to propagate, include native terrestrial orchids; trilliums and other lily family members; cacti; hardy ferns; and typical eastern woodland wildflowers. Ethical collecting of these species is possible, but the impossibility of determining what collection techniques were used by a dealer makes it advisable to buy only nursery-propagated plants. For responsible sources of native plants, see Appendix 1. Suppliers of nursery-propagated plants in some states can provide a written guarantee to that effect from their state department of agriculture; ask for one.

The wistful 1970s notion that we could rely on back yard "preserves" of wildflowers to replace our natural heritage is false, ecologists say. When a plant is taken out of nature, nature is gradually taken out of the plant, as it adapts to cultivation. The leap from the garden to human health and welfare is not a long one, when you consider even such obvious examples as the drug digitalis, obtained from the foxglove, or penicillin, developed from a lowly mold. From a global perspective, we need wilderness for its wealth of genetic diversity that enables species to adapt to environmental changes now and in the future. This is our global insurance against destruction of species on which life depends, now and in the future. We need to preserve wilderness for such self-interest, if not out of awe and love for the primal world from which we sprang, which predates humanity by eons and has sustained us from the beginning. Only if our methods serve the survival of the great green world from which our cultivated plants came can we continue to tend our gardens in good conscience.

Season-long color is provided by scarlet sage, pavonia, Mexican oregano, and oleander. San Antonio Botanical Center.

CHAPTER ELEVEN

Design with Perennials

"I should see the garden far better," said Alice to herself, "if I could get to the top of that hill: and here's a path that leads straight to it—"

—Lewis Carroll

Planning, plant selection, and color sense all enter into durable and eye-pleasing gardens. This expertise grows with experience. Some basic concepts provide a head start.

Kinder, Gentler Color

"Everyone wants nonstop color all season, with no maintenance!" is a common complaint of landscapers. There's no such thing. The industry consensus is, take your pick: the fabled season-long "riot of color" of annuals, or long-lived but intermittent color with perennials. Neither annuals nor perennials are labor-free. But then, neither is a Bermuda grass lawn. Many gardeners say a lawn is more work.

Subdue the unruly annuals in a garden governed by perennials, along with the subtle, lasting grays, silvers, and greens of small foliage plants and herbs and the seasonal surprises of bulbs, and you have a palette for a richer if quieter kind of year-round landscape color. Two-thirds perennials and one-third annuals is an ideal combination, suggests Gary Raith, past director of landscape services for the Mansion hotel and the Crescent office-retail complex in Dallas, unexpected but happy settings for these cottage plants.

"The lowest-maintenance color is from native and Texas-hardy perennials," says Raith. "I work with them more, for the cost savings in water and fertilizer." They were bedded out like annuals in the high-visibility plantings at the properties Raith oversaw, but they follow their natural cycles in permanent plantings at his home garden near Forney. He particularly appreciates "the good movement of color through the whole bed with perennials with different bloom times."

Perennial Myths

Perennials are a group of plants about which people seem to have a great number of misconceptions. In the process of practical garden-making with perennials, some common myths must be left behind.

TROPICAL VERSUS PERENNIAL

The term "perennial" comes in for some misuse in the South. This is in part because the farther south one goes, the less distinct are the habits of tropical plants and tender and hardy perennials.

In gardens in Zone 9, where winters remain mild, tropicals may fill roles played by perennials and flowering shrubs in temperate climates. They are natural, customary garden members and a welcome source of color here where perennials requiring winter dormancy don't "do." From a purely visual standpoint, drifts of tender Gerber daisies are just as effective as drifts of hardy Shasta daisies, although different. Some tropicals, such as tree Turk's cap (*Malvaviscus arboreus* var. *mexicanus*) are included in this book, because they lend themselves to the effects of herbaceous and mixed borders in places where herbaceous perennials traditional to those borders don't thrive. In sheltered microclimates or with winter protection, they will often winter over well outside their normal range. No part of Texas is entirely immune to hard freezes, however, so tropical plants are not failsafe here. Their chief values are fast growth, heavy bloom, and great performance in the worst season for most temperate perennials, late summer. There's no reason one can't defy orthodoxy and mingle tropicals with wildflowers and traditional perennials, after all. With the above limitations, semi-tropical and tropical plants have a proper place in perennial-style gardens in Zone 9. Because this zone makes up less than a third of the state, however, this book presents fewer tropicals than would a book exclusively for that region.

Similarly, a few plants are included that are suited to the Zone 6 and 7 portions of the state but do not do well farther south.

A PERENNIAL IS A PERENNIAL IS A PERENNIAL

This seems obvious. But many gardeners persist in describing perennials that die out under their care as "annual in my garden." Behaving seemingly like an annual in a garden outside a given plant's preferred climate range doesn't make the plant an annual—it makes it a dead perennial.

Annuals may, of course, maintain their presence in a garden by reseeding. The individual plants still fulfill only their one-year lifespan.

True annuals do appear in this book, not only in the chapter on "companion plants" but also, in a few cases, in the plant profiles, if they are truly persistent reseeders.

PERENNIAL, NOT PERMANENT

People often take the word "perennial" to mean that such plants can be planted and left to take care of themselves from then on, much as one installs furniture. This is akin to other gardening myths, such as the no-care, season-long "riot of color." Another is the universal wildflower seeds that sprout and bloom wherever you throw them. These are fond fictions, like natural-looking toupees and muscle-toning with no exertion. The grain of truth is that perennials generally require much less labor and expense in successive seasons than annuals, since it is not necessary to provide new plants every year. In addition to the periodic soil enrichment that all cultivated plants need, most perennials need occasional cutting back, staking, or winter protection, as well as division at least every few years. (Some few need none of these.) Their greater rewards are their generous self-propagation, ever-changing seasonal cycles, and the special beauty of plantings matured and interwoven over time.

Bloom Season

It is surprising to some people that most perennials do not bloom all season long, as many annuals do. Annuals must produce enough flower-borne seed in one season to reproduce themselves; perennials, by contrast, put some energy into reproduction and some into growth and survival of the individual plant. Some perennials do bloom all season; many are natives of the U.S. South and Southwest and other areas with long, hot growing seasons. More common bloom periods range from two to six weeks. Creative planning is needed to achieve a season-long succession of bloom in compatible colors from an assortment of plant varieties. But this also results in the special variety and surprise of perennial gardens.

Setting, Style, and Theme

There are many sources of inspiration for garden looks. Setting, style, or theme can all pose approaches to a garden that is uniquely one's own.

Setting is important. Your home may be your castle, but in the very small kingdoms of today, ignoring what's outside the fence can make the monarch look a fool. The natural terrain of your region may be visible in your property, an asset capitalized on in the case of Frankie Clark's hillside garden on Austin white rock, for example. Cultivated surroundings may dominate, as with adjoining manicured lawns, and large trees not native to the site. Despite this, you may still choose to make your perennial garden a rock garden, but smooth the transition with an irregular grassy area that merges into rock outcrops rather than abruptly starting a mock Alps at the property line. The architectural style of your home and those nearby is another cue to garden styles that will fit. A period garden style contemporaneous with the style of architecture may be a happy choice—if you are so lucky as to own a house built in a recognizable period style.

The world of style moves between two poles, of course, the formal and the informal. Classic examples of these opposites are the grand gardens of seventeenth-century France and the cottage gardens of late-nineteenth-century England, described in Part One. Louis XIV's Versailles displays absolute symmetry, order, and control, with even the forms of the shrubs in the *parterre* garden transformed by incessant clipping to perfect ribbons and cones. The artificiality and compulsive symmetry of those gardens does not exhaust the meaning of the word "formal," however; contemporary gardens may be formal in a completely different sense. A better summation of formal design in gardens may be subjugation of all the color, texture, and profusion of the garden to a strongly ordered, dominant form or plan. Japanese Zen gardens of only two or three major elements—raked sand, a grouping of stones—are highly formal. "Formal" describes some modern landscapes in the American landscape style that arose in the 1950s, as well. In addition to their asymmetry—a characteristic often seized on as informal—they are simple, spare, and sharp-edged, dominated by a single concept and strong plan like the skyscrapers of the time.

The mostly informal gardens depicted in this book suggest the many forms that informal gardens may take. Perennial borders like Bob Wilson's show both qualities: formality in their straight edges and symmetrical placement on the property and informality in their tousled, apparently casual plant placement.

It seems that the whole vocabulary of style from all periods is available to us now. In this era in which social customs are extremely informal, there is a returning interest in formal surroundings. The formality, symmetry, and ornament characteristic of earlier times and historic garden styles are newly popular, especially in conjunction with period buildings. Much that we had forgotten is classic and timeless. Garden designers are only beginning to go into the attic, so to speak, to pull out bygone fashions and see what is adaptable. A new wealth of garden pictorial and historical books offers abundant inspiration far beyond what can be presented here.

Themes for perennial gardens are as numberless as thoughts. What do you like best in a garden? Make that your theme. In addition to themes based on historic styles, there are theme gardens based on plant groups, colors, uses, seasons, ecosystems (bog, meadow), even wildlife the garden is meant to attract. Here is a partial list of perennial theme gardens:

    crinum lily garden
    garden of grasses
    meadow garden
    gray garden
    silver-and-gold garden
    rainbow garden
    children's garden
    edible ornamental garden
    Shakespeare garden
    daylily garden
    Louisiana iris bog
    vine garden
    red border
    white garden
    scented garden
    cutting garden
    moon garden
    butterfly garden

In past eras, landowners might devote an entire garden to one season, such as the June garden at Gertrude Jekyll's home, Munstead Wood. In spring and fall, when the June garden was out of bloom, activities centered in other areas. Now, few have, or care to have, this luxury. Gardens planned around one plant group today usually use one whose members bloom over a long period, like crinums or daylilies, or a many-seasoned grouping of plants with a shared characteristic like growth habit, such as vines.

Site Selection

A floral planting can be the landscape's focal point, suggests a Dallas landscape architect. In an existing, all-green landscape, a flower bed can add emphasis and interest, as a piece of statuary or a water feature would—for much less expense. Another landscape designer uses floral color "to move your eye around the landscape. I concentrate color where I want people to look."

Contrarily, a cutting garden for ready stock for flower and foliage arrangements is traditionally placed out of view, so that it can be plundered at will without concern for attractive garden display.

There are practical considerations in locating a garden, as well, such as sunlight and good drainage.

Many perennials need "full sun"—that is, unobstructed sunlight from dawn to dusk—to grow and bloom well. In hot southern climates, it seems that many plants generally described as needing full sun respond even better to a situation with two or three hours' shade in the hottest part of the day in summer. Many plants recommended for "shade" actually prefer the filtered light found in the high shade of tall trees, or "partial shade," that is, a half-day's shade, preferably in the afternoon. (In the South in summer, very few partial-shade plants, and these mostly tropicals, can adapt to shade broken only by hot midday sun.) True deep shade is good for only a few perennials, such as blue ginger and some violets.

Low, wet sites are to be avoided except for especially suited plants. Soggy soil will rot plant roots, especially in winter. Handsome perennials that are bog-dwellers are numerous enough for another book. Only a few plants that like standing water, such as Louisiana iris, are included here.

Garden Seasons

In various parts of Texas, as in adjoining states and the remainder of the Middle and Lower South, the growing season ranges from six to twelve months long. In the absence of one brief period of concentrated bloom such as occurs in the North, manageable bloom seasons must be organized within the long period of potential gardening time. Few plants flower for the duration. The diverse plants usable here, from cold-hardy perennials used in the North to true tropicals, afford many options for seasons-within-the-season.

In the Dallas–Fort Worth area, for example, the ten-month growing season can be divided into as many as six different bloom periods. One can span the season with a few spring-to-frost bloomers or punctuate it with several surges of bloom from different groups of flowers. It all depends on how intensively you want to garden and on the bloom cycles of the plants you select. The process is not like the seasonal "color changes" done with annuals, when beds are stripped, cultivated, and completely replanted. Rather, one season blends into the next, as the newly blooming perennials open and fading ones are cut back, and, if desired, seasonal annuals are used to fill in gaps. Local publications and area nurserypeople and extension horticulturists are good sources for seasonal bloom schemes for your locale. The following four bloom seasons are characteristic of the Dallas–Fort Worth area; not all gardeners aim for bloom in all four, of course.

AN EXAMPLE OF GARDEN SEASONS IN ZONE 8A IN NORTH CENTRAL TEXAS

Winter-spring: Perennials are visible in winter mostly as evergreen foliage rosettes, appearing with evergreen and evergray herbs and dried seed heads of flowers and grasses. Cool-season annuals such as pansy and cool-climate perennials used as annuals, such as calendula, English daisy, and English primrose, add color in early winter, through mild winters, and in early spring. Paperwhite narcissi, which often return here, bloom in mid- or late winter.

Early spring: Spring begins in February or March. Cool-season flowers squelched by brief freezes revive. Early daffodils and old-time "cemetery white," or "Florentine white," and "early purple" irises bloom. Perennial thrift, alyssum, and violets bloom. The second crop of cool-weather nursery annuals—snapdragons, calendulas, pansies, pinks, petunias—is available. Cool-climate perennials—delphiniums, stock, Iceland poppies, and foxgloves—are used as annuals.

Spring and summer: March 18, the average frost-free date here as of 1990, inaugurates spring proper. The first bloom comes from irises, daffodils, old roses, and many, many garden and wild perennials that were planted from divisions or nursery stock in fall or set out, with protection, in early spring. Certain cool-season annuals best planted from seed in fall bloom now: larkspur, cornflower, and native Drummond phlox. Spring brings the year's biggest bloom with excellent plant availability, peak wildflower season, the least temperature stress on plants and gardeners, and more well-known plants.

Many flowers that start blooming in spring continue well into early summer, depending on how hot it gets, such as coreopsis, wild foxglove, certain dianthuses, and rudbeckia. Garden phlox, daylilies, crinums, and true lilies have their heyday in early summer, prolonged to July in mild summers. Some few others bloom all summer no matter how hot, with a little water, such as prairie verbena, blackfoot daisy, prairie coneflower, lantana, Mexican mint marigold, Mexican oregano, and, with deadheading, gaillardia. Mediterranean herbs provide reliable green and gray foliage despite the heat.

Only a few perennials start blooming in late summer. Blue ginger and *Cuphea micropetala,* or hummingbird bush, a tender perennial from Mexico, are two. Many hot-weather annuals from the tropics and subtropics, started in May, do bloom from early summer right through the dog days. Cleome, cosmos, and celosia are three.

Fall: Fall here is a protean season. Mid-spring bloomers such as mealy blue sage that pall in August flower strongly with cool weather. Roses rebloom. Many fall perennials come on: hardy blue aster, fall rain lily, 'Autumn Joy' sedum, obedient plant. Hot-season annuals generally carry on, but weaken when night temperatures decrease to 40° F. A third crop of cool-season annuals is available for inter-planting. Some will weather light freezes and carry on into winter, providing a floral finish as the seasons cycle on.

Sizes and Shapes

A garden or a border? Starting small enough that you won't be overwhelmed is a good idea. Dabble first. A shallow strip limits the gardener to plants in a toy-soldier row. A short, blocky bed precludes use of some of the best tall perennials, because they appear too tall for the bed width. But about a 5-by-10-foot area, with stepstones to walk on, is ideal for starting out.

The traditional perennial border was a rectangu-lar bed, customarily backed by a hedge and fronted by a path or lawn. "Island" beds surrounded by lawn were soon to follow, attributed to respected English plantsman Alan Bloom. A more recent innovation is the small accent planting, just large enough to use one or a few plant varieties and provide color in a spot where it will be most noticed, such as near the front door or front walk. Shapes fancier than the rectangles and ovals of borders and islands have been familiar through history: crescents, knot patterns, circles or squares bisected by paths. The main practical considerations in garden layout are accessibility and, where a lawn is adjacent to the bed, a bed shape that can be followed by a mower. A bed width greater than 4 feet generally necessitates stepstones or interspersed blocks of paving or gravel contained by edging.

Color Schemes

Try to suit colors to the landscape's sun and season and time of use, as well as to your personal taste. A sunny patio may seem more comfortable with cooling pastels, not hot, bright colors. This is especially effective in areas used for entertaining at night, when whites and pastels show up best. White flowers predominating with a few very pale yellow or blue varieties, combined with gray and silvery foliage plants, form the traditional "white garden." A variation is to add splashes of intense color; for example, white, pale pinks, and light blues punctu-ated by spots of gold and deep rose. Small areas of intense color make a pale summer garden more vibrant at midday, when the sun reflecting off petals and leaves gives them a pale, glittering appearance and its heat actually bleaches flower color. They also give visual depth to the plantings.

Another effective scheme is complementary colors of equal intensity. Golden yellow Maximilian sunflowers and purple Mexican bush sage (*Salvia leucantha*) are an example. Any color can work, in the right company. Red flowers are a screaming contrast with flowers in many other hues but appear rich and warm among an array of red shades, paired with dark foliage plants. Arranging plants of different colors together in the nursery before you buy is a good idea.

All intense, analogous colors (those next to each other on a color wheel) make another scheme—for example, deep blue *Salvia* 'Victoria' and rose-red, red-leaf celosia with hot pink 'Summer Madness' petunias. Because the shades are all of similar intensity, the effect is soothing. Gray and silver foliage plants such as dusty miller, lavender, and lamb's-ears are good mixers in this and many other color schemes. Golden yellow heliopsis with medium orange zinnias and 'Rose Pinwheel' zinnias make a sunny analogous scheme of warm colors.

Planning

While soil preparation is serious business, planning and planting should be fun. "Playful experimentation" is the byword. New gardeners shouldn't take a few failures to heart. Not every plant thrives, even for the most experienced gardener. Beginners should rely on the tried-and-true but give something new or unusual a fling.

A simple approach to getting season-long color is to make the basic planting of some of the few perennials that bloom spring to frost, such as prairie verbena, blackfoot daisy, and hardy pink verbena, and then to add shorter-season perennials as desired. Shorter-season old reliables are purple coneflower, single pinks (if well-drained soil and good air circulation can be provided), and obedient plant. Add annuals such as native Tahoka daisy, long-blooming medallion daisy (a tropical *Melampodium*), larkspur, cosmos, and cleome. Plants with similar water needs are grouped together. Some gardeners team perennials with annuals in the same color to maintain the color pattern when the perennial goes out of bloom. Continuity is also created by interweaving plantings in somewhat irregular, diagonal drifts so that bands of different varieties overlap.

"Keep it simple" is another pointer. Gardeners can avoid confusion and create visual continuity by using a limited number of plant varieties. Eight to a dozen varieties can be plenty for a 5-by-10-foot bed. Group several plants of each variety together so they can fill in to make a mass, rather than mixing single plants of each kind. The latter method makes a spotty effect that I have heard gardeners call "box of Crayolas" and "a florist's garden."

A few long-blooming perennials and evergreen herbs define the space, and a couple more early, mid-, and late season perennials and/or annuals fill it out. Having two varieties for each month of the season ensures that, even if one doesn't thrive, the color continues.

Making a chart will help in selecting plant combinations. One way to do this is to list plant names grouped by height down the page, versus months of bloom across the page. This quickly shows if there are enough plants of varied heights and if they provide bloom at the desired times.

To plot a small area, you can simply purchase the number of plants needed for the space and set the pots in the bed, rearranging them until they look right. For more extensive plantings, drawing a simple plan will be a big help. It will aid in visualizing the space and the seasonal changes, and in estimating quantities and catching potential errors.

Rose 'Hermosa,' red dwarf carnations, early irises 'Gypsy Belle' and 'Peach Spot,' blue thrift, and rose 'Red Jacket.' Former home of Bob Wilson and Ray Hapes, Dallas.

CHAPTER TWELVE

Plant Selection and Growth Requirements

What the gardening public wants is a plant with evergreen leaves that don't shed, red flowers all season, and edible fruit. It doesn't exist.

—*A Texas nurseryman*

More than three hundred perennials, bulbs, foliage plants, and grasses are recommended here, the yield of a detailed process conducted over four years. As a result of gathering information and comparing notes around the state, an initial list of excellent perennials grew into the charts that appear in Part Four and the prose profiles of the plants in Chapters 13–15. The charts are designed both for speedy guidance to the plant descriptions of interest to the reader and as a quick reference to key details for garden planning. They give information on the regional adaptability and cultural needs of the plants and tell how they look and their bloom seasons. This information and other essentials are elaborated on in the plant profiles. Many comments by gardeners of various regions as to the plants' special attractions as well as their pests, diseases, or other problems, if any, are also included.

On Plant Names

Twenties garden writer Alfred C. Hottes admonished, "Do not shun one of these new acquaintances because its name is long—no doubt your name is also long, difficult to pronounce, and with far less meaning."

Learning Latin plant nomenclature is like tackling a foreign phrase-book—awkward at first but essential for safely embarking on new and interesting adventures. Once Swedish naturalist Carolus Linnaeus (Carl von Linné) published his new naming system in 1753, gardeners the world over, no matter what their spoken language, could read *Rosa canina* and *Monarda citriodora* and recognize the dog rose and lemon mint. Contrarily, the folksy, fun, but haphazard common names evolved in everyday speech, while a lasting delight to lovers of language, abound in possibilities for error in the garden. "Loosestrife," for example, may mean members of either of two entirely different groups of flowers, one with bright yellow blooms and the other, vivid purple-pink. Ask for "bleeding heart," and you may be given a shrub-like, tough native Texas mallow also called Turk's cap or a cool-loving little border flower that may not survive hot climates. Ask for *Malvaviscus arboreus* var. *drummondii*—*Malvaviscus drummondii* for short—and you'll always get the Texas native; order *Dicentra spectabilis,* and you're sure to receive the dainty northerner.

Don't worry about pronunciation. Latin names arise more often in writing than in speech. And by the time spoken Latin is transmuted by English pronunciation, Ovid himself might have a hard time recognizing it. Invariably, two people attempting to match Latin plant names are so unsure of the pronunciation that they gratefully seize on anything recognizable—and recognizing the word is, after all, what matters.

A plant may have four names. First on the list, as with all known living things, is the name of its *genus.* The first botanical name of any sunflower, for example, is *Helianthus.* (*Helios* means *sun*—it's actually Greek, which occasionally crops up in the mostly Latin lexicon.)

The second, or *species,* name denotes a differentiation in the genus. *Helianthus annuus* is the annual sunflower, distinguished from swamp sunflower, Maximilian sunflower, and others.

A plant that is the original, wild type of its kind may be referred to as "the species" or as, for example, "a species sunflower," to distinguish it from natural and garden hybrids.

Either genus or species name may be derived from a person's name, usually the individual credited with the discovery of the plant. *Muhlenbergia lindheimeri,* a beautiful prairie grass, is named after two people, Muhlenberg and Lindheimer. Other frequently seen names, such as *annuus,* refer to a quality of the plant: *procumbens,* procumbent, lying on the ground; *lanceolata,* lance-shaped; *multiflora,* having many blooms. Most such terms are similar to common Latin-derived English words.

Genus and species names are italicized, and genus names are capitalized. In this book all species names appear in lower case. *Hortus Third,* the authoritative plant encyclopedia, does not include some native Texas plants included in this book. Their names are as given in Donovan Stewart Correll and Marshall Conring Johnston's *Manual of the Vascular Plants of Texas* and in updates to that work by Johnston and by Hatch, Gandhi, and Brown.

A third, or "variety," name is given to a plant that clearly differs from the species, if these differences persist in its descendants. *Rudbeckia fulgida* var. *sullivanti* is an example. Among other differences from the species, its stem leaves are successively smaller up the stem.

A "cultivar" is a cultivated variety that appears, by accident or design, while a plant is in cultivation. The cultivar name is given in single quotes. *Rudbeckia* 'Goldsturm' is an example.

Finally, one sometimes encounters "×," a symbol used as part of the proper designation for plants that are bigeneric or bispecific hybrids, that is, plants bred from members of two different genera or species. *Sedum* × 'Autumn Joy,' for example, is a cultivar from two species, *Sedum spectabile* and *Sedum telephium.* × *Amarcrinum howardii* is a hybrid of two genera, *Amaryllis* and *Crinum.* Catalogs sometimes include the "×" and sometimes omit it.

Perennials Primer

Key factors in plant health and garden planning that appear in plant profiles and the charts are introduced in the following pages. This chapter provides a glossary of terms and an introduction to climate and plant care concerns addressed throughout the rest of the book.

SOIL

The recommendations of many gardening experts from other regions presuppose "good garden soil," that fertile, friable commodity, slightly acid, with correspondingly acid or neutral water. In much of Texas, this assumption could hardly be more wrong. This makes it doubly important to know soil characteristics of the planting site and needs of specific plants. While native plants thrive in soils to which they are indigenous, little native soil remains in its natural state. And many gardeners wish to grow other plants, as well.

Other factors important in garden soil are discussed in Chapter 18. These include organic content (compost, mulch, manure, and myriad other once-living materials) and mineral nutrients.

Soil Types

The relative density of soil is determined by the size of the particles of which it is composed. A balance between dense soils' moisture retention and loose soils' permeability to air and water is desirable. Plant preferences for heavy or well-drained soils are noted.

Adobe (A) is a fine-textured mixture of alluvial clay and silt with some sand. It is extremely compact, sticky when wet, and hard enough when dry to be made into brick.

Clay (C) is very fine-textured, dense, and retentive of moisture and nutrients. It is relatively resistant to air passage—vital to healthy plants—and slow to warm.

Good garden soil (G) is an ideal combination of loam and organic matter. Loam is a soil that combines the three basic kinds of soil particles, sand, silt, and clay. This composition provides an ideal medium between rapid drainage and moisture-retention.

Of course, some wild plants that thrive in poor soil run amok in garden earth; these tendencies are noted.

Sand (S), the coarsest-textured soil type, is easily aerated and warmed and quick-draining. Free from root rot and other common problems of soggy soil, it tends to dryness and infertility because of the quick passage of water and its consequent leaching.

The charts also indicate plants' needs for well-drained (WD) and/or moisture-retentive (MR) soils. The apparently contradictory description "well-drained but moisture-retentive" refers to soil on which water doesn't stand but that does retain moisture in the soil particles, as can be felt by squeezing a handful. For more on soils and soil improvements, see Chapter 8, Techniques.

Soil pH

Soil pH is an expression of the degree of what is commonly termed the soil's "acidity" or "alkalinity." It is given as a number on a scale from 1.0 to 14.0, with 7.0 representing "neutral" pH. Most soils fall between 4.5 and 8.0. A pH of 4.5 or below is considered very acid; 8.0 or above, very alkaline. The values increase geometrically; that is, a pH of 8.0 is *ten times* more alkaline than one of 7.0.

Most plants have a preference as to soil pH but will tolerate a wide range of pH levels. Violets in general prefer acid soil; hollyhocks like calcareous soil, which is one type of alkaline soil. A relatively few plants, such as azaleas, *must* have their preferred condition. The charts note the pH conditions each plant accepts, from alkaline (Al, above 7.0) to neutral (N, 7.0) to acid (Ac, below 7.0).

Soil tests available from agricultural universities, extension services, and commercial soil labs evaluate soil pH as well as fertility and levels of various minerals. A soil test is recommended as an easy, economical, efficient way to gauge what is needed and avoid spending money and labor on soil amendments that may be unnecessary or incorrect for your soil.

In some regions, such as the Plains Country and the Piney Woods, one general pH condition dominates (alkaline and acid, respectively), with varying intensity. Types of plants that thrive are fairly consistent region-wide. In other regions, belts of acid and alkaline soils may occur side by side. This is where knowledgeable gardener neighbors and local horticulturists or—for the greatest accuracy—a soil test can be helpful.

By continued treatment, your soil can be maintained at a pH level different from its normal range. Attention to soil alone is insufficient, however; pH of water may be acid or alkaline, also, and this is a continuing influence. The local water's condition persists, however one may alter the soil. This, along with water's leaching effect, gradually counteracts soil treatments; therefore regular, continued treatment is necessary. This may be simply a matter of using a different kind of fertilizer. Also, as has been mentioned, desirable soil characteristics that promote plant health and minimize the effects of an adverse pH condition can be fostered. These include high organic content, good aeration, and rapid drainage. Techniques for altering pH and counterbalancing its effects are noted in Chapter 18.

Many gardeners agree that, except when dealing with extreme pH levels or certain plants that must have a given condition—such as the acid-insistent azalea—soil aeration and organic content are more critical than a certain pH level.

Salinity

Saline soils, which occur widely in the Trans-Pecos, and air-borne ocean salt are tolerated by only a few plants. These are noted in the charts (tol. salt). Salinity can be caused by saline groundwater originating in mineral-laden areas hundreds of miles distant from the garden site. City water purification and excessive use of chemical fertilizers are other sources. Dry gardens of drought-tolerant plants are well suited to areas with salty soil and water. Their infrequent need for irrigation minimizes water's contribution to the salty soil condition.

LIGHT

In these regions, exposure recommendations on out-of-state plant tags and in Eastern garden books should be taken with a grain of shade.

HEAT TOLERANCE

Cold-hardiness is obviously only a partial indicator of plant viability in the South and Southwest. Absolute high temperatures, unbroken heat, and the long growing season all can spell the early demise of plants like delphinium and foxglove.

Humidity and elevation interact with temperature to influence plant heat tolerance. In the "medium"-range Piney Woods and Gulf Coast, parts of South Texas, and the southernmost Prairies and Cross Timbers, higher humidity reduces temperature variation. The narrower temperature range doesn't necessarily mean an easier life for the plants, however. High humidity also increases plant rates of transpiration (release of moisture through leaves, the floral equivalent of sweating). This increases demand on the plant's energy resources—"life in the fast lane," one horticulturist calls it. Combined with heat, especially around the clock, humidity increases root rot and virus problems.

Drier air further west reduces these problems in the "moderate" zone regions found at higher elevations and further from the Gulf. Cooler night-time temperatures give plant metabolisms a rest. Dry air results in higher evaporation rates, obviously, with less moisture retained on plants and soil to encourage rot and other problems caused by moisture-dependent microorganisms. Thus many northern plants "do" in the High Plains that don't in areas in the same cold-hardiness zone but at lower elevations that are warmer and damper.

MOISTURE

Moisture ranges given in the plant profiles indicate the optimum annual inches of rainfall/irrigation in which the plant is known to grow. There are three ranges:

Low: less than 15 inches average annual moisture.
Medium: from 15 to 30 inches.
High: over 30 inches, up to 50 inches.

Supplemental watering makes up the deficit for plants that require more moisture than the regions to which they are otherwise adapted usually receive in rainfall, of course.

Seasonally wet soil and drought are other variables in moisture other than total rainfall that are important to plants. Acceptance of these conditions by plants is also noted.

In addition to annual rainfall and seasonal moisture variations, there are less obvious moisture conditions. Persistent winds, as in the High Plains, increase evaporation rates, reduce available moisture, and speed up plant transpiration, the vegetable equivalent of perspiration. Humidity can give a misleading impression of moisture in arid areas, as in South Texas near the Gulf. Being aware of these conditions in their areas and how plants respond to them enables gardeners to water according to plants' real moisture needs, rather than on an arbitrary timetable.

Adapting conditions to a plant's moisture needs may be more than a matter of applying a garden hose. Amaryllis (*Hippeastrum*) requires considerable moisture but flourishes in dry South Texas with ample irrigation. The reverse—dryland plants thriving in moist regions—is not so easy. Still, plants can be grown in wetter-than-ideal locales by means of raised beds and other drainage improvements, good air circulation, and positioning out of the path of gutters and other water channels. Thus treated, Mexican oregano (*Poliomintha longiflora*) can grow attractively in Houston. More detail on proper moisture supply is given in Chapter 18.

PROPAGATION METHODS

Common methods of propagation are by seeding and root division and from root or stem cuttings. These basic techniques are explained briefly in Chapter 18. The methods suitable for each plant are listed in the plant profiles.

Perennial rose campion, yellow yarrow, sundrops, and tall spires of white foxglove brighten a misty day in May. Garden of John Fairey, Waller County.

CHAPTER THIRTEEN

Flowering Perennials

Given a few trees and shrubs, a plot of grass, and comfortable walks, the first three essentials of a garden, a collection of hardy herbaceous plants is the fourth essential feature, and may be the last . . .

—*James Shirley Hibberd*

Perennials, more dramatically than many plants, enact the cycle of life, death, and rebirth, from sprout to flower to seed to hidden winter root, and back again. Their many colors mark the seasons. They are small and easy to handle and likely to make a home of any spot that meets their needs. They mark each day with some minute and interesting change. With their powers of adaptability, growth, multiplication, and renewal, they embody characteristics of nature as a whole in one small, leafy package.

The plants presented here include both herbaceous perennials and subshrubs. Herbaceous perennials usually die back to the roots at some point in the year and regrow the following growing season. Subshrubs are perennial plants with woody lower stems; in them, some woody growth persists at all times.

Plants of all origins and pedigrees are included. Some are species, that is, the original or wild plants as they occur in nature. Many species flowers offer qualities lost in highly bred garden plants, such as fragrance, subtlety of shape and color, drought and disease resistance, longevity, and prolific self-propagation. Some are smaller-flowered and less brightly colored than their garden kin but are nonetheless invaluable for their hardiness and their ease and thrift of care. Self-perpetuating for thousands of years in their native regions, they bring the benefits of this perfect natural adaptation to other locales sufficiently like their own. Native species of this region, Mexico, Central and South America, the Mediterranean, South Africa, and Japan are included.

The heredity of many old hybrid garden plants, such as bearded iris, is lost in the mists of time. The twists of their family trees, rooted in many eras and several continents, are unlikely ever to be charted. Others of the garden flowers presented are comparatively new. Some are the result of selection of the best of several generations of the species, chosen for some improvement in color intensity, manageability in the garden, or another desirable trait. *Salvia farinacea* 'Victoria,' for example, is a selection of wild mealy blue sage that is the species' near-equal for hardiness, health, and drought resistance. It is widely preferred for its compact form, tidier in gardens, and its deep violet-blue color untinged by the species' sometime-gray. One's choice, as with other flowers, depends on which side of the fence is being planted and whether what's wanted is the free, wild spirit of woods and fields or the rich, composed civility of gardens. Of course, there are plants from both sides of the bed, so to speak, whose looks and manners enable them to cross over very well.

Rose yarrow *Achillea millefolium* 'Rosea'

℘ *Achillea*
Yarrow
COMPOSITAE

BLOOM: White, yellow, pink, red.
FOLIAGE: Fernlike; green or gray.
HEIGHT: 6–36″, depending on species.
BLOOM SEASON: Spring to summer; *A. millefolium* sometimes intermittent until frost.
REGIONS: All (depending on species; see Chart 1).
HEAT TOLERANCE: High (*A. millefolium*, 'Rosea,' 'Fire King,' 'Coronation Gold,' 'Moonshine'); medium, moderate (*A. tomentosa*).
LIGHT: Full sun to shade, depending on species and climate. Increase shade with high heat, intense sun.
SOIL: Any is acceptable, if well-drained.
MOISTURE: Medium (15–30″ annual average), high (30–50″). Tolerates drought.
PROPAGATION: By seed or root division in fall or spring, cuttings in spring. *A. millefolium* cultivars flower second year from seed. Hybrids generally propagated by division or cuttings, but 'Parker's' selection of *A. filipendulina* and *A. taygetea* 'Debutante' can be propagated from seed.

Common yarrow, *Achillea millefolium,* is one plant that gives the soft, lush look of a fern in conditions ferns would find fatal: full sun and dry soil. It also accepts shade. From early spring to frost—year-round in mild winters—yarrow adds greenery to the most difficult settings. The lacy flower heads, composed of many tiny florets like the wildflower Queen Anne's lace, bloom through spring to midsummer and sometimes intermittently until frost.

This is the classic white yarrow of England, with flower stalks 12–24 inches high above ferny green foliage. It grows in all eight regions of Texas, in some of which it occasionally suffers from powdery mildew or stem rot. When the flower heads fade, they should be cut promptly before they turn brown. The popular rose cultivars 'Cerise Queen,' 'Red Beauty,' and 'Rose Beauty' remain sightly as they fade, however. The others are "coarse" plants compared to 'Red Beauty,' in the eyes of Austin gardener Russell Weber. 'Fire King' is a well-liked red that blooms in mid- and late spring and off and on thereafter. In the Plains Country, the rose and pink varieties are said to have better color in semi-shade than in full sun. Both white and red yarrows are said to do better in the Gulf Coast area than do most yellow species and varieties.

Common yarrow is often described as "invasive." Whether its vigorous growth and spreading by stolons are assets or liabilities depends upon the site and the gardener's taste. In small, formal gardens, yarrow can rollick over the borders and out of its appointed space, taking over. It is easily pulled up, however. And, in large gardens or poor, hilly sites, this ground-covering ability can be a godsend. This plant is characterized as preferring acid, sandy soil but adapts quite well to alkaline soils of other types if well-drained. Giving the species less than its favorite conditions may in fact be desirable, in order to control its growth. A Lubbock gardener reports that he plants it in shade to slow its spread. Yarrow fills in nicely among other tenacious flowers in the border, for a bountiful profusion of greenery and blooms.

The many other species and varieties of yarrow also accept alkaline soil, tolerate drought, and take full sun or partial shade. In hot, humid areas, some shade appears to be better. All require good drainage.

A. filipendulina, fern-leaf yarrow, grows 3–4 feet tall, with 4–6-inch clusters of lemon-yellow flowers.

It blooms all summer. The hybrid cultivar 'Coronation Gold' is somewhat shorter and blooms deeper gold from mid-May to July and occasionally thereafter. 'Coronation Gold' likes moist soil, according to a Piney Woods gardener. In North Texas, however, it and the species often rot and do not regrow; this may be due to poor drainage, overwatering, or the combination of these with summer heat around the clock. They perform best there in dry soil and full sun with room to spread and breathe. Both may be aggressive in the Plains Country, reportedly. In the Trans-Pecos and South Texas, 'Coronation Gold' usually lives for three years.

A. taygetea, 12–18 inches tall, has silver-gray leaves and sulfur-yellow flowers. It makes an excellent cut flower. Light soil and up to half a day's shade are this plant's preference. The slightly taller hybrid 'Moonshine' has clear lemon-yellow flowers and silvery foliage. 'Moonshine' prefers well-drained but moisture-retentive soil, an apparently contradictory but important soil type you will encounter elsewhere in this book. It is the sort found in beds that don't get soggy or hold standing water but do retain moisture in the soil particles, which can be felt by squeezing a handful of soil. A raised bed of soil with high organic content is an example. Avoid crowding this plant.

A. tomentosa, woolly yarrow, is a minuscule, fuzzy, mat-forming ground cover that blooms from early to midsummer in sandy soil and full sun. The Piney Woods is one area where it is known to thrive. It spreads quickly in poor, loose soil but is difficult to divide.

The yarrows are excellent for drying.

Adenophora liliifolia
Ladybells, Lilyleaf Ladybells
CAMPANULACEAE

BLOOM: Pale lavender-blue spires.
FOLIAGE: Green, toothed, 3″.
HEIGHT: 18–48″.

Ladybells *Adenophora liliifolia*

BLOOM SEASON: Spring to late summer.
REGIONS: Edwards Plateau, Piney Woods, Plains
Country, Prairies & Cross Timbers. Hardy to Zone 4.
LIGHT: Filtered to half-day sun to full shade.
SOIL: Deep, well-drained, with organic matter;
neutral to acid.
MOISTURE: Said to tolerate drought, but Texas
reports to date are from regions with 30–50″
average annual rainfall.
PROPAGATION: Cuttings; easy from seed. Division
not advised. Transplants poorly; fleshy roots resent
being moved.

Adenophora liliifolia, a native of Central Europe to
Manchuria, has nodding, bell-shaped flowers about
¾ inch long that are lavender-blue and fragrant.
They hang from upright, usually branched stems.
The leaves are finely toothed and wedge-shaped.
This flower adds soft blue color and a tall, spirelike
form to the border in spring to late summer. The
plants are most effective in groups.

Half-day sun to full shade is recommended for
lilyleaf ladybells in Texas within 100 miles of the
humid Gulf. Sources from Oklahoma and the
Northeast, where there is less fungus-promoting
humidity, specify full to half-day sun. This plant has
no serious pests.

The adenophoras are often confused with the
campanulas, or bellflowers. They are distinguished
by the structure of the flower, which has a disk at
the base of the style. (That's the slender stalk of the
pistil that connects the stigma and ovary.)

❧ *Alcea rosea* and Hybrids
Hollyhock, *Amapola Grande*
MALVACEAE

BLOOM: White, pink, rose, red, yellow.
FOLIAGE: Large, coarse, green or gray-green, felted
or hairy.
HEIGHT: 3–9′.
BLOOM SEASON: Mid-May to July.
REGIONS: All. Single varieties generally perform
better than doubles in Gulf Coast, Lower Rio
Grande Valley, Piney Woods, and South Texas.
HEAT TOLERANCE: High (singles), medium,
moderate ranges.
LIGHT: Full sun to partial shade. No reflected light.
SOIL: Well-drained. Prefers garden loam, neutral
to alkaline. Survives all.
MOISTURE: High, medium, low rainfall/irrigation.
(See "Moisture" in Chapter 12 for explanation of
terms.) Drought-resistant even in extremely arid
Trans-Pecos.
PROPAGATION: Seed for all; division for 'Indian
Spring' and 'Indian Summer.'

No cottage-style garden would be complete without
a towering hollyhock against a wall or in a fence
corner. The garden hollyhocks are hybrids of *Alcea
rosea*. *Hortus Third* calls them "mostly biennial and
short-lived perennial herbs" but notes that there is
an annual strain that flowers its first year. In various
regions of Texas, almost certainly with different
strains of alceas, gardeners' experiences differ. A
veteran Austin gardener and nurseryman says all his

Hollyhock *Alcea rosea*

hollyhocks are true perennials, and that the old-fashioned single hollyhock and 'Chater's Doubles' are the longest-lived. Old hands in the High Plains and Lower Rio Grande Valley confirm the perenniality of old-fashioned hollyhocks at their homes. However, equally experienced San Antonio and Brenham horticulturists say that hollyhocks are annual or biennial at best. The San Antonian, Raydon Alexander of Milberger Nursery, adds that the longest-lived are lobed, blue-gray-leaved 'Indian Spring' and 'Indian Summer,' single-flowered hybrids of *A. rosea* and *A. ficifolia*. Double 'Powder Puff' "rusts just when it's looking good," says another San Antonio source. Asking by name for one of the types or named varieties mentioned

above is a good bet. In any case, short life is no serious drawback, because new plants are easily started from seed.

In warm regions, hollyhocks can be started from seed in very early spring for bloom the same year. In hot, humid areas, even perennial ones may decline in two to three years from root rot, but well-drained soil will prolong their lives. So will removing the bloom stalks as soon as flowering is over. Treatment for rust (Zyban) is sometimes necessary, and spider mites can be a problem in reflected sun. These problems may preclude perennation even with a long-lived strain. Singles can be treated as self-sowing annuals.

Anisacanthus quadrifidus var. wrightii
Flame Acanthus, Wright Acanthus, Hummingbird Bush
ACANTHACEAE

BLOOM: Orange-red to yellow-orange, tubular, 2″ long.
FOLIAGE: Shiny, green, lancelike.
HEIGHT: 3–5′.
BLOOM SEASON: Summer to frost.
REGIONS: All to Zone 7, in which it is root-hardy, but not top-hardy.
LIGHT: Full to half-day sun or filtered light.
SOIL: Any well-drained, preferably neutral to alkaline.
MOISTURE: Low, medium moisture ranges. Drought-resistant.
PROPAGATION: Seed in fall; softwood cuttings, division fall or winter; self-sown volunteers.

Flame acanthus is native to Texas, New Mexico, and northern Mexico. It is a small deciduous shrub that may freeze to the ground but is generally root-hardy to Zone 7. It likes heat and drought. The leaves are broadly lance-shaped, shiny, and green. The flowers, which appear in spikes on the stem-tips, are a great lure for hummingbirds.

This plant's season-long bloom is a wonderful source of color in late summer. The shrubby form

Flame acanthus *Anisacanthus quadrifidus* var. *wrightii*

adds volume to plantings, especially in fall, when gardens can look skimpy with spring perennials cut back, early-season annuals gone or past their prime, and newly planted fall annuals not yet full grown.

Flame acanthus plants should be spaced 3 feet apart and cut back to 1 foot in February.

❧ *Aquilegia*
Columbine
RANUNCULACEAE

BLOOM: Species, various shades of yellow, red and yellow, blue-violet. In garden hybrids, all hues and combinations.
FOLIAGE: Like maidenhair fern in effect; clear green or blue-green. Evergreen with moisture.
HEIGHT: 6–36″.
BLOOM SEASON: Varies from March–May to March–November, depending on species and locale.
REGIONS: Gulf Coast, Piney Woods, Prairies & Cross Timbers for *A. dichroa;* all for other species.
HEAT TOLERANCE: High, medium ranges; *A. dichroa,* moderate.

LIGHT: Partial to full shade. Full sun in some sites, with ample moisture and excellent drainage.
SOIL: Well-drained. Most prefer neutral to alkaline (to pH 8.5); *A. dichroa,* neutral to acid.
MOISTURE: Species, low and medium, except *A. canadensis* (also found in high rainfall) and *A. dichroa* (medium, high). Hybrids, medium and high. Never standing water.
PROPAGATION: Seed.
ENVIRONMENTAL STATUS: *A. hinckleyana* has less than six known populations on the globe; those are in Texas. It is under federal review for protection as an endangered species.

Columbines form mounds of clear green or blue-green foliage resembling maidenhair fern, but larger. The dainty spurred blossoms seem to float above the leaves. They have been beloved garden flowers for hundreds of years.

The native southwestern columbines are hardy but exacting flowers that demand certain conditions to thrive. In situations that they like, they grow and reseed vigorously. They typically live two to four years but often persist longer in a location by reseeding.

Columbines native to the Southwest appear in nature on solid limestone, black clay on a slope, and near water seeps. They are most commonly found in shade but also grow in full sun with their feet in a cool spot where water never stands but is held by soil particles or porous stone, such as a fissure in limestone. The High Plains is a region outside aquilegias' natural range where gardeners report that they succeed in full sun.

"Natives and their natural hybrids are the only aquilegias to use in Texas," says Paul Cox of the San Antonio Botanical Center; other gardeners are more inclusive. Native Texas species include red-and-yellow *Aquilegia canadensis,* 6–30 inches tall; *A. hinckleyana* and *A. chrysantha,* larger yellows; and big *A. longissima,* the "longspur columbine," 18–36 inches tall with clear yellow flowers spanning 8 inches from corolla to spur-tip. Each of the four species has its own distinct natural range, in the

Texas and Hinckley's columbines
Aquilegia canadensis and *A. hinckleyana*

Edwards Plateau and in three Trans-Pecos mountain ranges.

A. canadensis is ideal for rock gardens, raised beds, containers with plenty of soil space—small areas that make its delicate beauty visible. It is said to bloom the third year from seed, reseed heavily (at least in the Plains Country and Central Texas), and bloom less the larger the plant grows. In Central Texas, three to five years is reportedly the maximum life of individual plants.

Deep yellow *A. hinckleyana* blooms March to June around Midland. It is considered the best columbine for San Antonio. Golden yellow *A. chrysantha* and lemon *A. longissima* are short-lived there. Michael Shoup of the Antique Rose Emporium near Brenham finds *A. hinckleyana* and *A. canadensis* the most durable in his locale.

The showiest native columbine, *A. longissima*, creates an unforgettable scene at the foot of Cattail Falls below the Chisos Mountains in Big Bend National Park. The columbines cluster around a tree-shaded pond, their 8-inch yellow blooms with long, airy spurs gleaming in the cool shade. This species and *A. hinckleyana* bloom spring to November in their native sites. In Logan Calhoun's Dallas landscapes, *A. longissima* succeeds best of all;

A. canadensis doesn't reseed well there. However, *A. longissima* is short-lived further south.

Carl Schoenfeld of Hempstead touts *A. dichroa,* a deep blue-violet columbine native to Portugal, as the best columbine for his East Cross Timbers site northwest of Houston, where it blooms heavily over a long season. Carl finds that individual plants perennialize if they are not allowed to go to seed and if rot does not ensue from too-wet soil. Letting some plants set seed assures a supply of new volunteer plants.

Columbines hybridize freely if different species are grown close together.

As for garden hybrids, some horticulturists find that well-known ones considered short-lived here belie their reputation. Large, multicolored McKana hybrids and the 'Dragon Fly' and 'Music' series are grown successfully by nursery veterans in North Texas and Austin. They recommend "extra well-drained" soil and only moderate moisture in high heat.

As well as excellent drainage and adequate moisture, columbines need light enrichment of the soil.

Crown rot, which can occur in hot weather, can be prevented with Benomyl or another fungicide. Spider mites may appear in hot weather, but can be controlled by spraying. Leaf miners must be controlled early.

Butterfly weed *Asclepias tuberosa*

❧ *Asclepias tuberosa*
Butterfly Weed, Orange Milkweed

AND

Asclepias curassavica
Bloodflower, Tropical Milkweed

ASCLEPIADACEAE

BLOOM: Yellow or orange with red; all red.
FOLIAGE: Lancelike, green.
HEIGHT: 1–3′ (*A. tuberosa*); 3–5′ (*A. curassavica*).
BLOOM SEASON: Generally, 4–6 weeks in late spring for *A. tuberosa*. May bloom longer, start in late summer, or repeat in fall in various locales, soils, and weather conditions. Tropical *A. curassavica* blooms spring to fall in most areas, the entire growing season in the Lower Rio Grande Valley and South Texas.
REGIONS: All, *A. tuberosa*; *A. curassavica,* hardy to Zone 8b.
LIGHT: Full sun to partial shade, filtered light.
SOIL: Sandy preferred; most survived, if well-drained.
MOISTURE: *A. curassavica,* medium. *A. tuberosa,* all; occurs in well-drained sites in high rainfall regions, low areas in dry regions.
PROPAGATION: Seed, root cuttings. Division, *A. curassavica* only.

Butterfly weed grows wild from moist canyons in West Texas to the fencerows of East Texas and Louisiana. In spring, it is frequently attended by a flock of Monarch butterflies, hence its name. This orange milkweed can take two or three years to bloom from seed, but its long-lasting display of 4-inch showy orange-and-tangerine flowers is worth the wait—or worth a nursery purchase. There are also natural color variants, a light orange and a red one. In the Trans-Pecos, the form native to the Guadalupe Mountains blooms from April to August.

Butterfly weed sown directly into the ground cannot be easily transplanted, because its deep taproot is likely to be damaged. It must be direct-seeded in its permanent location or started as a container-grown nursery plant.

A tropical species, *A. curassavica,* flourishes in the subtropical Lower Rio Grande Valley and in South Texas. There, its smaller clusters of yellow blooms with red centers appear through the entire growing season, except for summer's hottest days. Grown as an annual in the Trans-Pecos, it freezes out at 15° F. Cutting the 3–5-foot plant back to 10 inches promotes heavier bloom. Cut it back again after leaves fall in winter. *A. curassavica* transplants well. It is scarce in the trade.

Pests of *A. tuberosa* are spider mites, yellow melon aphids, and Monarch larvae. Minor infestations of mites can be controlled with forceful water spray or insecticidal soap on both sides of leaves every five days, for four or five rounds. The best control for severe infestations, say entomologists, is Kelthane. If you want to enjoy Monarch butterflies, you must plant extra for the larvae to eat and refrain from using pesticides, however. Undesirable crawlers can be hand-picked. (For a perspective on overall plant health and insect life, see "Insect and Disease Control" in Chapter 18.) Monarch butterfly lovers will prefer the occasional sacrifice of an entire plant or of nibbled leaves to possible loss of the butterflies to pesticides.

A. curassavica is susceptible to no pests according to some, to melon aphids on new growth according to others.

Minnie Colquitt of Shreveport calls orange milkweed "a good garden plant at hemerocallis time." The two make a beautiful combination.

🌿 *Aster*
Aster
COMPOSITAE

BLOOM: Lavender-blue, pink, white, rose, purple; yellow eye.
FOLIAGE: Dark green, lancelike; tiny upper leaves needlelike in one common hardy blue aster found in Dallas, San Antonio.
HEIGHT: 18–48″.
BLOOM SEASON: Spring to fall, depending on species. Longer in moisture-retentive sites.
REGIONS: All.
LIGHT: Full sun to partial shade, depending on variety.
SOIL: Fertile, well-drained.
MOISTURE: Low, medium, high moisture ranges. General and seasonal moisture needs vary with species, varieties.
PROPAGATION: Root division, cuttings for hardy blue aster and Michaelmas daisy hybrids. Root division and basal cuttings for *A.* × *frikartii.* Seed and self-sown volunteers for species Michaelmas daisies.

Aster

There is a small-flowered lavender-blue fall aster that I have seen in Central, North Central, and South Texas and have heard blooms in the rest of the state. It has nickel-sized lavender daisies with yellow eyes and stubby, needlelike upper leaves. The plant's open, branching form composes a shrubby shape usually 18 to 48 inches high, depending on the strain and on the growing conditions, but capable of reaching 5 feet in rich soil. Hardy blue aster, as it is called, provides a fresh splash of lavender-blue among the yellows, golds, and bronzes of fall mums and sunflowers. It blooms for two to five weeks sometime between late August and November, depending on the locale, and occasionally to frost.

For years plantspeople have speculated as to the little blue aster's identity, thinking it might be *A. amellus,* a clone of another species, or "New England aster," *A. novae-angliae.* One fall aster common in San Antonio was positively identified as *A. oblongifolius* var. *angustatus* in 1989 by the leading specialist in the genus, Almut G. Jones of the University of Illinois at Urbana-Champaign. Dr. Jones writes that this plant, commonly called aromatic aster, resembles ones collected in southern Tennessee. San Antonio horticulturist Raydon Alexander finds it is "self-supporting, disease-free, indestructible." A "less spectacular" variety of the species, *A. oblongifolius* var. *rigidulus,* is said to appear in North Texas. The faithful hardy blue aster I know from North Texas and some San Antonio gardens differs from Dr. Jones' specimens in that the leaves vary from dark green, pointed-oval, smooth ones low on the plant like those of *A. oblongifolius* to fine, stubby, needlelike ones close to the branch tips, and the flowers are a little smaller.

Whatever their identification, these hardy blue asters' long, arching branches spill attractively over rock walls or walkways, inconspicuous green mounds in midsummer, but heaped with lavender-blue flowers for several weeks in fall. For compact plants in autumn, it is recommended to cut them back by half in midsummer, or to pinch them back in spring and again a month later. They can be increased by root division.

A. × frikartii is considered one of the best herbaceous perennials. Hardy blue aster is frequently sold by its name. Frikartii aster has larger flowers, which are fragrant and make good cut flowers, and it blooms from spring to frost. Light afternoon shade in summer is recommended in some locales, to prevent the blooms' fading in intense sunlight. Good ventilation reduces powdery mildew. Frequent division is not necessary with this hybrid. 'Monch' is considered a superior variety of Frikartii aster. *A. × frikartii* 'Wonder of Staffa' is less highly rated by some.

A. novae-angliae and *A. novi-belgii,* traditionally known as Michaelmas daisies because they bloom near St. Michael's Day, September 29, are also useful in the South and Southwest. Two-inch pale blue flowers appear on plants of arching form like that of hardy blue aster. They have sired many 1–4-foot hybrids of colors in the blue-purple-pink range.

Native asters abound in Texas, often eluding exact identification. Native plantswoman Rosa Finsley finds that a tall white and a mid-height blue form both adapt well to gardens, and that a purple form that spreads by stolons can be very invasive.

Generally, garden asters do best in full sun and fertile, well-drained soil that is kept moist in the growing season and not allowed to become soggy in fall and winter. However, in North Texas, Michaelmas daisies accept sun to partial shade and don't rot in moist soil. In San Antonio, all asters are said to need good drainage, air circulation, and full sun to avoid powdery mildew.

Prompt removal of faded flowers of all asters keeps the plants attractive and prevents hybrids from spreading seed that won't come true to type. Legginess can be minimized by cutting bare-stemmed old wood back to the base in spring and midsummer. Generally, plants should be divided every two to four years, and the outer portions of the rootstock replanted for quick-growing new plants. Otherwise, garden asters should not be

transplanted unless necessary; as an English gardener puts it, they "resent disturbance."

Bouvardia ternifolia
Firecracker Bush, *Trompetilla*
RUBIACEAE

BLOOM: Red tubular flowers, to 1¼″ long in clusters of 4 to 12.
FOLIAGE: Ovate, downy, green.
HEIGHT: To 6′; usually 2–4′.
BLOOM SEASON: Late spring or summer and early fall.
REGIONS: Lower Rio Grande Valley, South Texas, Trans-Pecos.
LIGHT: Full sun.
SOIL: Well-drained, neutral to alkaline. Rich soil preferred, according to horticultural references; occurs naturally in igneous soils, but considered widely adaptable as long as drainage is good.
MOISTURE: Low, medium rainfall ranges. Drought-tolerant.
PROPAGATION: Root cuttings and cuttings of fresh shoots taken with a heel and rooted over bottom heat.

Bouvardia is a member of the Rubiaceae, or Madder Family, which includes the coffee bush and the plant that supplies quinine. It is a source of long-lasting

Firecracker bush *Bouvardia ternifolia*

color for the warmer parts of the Southwest. The fiery scarlet-red, tubular blooms won it the nickname "firecracker bush." This shrubby plant can be kept 1–2 feet tall by clipping. It has thin, woody branches with ovate, downy leaves, terminating in clusters of firecracker flowers.

🌿 *Callirhoe involucrata*
Winecup, Poppy mallow
MALVACEAE

BLOOM: Deep, clear red-purple blooms, cup-shaped.
FOLIAGE: Finely cut.
HEIGHT: Low, trailing, 12″ tall.
BLOOM SEASON: Spring to early summer; all summer, if watered frequently.
REGIONS: All. Zones 3–9; evergreen in 8–9. Found from Missouri and Wyoming south to Texas.
LIGHT: Full sun.
SOIL: Any well-drained. Broad pH-tolerance.
MOISTURE: Low, medium and high rainfall ranges. Drought-tolerant.
PROPAGATION: Volunteer seedlings, stem cuttings, root division.

Winecup *Callirhoe involucrata*

This trailing perennial has attractive, deeply cut green leaves. When sunlight shines through the deep red-purple cups, they are translucent and lovely like stained glass. Occasionally, pale pink and white shades appear. Winecups are useful in the fronts of sunny borders, in rock gardens, or trailing over walls.

This plant's delicate appearance is belied by a constitution tough enough to win it the respectful appellation "a plant you can drive a garbage truck over" from landscape architects I know. Alley plantings driven over by garbage trucks have recovered to bloom—on shorter stems—in a matter of days.

There are several ways to propagate winecups. Seedlings grown from seed scattered by the parent plant can easily be transplanted to other locations. Because of the plant's deep taproot, small plants transplant more successfully than larger ones. Deep roots may be divided in spring or fall, with care to get the entire root. In addition, 3–4-inch stem cuttings taken in early summer are said to root quickly.

🌿 *Campanula*
Harebells, Bellflowers
CAMPANULACEAE

BLOOM: Medium clear blue, white, violet, 1–2″.
FOLIAGE: Bright green, lanceolate; 3 species listed are evergreen in mild winters.
HEIGHT: 4–36″, depending on species.
BLOOM SEASON: 3–4 weeks in April and May with fall rebloom, or late summer to fall, depending on species.
REGIONS: See Chart 1 and species descriptions below.
HEAT TOLERANCE: Medium, moderate ranges, depending on species.
LIGHT: Light shade, especially in summer; not tolerant of high heat.
SOIL: Varies with species from gritty, well-drained, to fertile and moist but well-drained.
MOISTURE: Low, medium, high moisture ranges, depending on species.
PROPAGATION: Seed, cuttings, division. *C. persicifolia* self-sows and spreads by root expansion.

Bellflower *Campanula poscharskyana*

There are about 300 known species of *Campanula* or bellflower. Two dozen are commonly cultivated. They offer many shades of blue-violet as well as white.

C. poscharskyana and *C. portenschlagiana,* two species usable in some parts of Texas, are blooming ground covers. *C. poscharskyana,* Serbian harebell, is the less heat-tolerant of the two and the more invasive. Its flowers are like small blue stars on 12-inch stems. Gardeners recommend it as a shady ground cover in the Piney Woods, Gulf Coast, Edwards Plateau, and Prairies and Cross Timbers. Summer heat stresses it, but if it is watered well, it will rebloom in fall. It is drought-resistant near the Gulf on heavy soil in shade. Cold-hardy to Canada, it probably does not thrive south of Central Texas. *C. portenschlagiana,* Dalmatian bellflower, forms clumps that spread but are controllable. The flowers are not as profuse as those of Serbian harebell, and it grows only about 4–6 inches tall. It likes gritty, well-drained soil and partial shade and is hardy to Zone 4 or 5. Both *C. poscharskyana* and *C. portenschlagiana* are evergreen in mild winters.

C. carpatica, Carpathian harebell, does well in the High Plains by the report of Marihelen Kemp, Ph.D., previously of Texas Tech University of Lubbock. Burr Williams of Midland, a half-zone south, says it is too hot for campanulas there. *C. carpatica* is cold-hardy to Zone 4 but sensitive to "drought and drowning," as garden writer Pamela Harper puts it. Late summer and fall are its bloom seasons. The flowers open nearly 2 inches wide on plants 6–12 inches tall. Partial shade or filtered sun and fertile, moist but well-drained soil are its preference. It should be shaded from the afternoon sun, especially in humid areas, and mulched in winter. This campanula is short-lived but quickly raised from seed.

C. persicifolia, peach-leaved bellflower, is reported to be fairly successful as far south as San Antonio. In the northern Prairies & Cross Timbers it typically "lives three years and you hope it throws some seeds," says one gardener. Its 1½-inch white to violet flowers rise above mats of bright green lance-shaped leaves. The bloom stalks reach 2 or 3 feet in height. Described as hardy to Zone 4, this species naturalizes by root spread and by seed but is said to be too variable from seed for starting from seed in a garden. It is evergreen in mild winters. Peach-leaved bellflower prefers moist soil. In summer in medium- and high-heat regions, shade or dappled light in afternoon rather than full sun will probably keep it more attractive and healthier. Removing faded flowers promotes rebloom.

Raised beds and pine-bark mulch, which contains a natural fungicide, are recommended for campanulas. Horticultural references say that in acid-soil areas they like dolomitic limestone, but Texas gardeners in acid soils grow campanulas very successfully, and others in alkaline areas rate the plants' preference acid to alkaline.

Ceratostigma
Plumbago
PLUMBAGINACEAE

BLOOM: Cobalt blue or pale blue with purple tubes.
FOLIAGE: Bright green; *C. plumbaginoides* tinged with red in fall.
HEIGHT: *C. plumbaginoides,* to 12"; *C. willmottianum,* 24–48".
BLOOM SEASON: Late spring or early summer to fall, often to frost. Heaviest bloom in July–August.

Hardy blue plumbago *Ceratostigma plumbaginoides*

REGIONS: All for *C. willmottianum. C. plumbaginoides* annual in Plains Country, unless planted 9–10″ deep, not reliably hardy in Trans-Pecos, perennial in all others.
LIGHT: Afternoon shade or filtered sunlight best. *C. plumbaginoides* tolerates full sun; *C. willmottianum* accepts it better.
SOIL: Any.
MOISTURE: Low, medium, high rainfall ranges. Tolerates drought, but medium moisture reduces rusty seed heads.
PROPAGATION: Seed, division.

Ceratostigma plumbaginoides, hardy blue plumbago, is one of nature's rare true blue flowers—in this case, cobalt blue. ". . . the perfect contrast for the lemon and orange of *Zinnia linearis* [now *angustifolia*]," wrote North Carolina gardener Elizabeth Lawrence. This vivid ground cover, which tolerates shade but not tree roots, offers a long bloom season and demands little care. The trick is to obtain its rich blue without the rusty-red remnants of dead flower heads that so often cover it. Bob Wilson, a Nicholson-Hardie nursery manager in Dallas, has his own formula for maintaining it at peak attractiveness. First, the plants should be situated where they get a maximum of six hours of sun, or in filtered sunlight. "Avoid hot, dry corners," he cautions. Abundant water will lessen heat stress. Finally, periodic fertilizing promotes new growth that hides the rusty-looking old flower heads and keeps this dependable perennial attractive.

Soil with ample organic matter and good drainage, especially in winter, is recommended. This plant is not reliably cold-hardy in the High Plains and Trans-Pecos, although a Lubbock gardener sustains it by planting it 9–10 inches deep. It should be mulched in winter in Zone 6. It spreads by runners (slowly in the southern Blacklands).

C. willmottianum, Chinese plumbago, is a small shrub native to western China and Tibet that forms mounded 2–4-foot plants. Its flowers are deep blue or pale blue with reddish purple tubes, and the dead flower heads are less conspicuous than those of *C. plumbaginoides.* A plant of this species reportedly lives no longer than two years in the San Antonio area. It is somewhat more drought-tolerant than *C. plumbaginoides.*

Chrysanthemum leucanthemum
Oxeye Daisy, May Daisy
COMPOSITAE

BLOOM: White with yellow center, 2″.
FOLIAGE: Evergreen.
HEIGHT: 24″ bloom stalks above 4–6″ foliage. Evergreen winter rosettes.
BLOOM SEASON: 3–4 weeks in mid-spring to early summer.
REGIONS: All.
HEAT TOLERANCE: Medium, moderate ranges preferred, high tolerated.
LIGHT: Full sun to light shade. Afternoon shade or filtered light best in hot, dry regions.
SOIL: Acid to alkaline, light to heavy, well-prepared. Less drainage-sensitive than Shasta daisy.
MOISTURE: Grown in low, medium, and high rainfall ranges, but prefers consistent moisture. More drought-tolerant than Shasta daisy.
PROPAGATION: Direct-seed in early spring. Division easy. Self-sows.

Native oxeye daisy has all the charm of the Shasta daisy, with a smaller bloom. A good, old-fashioned perennial, it is found in many old gardens. Less sensitive to poor drainage than Shastas, it often survives the summer better. The rosettes of ever-

Oxeye daisy *Chrysanthemum leucanthemum*

❧ *Chrysanthemum parthenium*
Feverfew

COMPOSITAE

BLOOM: White, yellow, buttonlike.
FOLIAGE: Pale green, ferny, strongly scented.
HEIGHT: 15–36″.
BLOOM SEASON: As long as June to frost in good weather conditions, if deadheaded.
REGIONS: All. Not widely used in Lower Rio Grande Valley.
HEAT TOLERANCE: Grown in high, medium, and moderate ranges but not at its best in summer in high zones.
LIGHT: Full sun to partial shade.
SOIL: Any well-drained soil.
MOISTURE: Ample and consistent. Avoid prolonged drying.
PROPAGATION: Seed.

green foliage are ground-hugging, not the long, sometimes rank leaves of the Shasta. The blooms, which stand above them on long stems, make excellent cut flowers.

In Europe, oxeye daisy came to be called Marguerite when Margaret of Anjou, queen of England's Henry VI, adopted this flower of her native Anjou as a personal emblem, according to Roy Genders.

Apparently conflicting information from various Texas regions yields the following conclusions. Oxeye daisy thrives in East Texas, the Gulf Coast, and Central Texas. South Texas gardeners claim success with it also. It needs watering in a typical Texas summer. More than one gardener described its preferred pH range as acid to mildly alkaline, but one from the South Plains reports success with it at the extremely high pH of 8.5. It should be planted in well-prepared, mulched garden soil from which weeds can be easily pulled without hoeing that could damage the daisies' shallow roots. The plant prefers cool weather; I have been told that it may die in August heat, and the foliage may burn in full sun, but I suspect that oxeye daisy is less sensitive in these respects than Shasta daisy.

Division of the clumps is simple. "Rip it apart with your bare hands," says Russell Weber.

Feverfew has been grown in home gardens for hundreds of years. Its name comes from the Latin *febrifuge,* "to drive away illness." It was recommended in 1557 in "One Hundred Points of Good Husbandry," a poem by English gardener Thomas Tusser, as an invaluable aid in keeping the home fresh and sweet-smelling. In Victorian times it was used as a summer bedding plant.

Feverfew *Chrysanthemum parthenium*

The long, arching branches, clustered with tiny white blossoms and pale green foliage, add freshness to the garden and set off stronger colors well. The plants are most effective as background plantings, to trail over the edge of raised beds, or combined with other flowers.

Ordinary soil is suitable, but the bed should not be allowed to remain dry. Feverfew prefers cool temperatures. A light mulch is beneficial, and in high temperature zones, afternoon shade is advised; foliage may burn in hot sun. Contrarily, one Austin gardener found the cultivar 'Aureum,' or 'Golden-feather,' thrived in midsummer heat; however, it lived only two years.

Feverfew can be sowed directly in early spring or started in a greenhouse in February.

Red spider mites can be controlled with repeated sprayings with a forceful jet of water on both tops and bottoms of the leaves daily; or with insecticidal soap; or, in severe cases, with miticides such as Kelthane until the pests disappear. The dried stalks should be cut down after the first freeze.

✺ *Chrysanthemum × superbum*
Shasta Daisy
COMPOSITAE

BLOOM: White with yellow centers.
FOLIAGE: Green.
HEIGHT: 8–48″, depending on variety.
BLOOM SEASON: 4–6 weeks in April to August, with fall rebloom by some varieties.
REGIONS: All.
HEAT TOLERANCE: Medium and moderate ranges preferred; high tolerated.
LIGHT: Full sun, partial shade, or filtered sun.
SOIL: Rich, well-drained, neutral to alkaline.
MOISTURE: Consistent. Moist but not soggy. Grows in all moisture ranges with supplemental watering.
PROPAGATION: Seed, division.

Shasta daisies are garden favorites, the essence of freshness and cheer. In warm regions, the earlier-

Shasta daisy *Chrysanthemum × superbum*

flowering dwarf forms enjoy a longer bloom period than the late-bloomers, because they flower before summer heat accelerates the bloom cycle to a premature finish. *Chrysanthemum maximum,* a botanical name frequently given for Shasta daisy, more probably identifies one of its forebears that originated in the Pyrenees. Both *C. maximum* and *C. × superbum* consist of white "ray flowers" (the petals) and yellow "disk flowers" (the center or "eye"). As many gardeners know, this form characterizes flowers of their family, the numerous Compositae.

Double-petaled daisies do better in partial shade. All are excellent cut flowers. Afternoon shade in summer is best in all but East Texas.

Shasta daisies need rich, well-drained garden soil with plenty of well-composted organic matter. Shallow-rooted Shastas require ample, consistent moisture but do not like soggy soil. Good drainage is a must. The foliage of this flower may brown in midsummer in warm regions. Shasta daisies may even die back completely at that time; the combined heat and high humidity of the season probably promote their nemesis, root fungus. Pull and dispose of sick, wilting plants immediately.

Shastas will bloom their first summer if set out from 4-inch pots in spring. Some bloom late the first year from seed.

For vigor, they should be divided every two to three years in fall. In areas with long, hot growing seasons, the plants are short-lived and are best treated as biennials.

'Alaska' is a longtime favorite large-flowered variety, described as a "dependable, rugged, good performer in San Antonio." 'Polaris' is said to equal or surpass it, forming 30-inch clumps with "huge" flowers.

C. × superbum 'Little Miss Muffett' is a dwarf, early form long recommended. Newer 'Silver Princess' is said to be indistinguishable. A Dallas gardener says that 'Silver Princess' is the only Shasta that never falls prey to "June decline." In the High Plains and North Central Texas 'Little Miss Muffett' can bloom for two months, starting in mid-June, and then rebloom in fall, if it is well watered and fertilized. 'Snow Princess' is extremely dwarf; it performed poorly for one Cross Timbers gardener.

'Snow Lady,' the All-America selection for 1988, is billed as the earliest-flowering Shasta, capable of all-summer bloom. A North Texas grower says that there it really blooms July to August. In Dallas, my 'Snow Lady' seeds, planted in partial shade too late for early bloom, germinated in great numbers and flowered when fall cool arrived. The second year they multiplied and, not having been thinned as seedlings, grew extremely thickly; blooms appeared in mid-spring and occasionally all season, with dead-heading. In San Antonio, by contrast, Nancy Brillos' first-year trials showed uneven germination, slow growth, and only fair heat tolerance.

An unnamed compact variety of Shasta daisy or possibly *C. leucanthemum* developed by Texas A&M University is on the market; it forms a dense ground cover with daisies on foot-long stems above the evergreen foliage.

Texas clematis *Clematis texensis*

✍ *Clematis*
Clematis

RANUNCULACEAE

BLOOM: White and many shades of purple, rose-red, pink, and blue; one yellow species.
FOLIAGE: Green. *C. armandii* is evergreen.
HEIGHT: Trailing stems climb 5–30´, depending on species.
BLOOM SEASON: Spring, summer, or fall, depending on species.
REGIONS: Depends on species or variety; see Chart 1.
LIGHT: Partial (afternoon) to light shade; full sun with shade over the roots from annuals or shallow-rooted perennials.
SOIL: Fertile, light, loamy. Well-drained. Slightly alkaline, generally.
MOISTURE: Medium to high annual rainfall. Even moisture, neither very dry nor very wet, except for Texas natives, which tolerate drought once established.
PROPAGATION: Stratified seeds, layering, division, cuttings rooted in summer. For *C. armandii* and *C. texensis,* softwood cuttings.

Two attractions of the vining clematises are their abundant bloom and their trait of climbing harmlessly over shrubs and trees. They like to clamber over evergreens, swathing them in color. "This is the only way I know to get an evergreen shrub with blue flowers in Texas," quips one landscape architect.

Common belief holds that the fancy large-flowered clematises seen in garden catalogs, such as *Clematis × jackmanii* and its many hybrids, will not thrive in Texas, and that Texas natives and ones naturalized in the South are our only choices. However, in North Texas, the Edwards Plateau, and the northern part of South Texas, a few gardeners report reliable success with popular old large-flowered garden clematises such as red 'Ernest Markham' and purple × *jackmanii*. I have heard Dallas, east San Antonio, and Austin gardeners enthuse over beautiful bloom from such stellar varieties. One told me that it took three or four years to create the right conditions and for the vines to get well established and large before they produced a mass display. In the Plains Country, of the hybrids only a white, probably 'Henryi', is said to perform satisfactorily, and only if its roots are kept cool. It seems that common wisdom should be amended to make the Hill Country and Blacklands large-flowered clematis country.

A few other old garden hybrids are also satisfactory here; some of the best-adapted ones are hybrids of *C. viticella* and native Texas scarlet clematis.

There are also several attractive small-flowered species, both native and naturalized, that are suitable for garden use across a wider area.

Species clematises include ones with urn-shaped pendant blooms and fall-blooming ones that are white with fleecy seed-plumes.

C. armandii, native to China, is evergreen and grows up to 20 feet tall. Its narrow 3–5-inch leaves are leathery. The 2-inch white flowers appear in panicles.

Korean *C. dioscoreifolia* and *C. maximowicziana* from New Zealand are two species that are frequently interchanged in the trade. (*C. paniculata* is the earlier name for *C. maximowicziana* and is still in use by most nurseries.) This is the old-time garden flower naturalized in the South that is traditionally known as "sweet autumn clematis." It sometimes reaches 30 feet in height. For three weeks in fall it is covered with masses of white, star-shaped, 1–4-inch fragrant blooms. These are followed by silvery plumed seed heads. *C. maximowicziana* freezes to the ground in the Plains Country but comes back from the roots. In Southeast Texas it is considered invasive. It is recommended in the northern part of South Texas, based on San Antonio reports.

A clematis native to Texas that produces a similar effect is *C. drummondii*, called "old man's beard" or "Texas virgin's bower."

C. pitcheri is a native Texas clematis with distinctive pendant, urn-shaped small blooms in various shades of purple. It generally grows no more than 10 feet tall.

C. texensis, "scarlet clematis," has showier red blooms of the same form as *C. pitcheri*. They are very pretty against the green to blue-green foliage. It may die to the ground in winter, then regrow and bloom the next year. It is not reliable in the Plains Country. On the basis of San Antonio results, it is recommended for northern South Texas, as is the hybrid 'Duchess of Albany.' *C. texensis* is reportedly the only clematis suitable for use in the Lower Rio Grande Valley.

Another clematis species worth trying is *C. tangutica*, a yellow, fall-flowering plant that grows 10 to 15 feet tall and is described as hardy in Zones 5–9. It has been grown successfully in the Post Oak Savannah and by Keeta Hodges, perennial grower for Nortex Nursery Industries in Wylie, Texas.

C. virginiana, traditionally called virgin's bower, is native to North America from Nova Scotia and Quebec to Manitoba, south to Louisiana and Georgia. Its creamy, 1-inch flowers appear on a 10–20-foot vine. As the flowers fade, they are replaced by silky tasseled seeds.

The English, enchanted with Texas scarlet clematis, crossed it with *C. viticella*, and produced some fine garden hybrids, such as red 'Madame Julia Correvon' and pink 'Duchess of Albany.' The *texensis* parentage is visible in the fascinating appearance of the flowers as they open. The buds resemble the dangling urns of the native clematis, but as they open they rotate upward, spreading like small pinwheels finally to flat, open stars. "'Madame Julia Correvon' is the only hybrid that blooms off and on all summer" in his garden, says Waller County gardener John Fairey.

Pruning is important to flowering. At planting, prune all clematises, especially large-flowered hybrids, to just above the lowest pair of strong leaf buds. In late January or February, established plants of species and hybrids that flower on new growth in summer and fall are pruned of all the previous year's growth above the lowest bud pair. (These include *C. tangutica, C. texensis* hybrids, *C. viticella* and its hybrids, and *C. × jackmanii* and some of its hybrids.) An exception is 'Henryi,' which flowers on both old and new stems; after the first year, pruning it is optional.

The old saw about clematis care is "Head in the sun, feet in the shade." The plants like sunshine best but only with cool soil around their roots. In hot climates, full sun with ground-level shade or, alternatively, light or afternoon shade is preferred. Shade can be provided by planting so that the vine's roots are on the shady side of the post it is to climb; shoots naturally climb around to the sunny side. Annuals, shallow-rooted perennials, and low shrubs all can be used to shade clematis roots; this is a plant that welcomes company.

The vining clematises adapted to Texas all need trellises or other support to grow on, as well as occasional tying up to direct their growth and keep them from strangling themselves. Clearance of ½ inch allows the tendrils to wrap around. They don't attach by suckers or grow into masonry as ivy does.

Sweet autumn clematis can be left unpruned or, in small spaces, pruned hard to keep it in bounds. Pruning hard in late January or February will eliminate bare stems low on the trunk and will make it bloom nearly to the ground.

When shopping or pruning, if grower tags give only the varietal name, consult a reference book such as Jim Fisk's *Clematis, the Queen of Climbers* to determine its parent species. Or use your own observation to tell you when to prune; you may have to postpone pruning to watch the first season's flowering. If blooms appear on new shoots, prune the following February. If blooms appear on old growth from the year before, prune right after flowering.

Coreopsis
Coreopsis, Tickseed, Golden-wave
COMPOSITAE

BLOOM: Yellow to yellow-orange.
FOLIAGE: Lanceolate or threadlike, depending on species. *C. lanceolata* and hybrids are evergreen.
HEIGHT: 4–36″, depending on species and variety.
BLOOM SEASON: *C. lanceolata* and hybrids, spring to midsummer with possible rebloom. *C. verticillata* and hybrids, early to midsummer and occasionally later.
REGIONS: All (except Gulf Coast for *C. verticillata*).
LIGHT: Full sun, afternoon shade, or light shade.
SOIL: Clay to well-drained, depending on species and variety.
MOISTURE: Low, medium rainfall ranges. Dry, *C. lanceolata* and especially *C. verticillata*; others accept moist as well as dry garden conditions.
PROPAGATION: Seed, division, new plantlets at stem tips. Self-sows.

American humorist James Thurber once wrote of a character who suffered from "coreopsis." In fact, this is a desirable condition, as you will discover if you grow it. *Coreopsis* includes many species and varieties of yellow-flowering, old-fashioned perennials. Gardeners in every region of Texas list them among their twenty favorite garden flowers. All are long-blooming daisy-type flowers that are good for cutting and provide vibrant color in spring and early summer.

Goldenwave *Coreopsis lanceolata*

C. lanceolata, or golden-wave, a spring-blooming Texas native, thrives even in heavy clay in the Blacklands, Trans-Pecos, and South Texas regions, as well as in more friable soils. It is best grown in rather infertile soil kept on the dry side; otherwise, it produces more foliage than flowers and falls over. In the South Plains it has a reported lifespan of two to three years.

Reportedly, the first improved hybrid of wild coreopsis, 'Goldfink' ('Goldfinch'), came from Germany. Several other good cultivars are available in the nursery trade. 'Baby Sun' offers 12–18-inch bloom stalks and a dense mound of foliage that stays evergreen in winter. It prefers full sun or light shade. 'Sun Ray' is a somewhat taller plant with 4-inch semi-double blooms. The 1989 All-American selection 'Early Sunrise' is another semi-double (but reportedly less double than 'Sun Ray') that is supposed to bloom early, but doesn't, according to one report.

C. auriculata 'Nana' is a 4–6-inch attractive evergreen ground-covering plant that puts up small flowers on 18-inch stems.

Lacy-leaved *C. verticillata,* or threadleaf coreopsis, grows in the Piney Woods and in the Blacklands to Zone 8, but does not do well in the heavy soils of the Gulf Coast or southern Blacklands. In dryish, well-drained, sunny locations in the Piney Woods, it blooms from June to July. Its foliage resembles asparagus fern, giving the effect of a 2–3-foot light-green cloud among other flowers. The small golden yellow flowers sport pointed petals. Reports from San Antonio indicate that this plant grows poorly there. 'Moonbeam' is a cool-looking pale lemon yellow that is somewhat shorter than the species.

Thelesperma filifolium, or greenthread, is another Texas wildflower that is similar in appearance.

Fall planting of seed is best for all varieties. Self-sowing is common; in hybrids, resulting volunteers are not true to the parent plant. Plants can also be divided in early spring or fall. Division every two to three years will keep them at peak vigor. Deadheading and removal of plantlets can prolong bloom and promote fall rebloom. The plantlets, or offsets, are also a source of new plants.

Threadleaf coreopsis *C. verticillata*

Cigar plant *Cuphea micropetala*

℘ *Cuphea micropetala*
Cigar Plant, Hummingbird Bush
LYTHRACEAE

BLOOM: Yellow and red-orange, tubular.
FOLIAGE: Dark green, lanceolate.
HEIGHT: 3–5′ with 8–12″ bloom spikes.
BLOOM SEASON: Late summer to frost. Best in October and November. Scattered blooms in spring.
REGIONS: All but Plains Country and western Trans-Pecos.
LIGHT: Full sun.
SOIL: Poor to good. Well-drained.
MOISTURE: Low, medium ranges. Tolerates drought.
PROPAGATION: Seed, division, cuttings.

Cuphea forms a large, rounded shrub covered with tubular flowers shaded from yellow to red-orange. Its bold form and vivid coloration give it a tropical look. When bloom in many other plants temporarily stops in the hottest days of summer, cuphea keeps flowering. It has flowers and leaves all the way to the ground, rather than the bare lower stalks seen in many shrubby perennials, and makes an excellent specimen plant or a background plant in a large border. Hummingbird lovers are thrilled by the way it attracts hummers to their gardens.

This tough plant is not particular about soil and has no significant pests. It dies to the ground north of Zone 9. Best cut to the ground after the first freeze, it springs up again the next summer. It tolerates drought but needs adequate moisture to bloom well, according to a San Antonio gardener. It is not winter-hardy in the western Trans-Pecos or the Plains Country.

There are several other native species and garden varieties of cuphea, mostly reseeding annuals and tender perennials, that grow well in the southern half of Texas.

℘ *Dianthus*
Pinks and Carnations
CARYOPHYLLACEAE

BLOOM: Pink, white, rose, magenta, red. Banded, edged, eyed, and streaked combinations.
FOLIAGE: Green to gray, grasslike to mat-forming depending on variety. Evergreen.
HEIGHT: 4–24″.
BLOOM SEASON: Late March or April to May; to fall for some varieties.
REGIONS: Edwards Plateau, Piney Woods, Plains Country, Prairies & Cross Timbers, Trans-Pecos (most varieties); Gulf Coast, South Texas (a few varieties).
HEAT TOLERANCE: Medium, moderate ranges.
LIGHT: Full sun, 2 hours late-afternoon shade in heat of summer; filtered light.
SOIL: Well-drained sandy loam, neutral to alkaline. Raised beds. Prefers calcareous soils.
MOISTURE: Low, medium, high moisture ranges. Prefers moderate moisture; do not overwater.
PROPAGATION: Seed, some varieties; division; cuttings; layering; "pipings."

Old-time gardens included many members of the genus *Dianthus:* the singles called pinks, cluster-flowering sweet Williams, and hardier versions of the very double form we now know as carnations. Traditionally, all were extremely fragrant, sweet, spicy-smelling flowers; the perfume has been lost in many of the modern hybrids.

Two members of this family are the progenitors of modern carnations and modern pinks. *D. caryophyllus,* or clove pink, is believed to have been brought into England during the Norman Conquest, perhaps on building stones from northern France. *D. plumarius,* the grass pink, was crossed with *D. caryophyllus* to produce the fancy double pinks and florist and border carnations we know today.

The clove pink was named for its spicy clove scent. The flower name brought the word "pink" into the language as a color designation; previously, "flesh" was the common term. "Sops-in-wine" was another early name for the pink, for its use in flavoring wines and ales. It is thus due only to the accidents of language that blushing brides are referred to as "pink-cheeked" rather than "sop-cheeked." The name "carnation," meaning flesh-colored (from Latin via Old French), was widely applied to *D. caryophyllus* from the sixteenth century onward.

Dianthuses were household standbys in medieval Europe. They were scattered on floors to scent the air, compensating for the limited personal hygiene of the time and the lack of indoor plumbing. Nobility and merrymakers were crowned with dianthus wreaths.

Dianthuses other than clove pink and grass pink and their hybrids also appear in today's nursery trade, although in scant numbers compared to the hundreds offered in the heyday of the dianthus in the early nineteenth century.

The most readily available dianthuses today are biennial sweet William (*D. barbatus*) and annual *D. chinensis* hybrids with names like 'Charm' and 'Snowfire.' Some gardeners report that these two have, uncharacteristically, lasted three years in their gardens. *D. barbatus* is extremely cold-hardy in well-drained sites. Other, truly perennial varieties are scarcer but increasing in availability: the species and hybrid forms of *D. caryophyllus* (clove pink), *D. plumarius* (grass pink), and *D. deltoides* (maiden pink); *D. alpinus* 'Allwoodii' and *D. × allwoodii* (Allwood pinks); and *D. gratianopolitanus* (Cheddar pink).

Pinks and stock *Dianthus plumarius* and *Matthiola*

Pinks *Dianthus* sp.

Clove pink is strongly clove-scented, grows up to 24 inches tall, and puts on its 1½-inch flowers in spring. The blossoms are slightly serrated ("pinked") around the edges.

Grass pink has gray, grassy, mat-forming foliage 8–10 inches high. Clumps are long-lived but prone to stem rot. The deeply fringed blooms are colored rose-pink to purplish, white, or variegated, with a strong, sweet, spicy scent. They appear in late spring.

Maiden pink produces a mat of tiny green leaves only 4–5 inches high, with a late-spring display of tiny bright pink or white flowers on 6–18-inch stems. It is especially insistent on good air circulation and calcareous soil. 'Zing Rose' is a popular low-growing pink cultivar that blooms all season in North Texas if deadheaded, watered, and fed consistently, and lives up to four years.

The Allwood pinks have blue-green foliage and red, pink, white, or variegated blooms, also clove-scented, mostly semi-double. In optimum conditions, their bloom season spans early May to September. There are two hybrid groups of different heights, both named for breeder Montagu Allwood, according to Russell Weber, previously of White Flower Farm in Litchfield, Connecticut, and Red Barn Nursery in Austin. Correctly, the 8–10-inch type, not properly called in the trade, is *D. alpinus* 'Allwoodii,' says Mr. Weber. The 12–18-inch type is *D. × allwoodii.*

D. gratianopolitanus, or Cheddar pink, is a very low-growing species that blooms in spring in fresh pink. Its choice double-flowered cultivar 'Tiny Rubies' is widely used.

Unnamed hardy pinks and carnations, produced by breeding that has gone on since the 1300s, are being brought back into distribution by growers here and there who have reclaimed them from abandoned houses and old churchyards. In Texas, a single pink-and-rose form and a single magenta that bloom in spring are among these. Another available unnamed dianthus is a short-stemmed, fragrant red carnation that blooms all spring and summer in most locales and as late as winter in the Piney Woods and southern Blacklands, if deadheaded regularly. It is often called "German red carnation," identified whether correctly or not with dianthuses grown by early German settlers. "Probably the most reliable of the small carnations," one gardener says. Shearing this plant back when only 15 percent remains in bloom, and the rest has brown, spent blooms, is recommended. Seedless, it is propagated by cuttings.

Even perennial dianthuses are fairly short-lived, but they are easily propagated by division, layering, or cuttings. Division every two years generates fresh stock. The best care for dianthuses is continual deadheading and fertilizing; given this attention, the ever-bloomers live up to their name. Many gardeners caution against using garden pinks in climates that are both hot and humid, such as the Gulf Coast, because of their susceptibility to root rot. Northeastern gardeners plant dianthuses in full sun; in hot Texas and southwestern summers, situations shaded briefly in the hottest part of the afternoon may help prolong their life. Good air circulation also reduces disease problems. Overwatering should be avoided. *D. deltoides,* maiden pink, is said to be particularly rot-prone. Luckily, it blooms vigorously with a half-day's sun. Filtered light, readers are reminded, means *bright* light, especially for good bloom in dianthuses.

In northern publications, much is made of southern exposure and mulch to protect dianthuses from winter cold. In Texas, a southern exposure could prove deadly in summer. The necessity of mulch in winter depends on the locale and the cultivar. In Zone 8 areas, perennial dianthuses in general are considered fairly cold-hardy, a distant second to pansies. They bloom as long as sunny days and temperatures of 40 to 60° F prevail, and they survive freezes into the twenties and briefly to 10°. *D. × allwoodii* 'Doris' seems hardy at least to Zone 8. However, dianthuses in general are considered hardy in the much colder (Zones 6–7) Plains Country. Opinion is that their survival there despite more severe cold is owed to the well-drained soils and low humidity. In light of Texas experience, I can account for the widely published U.S. hardiness ratings of Zone 4 or 5 (republished here) by the conjecture that dianthuses resist severe, unbroken cold better than our intermittent freezes and thaws. Perhaps everyone in Zones 4 and 5 follows the advice in garden books and uses mulch. At any rate, the delightful appearance and sweet scent of these age-old garden flowers make experimentation worthwhile in climates at least as cold as Texans encounter.

Dichorisandra thyrsiflora
Blue Ginger
COMMELINACEAE

BLOOM: Deep blue-violet, conelike.
FOLIAGE: Large, glossy, dark green.
HEIGHT: 3–5′.
BLOOM SEASON: Begins late summer or early fall; to frost in South Central Texas.
REGIONS: Gulf Coast, Lower Rio Grande Valley, Piney Woods, Prairies & Cross Timbers, South Texas; to Zone 8b.
HEAT TOLERANCE: High, medium ranges.
LIGHT: Filtered light to deep shade.
SOIL: Good garden soil with plenty of humus.
MOISTURE: Moderate to high average annual moisture. Keep moist, especially in the growing season, but not wet.
PROPAGATION: Seed, cuttings, division.

Dichorisandra thyrsiflora, native to Brazil, belongs to the same family as the lowly spiderwort and day-flower. It makes a very showy specimen plant, with 6–9-inch racemes of deep blue-violet blooms, each

Blue ginger *Dichorisandra thyrsiflora*

with a white eye. Blue ginger leafs out in late summer, relatively late in the Texas growing season. It blooms into fall and, in warmer parts of the state, continues to bloom until frost. The regions noted here are ones in which it has been grown successfully; its range of adaptation may be much wider.

This is not a true ginger at all but resembles the gingers in its broad, swordlike leaves and bloom form. It is a plant that makes a statement, in the same bold style as yucca or oak-leaf hydrangea. Mulch in winter protects it from freezing. It has no known pests.

Echinacea
Coneflower
COMPOSITAE

BLOOM: Many shades of rose and pink with orange center. White, rarely.
FOLIAGE: Grayish to green, fuzzy to waxy, depending on species.
HEIGHT: 18–48″, depending on cultivar.
BLOOM SEASON: 4–6 weeks starting in mid-spring to early summer; 3 months' bloom is not unusual with good care and consistent deadheading. Occasionally, with some varieties, to fall.
REGIONS: All (for *E. purpurea*).
HEAT TOLERANCE: Medium, moderate ranges for all; high, for *E. purpurea* only.
LIGHT: *E. purpurea,* full sun, filtered light; partial shade to almost full shade in hot, dry regions. Other species, bright filtered light, partial shade.
SOIL: Any, if enriched with humus. Well-drained soil best.
MOISTURE: Medium. *E. laevigata, E. pallida* also accept high. *E. purpurea* tolerates drought.
PROPAGATION: Seed, spring division (all). Late fall root cuttings (*E. purpurea*).

The pink, daisy-form prairie flowers of *Echinacea purpurea* are so widely used in gardens that few people think of them as wildflowers any longer. They are long-blooming and generally excellent in the border and as cut and dried flowers. Cut, they last two weeks. One San Antonio gardener finds

Purple coneflower *Echinacea purpurea*

them less reliable than desired in a border and instead relegates them to the cutting garden. Their color ranges from dusty rose to neon pink. Colors seem to be muted when the plants are grown in shade. The number of flowers increases the second year.

Purple coneflowers like good garden soil. They accept more shade in southern and western Texas, up to 75 percent in the Trans-Pecos and South Plains. The dead flower heads should be removed promptly to keep the plants attractive. New growth and re-bloom are encouraged by cutting back the top growth once flowers have bloomed and by consistent watering, which reduces heat stress, as with coreopsis. The plants reseed widely and interbreed freely. Pull up the new seedlings if a contained planting is desired.

'Bravado,' 'Mangus,' 'The King,' and 'Bright Star' are good pink cultivars, the last of which is said to bloom all season. 'Bravado' is the tallest, up to 48 inches.

'White Lustre' is an attractive white hybrid of *E. purpurea* with an orange-gold cone. 'White Swan' can be grown from seed.

For subtle flower form and color, try pale pink species *E. laevigata* and *E. pallida*. Their slender petals droop gracefully. Spring-blooming *E. laevigata*, smoothleaf coneflower, a woodland flower, likes slightly acid soil and partial sun. Its handsome foliage is waxy and smooth. *E. pallida* is native to

the Piney Woods and Cross Timbers of Texas to Indiana and Nebraska. It takes any enriched, well-drained soil and prefers afternoon shade. Its gray foliage is slightly hairy. The two create a succession of bloom from spring to fall.

✿ *Eustoma grandiflorum*
Texas Bluebell, Prairie Gentian
GENTIANACEAE

BLOOM: Deep blue-violet with gold-and-black eye; occasionally white. Hybrids pink, white, and blue.
FOLIAGE: Blue-green, oval.
HEIGHT: 12–24″, hybrids to 36″.
BLOOM SEASON: Summer. Species, typically 3–4 weeks in mid- to late summer or fall.
REGIONS: All.
LIGHT: Full sun, partial shade, filtered light.
SOIL: Heavy and alkaline preferred; survives all.
MOISTURE: Medium annual moisture. Ample during peak growth.
PROPAGATION: Seed. Controlled propagation is difficult.

Anyone who has seen drifts of Texas bluebells in a seep or low spot in the Central Texas prairies comes home wanting to grow them. Gardeners report varying results with these gorgeous wildflowers, but their beauty makes them worth trying. They are said

Texas bluebell *Eustoma grandiflorum*

to be more reliable in dry beds or cutting gardens than in mixed borders. The cut flowers last a week.

Eustomas are in fact biennials, not true perennials. They are started in the garden from tiny seeds or from nursery transplants. They are reported to regrow the second year only if the first-year seed heads are removed after blooming. If one plant is allowed to set seed, it will produce volunteer plants for the next season. Eustoma prefers seasonally moist sites in the wild but, paradoxically, it sometimes rots in gardens. It is also subject to borers.

'Lion' and 'Yodel' are good named garden varieties that reach 2–3 feet in height.

Another hybrid form of this plant is frequently sold in nurseries under the older genus name *Lisianthus*. Japanese hybridizers developed these pink, white, and blue forms from the native Texas wildflower. They bloom all summer but lack the distinctive gold and black markings inside the flower cup, the deep blue-violet color of the native, and its grace of proportion. The double forms add ruffles to the pastels and top-heavy form. I prefer the original.

৯৯ *Gaillardia*
Indian Blanket, Firewheel
COMPOSITAE

BLOOM: Many variations of red and golden yellow, with ray flowers surrounding maroon or yellow centers; 3–4″ flower heads.
FOLIAGE: Green.
HEIGHT: Mostly 12–30″, depending on species or cultivar; some hybrids reportedly to 60″.
BLOOM SEASON: Natives in the wild, mid-spring to early summer, 3–4 weeks. Garden varieties, early summer to frost if watered and deadheaded.
REGIONS: All.
LIGHT: Full sun, partial shade.
SOIL: Light, well-drained. Relatively infertile soil for natives. Tolerates range of pH.
MOISTURE: Low, medium moisture ranges best suited. Tolerates drought.
PROPAGATION: Easy from seed. Division in fall; late summer root cuttings.

Indian blanket *Gaillardia pulchella*

Wild Indian blankets are among the easiest native plants to grow. They begin blooming as the bluebonnets are finishing up. *Gaillardia aristata* is perennial, with yellow or purple disk flowers and yellow rays, sometimes purplish at the base. *G. pulchella,* yellow banded with red, is the common roadside annual. *G. amblyodon* is a gorgeous, deep-red annual native to West Texas. Other native and endemic blanket flowers grow in various parts of the state. If the garden perennials don't thrive in a given locale, chances are a home plant will. Wide variations in color and marking distinguish wild populations. In gardens, where soils are fertile and watering consistent, the wild gaillardias are likely to become overgrown with more foliage than flowers.

The garden flower *G.* × *grandiflora* is a hybrid of *G. aristata* and *G. pulchella.* Its numerous named cultivars offer a variety of sizes and colors. These must be propagated vegetatively to keep offspring true to the parent variety. 'Burgundy' has wine-red, 3-inch flowers on 2–5-foot stalks. Foot-high 'Goblin' is a popular hybrid that has large, dark-red flowers with a wide, irregular yellow border. It will rebloom if it is cut back. The 'Monarch' strain in a variety of red and yellow combinations can be grown from seed. It grows about 30 inches tall and reportedly to 5 feet. 'Baby Cole,' a widely advertised variety, in the estimation of one Dallas nurseryman, "stinks."

Light, well-drained soil is essential for gaillardias. Short-lived even in good conditions, they decline quickly in unimproved heavy clay, especially in winter. Late to sprout in spring, gaillardias are easily hoed up or overplanted if the gardener isn't careful. In late summer, cut them back to encourage fall bloom.

Gaillardia is named for an eighteenth-century French patron of botany.

Rain-of-gold *Galphimia glauca*

❧ *Galphimia glauca* (*Thryallis glauca*)
Rain-of-gold
MALPIGHACEAE

BLOOM: Yellow ¾″ flowers in showy panicles.
FOLIAGE: Leathery oblong evergreen with waxy bloom.
HEIGHT: Shrub usually 3–6′; can reach 10′.
BLOOM SEASON: Year-round except briefly during light frost periods in regions where it is adapted.

REGIONS: Zone 9b in Lower Rio Grande Valley, South Texas. Not freeze-hardy.
HEAT TOLERANCE: High.
LIGHT: Full sun.
SOIL: Well-drained, dry.
MOISTURE: Low annual moisture range. Tolerates drought.
PROPAGATION: Seed; cuttings with heat.

Galphimia glauca is a neat, free-flowering tropical shrub, native from Mexico to Guatemala and Panama. It provides volume and dense foliage in the back of the border or makes a tall screen. It could serve as an annual in warm regions, subject to killing freezes in winter, much as *Hamelia patens,* or firebush, does. In Harlingen in the Lower Rio Grande Valley, it weathered the severe winter of 1983 with no problems.

The leaves of rain-of-gold, as it is commonly called, are covered with a waxy "bloom" formed by a whitish powder that rubs off easily. The flowers are a bright, clear yellow.

❧ *Gaura lindheimeri*
False Honeysuckle
ONAGRACEAE

BLOOM: Delicate, airy 1″ four-petaled white flowers that open from pale pink buds and deepen to rose-pink with age. Long stems. Honey-scented.
FOLIAGE: Green, willowlike, wavy, and toothed.
HEIGHT: Wiry stalks 18–48″ tall.
BLOOM SEASON: Spring to fall.
REGIONS: All. Native to Louisiana, Texas, and adjacent Mexico, Zones 6–10. Tolerates extremes of both heat and humidity.
LIGHT: Full sun.
SOIL: Any well-drained. Grows wild in relatively infertile, dry soil and adapts to good garden soil.
MOISTURE: All moisture ranges. Tolerates drought.
PROPAGATION: Seeds and division. Self-sown seedlings reach flowering size in a year. Long taproot necessitates deep digging to transplant.

This vase-shaped plant with tall, slender wands of bloom is a common wildflower here. I was surprised

False
honeysuckle
*Gaura
lindheimerii*

when I first heard that attendees of a national perennial conference exclaimed over it as a garden flower. On reflection I saw why; I know that I am always delighted to see it each year. It comes up in a crack between the driveway and a concrete retaining wall and blooms for weeks. It has no serious diseases or pests.

The white-and-pink wands of gaura can lend fullness to a border and provide delicate contrast to more substantial flowers, much as baby's breath does, but for a much longer bloom period. Gaura should be planted in clumps in order for the slender, delicate-looking plants to have visual impact.

Gerber daisy
*Gerbera
jamesonii*

৯৯ *Gerbera jamesonii*
Gerber Daisy
COMPOSITAE

BLOOM: Rose or scarlet, slender-petaled. Hybrids also pink, red-orange, white, yellow.
FOLIAGE: Green.
HEIGHT: 12–24″.
BLOOM SEASON: Spring to fall.
REGIONS: All but Plains Country and Trans-Pecos. Hardy to Zone 8.
HEAT TOLERANCE: Medium, moderate ranges. Adapts in high-heat regions with more shade, mulch over roots.
LIGHT: Morning sun, filtered light, full shade.
SOIL: Well-drained. Prefers neutral garden loam.
MOISTURE: Medium to high.
PROPAGATION: Seed or cuttings of side shoots.

The Gerber daisies best known from garden centers and florist shops are what Dallas nurseryman Bob Wilson calls "bred-to-death" hybrids. They are large-flowered, Crayola-colored, and too sensitive to heat and cold to go out of doors. The only part of the state in which they thrive—with shade, that is—is the subtropical Lower Rio Grande Valley. For other parts of the state, the simpler species *Gerbera jamesonii* and hybrids not far removed from it are better. These are longer-stemmed than the florist hybrids, and the flower petals are long and slender, rather than stubby.

A site with well-drained and well-prepared soil, shaded from summer's afternoon sun, is the key to success with Gerber daisies. Jameson's gerbera tolerates summer heat if given afternoon shade. Pine-straw mulch will protect it from winter freezes; the mulch must be removed early in spring to allow the re-emerging plant to sprout. In the High Plains and colder parts of the Trans-Pecos, even mulch does not protect gerberas from freezing.

Applications of soil acidifiers or acid organic matter and fertilizers may be needed to keep the leaves a healthy green in iron-poor and alkaline soils, such as those in South Texas, where the plant is prone to chlorosis.

In bouquets, old-fashioned Gerber daisies are subtle, charming, and long-lasting.

Hedychium × *kewense*

Ginger

ZINGIBERACEAE

BLOOM: Multitudes of pale orange flowers surround the tops of tall, stout stalks.
FOLIAGE: Green, long, lancelike.
HEIGHT: 5–8′.
BLOOM SEASON: Early summer to frost.
REGIONS: Gulf Coast, Lower Rio Grande Valley, southern Prairies & Cross Timbers, South Texas; Zones 8b–9b.
HEAT TOLERANCE: High, medium ranges.
LIGHT: Filtered sunlight, but adapts to full sun with adequate watering.
SOIL: Rich garden soil high in organic matter.
MOISTURE: Medium, high. Prefers moist sites but tolerates occasional drought.
PROPAGATION: Division.

This plant is one of many ornamental gingers distantly related to culinary ginger. It is very fragrant and long-blooming. This lovely flower has been known to weather 13° F cold in San Antonio. It is effective against a background of evergreen shrubbery.

Another "ginger" widely grown in gardens in similar conditions is white *Hedychium coronarium,* butterfly ginger. It is said to withstand brief freezes to 10° F if mulched.

Ginger *Hedychium* × *kewense*

Helenium flexuosum. Photo © 1987 by Carl Schoenfeld.

Helenium

Sneezeweed, Helen's Flower

COMPOSITAE

BLOOM: Yellow, bronze, red-brown, red-orange.
FOLIAGE: Green, lanceolate. Often prematurely deciduous.
HEIGHT: 1–6′.
BLOOM SEASON: Late spring to early fall, depending on species and variety.
REGIONS: All but Lower Rio Grande Valley, depending on species and variety. See Chart 1.
LIGHT: Full sun.
SOIL: Fairly rich garden soil to moist sand, depending on species.
MOISTURE: Moderate to high. Prefers damp sites and, for several species, moisture-retentive soils.
PROPAGATION: Seed, except for named hybrids. Division.

None of the sources on this plant report whether it in fact causes sneezing. The more attractive early common name was Helen's flower. It sprang up, legend has it, from the spot where Helen's tears fell when she wept over the fall of Troy.

Heleniums belong to the Compositae, along with daisies and sunflowers. Mainstays of the garden from July to September, they are excellent cut flowers, as well. In heleniums, the disk is a prominent, raised knob, usually in a color that contrasts to the ray flowers, or petals. The disk may be yellow, chestnut, or brownish-purple, attractively ringed by open disk flowers in contrasting yellow. The ray flowers are scallop-edged like those of coreopsis and may be yellow, red-orange, or bronze.

There are heleniums for most regions. The fall-blooming species *Helenium autumnale* does best in the Blacklands, Post Oak Savannah, Piney Woods, Edwards Plateau, and Plains Country. Its 5´ height may not fit into all settings. This helenium prefers damp soils where daisies would rot. A mahogany-red cultivar, 'Crimson Beauty,' has been successful in a smaller area, based on limited trials. Yellow 'Sunny Boy' does well on the Edwards Plateau, and probably elsewhere. *H. flexuosum* grows wild in Southeast Texas to Calhoun County and rarely in the Piney Woods, blooming from spring until early June. Nationally, it ranges from Massachusetts to Florida, west to Missouri and Texas.

Heleniums are most easily propagated by division. Disbudding will control rangy growers. Space the plants 1½–2 feet apart and divide them every third year.

Yellow 'Butterpat' and burnt-orange-and-dark-brown 'Brilliant' are two hybrids of *H. autumnale* available by mail order. 'Sunshine Hybrids,' in a range of solids and bicolors, are reportedly easy to propagate by spring division but difficult from cuttings.

Although perennial heleniums are not long-lived, they are easy to grow, handsome, useful in borders, and invaluable in wet areas.

❧ *Helianthus*
Sunflower
COMPOSITAE

BLOOM: Yellow, with yellow or purple-brown eye.
FOLIAGE: Green.
HEIGHT: 3–7´.
BLOOM SEASON: Summer to fall, or fall, depending on species.
REGIONS: All for *H. maximiliani* and *H. ×*

multiflorus; all but Plains Country and Trans-Pecos for *H. angustifolius.*
LIGHT: Full sun; also partial shade for *H. angustifolius.*
SOIL: Fairly infertile to good garden soil, depending on species. Neutral to alkaline.
MOISTURE: Low, medium, high ranges. Dry to wet sites depending on species. All accept seasonal drought.
PROPAGATION: Seed; division in spring. For *H. × multiflorus,* division or root cuttings in late fall.

Helianthus angustifolius is commonly called swamp sunflower, because it is found in low, wet places. It is nonetheless tolerant of drought, except at summer's peak. Soil should not be too rich. This plant's range includes the Prairies and Cross Timbers, Edwards Plateau, Gulf Coast, Lower Rio Grande Valley, Piney Woods, and South Texas. The plants grow as

Maximilian sunflower and Mexican bush sage
Helianthus maximiliani and *Salvia leucantha*

tall as 7 feet. They branch out at the top and bear brown-eyed yellow flowers in fall. This plant spreads freely in its preferred conditions.

H. maximiliani, Maximilian sunflower, bears large double daisies all up its stalks in late summer or fall, or even as early as June in the Plains Country. It is unforgettable to wander a meadow in October when these 7-foot spires of gold tower overhead—a treat that is becoming unfortunately rare.

In gardens, Maximilian sunflowers need fairly poor soil and absolute sun. They do very well in the Prairies and Cross Timbers, Edwards Plateau, and Plains Country and satisfactorily in most of the rest of the state. Infrequent, deep waterings are best; ample water promotes rank growth with sparse bloom. Avoid fertilizer for the same reason. These tendencies make Maximilian sunflower a candidate for inclusion in a dry garden with other plants that react similarly, such as liatris and gaillardia. It is best positioned against a wall or at the back of a dry border. To keep the plants compact, cut them back three times during the growing season, the last cutting in July. The clumps should be divided in early spring every few years to keep the plant in good form in a garden. By summer, attractive clusters of sage-green, lance-shaped foliage will be knee-high.

Maximilian sunflower was named for Prince Maximilian of Germany, who explored the western frontier in the 1800s, recording the flora and fauna.

H. × multiflorus is a summer bloomer that grows 3 to 5 feet tall, with double flowers like shaggy chrysanthemums up to 5 inches across. It needs good, well-drained garden soil, plenty of room, and the chance to dry completely between heavy waterings. Divide it in spring every three to four years. Although little known and thus rarely used, *H. × multiflorus* does excellently in the San Antonio area, the Prairies and Cross Timbers, and the Edwards Plateau and satisfactorily in many other locales. It can be grown in containers. Perennial sunflower, as it is commonly called, is a cross between the annual western sunflower and wild perennial *H. decapetalus.*

Two cautions with the species sunflowers: first, they are said to secrete a substance that inhibits the growth of other adjoining plants. Its effect is variable; certain salvias, at least, don't appear to be affected. Second, weedkillers should be used with more than usual caution near Maximilian sunflowers; they can be killed by chemicals that other perennials tolerate.

Cut, the flowers last indoors for a week or even two. The stalks with dried flower heads can be left standing for winter bird food.

ℬ *Heliopsis helianthoides*
Heliopsis, False Sunflower
COMPOSITAE

BLOOM: Golden yellow semi-double 3″ blooms.
FOLIAGE: Dark, attractive.
HEIGHT: 24–48″.
BLOOM SEASON: July or earlier to frost, depending on variety.
REGIONS: All but the Lower Rio Grande Valley.
LIGHT: Full sun. Tolerates partial shade, filtered light.
SOIL: Any.
MOISTURE: Medium, high annual moisture preferred. Tolerates drought.
PROPAGATION: Seed, division in spring, basal cuttings.

Heliopsis helianthoides 'Summer Sun'

Heliopsis' several varieties are all considered quite hardy. The species blooms from July or earlier to frost, a boon to gardeners who don't care to replant in fall. These sun-loving flowers do better in dry soils than most perennials. They make excellent cut flowers.

'Summer Sun,' a cultivar variously designated as *H. scabra* (a subspecies of *H. helianthoides*) and *H. helianthoides* var. *scabra,* is a favorite of gardeners in both the Prairies and Cross Timbers and the Piney Woods. Its large double flowers top 3–4-foot stalks. Horticulturist Eric Lautzenheiser, who began gardening as a boy in Medina, Texas, reports great success with 'Summer Sun' in a garden he grew in East Texas. Planted from seed in March, it bloomed by midsummer, rested, and bloomed for three more three-week periods.

Heliopsis is divided in spring for longevity and vigor. It can be propagated by seed, as well. Russell Weber of Austin recommends sowing seed early in a greenhouse for same-season bloom. Planted beside red or deep pink late-season daylilies, heliopsis is smashing.

✿ *Hemerocallis*
Daylily
LILIACEAE

BLOOM: Near-white, yellows, oranges, pinks, mauves, reds, purples, near-blues, blends, bi- and tricolors, and many markings.
FOLIAGE: Green, swordlike.
HEIGHT: 8–48″. *H. fulva,* to 6′.
BLOOM SEASON: With a range of varieties, March–October, generally with a late July–August lull. Each plant generally blooms for 2–3 weeks. Some rebloom later in the season.
REGIONS: All.
LIGHT: Full sun, partial shade, filtered sun. Afternoon shade in summer desirable in hot, humid areas.
SOIL: Tolerates any well-drained soil. Slightly acid, well-drained, with ample humus is best. Clay or sand satisfactory if improved.

MOISTURE: Moderate preferred. Essential in spring. Survives drought, but subsequent growth and bloom are reduced.
PROPAGATION: Root division, preferably in fall.

The daylily has long been a favorite garden flower of easy culture, suited for most locales. It is ranked among the top ten perennials for easiness by many gardeners nationwide.

Daylilies are herbaceous perennials with swollen roots, not true lilies, which grow from bulbs. The botanical name *Hemerocallis* is derived from Greek words meaning "beauty for a day." Individual blooms do live only a day, but the bloom period of most plants is two weeks or more, and some varieties rebloom. A single plant may have multiple bloom stalks, or "scapes," and many buds per stem.

With varieties that bloom early, midseason, and late, bloom can be obtained from March to October with only a late-summer lull.

The foliage, something between iris blades and liriope or monkey grass, spreads fountain- or fanlike. Heights of the plants in flower range from 8 inches to 4 feet or more, with the blooms positioned anywhere from slightly above the leaves to well aloft.

Daylilies grow throughout the United States, Europe, and Asia. Their cultivation in China predates the written word. There, every part of the plant was used for medicine or food. In Chinese culture, the daylily symbolizes relief from worries and cares, the equivalent of our "heart's ease," the pansy.

At one time, the tawny daylily and the lemon lily, two Asian plants introduced to the New World from Europe, were the most popular daylilies in America. The tawny daylily, *H. fulva* 'Europa,' is deep orange, its bloom stalks towering as high as 6 feet above a mass of arching foliage. In the New World, this naturally occurring clone acquired another common name, roadside lily. It followed farmers and roadbuilders into broken ground throughout the northeastern United States, spreading vigorously by rhizomes. The yellow-flowering lemon lily, *H. lilioasphodelus* (*H. flava*), was less aggressive and slower to multiply than its kin and so did not establish itself in such numbers in the wild. Its early bloom time, clear yellow hue, and sweet scent made it a favorite of American gardeners, however, as it had been in Victorian England. Both tawny daylilies and lemon lilies are considered good plants for the High Plains, Piney Woods, Prairies and Cross Timbers, and Gulf Coast of Texas.

H. fulva rosea, a naturally occurring pink or rosy variation in the species, is the source of the red and pink colorations brought out by mid-twentieth-century hybridizers.

Now, a couple of hundred years after the arrival of the daylily in America, many types of modern daylilies fill gardens. Their hues range from sherbet pastels to deep jewel tones, a rainbow palette of all colors but pure white and true blue, which hybridizers still pursue. Flower colorations defy description, with every possible combination of hues of petal and flower throat and various patterns of banding, midribs, and edging, as well as showy freckled and shimmering "diamond dust" effects. Such variations appear in thousands of showy named and registered hybrids.

Daylilies thrive in all regions of Texas and the South. The single forms do well in dry gardens. Double-flowering 'Kwanso,' an early *H. fulva* cultivar, is also very drought-tolerant. In fact, after their spring bloom period, all daylilies can go for three or four weeks without moisture, with some sacrifice in growth vigor and bloom the subsequent year.

Adaptation to the region is the most important factor in selecting daylilies. Daylily hardiness is often discussed in more general terms, but categories by foliage-hardiness are recognized by the American Hemerocallis Society and are used—with some license—in nursery catalogs. In general, daylilies of

Tawny daylily *Hemerocallis fulva* and modern 'Aztec'

every type can be grown in some part of Texas. In *dormant* daylilies, the top growth yellows and dies back after several hard freezes. *Semi-evergreen* varieties leave a few inches of greenery above ground in winter and, in general, perform well throughout the United States. *Evergreen* varieties do not die back and may be damaged by rotting of frozen foliage in alternate freezes and thaws.

The colder winters of the High Plains and Central Texas north of Dallas–Fort Worth make dormant daylilies the best choice there. Dormant varieties do well in all regions of Texas other than the Gulf Coast, Lower Rio Grande Valley, and South Texas, in fact. Semi-evergreen varieties are suited to all but the Plains Country, although only fairly so in the Edwards Plateau and Trans-Pecos. The Lower Gulf Coast and subtropical Lower Rio Grande Valley are best suited for evergreen varieties. There are exceptions to these general guidelines, of course, and there are gardeners willing to do whatever it takes to make a favorite daylily grow outside its preferred range.

Other concerns in selecting daylilies are aesthetic. Knowing the range of choices and basic terminology is helpful.

There are three classes by bloom size, from under 3 inches to over 4½ inches in diameter: miniature, small-flowered, and large-flowered. Height divides daylilies into groups from 6 to more than 36 inches: low, medium, and tall. "Dwarf" refers to plants less than 12 inches tall. These measurements are of the plants with bloom scapes; the foliage may be much shorter.

Balanced proportion of foliage height and mass to height of bloom scape is desirable. In the back of a border, tall scapes will be preferred. As a low border around a patio or in the front of a bed, daylilies whose flowers rise just above the foliage will be more attractive, even though they would not win prizes in a daylily show.

Daylily blooms come in nine recognized forms, from star-shaped to triangular and flat to recurved.

Finally, daylilies include night owls and early birds, "nocturnal" and "diurnal" types. And some in each

Table 1. Recommended Companion Plants for Border Daylilies

Beebalm, bergamot	*Monarda didyma, M. fistulosa*
Columbine	*Aquilegia*
Cosmos, annual	*Cosmos bipinnatus, C. sulphureus*
Feverfew	*Chrysanthemum parthenium*
Lythrum	*Lythrum salicaria*
Pinks	*Dianthus*
Garden phlox	*Phlox paniculata*
Louisiana phlox	*P. divaricata*
Prairie phlox	*P. pilosa*
Salvias, perennial	*Salvia farinacea, S. × superba, S. × 'Majestic'*

group are "extended" bloomers that stay open at least sixteen hours. It is best to choose ones with habits similar to your own, or you'll never be awake to see them open.

All of these variations represent an endless playground for personal taste that can be explored at leisure. All that is needed to begin to grow daylilies is to choose among those of the proper hardiness class for one's region and to provide the needed care.

How to Plant Daylilies

Good garden soil as for most perennials is best. New beds should be prepared at least six weeks in advance of planting to allow the soil to settle. Dig to a depth of 1 foot, add humus, and if drainage is poor, raise the bed level. (Good drainage is a must to avoid crown rot.) Alkaline soils can be amended to the preferred slightly acid condition. If there is not time to prepare the bed well in advance, plant each daylily atop a small mound of soil to compensate for later settling. Situations near the competing roots of broad-leaved trees and shrubs are to be avoided, but locations beneath pine trees are desirable.

Potted daylilies are planted any time, at the same height in garden soil as in the pot.

Bare-root daylilies should be kept moist, but not in standing water, prior to planting. Some gardeners recommend an overnight soak in a mild fertilizer-and-water solution. Putting them in perlite, available in garden centers, in a container with drainage holes and then running water over them is Garland gardener Natalie Thompson's recommendation to hold them up to a week. Plant bare-root daylilies to the crown, where the roots join the top growth.

In hot climates, daylilies are best planted in fall.

Mulch is recommended to conserve water and to suppress weeds. Some gardeners say fertilizer should be added along with organic mulch to be sure that soil fertility is not depleted as the mulch decomposes; others say this is necessary only if the organic matter is dug into the soil.

Daylily beds are allowed to dry between waterings. Probing the soil an inch or two below the surface with your finger is the best way to know when to water. Deep watering at soil level to 8–10 inches' depth is best; overhead watering spots the blooms.

An annual application of a complete fertilizer such as 5-10-5 in spring is sufficient in most good garden soil, experienced daylily growers say. A controlled slow-release fertilizer is best. Poor or extremely sandy soils may require several applications. Composted organic matter is always beneficial. High-nitrogen fertilizers are to be avoided; they yellow foliage and promote rank growth with few blooms.

Daylilies have few pest problems. Hardy evergreen varieties can harbor aphids. Spider mites may appear in dry springs and summers. Never use Kelthane on daylilies; it kills them.

Division every two or three years will keep the plants in peak condition and provide new roots for planting. Older types may need division less often.

Daylilies *Hemerocallis* hybrids

Table 2. Peggy Hammel's Daylilies for All of Texas

VARIETY	BLOOM SEASON	BLOOM	HEIGHT	COMMENTS
'Apple Annie'	Early	Apple red	24″	
'Bitsy'	April–July	Yellow miniature-flowered	20″	
'Bridget'	Late	Dark red	14″	
'Country Honey'	Midseason	Miniature dusty-rose with maroon banding	20″	
'Dumpy'	Late	Yellow	14–16″	
'Gertrude Lanham'	Late	Copper-pumpkin	22″	
'John Doe'	Late	Yellow	34″	
'Mae Graham'	Early	Rose-pink	22″	
'Mattie Mae Berry'	Early	Yellow, small	20″	
'Stella de Oro'	Early midseason; reblooms	Gold miniature	10″ (dwarf)	Reblooms as many as 4 times in Texas
'Sweet Patootie'	Early	Lemon-yellow	24″	
'Tetrad'	Early	Yellow	14″	

Bloom Seasons by Region

On the Gulf Coast, daylilies bloom longer and re-bloom more heavily than in most of the Southwest. Typically, bloom starts in March, peaks in mid-May, and resumes in late September after an August pause.

In North Central Texas, the late summer bloom hiatus is longer. Watering and feeding in late summer is necessary to encourage fall rebloom.

On the High Plains, daylilies bloom from June to August. Gardeners there report that they are "as reliable as Shasta daisies" and that, generally, hybrids are not aggressive spreaders there.

Varieties

Some of the older daylily varieties are more vigorous and can be aggressive in the flower bed. However, "newer hybrids have fewer flowers than the old-timers," says Margaret Kane of San Antonio. Some of the best-known daylilies are fragrant, clear yellow 'Hyperion' (an older hybrid), long-blooming gold dwarf 'Stella de Oro,' and ruffled yellow 'Mary Todd.' There is a daylily for every taste and situation. The daylily growers' favorites are listed in Tables 2 and 3. Peggy Hammel of Euless, a home gardener and wholesale grower, selected twelve daylilies suited to gardens statewide, representing a range of heights, colors, and bloom seasons. Carl Schoenfeld, who gardens in Waller County 50 miles inland from Houston, grows daylilies in acid soils and high rainfall. Here, he shares his personal favorites. My own favorites include 'Hyperion' and 'Tone Poem.'

Table 3. Carl Schoenfeld's Daylily Picks for the Southern Post Oak Savannah

VARIETY	BLOOM SEASON	BLOOM
'Aabachee'	Midseason to late	Antique ruby spider form
'Black Hills'	Early midseason	Small, semi-spider form, dark wine with darker throat
'Concubine'	Very late (2d week of July)	Pale cream, trumpet-shaped
'Driven Snow'	Midseason	Near-white with green throat
'Harry Barras'	Early midseason	Huge creamy yellow
'Hyperion'	Midseason	Very large, canary-yellow, green throat, fragrant
Lemon lily (*H. lilioasphodelus* [*H. flava*])	Very early	Clear yellow with grasslike foliage
'Little Hustler'	Early to early midseason	Peach to melon, semi-spider form, fragrant
'Orange Bowl'	Early midseason	Brilliant clear orange, wide petals, lightly ruffled
'Sky Country'	Early midseason; extra long bloom	Greenish near-white
'Subtle Serenity'	Midseason, prolonged bloom	Ruffled near-white with olive throat
Tawny daylily (*H. fulva* 'Europa')	Summer	Orange; cultivar 'Kwanso' is double
'Tone Poem'	Midseason to late	Polychrome blend of melon, gold, and peach
'Valentine's Day'	Midseason to late	Cerise-red

[a]Tetraploid daylilies are genetically altered to possess four sets of chromosomes. They are characteristically large-flowered and vigorous.

HEIGHT	CLASS/TYPE	COMMENTS
32″		A 1957 hybrid that lasts. Beautiful, elegant large spider.
18″		Best in shade so that sun doesn't fade the fabulous color.
26″	Tetraploid[a]	
24″	Evergreen	"One of the best." Flowers are in the foliage.
26″	Evergreen, tetraploid[a]	Blooms larger than any other. Large clump.
48″		Introduced in 1925. Blooms up to 6 weeks. "Unsurpassed yellow." Prolific bloomer. Choice cut flowers.
To 24″		An ancient species from China and a favorite in Victorian gardens. Slow-spreading. Sweetly fragrant.
15″		A great plant that blooms well in shade. Heavily branching.
24″	Dormant	"The most orange one can imagine." Tight, slow grower. Takes much sun.
24″	Evergreen	"Great refreshing color that stands out in heat."
24″		One of the finest for color and duration of bloom.
To 6′		Very tough. Withstands drought. Vigorous spreader. Long scapes over low foliage are ungainly compared to modern cultivars, but no daylily is less demanding of care. A sterile clone.
29″	Dormant, tetraploid[a]	Lovely, hard-to-describe color. Huge blooms. Divide every 2 years.
27″	Dormant, tetraploid[a]	A very special color.

☙ *Hibiscus*

Hibiscus, Rose Mallow

MALVACEAE

BLOOM: Pink, white, rose, red, and combinations.
FOLIAGE: Green; shape varies among species.
HEIGHT: 1–8′, depending on species.
BLOOM SEASON: June to October; to frost for
H. martianus and *H. laevis.*
REGIONS: All. See species descriptions and Chart 1
for best species for each.
LIGHT: Full sun, filtered sun, partial shade.
SOIL: Moist clay, garden soil. *H. martianus* also
grows in adobe and sand. Acid to alkaline,
depending on species. One salt-tolerant species,
Kosteletzkya virginica.
MOISTURE: Medium, high annual moisture,
generally; *H. martianus* grows in dry ranges, and
only it tolerates drought.
PROPAGATION: Seed; also softwood cuttings,
H. laevis; these methods and hardwood cuttings,
H. moscheutos and hybrids.

Hibiscus laevis, halberd-leaf hibiscus (formerly called
H. militaris), is a 3–8-foot-tall native Texas plant
that deserves trial in a wider range of the state than
East Texas and the Upper Gulf Coast, where it is
indigenous. It prefers acid to slightly alkaline soils.
Its adaptation to filtered sun or high shade makes it
ideal for treed lots where other hibiscus would not
thrive. The dainty 4-inch pastel blooms lend a
delicacy and grace unequaled by the large-flowered
hybrid mallows common in the trade. The blooms
are pale pink or white with a pink throat; they close
at night. Their long bloom period spans summer
and part of fall. Tolerance of extreme cold and heat
in other parts of the state has been tested by only a
few gardeners, who report success in the High Plains
and North Central Texas. The species' natural range
from Pennsylvania and Minnesota to Florida and
Texas indicates that it is quite cold-hardy.

Good garden soil and ample moisture are this
plant's only requirements. In the South Plains it has
been found to tolerate high alkalinity. Like the
canna, it prefers a bed to itself. After frost the bloom

Halberd-leaf hibiscus *Hibiscus laevis*

stalks should be cut down and discarded. Propagation is by seed or softwood cuttings.

Another native mallow is *Kosteletzkya virginica,*
salt marsh mallow. It resembles *H. laevis* in pink
flower color and growth habit, reaching 6 feet in
height in good soil. While *H. laevis* grows in fresh-
water marshes, *K. virginica* is native to both fresh-
and saltwater areas, an asset for Gulf Coast dwellers.
It is less cold-hardy and should be cut down after a
hard frost and mulched for winter protection in
Zones 8 and 9a.

H. martianus, heart-leaf hibiscus or *tulipán del
monte,* is a short, dryland mallow native to South
Texas, the Trans-Pecos, and the Lower Gulf, with
attractive heart-shaped green leaves and soft rose-red

Species hibiscus *H. rockii* and *H. moscheutos*

single 1½–4-inch blooms. It is native to droughty regions and poor, alkaline soil. In well-watered garden soil, it can get taller than its usual yard-high maximum stature, but it still grows smaller than other mallows here. Well-drained soil ensures against rot and mildew. Mulch in winter improves its winter-hardiness further north and inland. One Piney Woods gardener reports that it survived 20° F in a pot. It was known until recently as *H. cardiophyllus.*

H. moscheutos is the species from which the popular hybrid 'Mallow Marvels' were developed. The species grows wild through the eastern third of the United States from Massachusetts and Michigan south to Georgia and Alabama, and reportedly in East Texas as well. The hybrid forms do not close in the afternoon like the species, but stay open to late evening. Both species and hybrids prefer fertile, iron-rich soil and full sun and need ample moisture. They are adapted throughout Texas. The species tolerates poor, dry soil. In the Lower Rio Grande Valley, overwatering can make this mallow rot-prone.

"Clown flowers," Dallas gardener Ray Hapes calls the enormous hybrids like 'Dixie Belle' and 'Frisbee,' hibiscus with blooms the size of dinner plates. Other gardeners may find them appealing or, as Ray does, appalling. They grow on broad, bulky plants 3–4 feet tall (grown as standards) or 18–24

inches (as shrubs). The daintier species flowers are white, pink, or rose, usually with a dark red eye, and up to 8 inches wide, on a plant that can reach 8 feet in height. Both groups are hardy garden plants. They can be grown in beds by themselves or at the back of the border. North Carolina gardener and author Elizabeth Lawrence recommended 'Mallow Marvels' as partners with monardas, to bloom when the monardas are in full swing and continue after they wane. Cut mallows back after hard frost for regrowth in subsequent years.

H. mutabilis, the Confederate rose, is an old-time garden perennial. Its double flowers are 4–6 inches across. They gradually change from white in the morning to pink or deep rose by nightfall. Its cultural requirements and bloom season are similar to those of *H. moscheutos.* Confederate rose makes a bush 6–8 feet tall in regions where it does not freeze.

Kniphofia uvaria (*Tritoma*)
Red-hot Poker, Torch Lily
LILIACEAE

BLOOM: Yellow shaded to orange and red; hybrids, cream to red.
FOLIAGE: Gray-green, sword-shaped.
HEIGHT: 24–48″.
BLOOM SEASON: April or May; sometimes several bloom flushes; sometimes repeats in fall.
REGIONS: Edwards Plateau, Plains Country (reliable to Canyon), Prairies & Cross Timbers, Trans-Pecos.
HEAT TOLERANCE: Medium, low ranges; high range in low humidity.
LIGHT: Full sun to light shade.
SOIL: Garden soil, sand. Well-drained. Neutral to alkaline; tolerates acid.
MOISTURE: Low, medium annual moisture. Ample in early summer, dry after blooming and in winter. Dry air best.
PROPAGATION: Division.

"Red-hot poker" and "torch lily" convey much better than its botanical names the fiery gradation

Red-hot poker *Kniphofia uvaria*.
Photo © 1986 by Paul Cox.

Midsummer decline of kniphofia in the Blacklands may be attributable to this combined damp and heat. Even in dry areas this plant is not problem-free. "One out of four people has success with it. Why? No one knows," says Burr Williams of Midland.

Kniphofia requires copious moisture in early summer, when it grows actively, and minimal moisture after it blooms and in winter. In areas with over 30 inches of rainfall per year, encourage summer dormancy by withholding water after bloom. Fast growers, the plants require about a square yard of space each. Clumps are best left undisturbed; gaps can be filled in with annuals or shallow-rooted perennials. Kniphofia reportedly can be rapidly increased by division of the crowns in autumn. 'Earliest of All' is an excellent hybrid that blooms in April and is fairly easy to find.

from yellow to red of this unusual flower. It is native to South Africa, and appeared in the English cottage garden in the early 1700s. *Tritoma* is an earlier botanical name by which many catalogs still list it. Many of the plants sold as *Kniphofia uvaria* are not the species, but hybrids whose colors range through ivory, coral, orange, and scarlet. Stately clumps of kniphofia make striking displays in the lawns of the Davis Mountains town of Alpine, where the iron-rich, fast-draining soil and dry air suit it perfectly. More humid areas may accommodate it, with good drainage and air circulation. Fungicides are sometimes applied to prevent root rot. It is of critical importance, however, that the soil not hold moisture in winter. Raised beds should be used in humid areas with heavy soil.

Carl Schoenfeld, partner in Yucca Do Nursery near Hempstead, theorizes that plants preferring full sun in dry regions do better in afternoon shade where the air is humid. This avoids the combination of hot sun and humid air that often proves deadly, perhaps because of heat in the rhizomatous roots.

✍ *Lantana*

Lantana

VERBENACEAE

BLOOM: Pink-and-yellow, orange-and-yellow, lavender; cultivars white, orange, gold, red, and combinations.
FOLIAGE: Dark green, gray-green, or sage green, depending on species/variety.
HEIGHT: Shrub, usually 36–48″, taller in old plants; trailing stems to 24″ long, standing up to 12″ high.
BLOOM SEASON: Spring to frost.
REGIONS: All; Plains Country only below Panhandle, and not all species and varieties.
HEAT TOLERANCE: All ranges. Accepts extreme heat of reflected sunlight.
LIGHT: Full, partial, or reflected sun. Minimum 6 hours per day.
SOIL: Adobe, clay, garden soil, sand. Most species, generally neutral to alkaline, tolerate acid; *L. montevidensis,* acid to alkaline. Well-drained. Salt-tolerant.
MOISTURE: Drought-tolerant but more attractive with moderate watering.
PROPAGATION: Seed, except 'New Gold' and other sterile cultivars; softwood cuttings, division.

"So much color for so little effort," one gardener describes these long-blooming, heat-loving plants. There is a lantana for every region of Texas, the South, and the Southwest. Their flat clusters of bloom, often bicolor, resemble flowers from an old cross-stitch sampler, an "×" for each floret.

Lantana camara, native to the American tropics, is naturalized through most of the South. Its blooms are pink to red with yellow. Tolerant of acid soils and high moisture, it is the best lantana for East Texas. Its blooming is not slowed by cool weather. It is not as freeze-resistant as *L. horrida,* however, dying in two out of four winters in the South Plains. It is grown as an annual in the northern Plains Country (Zones 6a–7a) and is inconsistently hardy even in Zone 8.

'New Gold' and 'Silver Mound' are two compact *L. camara* cultivars that thrive as far south as the Lower Rio Grande Valley, where they bloom as long as eleven months of the year. Their foliage is more refined and a truer green than that of *L. horrida,* and they seed less heavily, so they are more everblooming. There are a number of other excellent *L. camara* cultivars in a wide range of colors that are widely used for seasonal color in commercial landscapes statewide.

L. horrida, hierba de Cristo, is the Texas lantana native to the Hill Country, the Prairies and Cross Timbers, and most of the rest of the state except the Panhandle. This shrubby plant bears gray-green, fuzzy foliage and deep orange-and-yellow florets. BB-sized green seeds appear as the blooms fade and turn black when ripe. *L. horrida* is the only lantana winter-hardy in the South Plains and outperforms others in the Edwards Plateau. Winter-hardiness of large, older plants with thick woody stems is better than that of young plants. The foliage can be quite woolly and gray-green in summer drought but smooth and clear green in the cool of fall.

L. montevidensis, previously named *L. sellowiana,* is a lavender trailing species excellent for hanging baskets, as ground cover, and to mound over retaining walls. Native to South America, it is naturalized in Southeast Texas. One of its common names is polecat geranium, for its pungent foliage. Lavender weed is another. Sun or light shade is *L. montevidensis'* preference. It goes out of bloom in the worst summer heat in Zones 8b and 9 and resumes blooming in cooler weather. Trailing lantana can be aggressive in flower beds. Its long use in the hanging baskets at the Six Flags over Texas amusement park is testament to its toughness and lavish color.

An excellent companion plant for the shrubby lantanas is *Campanula poscharskyana.* This carpet-forming soft blue campanula will bloom in spring when the lantana is just leafing out.

Lantana 'New Gold' and 'Silver Mound'

In cold-winter areas, lantanas should be cut back to a nub after hard frost and mulched. Winter annuals can fill in the space until spring. Out of their hardiness range, lantanas can be wintered over in the garage, scantly watered. These plants have no known diseases or pests. Regular removal of seedpods prolongs bloom. Deer won't eat lantana. It has been described as "just too easy for some people."

Perennial sweet pea *Lathyrus latifolius*

᪈ *Lathyrus latifolius*
Perennial Sweet Pea
LEGUMINOSAE

BLOOM: Pink, red, purple, blue, 1″.
FOLIAGE: Gray-green, pointed ovals or lancelike.
HEIGHT: 4–9′ vine with mounding habit.
BLOOM SEASON: Spring to summer. June–August in Plains Country; April–May in El Paso.
REGIONS: All but South Plains. Freezes to the ground in Plains Country.
LIGHT: Reflected sun, full sun, partial shade, filtered light.
SOIL: Any well-drained.
MOISTURE: Moderate. Drought-tolerant.
PROPAGATION: Seed in late spring; germinates in 2–3 weeks at 55–65° F. Soak seed in water before planting. Difficult to transplant, unless started in peat pots (transplant pot and all).

This plant provides exuberant color and rambunctious growth over a long season. Its enthusiastic spreading is considered a nuisance by tidy gardeners with small beds and a blessing by laissez-faire gardeners with lots of bare ground to cover. It is durable and good for low-maintenance sites. Sweet pea is best used on fences and trellises or trailing over walls or terraces; otherwise it can be a formless mass. Sequester it, or watch it overwhelm its neighbors. Flower-covered stems with their curling tendrils look wonderful in bouquets, trailing over the side of the vase.

᪈ *Lavandula*
Lavender
LABIATAE

BLOOM: Lavender or white. Fragrant.
FOLIAGE: Gray or silver.
HEIGHT: 12–36″.
BLOOM SEASON: Summer to early fall.
REGIONS: Edwards Plateau, Gulf Coast (*L. dentata, L. stoechas*), Piney Woods, Plains Country (*L. angustifolia*), Prairies & Cross Timbers, South Texas, Trans-Pecos (*L. angustifolia, L. stoechas*).
LIGHT: Full sun to part shade. Tolerates reflected light.
SOIL: Well-drained garden loam or sand, neutral to alkaline.
MOISTURE: Grows in all ranges in well-drained soil. Tolerates drought.
PROPAGATION: Late summer or fall cuttings, root division in spring.

Lavender *Lavandula* sp.

True lavender or English lavender, *Lavandula angustifolia,* was an age-old source for sachets, perfume, and a dozen other toiletries as well as medicines in Britain and on the Continent. Today *L. angustifolia* and *L. stoechas,* Spanish lavender, still provide oil of lavender for the perfume industry. There are many lavender species, mostly gray-foliaged and lavender to purple in bloom. Lavender is appreciated in the garden not only for its flowers, but also for the leaf color and for the scent when one brushes against it along a garden path. The gray foliage with its velvety-white nap is a perfect foil for purple, yellow, lavender, white, and blue flowers.

Lavender is native to the Mediterranean, blooming from midsummer to early autumn. A true classic of the old-fashioned garden, it is well suited to dry, sunny Texas sites and can withstand the reflected heat of stone or concrete walls and terraces. Sandy, well-drained soil is best. Drainage is the key to winter-hardiness. The plant's 1–3-foot height, wand-like shape, and soft color make its best position in the garden near the front of a bed, backed by a contrasting or paler color. It is also nice for lining a path.

Lavender is propagated from seeds and cuttings and by root division, but seeds are very difficult to start. Late-summer cuttings are said to be the easiest method. Spring division also works. Fall or very early spring is the best time for planting small plants.

Popular cultivars of English lavender are 'Munstead,' 'Hidcote,' and 'Alba.' The species *L. stoechas* is liked for its intense color and fragrance. *L. dentata,* French lavender, is also easy to grow. *L. angustifolia* is reportedly the most cold-hardy.

✿ *Liatris*
Gayfeather, Blazing Star, Indian Plume
COMPOSITAE

BLOOM: Pinkish-purple to purple; rarely, white.
FOLIAGE: Long, narrow, grasslike, green.
HEIGHT: 12–48″.

Gayfeather *Liatris* sp.

BLOOM SEASON: 3–8 weeks; late summer to fall for species in nature, timed by rainfall; spring to fall for garden varieties.
REGIONS: All. Various species are indigenous to different regions.
LIGHT: Full sun, bright filtered light, to 2 hours' shade in South Plains, Trans-Pecos.
SOIL: Infertile and well-drained. Alkaline to pH 8.5. Prefers sandy soils, tolerates clay. Intolerant of soggy soils, especially from midsummer through winter.
MOISTURE: Wild species, dry from midsummer on.
PROPAGATION: Grows from corms. Divide in spring. Some species and cultivars from seed (as listed), reportedly blooming in 2 years. Some reseed heavily.

Gayfeather or Indian plume, *Liatris* in all its species, harks back to pioneer days. Various liatrises adorned the prairie from Nebraska to Texas in fall. They can be seen in rocky limestone hills and lightly shaded mesquite meadows today, 1-foot fuchsia spikes atop 2–3-foot stalks. They also arrive by air freight from the Netherlands as cut flowers, adopted from America for the florist trade. Their virtue as long-lasting cut flowers is an added delight to the home gardener. In the wild, liatrises bloom a minimum of three weeks and may continue longer, if fall rains are light. Heavy rains may shorten the bloom period by rotting the budding flowers. They are hardy to Zone 4.

Gayfeathers deserve a place at the back of a flower border or the center of an island bed, with plants of similar requirements. They grow best in light soils but are known to grow in clay. The native forms do best without fertilizer, which may cause them to bloom so heavily that the bloom stalks flop over. Arguments are made for segregating this exuberant grower with other meadow flowers in a dry, infertile bed approximating their natural habitat. In watered, fertilized gardens, they can grow leggy and rank. Garden cultivars accept garden conditions. All are susceptible to borers.

The strong color common in the species requires some discretion in combining with other flowers. Pale yellows, light mauve-pink like the color of *Monarda fistulosa,* and whites are good complements. The flowers keep their color when dried. If these plants catch on with regional nurserypeople, growers will probably develop more compact forms and varied color shades, as happened with wild lythrum in the Northeast. Several species and cultivars are available in the trade, as listed below. 'Kobold' ("Gnome") is a good one that is grown in Texas.

From seed:

L. pycnostachya, Kansas gayfeather, cattail gayfeather, 36 inches tall, rose-purple.
L. scariosa 'White Spires,' 36 inches, white.
L. spicata, 24 inches, purple.

L. spicata 'Kobold,' 15–18 inches, rose-purple to deep purple.

Corms and plants:

L. pycnostachya 'Alba,' 36 inches, white.
L. scariosa 'September Glory,' to 48 inches, purple.

Cardinal flower *Lobelia cardinalis*

Lobelia cardinalis
Cardinal Flower
LOBELIACEAE

BLOOM: Red terminal flowers on slender, erect stalks.
FOLIAGE: Green or deep red, lance-shaped, pointed and toothed.
HEIGHT: 18–36″, rarely to 6′.
BLOOM SEASON: Early to late summer; to October in Trans-Pecos.
REGIONS: All but Lower Rio Grande Valley.
LIGHT: Afternoon shade or partial shade. Full sun with abundant moisture.
SOIL: Clay, garden soil; sand if wet. Alkaline to acid. Rich, moisture-retentive.
MOISTURE: High annual moisture or ground water. Moist to wet.
PROPAGATION: Seed in fall; cuttings, layering, division. Self-sows.

Cardinal flower is loved by those who grow it, even though it is difficult and not long-lived, particularly in the border. In summer or fall, its wand of rich, red flowers rises out of large, ragged leaves. It grows in most of Texas but the southern tip, in moist soil along streams, in meadows, and by springs and ponds. West Texas seeps and canyons and East Texas creeks where the supply of moisture never disappears are typical. The trick is to create similar conditions. In South Texas, the Edwards Plateau, the southern Plains Country, and the Trans-Pecos, it grows best on the margins of ponds, not as a border plant; it fails in dry culture. The shade of deciduous trees is a good place, also, with moisture. Standing water will rot cardinal flower; conversely, drought will burn it and cause it to wilt.

Since Canadian garden hybrids have poor success here, it is best to use the native species. Native cardinal flower will reseed itself, and it can also be propagated by division. Mulch is recommended to keep its roots cool in summer and for frost protection in winter months.

Rose campion *Lychnis coronaria* (behind *Salvia superba*)

✤ *Lychnis*
Rose Campion, Catchfly
CARYOPHYLLACEAE

BLOOM: Pink to crimson or magenta, depending on species.
FOLIAGE: *L. coronaria,* gray-white and woolly; *L. viscaria,* grasslike, evergreen.
HEIGHT: 12–36″, depending on species.
BLOOM SEASON: Spring and summer.
REGIONS: All but Gulf Coast. In Plains Country, only *L. coronaria,* and only in southern part.
LIGHT: Full sun, partial shade, filtered light.
SOIL: *L. coronaria,* dry; *L. viscaria,* porous but not too dry.
MOISTURE: All ranges. Dry or moist with seasonal drought, depending on species.
PROPAGATION: Seed. *L. coronaria* self-sows, is not easily divided. Others, spring or fall division.

Lychnis coronaria and *L. viscaria* are flowers for two different situations. Both are long-blooming and hardy.

L. coronaria is ideal for dry, sunny spots. The soft gray foliage is an excellent foil for the magenta flowers, as well as for other flowers in pale yellow, blue, lavender, and white. It benefits from being cut back after flowering. This plant likes alkaline soil and full sun. It grows up to 3 feet tall. Although it is short-lived, it produces many seedlings that bloom in the first year. Its place of origin is southeastern Europe.

L. viscaria, or "catchfly," prefers full sun, dappled light, or high shade and porous, moist soil, but will tolerate drought. Filtered light is best in the Prairies and Cross Timbers and the Gulf Coast. Twelve inches tall, *L. viscaria* bears reddish-purple flowers in interrupted clusters on upright stalks. Its sticky stems may have given rise to the name "catchfly." 'Zulu' is a good cultivar with deep salmon blooms. Others are magenta, white, and white with a pink eye.

Seed of at least ten *Lychnis* species and cultivars is available in the trade. Refrain from dividing seed-grown plants until their second year. The divisions, except for *L. coronaria*'s, "take" very easily.

✌ *Lythrum*

Loosestrife

LYTHRACEAE

BLOOM: Magenta-pink to rose-pink.
FOLIAGE: Green, willowlike.
HEIGHT: 18″–6′.
BLOOM SEASON: 6–7 weeks, late April to mid-August, with fall rebloom if cut back.
REGIONS: All but Trans-Pecos and Lower Rio Grande Valley.
LIGHT: Full sun. Partial shade to filtered light tolerated, with reduced bloom.
SOIL: Not too rich preferred. Accepts heavy to light.
MOISTURE: Moist preferred but also does well in border conditions (moderate moisture). Quickly revives from drought.
PROPAGATION: Division, soft stem cuttings.
L. salicaria easy from seed, self-seeds freely.

Loosestrife *Lythrum salicaria*

Lythrum salicaria, willow-leaf loosestrife, was introduced to the Northeastern United States from the wet lowlands and ditches of Europe, Western Asia, and Russia, and it naturalized there. In the past few years, Southern gardeners have discovered its tall, feathery hot pink spires, vigorous growth, and two-or-three-month bloom time. It blooms from spring or summer and repeats through fall, a time when bloom may be in short supply, and is hardy in Zones 4–9.

Lythrum will grow in most moderately fertile soils, from boggy to dry. The native forms are often accused of being invasive, but named cultivars are not. Lythrum is easily propagated by division or soft stem cuttings.

Lythrum flowers from flower stalk base to tip. When the lower stalks begin to look bare, cutting back half the plant will encourage it to rebloom. Lythrum's preference for moist sites makes it useful in modern sprinklered beds, provided there is plenty of sun.

L. virgatum 'Morden Pink' is magenta-pink and blooms later in the season than the others, with as little as three hours' sun. 'Morden Gleam' is a 4-footer that blooms from July to September in bright carmine, as close as lythrum gets to red. *L. salicaria* 'Robert' is a more compact plant, 18–24 inches tall, with the added attraction of scarlet fall foliage. Its blooms are rose-pink. It has been reported to be a poor bloomer in the southern Prairies and Cross Timbers. 'Robert' is said to tolerate wetter soil than other cultivars, in full sun.

The strong magenta-pink of some selections can be softened by using it with silver and gray foliage or in a monochrome scheme of related colors. Flea beetles can be a pest in South Texas. Otherwise, lythrum is generally problem-free.

French hollyhock *Malva sylvestris*

❧ *Malva sylvestris*
French Hollyhock
MALVACEAE

BLOOM: White to pink, striped with rose to purple.
FOLIAGE: Dark green, palmately lobed. Dies back to ground with freeze.
HEIGHT: 12–48″.
BLOOM SEASON: Mid-May to June or July.
REGIONS: All but Plains Country and Lower Rio Grande Valley.
LIGHT: Full sun to partial shade or filtered light.
SOIL: Prefers garden soil, neutral to alkaline; accepts any well-drained.
MOISTURE: Low to high moisture ranges. Drought-resistant.
PROPAGATION: Seed, division.

Malva sylvestris is often called *Alcea zebrina,* although this is not a recognized botanical name. This sprightly little mallow features large, lobed leaves like those of its relative the hollyhock, and small, zebra-striped pink and magenta flowers. The plant forms a mounded shape as wide as it is tall. It is not widely known and is probably adapted to a far wider range than it is now grown in.

This mallow is considered a biennial, but many gardeners report several years' growth from one plant. In any case, it reseeds so vigorously that it maintains its presence in the garden. Its care is similar to that of the larger hollyhock. It is less susceptible to rust.

❧ *Malvaviscus arboreus*
Turk's Cap, Bleeding Heart, Wax Mallow
MALVACEAE

BLOOM: Turk's cap, scarlet, 1–1¼″ long; wax mallow, scarlet or pink, 3″ long.
FOLIAGE: Large, soft green leaves on long basal stalks.
HEIGHT: Turk's cap, 30–36″; wax mallow, to 5′.
BLOOM SEASON: Late spring to frost.
REGIONS: Turk's cap, all but north portion of Plains Country. Wax mallow, Gulf Coast, South Texas, Lower Rio Grande Valley, southern Plains Country (Zone 7b) with mulch.
LIGHT: Full sun, filtered sun, partial shade; also deep shade for Turk's cap.
SOIL: Moist to well-drained. Accepts poor soil, clay.
MOISTURE: All ranges. Survives extreme drought but shows heat stress.
PROPAGATION: Easy from seed, softwood cuttings.

Malvaviscus arboreus var. *drummondii,* Turk's cap or bleeding heart, provides a mound of soft greenery and scarlet blooms like spiral florets of red frosting on a store-bought birthday cake. A curious frill-tipped filament sticks out of each flower tip. The flowers are followed by attractive red, tomato-like fruits that are edible and fairly tasty. Such color in the shade, especially along with a nice massy form, is not easy to come by.

Turk's cap *Malvaviscus arboreus* var. *drummondii*

The leaves curl and become lackluster in severe drought and afternoon summer sun, but the plant survives. Dying back in winter in all regions but the Lower Rio Grande Valley, it returns in spring except in the northern Plains Country.

"A wonderful plant," says one gardener. It attracts hummingbirds; "I've never seen so many," says another.

In the Rio Grande Valley and South Texas dwells tree-size tropical *M. arboreus* var. *mexicanus,* wax mallow. With its 5-foot trunks and arching branches dripping larger scarlet blooms, it is very showy. There is also a pink form. It blooms all summer and is reportedly hardy into Zone 8 if the roots are well established and protected with mulch. One gardener in Midland, Zone 7b, says it survives winter there reliably; he mulches it after frost kills the top growth back.

Melampodium
Blackfoot Daisy
COMPOSITAE

BLOOM: White with yellow eye.
FOLIAGE: Slender, green to gray-green. Evergreen in mild winters, but sparse.
HEIGHT: 6–12″.
BLOOM SEASON: April to frost; intermittently year-round in South Central Texas and Lower Rio Grande Valley.
REGIONS: All but Gulf Coast.
LIGHT: Full sun. Tolerates partial shade, filtered light, but becomes sparse, lax-stemmed.
SOIL: Thrives in poor, alkaline soil or well-drained garden soil.
MOISTURE: Prefers low moisture range; grown in raised beds in medium and high ranges. Thrives in drought.
PROPAGATION: Seed. Self-sows.

This neat little mounding flower seems ideal for the edge of the border in a dry garden. In the most arid stretches of the Hill Country and the Big Bend, *Melampodium cinereum* crops up in small, single-stemmed bouquets, fistfuls of white daisies with yellow eyes. Blackfoot daisy blooms in spring and repeatedly thereafter, up to ten or eleven months. As seen in its natural habitats, well-drained sites are its preference. It is a sparse evergreen in North Texas and deciduous in the Plains and Trans-Pecos, unless the winter is mild. Grown in garden conditions, the plant is taller and more open, losing the nosegay effect. The South Texas species is *M. leucanthum.* It is said to be visually indistinguishable from *M. cinereum.*

Blackfoot daisy *Melampodium cinereum*

Propagation is from seed. Blackfoot daisy self-sows prolifically. It cannot be transplanted easily, because of its long taproot. Its intolerance for high moisture when container-grown in lathe houses and, possibly, for overpotting was an obstacle to its commercial propagation, but a few growers have solved the problem and make it available. In gardens, poor drainage and overwatering will rot its roots. When watered in the South Plains, it is said to "grow itself to death in a year."

ஓ *Monarda*

Bee Balm, Bergamot, Monarda, Oswego Tea
LABIATAE

BLOOM: Red, pink, lilac to purple, white.
FOLIAGE: Dark green (*M. didyma*); gray-green (*M. fistulosa*).
HEIGHT: 12–48".
BLOOM SEASON: 3–4 weeks in summer.
REGIONS: Edwards Plateau, Piney Woods, Prairies & Cross Timbers; some types in Plains Country, Gulf Coast, and Trans-Pecos—see below and Chart 1.
LIGHT: Full sun to partial shade.
SOIL: Sandy loam or clay. *M. didyma* hybrids, acid to neutral, alkaline tolerated; *M. fistulosa,* acid to alkaline.
MOISTURE: Medium, high ranges. *M. fistulosa* also tolerates low range.
PROPAGATION: Species by seed. Division any time of year.

Lovers of monarda gladly accept eleven months of floppy, weedy foliage for a few weeks of gorgeous, glowing bloom. The aromatic, lemony scent is another of monarda's attractions, "as reviving in hot weather as a whiff of *eau de cologne*," wrote gardener and author Elizabeth Lawrence.

Horticulturist Logan Calhoun notes that scarlet *Monarda didyma* is native to 7,000–9,000-foot elevations of the Appalachian Mountains. He considers it the most difficult monarda to grow in warm regions. Bette Edmundsen of Fort Davis in Texas'

Monarda didyma

Davis Mountains gave one hybrid, 'Adam,' an enthusiastic report for her area, however.

Neither *M. didyma* nor its cultivars are long-lived where summers are long and hot. But at least one gardener in each region of Texas, whether in acid or alkaline soils, reported success with *M. didyma,* as long as it received ample water. Occasionally it fails to bloom for unknown reasons. There are other monardas easier for this region, such as native *M. fistulosa* and annual species, but *M. didyma* is a very showy one. It likes moist soil. *M. didyma* is biennial in the High Plains. Where it grows, rust and mildew are its only problems. Good named hybrids include bright red 'Adam,' 'Croftway Pink,' and 'Cambridge Scarlet.'

Situating this plant where other blooms become the focal point during its off-season is the key to using it effectively. Lawrence accomplished this by pairing it with 'Mallow Marvels' and garden phlox, which bloom in midsummer and continue after the monarda fades. This also solved the problem of finding a complement for the purple-tinged roses and pinks of garden phlox that are so inhospitable to many colors.

Monarda needs to be divided every two or three years, in fall. Carefully dig it up. Separate the center of the root clump and discard it. Replant the outside portions for new, vigorously blooming plants. Monarda is a rapid spreader, but its roots are shallow. Species are easily grown from seed started in cold frames.

Both the leaves and the flowers may be eaten in salads. Leaves, stems, and roots release their perfume when crushed. The leaves may be steeped in hot water to make Oswego tea, ostensibly named for its originators, the Oswego Indians of the eastern United States. This is the flavoring for English Earl Grey tea.

M. didyma's spreading root stolons can be invasive in light, moist soil or rich soil in shade. "Beautiful, fragrant, and must be controlled," cautions Shreveport gardener Cleo Barnwell.

Later-blooming *M. fistulosa* is good for drier sites. It is lilac, pink, or white and reaches 4 feet in height. It grows wild in East Texas. In Zones 7 and 8, the bloom season starts in July and lasts four weeks.

All the monardas are good cut flowers.

৪ৈ *Oenothera*
Showy Primrose, Evening Primrose, Sundrop
ONAGRACEAE

BLOOM: Yellow, pink, or white; morning- or evening-blooming, depending on species.
FOLIAGE: Dark green to gray-green lanceolate leaves, 4–6″.
HEIGHT: 9–30″.
BLOOM SEASON: Mid-spring and summer.
REGIONS: All.
LIGHT: Full sun, afternoon shade.
SOIL: Thin, dry soil preferred, except for *O. missouriensis,* which does best in deep, fertile soil but tolerates poor. Excellent drainage a must.
MOISTURE: Scant to moderate. Adapted to high-rainfall areas, but grows in dry sites there.
PROPAGATION: Seed, division.

Oenotheras are mostly sun-loving plants that are easy to grow, long-blooming, and tough. Many have large, showy flowers. Several species are native to the Southwest.

The genus originated in the New World. Its name is Greek for "wine-tasting," presumably for the flowers' cup shape. Many sources report that oenotheras whose flowers open in the daytime are commonly called sundrops and those that bloom from late afternoon to the next morning are called evening primroses, but common usage in Texas differs. As children here we called the yellow ones "buttercups," and seeing who could smear the most yellow pollen on the other's nose was a favorite sport. The pink or white one called showy primrose or pink evening primrose in fact has two forms, one day- and one night-blooming. These primroses bear no relation or similarity to the English primroses of the genus *Primula.*

Oenothera missouriensis, Missouri primrose or Ozark sundrop, has "enormous, fragrant, lemon yellow goblets," as Ruth Rogers Clausen and Nicolas H. Ekstrom so aptly put it, that open from reddish buds late in the day. Faded blooms that have turned shades of orange often add a second color to the plant. Velvety hairs cover the leaves. *O. missouriensis* is native from Missouri and Kansas to Texas.

Primrose *Oenothera speciosa*

O. speciosa, showy primrose, is pink with a white center or solid white, with soft yellow stamens. The foliage is green and mound-forming. It reaches about a foot in height. The roots run aggressively. A dry slope, not a cultivated garden, is the right sort of spot for this native primrose. "Showy primroses make good cut flowers, although they look as if they would wilt the minute you picked them. If you cut stems with a lot of buds, they will keep opening in a vase for several days," says Austin gardener Carolyn Wylie.

O. berlandieri, Mexican evening primrose, is more compact than *O. speciosa,* with deeper pink flowers on 6-inch stems. It takes hot, dry conditions and is somewhat less hardy than *O. speciosa.* This, also, is an invasive, ground-covering plant. It is native to Texas and Mexico.

Both showy primrose and Mexican evening primrose become rank and overgrown in fertile garden soil. They are compact and floriferous in relatively poor soils like those to which they are native. Both are so tough that they can be trampled flat and, if watered, recover and continue blooming on shorter stems—true "garbage truck" perennials.

✿ *Pavonia lasiopetala*
Rock Rose
MALVACEAE

BLOOM: Soft pink.
FOLIAGE: Green, heart-shaped.
HEIGHT: 12–36″.
BLOOM SEASON: May to frost; year-round on Edwards Plateau in mild winters and in the Rio Grande Plains.
REGIONS: All to Zone 7, with winter mulch.
LIGHT: Full sun to afternoon shade or filtered sun.
SOIL: Adobe, clay, garden soil, sand. Alkaline preferred. Must be well-drained.
MOISTURE: Tolerates drought. Overwatering in winter can be fatal.
PROPAGATION: Seed, softwood cuttings.

Rock rose *Pavonia lasiopetala*

Pavonia is one of those native Texas plants so well adapted here that it may bloom the entire growing season. "Superb!" is a South Plains grower's opinion. Pavonia's shrubby shape makes it ideal to fill in the back of a border. It may need frequent shearing to remain dense. Its height does not usually exceed 2 feet in North Texas. It is reportedly reliably root-hardy in Knox City, in Zone 7a on the Red Rolling Plains; however, a gardener in Fort Davis, in Zone 7b in the Trans-Pecos, reports that it does not always winter over there. An Edwards Plateau nurseryman points out the minor drawback that it is browsed by deer; plants deer won't eat, such as lantana and most salvias, are prized in the Hill Country.

Pavonia's scalloped 1-inch pink flowers, which resemble tiny hibiscus blooms, close in the afternoon unless it's shady. Heart-shaped green leaves are another attraction of this little subshrub. No particular pests beset it, although it is sometimes subject to powdery mildew. The driest reaches of the Trans-Pecos are not too dry for this plant, which also accepts ample moisture when available. Once the plant dies back in winter, it should be cut down, to regrow the next spring. It generally lives three to four years.

❧ *Penstemon*

Penstemon, Beard-tongue
SCROPHULARIACEAE

BLOOM: White, pink, coral, red, lavender to deep wine-purple.
FOLIAGE: Green or gray-green. Frequently evergreen.
HEIGHT: 6–36″, depending on species.
BLOOM SEASON: Spring or summer, depending on species. Some repeat in fall.
REGIONS: All; see chart for species for each region.
LIGHT: Full sun to partial shade, depending on species.
SOIL: Most, gravelly loam or sand. *P. digitalis* and *P. tenuis,* also clay. Most neutral to alkaline. Well-drained or moist, depending on species.
MOISTURE: Scant or ample, depending on species. Various species live in all ranges.
PROPAGATION: Seed in late summer, except for *P. barbatus* and var. *torreyi* in Plains. Division in autumn or spring. In summer, cuttings can easily be taken from plants that put out side shoots.

Penstemons are tubular, dainty flowers with foliage that usually persists through winter as evergreen rosettes. They vary greatly in size. They resemble the tall and stately northern foxglove, *Digitalis purpurea,* but are smaller, freer in form, and less symmetrical—among the most beautiful American wildflowers. Penstemons, mostly native to North America, are primarily western dry-country plants. *Penstemon tenuis,* however, thrives in East Texas, the Upper Gulf Coast of Texas, and Louisiana and Arkansas.

P. baccharifolius, known as rock penstemon, lives on the rock outcrops of the Edwards Plateau and the Trans-Pecos. It ranges from 6 to 18 inches in height. Its clear, bright coral blooms are elfin and pretty. The succulent leaves may get fungal spots treatable with fungicidal sprays. They die back in winter in the South Plains. For best results, rock penstemon should be grown in a dry, well-drained gravelly loam. This penstemon generally blooms at least two or three times in a year, starting in May. Some gardeners find it blooms continuously in the

Rock penstemon *Penstemon baccharifolius*

summer. In the southern Blacklands in its preferred conditions, it may bloom almost year-round.

P. barbatus var. *torreyi,* or *jarritos,* is native to the Chisos and Davis mountains of Texas. Its brilliant scarlet 2-inch blooms appear from June until as late as October. The species, *P. barbatus,* is hardy in the Zone 5 regions of New Mexico. Its blooms are strongly two-lipped like the Texas endemic, but the lower lip is marked with yellow. *P. barbatus* and its many cultivars are popular perennials elsewhere but have been little tried in Texas' heat and then with poor to moderate success.

Wild foxglove
Penstemon cobaea

P. cobaea is often called wild foxglove. Of the penstemons, it looks most like the northern foxglove. An April or May drive through the Lampasas Uplift of Texas discovers *P. cobaea* in bar ditches all the way, in shades ranging from white to pale lavender to deep pink, all with lavender-speckled throats. It accepts partial shade and does well in good garden soil or poor alkaline soil. In loam in South Texas, it is said to die the second year from fungi, however. Propagation is by stratified seed or division. This penstemon is native not only to the Edwards Plateau, but also to the Prairies and Cross Timbers, Upper Gulf, Piney Woods, and Rolling Plains. It is said to be the longest-lived of the spring penstemons.

P. digitalis is the identification collectors gave to a white, airy penstemon of the Ozarks that was gathered in East Texas near Woodville by Lynn Lowrey. It is known to grow well in the Prairies and Cross Timbers, also. Morris Clint of Palm Garden Nursery in Brownsville recalls his parents growing a white penstemon in years gone by that he believes may have been *P. digitalis*. In April and May, *P. digitalis* flowers in yard-long sprays of blooms larger than those of *P. tenuis* but not so large as *P. cobaea*. Bloom time is usually about three weeks after *P. tenuis*. *P. digitalis* tolerates partial shade and will grow in damp or dry soil, though it prefers moist. Margaret Kane of San Antonio reports that it tolerates standing water for a week or more after a heavy rain, in heavy black clay. The foliage rosettes remain green in winter. The blooms make excellent cut flowers.

P. tenuis is the penstemon for the Gulf Coast. It is a delightful plant with low, ground-covering foliage and 12–30-inch sprays of profuse, tiny flowers that create a haze of color. The blooms are lavender-pink in the southern Blacklands and described by natives as blue to white in the Piney Woods and sometimes deep wine-purple on the Gulf Coast. This species also grows in Louisiana and Arkansas. The plants grow easily even in unadulterated clay, from transplants, divisions, or seed. They self-sow prolifically. Moist and even boggy soil is preferred. If spent

White penstemon *Penstemon digitalis*

Brazos River Valley penstemon and mealy blue sage *Penstemon tenuis* with *Salvia farinacea*

blooms are cut, this plant often reblooms, especially in fall. The foliage turns wine-red in winter.

Fertilizer and organic mulches are generally discouraged for these plants. Fertilizer is said to "grow them to death" prematurely. Organic mulch may promote crown rot; mulch with gravel instead. Penstemons' most important problems are fungal leaf spot and crown rot, which can be prevented by providing the proper soil and situation for each plant.

Phlox

Phlox (Border Varieties)

POLEMONIACEAE

BLOOM: White, pink, salmon, rose, red, lavender, purple. Contrasting eyes in some.

FOLIAGE: Green.

HEIGHT: 4″–5′.

BLOOM SEASON: Early spring to fall, depending on type.

REGIONS: While chart ratings reflect at least fair success reported by one or two excellent gardeners in each region of Texas but the Lower Rio Grande Valley and Zone 9 of South Texas, all the phlox included here other than *P. pilosa* thrive best in the northeastern fourth of Texas. *P. pilosa* also flourishes in the Edwards Plateau, where it is native.

HEAT TOLERANCE: All ranges, but not tolerant of combined high heat and humidity.

LIGHT: Full sun, partial or light shade.

SOIL: Generally, rich, deep, moist but well-drained. *P. pilosa* accepts poor but still well-drained soil, *P. divaricata* moist or dry.

MOISTURE: Medium and high ranges. Most prefer to be moist but not wet; *P. pilosa*, moist to dry.

PROPAGATION: Seed. Summer tip cuttings, fall root cuttings, division in spring or fall.

Garden phlox *Phlox paniculata*

Phlox paniculata, variously known as garden phlox, border phlox, and summer phlox, provides a long-blooming backdrop to the garden, with flower heads 2 to 4 or even 6 feet in the air. It is a strong magenta-pink. Midsummer begins its bloom time; it often lasts into fall, looking rather dry and burned by August unless it is deadheaded and well tended. Avid hybridization of this old-fashioned favorite has produced colors of various pinks, rose, red, lavender, white, and salmon—every shade but yellow and true blue. The tiny florets that make up the panicles of bloom may be bicolored, such as white or pink with a rose "eye."

Border phlox likes rich, well-drained soil and tolerates a few hours' shade. It has a reputation as difficult, given, I believe, for poor performance by phlox whose specific needs weren't respected. "Feet wet, clothing dry" is how these phlox like to be. Their resistance to powdery mildew varies from one cultivar to another. To reduce mildew and fungus diseases, phlox should be watered by soaking the soil, not sprinkling the plants. Spacing at least 2 feet apart provides good air circulation, another mildew preventive. Thinning the stalks helps, as well. Russell Weber of Austin says, "if you allow each clump to have no more than five flowering stems each year, you will achieve success." Planting away from moisture-retentive stone and brick walls also helps.

Propagation is by seed, cuttings, or division. Border phlox should be divided and the outer portions of each clump replanted every three to four years. With hybrids, cutting the flower heads before they go to seed will prevent garish magenta upstarts that may crowd the named varieties. Not everyone finds this reversion to magenta objectionable, of course. In the trade, the species is replaced by hybrids, but it is the magenta-pink original that one sees coming back in Texas gardens year after year with little evident care.

The Symons-Jeune hybrids from England are considered fungus-resistant and strong-stalked. Their height is 24 to 42 inches. They bloom from June to fall, in combinations of pink, rose, and white such

Louisiana phlox *Phlox divaricata* with tulips

as widely popular rose-on-pink 'Bright Eyes' and white 'Everest.'

A group called simply "border phlox hybrids" includes pure whites. 'Mount Fuji' is a very good one. Other named cultivars in this group come in a range of colors. All are strong, weather-resistant plants.

P. maculata 'Miss Lingard' has been a favorite phlox of many gardeners over many years. This valued pure white phlox, once known as the wedding phlox, is often found to bloom a month earlier than *P. paniculata* and into August. It is also mildew-free. Its typical height is 2–4 feet. 'Rosalinde' is lilac-pink. The species is purple or pink or sometimes white. *P. maculata* hybrids are mildew-resistant and strong-stemmed, seldom requiring staking.

P. pilosa, downy phlox or prairie phlox, is native to the Edwards Plateau of Texas and dry, rocky areas of Louisiana. It is fragrant. Its native range in the United States in areas from Southeastern Connecticut to Wisconsin, south to Southern Florida and Texas, suggests it may be grown further south and northwest in Texas than is commonly done now.

P. divaricata, wild sweet William, is referred to in Texas as "Louisiana phlox." It is native to the eastern third of the United States and Quebec. Caroline Dormon described it growing on rocky slopes at the edge of woods in her garden in southern Louisiana in her classic little book, *Natives Preferred.* There are two flower colors, lavender-blue and lilac-pink. The

pink form is sometimes called "Missouri phlox," but it is not a separate species. The evergreen foliage is a lovely deep green color. *P. divaricata* subsp. *laphamii* bears large, rich blue flowers and grows like a ground cover. It is said to accept more sun than *P. divaricata.*

Phlox subulata
Thrift, Moss Pink
POLEMONIACEAE

BLOOM: Pink to rose, lavender-blue, white.
FOLIAGE: Green, mat-forming.
HEIGHT: 6–10″.
BLOOM SEASON: March–April; scattered bloom in May.
REGIONS: All but Lower Rio Grande Valley and South Plains; best results in northeastern fourth.
HEAT TOLERANCE: Medium, low ranges; barely tolerates summer heat in high range.
LIGHT: Full sun to partial shade.
SOIL: Any well-drained soil; sandy best. More drought-resistant in deep soil.
MOISTURE: Grows best in medium, high ranges. Consistent, moderate irrigation is best.
PROPAGATION: Spring or fall division is easiest. Summer cuttings. Spreads by self-layering.

Thrift
Phlox subulata

This dense, mat-forming ground cover is one of the first flowers of spring. Illustrated is the "screaming pink" variety that seems to be the most popular. The other shades are softer but reportedly less frost-resistant. The foliage of the lavender-blue type remains greener and thicker in the heat of summer than that of the pink. The 'Emerald' hybrid series is recommended for its fine, shiny green foliage.

Thrift is ideal for edging a border or filling in a rock garden. Raised planters are another good place for it. This plant is evergreen. It dislikes hot weather but survives if given ample moisture, at least to the satisfaction of most gardeners. However, Midlander Burr Williams assesses it succinctly: "Yuck." When the weather cools, it bounces back. Shearing the stems halfway after flowering will encourage denser growth. *Phlox subulata* should be divided every few years, or it degenerates.

Obedient plant *Physotegia virginiana*

℘ *Physostegia virginiana*
Obedient Plant, False Dragonhead
LABIATAE

BLOOM: Pale pink to purplish-pink or white; cultivars, shades from red-violet to white.
FOLIAGE: Green.
HEIGHT: 12–36″.
BLOOM SEASON: Fall or summer to fall, species and most cultivars; one, June to frost. In many, blooming can be prolonged to frost by deadheading.
REGIONS: All but Lower Rio Grande Valley.
HEAT TOLERANCE: All ranges.
LIGHT: Full sun (species only); partial to deep shade.
SOIL: Any.
MOISTURE: Medium, high ranges. Tolerates wet areas generally, but not standing water in summer. Survives drought.
PROPAGATION: Seed, division.

Physostegia's common name, obedient plant, refers to a trick its blooms have of staying fixed in whatever position they are turned. It is also called false dragonhead to distinguish it from the dragonheads, genus *Dracocephalum*. With the species and an assortment of cultivars, one can have the white, pinks, and red-violets of these shade-loving, wet-tolerant plants all season. Their only fault to some minds is growing over-enthusiastically.

Physostegia virginiana is native to North America from New Brunswick to Minnesota and south to South Carolina and Missouri. Producing a wealth of violet-pink or white blooms in fall, it is considered the most adaptable in Texas of the species and cultivars. It blooms in deep shade where most plants will not. The white cultivar 'Summer Snow' is the earliest and longest-blooming; in the High Plains it reportedly flowers as early as June and as late as frost. 'Vivid,' an old, intensely red-violet cultivar, blooms last of all. (Current catalog offerings by this name are a medium purple-pink shade.) 'Vivid,' 'Rosy Spire,' and 'Summer Glow' are all reported to bloom to frost if the spent blooms are removed.

Adequate moisture is needed for these plants to bloom well, but if it is allowed to stand on their roots, rot may ensue, especially in summer. They survive in dry soils but are said to bloom more sparsely and at a lower height. However, some gardeners recommend dry soil for the species and well-drained for 'Summer Snow,' perhaps to slow down their spread.

Pinching the tips of the bloom stalks early in the season will keep them from getting lanky.

Obedient plant can be invasive in moist, light soil but is controlled by pulling it up and replanting it every other year to slow down the runners. James Taylor of Lubbock finds that partial shade also slows the rapid expansion typical of obedient plant when grown in full sun there.

The flower heads resemble pointed clusters of snapdragons. The intense "primal pink" shade of some specimens, common in native plants, can be a little difficult to use in gardens. Gray and silver herbs and foliage plants such as lavender and lamb's-ears tone its screaming shade to a gentle murmur.

Propagation is from seed as well as by division, although seed of all varieties may not be available. Division is recommended not only to keep obedient plant's enthusiastic growth in bounds but also to obtain new starts.

Balloon flower *Platycodon grandiflorus*

Platycodon grandiflorus
Balloon flower
CAMPANULACEAE

BLOOM: Deep to pale blue, white, or lilac, single and double, 2–3″.
FOLIAGE: Green.
HEIGHT: 18–30″.
BLOOM SEASON: Summer; long-blooming.
REGIONS: Edwards Plateau, Plains Country, Prairies & Cross Timbers only Texas regions reporting. Zones 4 to 9a, possibly 9b. Probably not for the Gulf Coast.
HEAT TOLERANCE: All ranges, with low to medium humidity.
LIGHT: Full to half-day sun.
SOIL: Slightly acid loam preferred, alkaline tolerated. Good drainage a must.
MOISTURE: Moderate to high ranges; won't tolerate wet soil.
PROPAGATION: Seed.

This delightful plant holds aloft blue-violet miniature hot-air balloons that open to shallow five-pointed bells. Blooms of the Japanese strain 'Komachi,' which I have not yet seen in commerce, are said to stay balloon-fashion. The Greek botanical name means "broad bell," but then, the Greeks did not have hot-air balloons.

Balloon flower perennializes well; horticulturist Raydon Alexander has grown one plant for fifteen years. It has no significant diseases or pests, except for small children who insist on pinching the buds.

There are many cultivars. 'Mariesii' is a popular one in shades of blue, white, and pink and a double form.

The plant blooms from seed the second year. Division is said to be difficult. The plants should be grown massed together to hold each other up or staked, as they have weak stems. They are slow to emerge in spring and therefore should be marked to avoid hoeing up the crown during early cultivation.

Platycodon is native to East Asia.

Plumbago auriculata (*P. capensis*)
Tropical Plumbago, Cape Plumbago
PLUMBAGINACEAE

BLOOM: Dark to pale blue, white.
FOLIAGE: Medium green.
HEIGHT: To 36″. Can be kept shorter by clipping.
BLOOM SEASON: May to frost.
REGIONS: Gulf Coast, Lower Rio Grande Valley, South Texas; used as annual in all other regions.
LIGHT: Full sun to partial shade.
SOIL: Clay, garden soil, sand; acid to alkaline.
MOISTURE: Prefers moderate moisture but tolerates both drought and high moisture.
PROPAGATION: Seed, summer cuttings of nearly mature wood, division.

Tropical plumbago is a large, arching shrublike plant with cool pale blue, dark blue, or white flowers most of the growing season. A native of South Africa, it is also known as Cape plumbago. Despite its drought tolerance, it will thrive where water is ample.

Plumbago grows well in alkaline soils, but its foliage yellows from chlorosis in high alkalinity, particularly in summer. This can be prevented by acidifying the soil. It shows frost damage at about 28° F or below, so in more northerly areas it belongs in a sheltered spot against a south-facing wall or in some other warm microclimate. It is treated as an annual in many locales. It can survive a normal winter in Zone 8 with mulch.

This plant is excellent to cover a bank, fill a mixed border, or cascade from a planter box. It is beautiful espaliered or, with support, as a climber. Plumbago is not particularly attractive when out of flower, but this is not much of the year. During that time, it can be cut back, and shallow-rooted annual flowers can be planted with it. Mulch after frost protects plumbago's roots from freezing. It will take reflected heat from house walls, making it an excellent choice for large patio pots or a trellis in a container. Reflected heat from below, as from a sidewalk, can damage it, however. This plant is propagated from cuttings of nearly mature wood—especially summer cuttings—by division, and from seeds.

A red species, *P. indica,* resembles blue tropical plumbago and requires the same conditions and care.

A deeper blue selection, *Plumbago* 'Royal cape,' representing decades of breeding by an avid amateur, was introduced to the trade in 1993.

Poliomintha longiflora (*P. incana*)
Mexican Oregano
LABIATAE

BLOOM: Pale pink to lilac.
FOLIAGE: Light green, pungent. Evergreen if protected from north wind.
HEIGHT: 2–5′. Can be maintained shorter.
BLOOM SEASON: Late spring to frost.
REGIONS: All, to Zone 7b.
LIGHT: Full sun. Tolerates some shade; grows shorter, blooms paler.
SOIL: Any type, if well-drained; tolerates clay. Prefers neutral to alkaline pH.
MOISTURE: Grows in all ranges; probably best in low to medium. Drought-tolerant.
PROPAGATION: Softwood cuttings, division.

For months I visited gardens around the state. Every other one, it seemed, had a shrubby, light green

Tropical plumbago *Plumbago auriculata* (*P. capensis*)

Mexican oregano *Poliomentha longiflora*

plant brimming with pink tubular blooms in a spot someplace. "What's that? Where'd you get it?" I would ask. "It's something called Mexican oregano," the answer would come. "Lynn Lowrey gave it to me."

This zealous horticulturist for years combed the southwestern United States and northern Mexico in search of plants deserving of wider use. When he found one he considered worthy, every friend he saw received a sample. Mexican oregano was definitely one of Lynn's prizes. It forms a rounded, broad shrub and, once established, blooms profusely from late spring to frost. Its leaves are used to flavor food in Mexico as a substitute for *origanum*. Bees love it. It grows where soil and water are so alkaline that they are toxic to many other plants. There are handsome shrubs of it in the Iron Mountain Ranch garden designed and managed by Dr. Barton Warnock in the arid Davis Mountains. Dr. Warnock advises that botanists differ as to the proper naming of this plant; some identify it as *Poliomintha incana*.

Mexican oregano has no known pests and needs no special treatment. Give it a periodic haircut to keep it compact. Dry sites are probably best. One gardener finds that it self-sows and spreads overly enthusiastically in garden soil in his Zone 8 garden. Another reports its demise in shade in Blackland

clay in Zone 8a. The bloom display the second year is better than the first. Propagation is from softwood cuttings or by division.

Ratibida columnifera
Mexican Hat, Prairie Coneflower
COMPOSITAE

BLOOM: Red-brown and golden yellow; occasionally solid yellow.
FOLIAGE: Green, fine.
HEIGHT: 24–36".
BLOOM SEASON: In the wild, mass bloom April–July and scattered repeat bloom to frost, with continued rainfall; in cultivation, through fall, if deadheaded.
REGIONS: All except extreme eastern Piney Woods.
LIGHT: Full sun; partial to light shade in well-drained soil.
SOIL: All types, if well-drained. Prefers neutral to alkaline, tolerates acid.
MOISTURE: All ranges. Drought-tolerant but accepts ample moisture.
PROPAGATION: Seed, division.

Mexican hat *Ratibida columnifera*

This is a plant with a sense of humor. The flower is like a small, droopy sombrero, or a propeller, or a fancy thimble. Considering omitting it from this book on the grounds that it is just too common, I faced it gaily dancing on the roadsides for months in late spring and summer—and gave in. Lots of flowers are solid and substantial and suitable for mass plantings. This one adds an airy, free form to the garden and to bouquets. The whimsical flowers are long-lasting in cut arrangements.

The blooms are usually mahogany-colored with a yellow edge to the drooping ray flowers and a tall, corklike cone of disk flowers. Occasionally, the yellow wins out, and entire blooms and even colonies of solid yellow appear. *Ratibida* is biennial or perennial. Propagation is from seed in spring or fall or by division.

⚘ *Rudbeckia*
Black-eyed Susan, Coneflower, Gloriosa Daisy
COMPOSITAE

BLOOM: Golden yellow with dark brown cone. Cultivars in various golds and oranges, some with bicolor petals.
FOLIAGE: Green. 'Marmalade' gray-green, felted.
HEIGHT: 16″–8′, depending on type.
BLOOM SEASON: Summer. Some continue to frost if deadheaded and watered through late summer without fail.
REGIONS: All; some annual in northern Plains Country.
LIGHT: Full sun to afternoon shade; some cultivars also in filtered light.
SOIL: Adobe, clay, garden soil, sand; well-drained. Generally, neutral or neutral to alkaline preferred, but wild *R. hirta* grows in acid Piney Woods, and all tolerate acidity.
MOISTURE: Somewhat drought-tolerant but accepts ample moisture in well-drained soil, especially in late summer.
PROPAGATION: Seed; easy by division; summer cuttings.

The rudbeckias are familiar not only as garden flowers but also as North American wildflowers. All varieties do well in the garden, and everyone has a favorite.

Rudbeckia hirta, the wild black-eyed Susan, is an annual, biennial, or short-lived perennial that self-sows easily and thrives in hot, dry areas. *R. hirta* has many named cultivars, including the large-flowered, often bicolor, tetraploid 'Gloriosa Daisy.' Other *R. hirta* varieties are dark yellow double or semi-double 'Goldilocks' and yellow-orange 'Marmalade,' also a self-sower.

Black-eyed Susan *Rudbeckia fulgida* 'Goldsturm'

Perennial rudbeckias in general are short-lived and easily lost; one Austin gardener winters over starts from fall divisions in containers, for insurance. *R. fulgida,* a 2–3-foot-tall species that flowers from midsummer to fall, is a true perennial, however. It has orange-yellow rays and a brownish-purple buttonlike cone. Its hybrid *R. fulgida* var. *sullivantii* 'Goldsturm' is liked for its slightly more compact stature, strong whiskery foliage, and abundant flowers. In the Piney Woods it blooms from mid-July to fall in favorable conditions if cut back after blooms fade.

R. laciniata, cutleaf coneflower, has green, raised cones and drooping golden petals. Double-flowered 5–8-foot 'Golden Glow' is an old *R. laciniata* hybrid—reportedly the first rudbeckia grown in gardens—now called 'Hortensia' by at least one grower. It's perfect for lovers of "huge weeds," as one grower calls it who knows it from Connecticut, Illinois, and northern New Mexico. It spreads freely. *R. laciniata* 'Goldquelle' is a more recent dark yellow double cultivar that is less aggressive and only 30 inches tall.

R. maxima is a gigantic six-footer native to the Gulf Coast and East Texas that many people delight in.

Over successive seasons, moderate-sized *R. fulgida* can grow into a handsome clump covered with daisy-shaped, school-bus-yellow flowers. In winter, the ground-hugging rosette of evergreen leaves that remains is attractive.

Rudbeckias are excellent cut flowers. The garden varieties prefer good garden soil, adequate moisture, and full sun. Good drainage is best. In Houston's heavy clays, "hybrids last one year, natives two," says one gardener. Propagation is by seed in fall or early spring, summer cuttings, and root division, necessary every two or three years for plant vigor. Hybrids don't come exactly true from seed. 'Goldsturm,' for example, definitely gives best results when propagated vegetatively. Some double-petaled types reportedly don't become that until their second year of growth.

❧ *Ruellia*
Mexican Petunia
ACANTHACEAE

BLOOM: Blue-violet, lavender, white.
FOLIAGE: Dark to medium green. Long, narrow, and straplike to dull, pointed-oval with wavy margins.
HEIGHT: 1–5´.
BLOOM SEASON: Starting mid- to late spring or as late as August, to frost.
REGIONS: All; used as annuals in Panhandle.

Mexican petunia *Ruellia brittoniana*

LIGHT: Full sun to full shade.
SOIL: Adobe, clay, garden soil; *R. brittoniana,* also sand; *R. nudiflora* is native to clay and adobe but also accepts garden soil and sand; pH appears not to be critical.
MOISTURE: Drought-resistant.
PROPAGATION: Seed, division. Cuttings, *R. malacosperma* and *R. brittoniana.*

Ruellia brittoniana, narrowleaved Mexican petunia, is an old garden plant in the United States that escaped from cultivation and has naturalized in the southeastern states. It is one of those tough plants that have earned the gardener's grudging praise, "You can't kill it." It disappears altogether in winter and pops back up in mid-spring. In North Texas, it is in bloom around July. This sizable ruellia is good for a middle or background place in the flower border, where you might use *Cuphea micropetala* or Mexican oregano. Like these, it blooms profusely in the dog days of summer when many plants go on vacation. Although it can get quite tall, cutting it back by half in midseason will keep it more compact. The very long and straplike narrow leaves are dark green and grow thickly, providing a good backdrop for shorter flowers of almost any colors except red and orange and for gray and light-green foliage plants. Propagation is from seed or by division or cuttings.

'Katy' is an adorable, ground-hugging rosette of lanceolate foliage and vivid blooms. It was named for the late Katy Ferguson, nurserywoman, of Houston.

R. malacosperma is a readily available ruellia for the southern half of Texas. Its height and growth habit are similar to those of *R. brittoniana,* but the leaves are broader and shorter. It blooms all season, albeit sparsely. Drought-tolerant, it grows in most soils and accepts full shade. It reportedly takes six months to spread and is evergreen to Zone 9b and in mild winters in Zone 9a.

R. nudiflora, lavender or white, is native to the Texas Hill Country, West Texas, and adjacent New Mexico. Either it or lavender *R. humilis* is probably the wild petunia seen in vacant lots and roadsides in North Texas, sometimes blooming at 3–4-inch height in mowed areas. *R. humilis* likes partial shade and is shorter than the other species. It does not occur in the Panhandle, South Texas, or the Trans-Pecos. *R. drummondiana* is native to South Texas west to Langtry and blooms over a long period.

The ruellias are not true petunias.

Firecracker plant *Russelia equisetiformis*

Russelia equisetiformis
Firecracker Plant, Coral Plant, Fountain Plant
SCROPHULARIACEAE

BLOOM: Tubular, two-lipped flower, scarlet-red with 1″ corolla.
FOLIAGE: Green.
HEIGHT: Rushlike stems to 6′ long make arching fountainlike mounds about 4′ tall.
BLOOM SEASON: Spring and summer; nearly continuous in warm regions to which it is adapted.
REGIONS: Gulf Coast, Lower Rio Grande Valley, South Texas, Zone 9. Frost-tender.
HEAT TOLERANCE: High.
LIGHT: Full sun to partial shade.
SOIL: Grows and flowers well in well-drained, only moderately fertile soil. Salt-tolerant.
MOISTURE: Medium to high ranges.
PROPAGATION: Root division.

Russelia is a striking, willowy shrub. Its species name, *equisetiformis,* describes the long stems that resemble horsetail reeds. Light green, they arch and cascade down like a waterfall, very attractive over a retaining wall, at the edge of a raised bed, or in the back of a tropical border. The tubular flowers are fiery scarlet-red and appear singly or in clusters of two or three.

This plant is very heat-tolerant, easy to grow, and almost continuously blooming in the warm locales to which it is suited. Native to Mexico, russelia is naturalized in Florida, the West Indies, and other warm regions of the world. It is widely grown in South Texas and the Lower Rio Grande Valley.

Salvia azurea
See under *Salvia farinacea*

Salvia coccinea
Scarlet Sage
LABIATAE

BLOOM: Scarlet, salmon, white.
FOLIAGE: Green.
HEIGHT: 12–36″.
BLOOM SEASON: April–June, August–November.

Texas scarlet sage *Salvia coccinea*

first started and in prolonged drought. It accepts full sun with moderate moisture and is propagated by seed, division, or cuttings.

The 1991 All-America Selections winners included a salvia called 'Lady in Red,' a cross between the popular, garish tropical *S. splendens* and native scarlet sage. It has all the vivid, dainty appeal of the wild plant and doesn't appear to get overgrown in garden conditions.

The pink form of *S. coccinea* is a delightful pale salmon. It is not as cold-hardy as the red. In North Texas and the lower South Plains, where it may winter over, both color forms should be protected with a winter mulch after a mild frost has hardened them. After a hard frost, cut them to the ground.

REGIONS: All, to Zone 7b. Used as annual in most of Plains Country and far North Texas. Winter mulch improves freeze survival in all regions.
LIGHT: Full sun to partial and dappled shade.
SOIL: All types. Best in fairly infertile, well-drained soil.
MOISTURE: All ranges. Drought-resistant; also accepts seasonally wet soil. Needs deep, infrequent watering.
PROPAGATION: Seed, division, cuttings. Self-sows heavily.

In Texas, scarlet sage is often found in woods or on rocky hillsides, growing single-stemmed and low, its splash of scarlet made even more vivid by its contrast with shade or white limestone. For a plant to like both drought and shade is unusual; this combination is especially useful in the wooded, rocky hills and escarpments that mark Texas' Hill Country and Prairies and Cross Timbers. Scarlet sage offers not a mass of color but brilliant dashes, and it is one of the longest-blooming flowers. But it needs to be kept on a lean diet.

Given rich garden soil and consistent watering, *Salvia coccinea* can become an ungainly green giant, far more leaf than bloom. It is better grown in poor, dry soil with only rainfall for moisture, except when

Salvia farinacea
Mealy-cup Sage, Mealy Blue Sage, and Other Blue and Purple Salvias
LABIATAE

BLOOM: *S. farinacea*, dusty blue to blue-violet, often tinged with white; white. Hybrids and other species, sky-blue to blue-violet, dark blue, purple, white.
FOLIAGE: Green. Variously smooth, felted, veined.
HEIGHT: 18″–6′.
BLOOM SEASON: Varies with species and locale.
REGIONS: All.
LIGHT: Full sun to partial shade.
SOIL: Average to dry, well-drained. See Chart 1 for pH preferences.
MOISTURE: Tolerates drought.
PROPAGATION: Seed, cuttings, division.

Salvia farinacea is one of the top ten perennials for Texas. Few plants could be more at home in their native range, free of pests (including browsing deer), drought-tolerant, and long-blooming. Its typical bloom season in nature is full bloom from April through May or June and light bloom in summer, with good fall rebloom with rainfall. Foliage is unveined, narrow, and sage green in poor, hot, dry conditions; medium green in cooler weather, and broader in garden conditions.

Salvia farinacea 'Victoria'

'Victoria' is a selection of *S. farinacea* with consistent deep blue color, dense flower heads, and more compact form. 'Alba' is white. Shearing both the species and the selections two or three times a season keeps them dense and free-flowering.

S. × superba (*S. pratensis*) is deep purple. It grows shorter than *S. farinacea,* and its flower heads are compact, slender spikes. 'East Friesland,' a deep blue cultivar, is available as transplants. Dark violet 'Blue Queen' and deep pink 'Rose Queen' are two that are available from seed.

S. × 'Indigo Spires' is a 2-foot, spiky blue-violet salvia with smooth, shiny, quilted-looking pointed-oval leaves. It was hybridized from *S. farinacea* and *S. longispicata.* It grows well from deep South Texas at least to Zone 8a in North Central Texas.

S. azurea, giant blue sage or sky blue sage, grows 3 to 6 feet tall. It is frequently seen in grassy meadows and roadsides, like a splash of fallen sky. In North Central Texas it blooms from late May through the summer, sometimes continuing through fall or pausing and resuming bloom in fall. In the Edwards Plateau it often blooms through fall.

Flowering may be timed by availability of moisture. The flower color, while most often pale blue, may be deep blue or white. *S. azurea* var. *grandiflora,* known as Pitcher's sage, is said to have larger and more numerous flowers. It is native throughout Texas. In one Prairies and Cross Timbers garden I have seen it growing both 30 inches tall and full, and 5 feet tall, slender and swoopy. Although both the species and the variant are native from Minnesota and Nebraska south to Arkansas and Texas, some question the species' cold-hardiness in Zone 8a and northward in Texas.

Two exotic blue-purple salvias with which John Fairey and Carl Schoenfeld of Waller County have good results are *S. moorcroftiana* and *S. forskahlei.* Moorcroft sage is native to the Himalayas. Surprisingly, it grows well in the low altitudes and high heat and humidity 50 miles northwest of Houston. It accepts moist or dry conditions. The white and violet-blue flowers appear from April to May. The enormous, lobed woolly gray-green leaves are striking winter evergreens. *S. forskahlei* is Iranian. So far, the Prairies and Cross Timbers is the only Texas region where I know it is being grown. It blooms heavily in blue-violet and white, continuing for a month after the other sage is done, and colonizes well, self-sowing. The felted gray-green leaves are evergreen. Afternoon shade is desirable for both these exotic salvias.

See also the separate listing below for *S. guaranitica.*

Salvia forskahlei
See under *Salvia farinacea*

Salvia greggii
Cherry Sage, Autumn Sage, Gregg's Sage
LABIATAE

BLOOM: Pink, dark red, white, salmon.
FOLIAGE: Dull green, small.
HEIGHT: 24–36″.
BLOOM SEASON: Mid- or late spring to frost.
REGIONS: All to Zone 7b.

LIGHT: Full sun to partial or light shade.
SOIL: Well-drained adobe, garden soil, or sand preferred. Tolerates clay. Accepts extreme alkalinity to pH 8.5; tolerates acid soil if well-drained.
MOISTURE: Moderate to low ranges; tolerates high in well-drained sites. Tolerates drought when well established.
PROPAGATION: Cuttings, division.

Autumn sage *Salvia greggii* (background)

The name cherry sage describes the cherry pink strain of this hardy native. It is a persistently woody perennial or subshrub. There are several naturally occurring colors; the wine-red and cerise-pink are considered respectively the most and next most cold-hardy. None are winter-hardy in far North Central Texas and the Panhandle. Gregg's sage does well in South and West Texas, however, and in East Texas in porous soils.

Once *S. greggii* is established, rainfall will sustain it. Deep, infrequent watering during droughts and periodic fertilizing promote repeat flowering. An occasional shearing keeps the plant compact and in good bloom most of the growing season.

Of the red salvias, *S. coccinea,* discussed elsewhere, is scarlet; Gregg's sage is a deep, dark red.

❧ *Salvia guaranitica*
LABIATAE

BLOOM: Cobalt blue.
FOLIAGE: Green.
HEIGHT: 12–48″.
BLOOM SEASON: May to frost.
REGIONS: Southern Piney Woods and Plains & Cross Timbers to Zone 8. Probably adapted elsewhere but not yet widely grown.
LIGHT: Full to filtered sun, half-day shade.
SOIL: Thrives in moist but well-drained, humus-rich soil. Accepts acidity well; results in alkaline soils pending.
MOISTURE: All ranges.
PROPAGATION: Cuttings, division.

The color of this salvia is at the opposite end of the blue spectrum from *Salvia azurea*. Deep cobalt is the hue of its 2-inch hooded flowers. Of the several shades of blue among the salvias, this is the most intense. At the bottom of Peggy Hammel's large daylily garden in Euless stand yard-high clumps of *S. guaranitica* paired with tangerine-red montbretia, *Crocosmia crocosmiflora*. The two strong colors clash superbly.

In the garden, *S. guaranitica* fares well in most well-drained, humusy soil. Bloom time is mid-spring to frost.

Salvia guaranitica

The thin, upright stems bear veined, wrinkled opposite leaves that are heart-shaped with crenate edges. The flowers are long, narrow, and strongly two-lipped.

There is some dispute as to whether this plant is properly identified; some sources hold that *S. guaranitica* doesn't start blooming until late summer or fall. As of publication, botanical clarification of this point was not yet available. In any case, *S. guaranitica* is the name by which it can be found.

✿ *Salvia leucantha*
Mexican Bush Sage
LABIATAE

BLOOM: Amethyst and white.
FOLIAGE: Gray-green, slender.
HEIGHT: To 6´; typically, 3–4´.
BLOOM SEASON: September to frost. Best in late October, November.
REGIONS: Edwards Plateau, Gulf Coast, Lower Rio Grande Valley, Piney Woods, southern Plains Country by some reports, Prairies & Cross Timbers, South Texas, Trans-Pecos.
LIGHT: Full to filtered sun or afternoon shade.
SOIL: Any well-drained. Accepts high alkalinity.
MOISTURE: Deep, infrequent watering. Drought-resistant.
PROPAGATION: Cuttings, division.

This tall sage with gray-green foliage and foot-long blooms puts on quite a show in late autumn. Its height and light violet color make it an ideal backdrop for a medium-sized gold or white flower; *Heliopsis* 'Summer Sun' would be nice. Combined with Maximilian sunflower, it makes a head-high wall that is spectacular as a background. Broad paths lined with *Salvia leucantha* would make a marvelous maze to wander in fall, one that would disappear completely in winter and early spring. A plant from a 3-inch pot set out in spring reaches 2 feet by August. *S. leucantha* is excellent as a cut flower. It also attracts butterflies.

Mexican bush sage *Salvia leucantha*

In the Prairies and Cross Timbers, the hardiness limit for this plant appears to fall just north of Mexia. I would be tempted to call it hardy only through part of Zone 8a; however, one Midland gardener (Zone 7b) reports it hardy there, if scant-blooming. To further confuse the issue, I have been told that a sudden 18° F cold snap may kill it. Of course, sudden arrival worsens the effect of any freeze. My advice is to try it and see; planted in spring, it gives fall bloom worth its keep even if it fails to come back a second season.

Mexican bush sage is very drought-tolerant and suffers no particular pests or diseases. Deer don't eat it. Propagation is from cuttings or division. "Better and bigger every year" is how one Medina native describes it.

✿ *Salvia moorcroftiana*
See under *Salvia farinacea*

꙰ *Salvia × superba* (*S. pratensis*)
See under *Salvia farinacea*

꙰ **Sedum**
Sedum
CRASSULACEAE

BLOOM: Brick red, rose, pink.
FOLIAGE: Fleshy, succulent, gray-green to blue-green.
HEIGHT: 12–30″.
BLOOM SEASON: July to frost.
REGIONS: All.
LIGHT: Full sun. Light shade in hot, dry areas. Tolerates reflected sun.
SOIL: Rich and well-drained but moisture-retentive preferred. Any well-drained tolerated.
MOISTURE: Grows in all ranges; in high, needs good drainage. Prefers moderate moisture. Tolerates drought.
PROPAGATION: Division; easy from cuttings.

Sedum × 'Autumn Joy'

Sedum × 'Autumn Joy,' thought to be a hybrid of *S. spectabile* and *S. telephium*, is considered one of the top ten perennials for the United States. "One of our top ten for ease and effect," Raydon Alexander of San Antonio calls it. It presents a bold, sculptural form and dense brick-red-to-bronze flower heads that remain attractive even when dry in winter. This sedum looks good year-round, unless there is a hard freeze. It is upright without staking. "I remember old ladies growing it in iron pots outdoors, winter and summer," Cathy Kyle of Raintree Nursery in Fort Worth says. "There is nothing much colder in winter or hotter in summer than an iron pot—it's a tough plant." It can be aggressive in the northern Plains Country. In the South Plains, "all sedums are worth using in dappled shade," says Midlander Burr Williams.

A succulent, 'Autumn Joy' sedum has large, scalloped, fleshy green leaves. It does well in light shade and full sun and tolerates moist soil. The plant begins blooming at 6-inch height in 4-inch nursery pots and will grow from that size to 1 or 2 feet tall in the first season. The ultimate height is 1 to 2½ feet, good for middle position in a flower border or as a specimen plant. Containers are also good places for this stately sedum. The flowers are pink when they open, gradually darkening to brick red and then to brown seed heads, a transition that takes several weeks and is interesting to observe.

This sedum propagates easily by cuttings—even a leaf will root.

S. spectabile hybrids 'Brilliant' and 'Meteor' are somewhat shorter than 'Autumn Joy' and similar in appearance. Their lilac-pink and rose-red tones are distinct from the brick red of 'Autumn Joy.' Mr. Alexander notes that seed-grown varieties have "very poor" color. Division and cuttings are the best means of propagation. Divide every few years to maintain these plants' compact shapes.

Besides these upright sedums, there are trailing and ground-cover types that are excellent additions to the garden. *S.* × 'Ruby Glow' is a large-leaved hybrid with showy rose-pink blooms and a sprawling habit. Low-growing sedums excellent as small-leaved ground covers—but not for foot traffic—and for rock gardens and chinks in stone retaining walls are gray-blue *S. reflexum* and green *S. floriferum*, both with small yellow flowers.

Goldenrod *Solidago* sp.

℘ *Solidago*
Goldenrod
COMPOSITAE

BLOOM: Golden yellow.
FOLIAGE: Green.
HEIGHT: 1–6½′ tall, species; various hybrids, 1–3′.
BLOOM SEASON: Late summer or fall.
REGIONS: All.
LIGHT: Full sun to light shade.
SOIL: Tolerant of most. Some goldenrods become
weedy in rich soil.
MOISTURE: Grows in regions with annual rainfall
of 15 to 50 inches. Tolerates both wet soil, when
actively growing, and drought.
PROPAGATION: Easy from seed, for bloom the
second year. Division of mature plants in spring
or fall.

Goldenrod is one of the less numerous and therefore
doubly appreciated fall flowers—appreciated, that is,
except by misinformed hay-fever sufferers. Its bright
golden pyramids of bloom are mistakenly blamed
for this malady, which is more probably caused by
the inconspicuous blooms of ragweed that appear at
the same time and produce airborne pollen. Easy to
grow, goldenrod makes excellent cut flowers as well
as garden and meadow flowers.

The wild species of Texas are generally considered
very invasive, except for *Solidago petiolaris,* which is
not stoloniferous. In meadows, wild gardens, rough
ground at the back of a property, and other situations where an aggressively spreading plant may be
welcome, a recommended wild species is *S. rigida,*
which grows to 5 feet tall with dense, flat-topped
bloom clusters.

In gardens, the hybrids are probably a better bet.
They range in height from 12 to 36 inches. Because
the exact parentage of most hybrids is unknown, I
am unable to recommend ones of Texas native parentage that would make likely successes in gardens
here. Several to try are foot-high 'Golden Thumb'
and 'Gold Dwarf,' 18-inch 'Cloth of Gold' and
'Crown of Rays,' and 2–3-foot 'Goldenmosa,' 'Peter
Pan,' and 'Golden Baby.'

Seed are sown indoors 6 to 8 weeks before last
frost or outdoors after last frost. Divide plants every
two or three years.

℘ *Tagetes lucida*
Mexican Mint Marigold, *Yerba Anís,* Sweet Mace
COMPOSITAE

BLOOM: Masses of golden yellow, ⅜″ blooms.
FOLIAGE: Light to dark green, anise-scented.
HEIGHT: 24–48″.
BLOOM SEASON: Late summer and fall.
REGIONS: All; survives to 0° F in Zones 8 and 7b,
so probably hardy further north. Usable as annual
where not cold-hardy.
LIGHT: Full to filtered sun, half-day shade.
SOIL: Any well-drained. Prefers alkaline to neutral.
MOISTURE: Grows in scant to heavy rainfall ranges
in well-drained situations. Tolerates drought.
PROPAGATION: Sow seed outdoors in full sun after
danger of frost is past, or indoors 8 weeks before
average last frost date. Easy from summer cuttings,
semi-hardwood cuttings in fall or early spring, or
division.

Mexican marigold *Tagetes lucida*

Native to Mexico and Guatemala, *Tagetes lucida* is a cousin to the familiar garden marigolds, common *T. erecta* and smaller-flowered *T. patula,* or French marigold. It doesn't much resemble either of them except in scent. *T. lucida* makes a green, full, shrubby form in gardens, with small gold flowers at every stem tip in fall. It is an excellent source of fall color and is apparently not susceptible to spider mites, which wreak havoc on the other marigolds in hot weather if they are not treated repeatedly. Its smooth leaves are evergreen in the Gulf Coast area. A sudden freeze may kill back the top growth, but it can be cut to the ground and will regrow whenever warm temperatures return. It survived 4° F in Collin County in December 1989's sudden hard freeze.

Known as *yerba anís* in Mexico, this herb has leaves that taste like anise, the familiar flavoring used in licorice candy, Italian sausage, and French *anisette* liqueur. The leaves are used to flavor soups, in herbal teas, and in potpourri. They are also used in Mexico as an excellent substitute for the culinary herb tarragon, which is difficult to grow in hot, humid areas. *T. lucida* offers excellent cut and dried flowers as well. The cut blooms are used *en masse* to adorn graves on the Mexican Days of the Dead, October 31 and November 1 and 2. Magazine articles touting this as a houseplant are incorrect—too little light.

❧ *Tecoma stans*
Yellow-bells, *Esperanza*
BIGNONIACEAE

BLOOM: Bright yellow 2″ flowers, funnel-shaped with a flaring, bell-like mouth and scalloped edges.
FOLIAGE: Bright green hairless leaves with toothed edges.
HEIGHT: Usually, 3–4′ shrub or small tree. In subtropical and tropical regions, 10–16′.
BLOOM SEASON: May to October.
REGIONS: Lower Gulf Coast, Lower Rio Grande Valley, South Texas, southern Trans-Pecos. Withstands only a few degrees of frost.
HEAT TOLERANCE: High, medium ranges.
LIGHT: Full sun.
SOIL: Any well-drained.
MOISTURE: All ranges. Tolerates drought.
PROPAGATION: By seeds and by cuttings of green wood under glass.

Tecoma stans is a very popular landscape plant in the southern third of Texas. It withstands high heat and blooms profusely all season. Native from Florida and Mexico south to South America and in volcanic and limestone soils of the Trans-Pecos, it is reliably perennial only in frost-free regions and in protected microclimates in Zone 9 locales. It provides both a full, shrubby form and ample color in the border, and can be used as an annual outside its winter hardiness range. In the subtropical toe of Texas, *Tecoma stans* forms shapely small trees 10 to 16 feet tall.

Yellow-bells *Tecoma stans*

Spiderwort *Tradescantia* sp.

❧ *Tradescantia*
Spiderwort, Widow's-tears
COMMELINACEAE

BLOOM: Three-petaled deep blue, purple, rose, or white flowers, borne in flat clusters at stem ends or in leaf axils.
FOLIAGE: Linear to lance-shaped, 12–24″ long, in clumps. Evergreen.
HEIGHT: To 36″.
BLOOM SEASON: Spring to fall.
REGIONS: All.
LIGHT: Half-day shade, filtered light best. Tolerates deep shade with less bloom, full sun with less sightly foliage in late summer.
SOIL: Poor to rich, slightly acid to slightly alkaline, moist to boggy. Tolerates dry.
MOISTURE: All ranges. Tolerates both drought and wet conditions.
PROPAGATION: Blooms second year from seed. Cuttings of growing shoots; division. Divide every 3–4 years to keep in bounds.

Tradescantia, spiderwort or widow's-tears, nestles at the feet of large trees and next to shrubbery, displaying vivid, three-petaled blue, white, or rose flowers every day until the sun gets high. Then the blooms close for the day. The common name "widow's-tears" refers to the droplets of deep blue fluid that often hang from the spent blooms.

These undemanding, shade-blooming plants are useful naturalized on the edge of woods and in wild gardens. They accept boggy and poor soils quite happily.

Some gardeners find the wild spiderworts coarse-foliaged for refined gardens, however. The plants may also become sprawling and untidy by late summer. However, in poor soils, excessive vegetative growth is not a problem. Also, the foliage can be kept more attractive through hot Texas summers if the plants are situated in locations with afternoon shade or filtered light. When the leaves become overgrown or sunburned, they can be cut back to encourage fresh new growth. These faults are more than compensated for by the long season of deep, richly colored bloom, acceptance of shade and soggy soil, and ease of care.

Several species of tradescantia are native to Texas. The hardy garden hybrids belong mostly under the name *T.* × *andersoniana,* which represents crosses of three species. In the trade these hybrids are often miscalled *T. virginiana,* the common spiderwort native to the eastern third of the United States to Connecticut. The many named *T.* × *andersoniana* hybrids offer colors from white to mauve, magenta, red-violet, pale and deep blue, and purple.

Tradescantia was one of the first New World flowers taken to England. John Parkinson, royal botanist to Charles I, named the plant for John Tradescant the Younger, whose journeys to the New World in the mid-1600s yielded many new botanical introductions to England. It quickly became common in English cottage gardens and has been widely hybridized there, while little-used in American gardens.

Because the plant's cells are so large that all parts of them can be easily seen with a simple microscope, tradescantia has been widely used in research in plant genetics and as demonstration material in medical schools.

Tradescantia is slightly susceptible to a few garden diseases and pests: botrytis blight, leaf tier, leaf cutter, and orange tortix caterpillar.

Verbena
Verbena
VERBENACEAE

BLOOM: Red, rose, pink, lavender, lilac, purple, white, bicolor.
FOLIAGE: Gray-green to green, depending on species and season.
HEIGHT: 2–24″.
BLOOM SEASON: Spring to frost.
REGIONS: All.
LIGHT: Sun to half-day or light shade. *V. peruviana* tolerates reflected light.
SOIL: Well-drained garden soil is best. Most prefer neutral to alkaline pH; *V. canadensis* and *V. rigida* also accept acidity, and *V. tenuisecta* prefers it.
MOISTURE: All ranges. Moderate, consistent preferred. Native species tolerate drought.
PROPAGATION: All from seed, division. *V. peruviana* and *V. rigida* also from cuttings.

Verbena *Verbena canadensis*

The verbenas are a genus of flowers native mostly to tropical and subtropical North and South America. They are so widely interbred that it is often difficult to distinguish among all the different varieties. This is no great practical problem, however, since all are good, if short-lived, garden flowers suited for the edges of beds and places where they can sprawl or trail. The blooms are flat-faced clusters a little like lace doilies, each rising from a single stem, and the foliage is serrated and sometimes spicy-smelling. Verbenas are easy to grow, for the most part. Some are longer-lived and more reliable than others. Although many are claimed to be hardy to Zones 4 or 5, Texas gardeners' reports bear this out only for *Verbena canadensis* and its hybrids.

Few flowers give as long a season of profuse bloom as *V.* 'Elegans,' often referred to as *V. elegans,* a name of no botanical standing that has adhered to a very popular horticultural hybrid widely sold in Texas. According to nurseryman Ralph Pincus, this verbena was first introduced to the Texas trade from a Minden, Ohio, supplier thirty years ago. Its hot pink variety is best known, but other bright colors exist. A well-drained site, deadheading, and consistent moisture will keep it blooming all season. Spider mites may affect it in South Texas. This verbena is hardy in freezes to 25° F, if they don't come suddenly. When freezes are predicted, covering the plant with burlap is a good idea.

V. canadensis is a dark purplish-pink species native from Virginia and Florida west to Iowa, Colorado, and Mexico. Some of the red-purple, lilac, rose, and white verbenas in the trade owe breeding to this plant. It prefers well-drained, dry soil and airy open spaces. It is susceptible to mildew.

A large group consists of the garden verbenas, *V.* × *hybrida* (*V. hortensis*), of undetermined hybrid ancestry. They are only half-hardy, the least hardy of the verbenas, and are most often grown as annuals. They include familiar white, bright red, purple, pink, and bicolor forms. Some gardeners term them "temperamental."

V. peruviana is a desirable deep red South American species with dark green, deeply cut evergreen foliage that hugs the ground. Its white, purple, and pink cultivars are also popular. 'Apple Blossom' is a lovely pink-and-white bicolor; 'St. Paul' is red, and 'St. Peter' is pink. *V. peruviana* is considered the second-longest-blooming and one of the most reliable perennial verbenas. It is more mildew-resistant than the garden hybrids and a smaller plant with smaller blooms than *V.* 'Elegans.' Like *V.* 'Elegans,' it is fairly short-lived in West Texas. Elsewhere, *V. peruviana* is considered generally the longest-lived of the verbenas. The red cultivar 'St. Paul' is considered hardier than pink 'St. Peter.'

Deep purple *V. rigida,* tube vervain, is a superb grower out west and easy, if a little coarse-leaved. Of the verbenas listed here, this is said to be the only one that is truly perennial in the South Plains. Native to Argentina and southern Brazil, it is naturalized over the western range of the state, East Texas, the Upper Gulf, the Blacklands, and the Post Oak Savannah.

Prairie verbena *Verbena bipinnatifida*

Native lavender-flowering *V. bipinnatifida,* prairie or Dakota verbena, is a tough-as-nails perennial "you can drive a truck over." It grows almost all over the state, with the exception of most of the Trans-Pecos. In the Southwest, it is the longest-blooming verbena. The foliage is gray-green and hairy in summer, deep green in winter. Prairie verbena is native from South Dakota to Alabama and west to Arizona and adjacent Mexico. Russell Weber of Austin writes that he once sent off for seed of prairie verbena for a new home in San Antonio, only to find it sprouting in the fill dirt in his yard.

V. tenuisecta, moss vervain, is a lovely ferny-leaved species that blooms white, pale pink, and lavender from March to frost. It is effective in borders and hanging baskets.

The verbenas in general like well-drained sandy soil and full sun. Most benefit from a winter mulch of fine pine bark or straw or from being planted with roots under a rock.

There is an old hybrid strain of garden verbena that bears very large pink-and-white flowers. Some selections of it radiate a honey-sweet fragrance for several feet around them. 'Pink Parfait' is one of these. They are more often found in old gardens than in the trade. Other members of the family, such as lemon verbena, possess deliciously scented leaves used in sachets and potpourri.

Propagation is by seeds in fall or early spring or from early fall cuttings, or by division.

℘ *Viola*
Violet
VIOLACEAE

BLOOM: Purple, blue-violet, blue, and white; hybrids, yellow to orange, rose to maroon, pale violet to deep purple, blue-violet, and bicolors. Various markings.
FOLIAGE: Clusters of heart-shaped to rounded green leaves.
HEIGHT: 2–12″.
BLOOM SEASON: Late winter or early to late spring, some reblooming in fall.
REGIONS: See Chart 1 for species adapted to each region.
LIGHT: Acceptable sun exposure varies inversely with heat and light intensity. Partial to light shade generally preferred. Full sun only in cooler regions with mulch over roots.
SOIL: For most, moist, fertile, well-drained soil with high organic content is preferred. Slightly acid preferred, but many tolerate slight alkalinity if other soil conditions are favorable.
MOISTURE: All ranges. Moderate to ample, consistent moisture preferred.

PROPAGATION: From seed in late summer or in fall in a closed cold frame with wet burlap over it. Winter plants over in the ground. Offsets late winter to early spring, division in early spring. Many self-sow and/or spread by runners.

Many people remember orchid corsages at proms and Mother's Day affairs, but fewer recall when clusters of violets were the feminine adornment of choice. In fact, sweet-scented violets were leading florist flowers through the twenties and thirties. They are the earliest flowers to bloom in North and East Texas woods and still linger as walkway borders and flower bed edging at many older homes. Now, most Texans are familiar only with *Viola odorata,* the wild sweet violet that comes up in their lawns, and don't know the larger-flowered hybrids and other species. These are richly colored, fragrant, and fairly easily grown. There is a violet for almost every part of the state.

Violets are members of the genus *Viola,* as are pansies, violas, and violettas. Their natural range is in the temperate regions of North America and in northern Europe from the British Isles to the Ural Mountains. Tidy and almost evergreen where temperatures don't often fall below 10° F, they are significantly bothered by few pests or diseases.

Violets are flowers for late winter, early spring, and fall in the South and Southwest, rather than spring and summer bloomers as they are in the Northeast. Most species prefer partial shade and moist, fertile, well-drained soil. Their intolerance of hot, dry conditions—with one or two exceptions—makes light shade, good air circulation, and plenty of humus desirable in Texas sites. They are susceptible to spider mites in summer heat. Where it is cool and moist, slugs and snails may disfigure the leaves. Other possible problems are crown rot, leaf spot, and downy mildew.

Violets' ability to stay evergreen in winter as far north as Zone 7b makes them good ground covers and gives them a head start on spring bloom, which can come as early as February. Some go semi-dormant in summer heat, resuming active growth

and even blooming in fall. Their deep green heart-shaped or elongated leaves make them attractive ground cover under trees where grass won't grow, provided there are a few inches of good soil.

Sweet violet, *V. odorata,* has been in cultivation since before the time of Christ. In medieval England, this busy violet served as seasoning for food, room deodorizer, and cure for many ills. For centuries it has been a mainstay of the French perfume industry.

Sweet violet and its hybrids can be grown in every part of Texas except, reportedly, the South Plains. They should be dug and divided every year or two to prevent such crowding that bloom is reduced. They spread by reseeding and by long runners from which new plants sprout. Rooted runners may be separated and replanted 1 foot apart in late winter to early spring to produce new plants. Planting in heavier soils or in confined areas also helps control their spread. Fertilize them in very early spring for better blooming. Seeds may be toxic if eaten.

'Royal Robe' is probably the most popular deep purple sweet violet hybrid. Keeta Hodges, perennial grower for Nortex Nursery Industries, considers it one of the best. In her northeast Texas location, it reblooms from October to frost. 'Rosina' is a beautiful rose cultivar. 'White Czar' is a gorgeous burgundy-striated white with deep purple calyxes. 'Freckle,' white with purple dots and only 2½ inches tall, is considered a "good spreader," ideal as ground cover. These excellent hybrids are usually classified as sweet violet hybrids, although some growers consider them offspring of the northern early spring violet, *V. cucullata.* They are semi-evergreen to Zone 8.

Bette Edmundsen, who owns High Country Nursery in Fort Davis, grows the horned violet, *V. cornuta,* native to Spain and the Pyrenees. This Davis Mountains location is more hospitable to violets than most of the Trans-Pecos. Horned violet insists on well-drained soil and protection from the sun and will not tolerate sunbaked ground. While it blooms spring to fall in some locales, this is unlikely in high heat zones and hot, humid areas, even though this species is more heat-resistant than most. The large purple flowers are very showy. Hybrids are available in many shades from pale yellow to apricot and blue to violet, as well as striking combinations like gold and blue or purple with a yellow center. Propagation is by seed, division, and runners or plantlets set 6 inches apart.

Violet *Viola walteri*

Also in the trade is *V. sororia,* woolly blue violet, a low 3-inch species native to the eastern United States that flowers blue-violet, sometimes sold as *V. priceana.* It does not spread by stolons like many violets.

In East Texas, native bird's-foot violet, *V. pedata,* shows its golden eye, with either velvety dark violet upper petals and lilac lower ones, all lilac, or, less often, white or pinkish. Atypically, it likes dry, sunny spots in acid, rocky, poor soils, especially sandy or gritty ones. However, "sunny" doesn't mean afternoon sun—or direct sun at all in summer—unless the roots are mulched or sunk in a crevice in rock. Growing it on a slope or in a raised bed reduces its susceptibility to a common disease, crown rot. It is propagated from seed.

Arrowleaf violet, *V. sagittata,* also grows in East Texas. It is a non-invasive species propagated from seed that likes moist, humus-rich spots in semi-shade or light shade. Deep violet-purple, it is native from Maine to Minnesota south to Georgia, Louisiana, and East Texas.

V. hederacea is an Australian species in the trade that can withstand a few nights of temperatures in the teens.

V. walteri is a ground-hugging violet native from South Carolina to Florida and west to Southeast Texas. In Zones 8 and 9, it usually blooms in February in a haze of pale purple that continues until mid-April. The leaves are rounded. Even moisture is necessary for it to make a dense cover. It spreads from rhizomes and stolons and is propagated from seed and by root divisions set 9 inches apart.

Violets are good as low floral edging for flower and shrub borders. An ideal place for the more invasive types, such as wild sweet violet, is between a walkway and lawn grass. Its use as ground cover should be limited to places where aggressive coverage is desired, such as under a grove of trees or on a shaded, rugged slope. Violets are excellent in hillside or rock gardens in Texas, provided there is light shade and rock or mulch over the roots. It would be interesting to put oxalis and violets together and let them battle it out. Some people like to let violets and St. Augustine grass do the same in their lawns.

Even in generally alkaline soils such as characterize many parts of Texas, acid microclimates suited to violets are found. One such likely spot is beneath oak trees where the leaves have decomposed. In many alkaline areas, the gardener who has a partially shaded area and takes time to add soil sulfur (strictly by directions) and ample well-rotted compost may be able to grow these shy-looking but tough little flowers outside their usual range.

𝒮𝒶 *Zinnia*

Zinnia

COMPOSITAE

BLOOM: Species include clear yellow, white with a yellow center, and orange with a black-purple center.
FOLIAGE: Needlelike 1″ leaves.
HEIGHT: 4–10″ subshrub.
BLOOM SEASON: Spring or summer to fall.
REGIONS: *Z. grandiflora* native from Colorado and Kansas south to Texas' Plains Country and Trans-Pecos, Mexico, and rest of southwestern U.S. See below for others.
LIGHT: Full sun, including hot reflected sun. *Z. angustifolia* accepts half-day shade.
SOIL: Almost any well-drained. Spreads best in loose soil.
MOISTURE: Low, medium ranges with moderate to scant watering. Very drought-tolerant.
PROPAGATION: Direct-sown seed in spring or fall, spring division of young plants. Division of mature plants and transplanting are difficult.

Zinnia grandiflora forms a cushion of yellow flowers all summer in the hottest, driest conditions. New Mexican growers say they've seen it on "almost vertical" hillsides. With its acceptance of reflected heat, prairie zinnia is a candidate for street medians as well as rocky slopes and dry beds. It is semi-evergreen in Central Texas and Zone 8 portions of the Trans-Pecos and disappears in winter in colder areas. A Midland gardener says it "crawls around the garden to new places."

White *Z. acerosa,* called dwarf zinnia, resembles *Z. grandiflora.* It is another native that grows from West Texas through, reportedly, New Mexico and Arizona. Its five to seven white petals surround a yellow eye; the foliage is grayish. In Texas, dwarf zinnia is native to limestone soil from the Guadalupe Mountains to Del Rio and through the Lower Rio Grande Valley. It is said to be even more drought-tolerant than prairie zinnia in areas with hot summers, but somewhat less winter-hardy. As of 1990 it was not yet in commercial production.

Z. angustifolia, native to Mexico, looks similar to these other little zinnias. Long known as *Z. linearis,* it has bright orange petals with black-purple disc flowers and narrow leaves. A popular hot-climate bedding plant, it has been crossed with the annual common zinnia, *Z. elegans,* to produce small-flowered zinnias that are free of the powdery mildew that plagues hybrid garden zinnias. 'Rose Pinwheel,' a bright pink, is one of these. A white that resembles blackfoot daisy is another. These hybrid strains, now in the mail-order trade, promise to be long-season, easy-care annuals in the border.

Prairie zinnia *Zinnia grandiflora*

Species narcissi and old hybrids planted more than sixty years ago on this farm in northern Louisiana continue to bloom every year. Sisters' Bulb Farm, Gibsland.

CHAPTER FOURTEEN

Bulbs

"There's magic in bulbs!"
—*Alfred F. Scheider*

The charms of bulbs have beguiled Westerners since the 1500s, when European nobility first corrupted *tülbent,* the Turkish word for "turban," to "tulip" and crammed their gardens with them. The popularity and value of tulips eventually inflated to such an extent that a house could be purchased with the price of three bulbs. Speculation in the Dutch bulb market finally resulted in a crash that wiped out many fortunes overnight. While bulbs' cash value has never again reached such heights, their popularity continues to grow.

Bulbs delight—and surprise. Few plants give as much for as little effort. Many bulbs offer a vivid two-or-three-week show that is as eagerly awaited, despite its brevity, as the robins in spring or the Monarch butterflies in fall. And many have multiple varieties that provide a long succession of bloom. Most prefer neglect to overly solicitous care in their off-season.

With bulb varieties selected for the South and Southwest and special techniques, year-after-year bloom (which is difficult to achieve here with many of the top-selling Dutch bulbs) can be a matter of course.

These persistent bulbs give gardeners an alternative to the one-shot bloom of popular large Dutch tulips and hyacinths and some large-flowered daffodils. These, originally species of southern Europe and North Africa, were hybridized over centuries in northern Europe's damp, mild summers and cold winters—a history which means that the hot summers and erratic winters of Texas and adjoining states generally spell their early death. But the wild forebears of the Dutch bulbs, as well as other bulbous plants from areas of the globe similar to the arid Southwest, take to Texas conditions like a horned toad to a sandpile. And, with special techniques, some gardeners induce successive years of flowering in even the big Dutch-bred beauties, despite our climate.

Success with bulbous plants is easy once you understand them. Bulbs are storage capsules. They store the sugars produced in the plant's leaves during the growing season. Most bulbous plants go dormant during part of the year. When they are dormant, the roots do not actively grow and thus do not penetrate and aerate the soil. During this period, the bulbs are extremely vulnerable to rot from soil moisture. This is a particular problem in heavy clay soils that are poorly drained. For this reason, many bulbs fall prey to inappropriate soil or overwatering. There are other cultural practices that also deter repeat-flowering, discussed under "General Bulb Culture" below.

Included here under the generic term "bulbs" are plants that grow from several underground energy-storage systems.

True bulbs are of two types—those that are onion-like with an outer skin, such as tulips, and those that are made up of overlapping scales like those of garlic and lack the outer membrane, as lilies do.

Other organs that perform a storage function similar to that of true bulbs are corms, tubers, rhizomes, and tuberous roots.

A *corm* is a solid, swollen part of a stem, usually subterranean, with a "basal plate," or flat tissue layer, at its base. Gladioli grow from corms.

A *rhizome* is a thickened stem, usually horizontal, that grows on or under the ground. It sends up leaves or stems at its tip. Bearded iris is an example of a rhizomatous plant.

A *tuber* is a short, thick, generally underground stem or branch with buds or eyes, such as that of the tuberous begonia.

A *tuberous root* has eyes located not on the root but on the base of the plant stem.

GENERAL BULB CULTURE

Certain bulbs naturalize well in lawns or ground-cover areas, where the other plants consume much of the water that would otherwise rot the bulbs during their dormant season. In a flower bed, shallow-rooted annuals may be planted over the bulbs to provide color when the bulbs are dormant, to drink up the excess soil moisture, and to help camouflage fading foliage. For directions for planting of bulbs, see pages 236–237.

Bulbous plants' leaves are their food factories; over-zealous gardeners should refrain from lopping off the leaves when the flowers finish blooming and, in the case of lilies, taking too much stem with cut flowers. Common wisdom has been that leaves of true bulbs such as narcissi and tulips should not be removed until they droop and turn brown. However, the Royal Horticulture Society's most recent findings on narcissi indicate that it is best to cut back foliage six weeks after cessation of bloom; experienced Texas bulb growers say when the foliage is half to one-third wilted. To hide the dying leaves in the meanwhile, bulbs are combined with small shrubs in a shrub border, with ground cover, or with flowers that leaf out as the bulbs fade, such as summer annuals. Braiding bulb foliage or bundling it with twine, once a common practice, is not recommended.

Some bulbs can be heirlooms. Crinums may last longer than a human lifetime. Some narcissi and rhodophiala, the oxblood lily, also remain from generation to generation.

Bulb plants range in height from 6 inches to 6 feet. The flowers offer every color in the spectrum, for bloom every season of the year. An ample selection, many little-known, will thrive in the South and Southwest.

❧ Agapanthus
Lily of the Nile
AMARYLLIDACEAE

BLOOM: Large umbels of up to 100 blue, purplish, or white flowers. Usually funnel-form, they flare outward into star-shaped tips.
PLANT FORM: Handsome clumps of strap-shaped foliage 12–40″ tall (including dwarf 'Peter Pan'). Evergreen and deciduous types.
BLOOM SEASON: Summer.
REGIONS: All but Plains Country and Trans-Pecos.
HEAT TOLERANCE: All ranges with ample water and some shade.
LIGHT: Afternoon shade, filtered light, or full shade.
SOIL: Prefers deep, well-drained, fertile soil with ample humus. Tolerates most soils.
MOISTURE: Grows in areas receiving from 15 to 50 inches rainfall annually, with good drainage. Moist through the growing season and dry in winter. Drought-tolerant once established but may not bloom if left dry prior to flowering time.
PROPAGATION: Root division. Divide every 3 or 4 years. Takes 3 or more years to reach flowering size from seed.

Lilies of the Nile, striking plants native to southern Africa, are poetically if inaccurately named. In colder climates where they cannot be grown out-doors year-round, they make fine container plants. The blooms are attractive to butterflies and make elegant, airy cut flowers. There are hundreds of varieties of these stately, elegant plants. They contrast handsomely with daylilies.

There are two species that are widely hybridized, *Agapanthus orientalis* and *A. africanus,* as well as a third one in the trade, *A. campanulatus. A. africanus* is evergreen; the other two are deciduous and are considered slightly more cold-hardy. Telling a nursery plant's parentage on sight and predicting its probable hardiness are difficult. Variations within species and free hybridizing among them make this a confusing genus, plants of which are unlikely to be accurately identified in the trade. However, all are excellent summer flowers for shade that may weather mild winters outdoors if protected and will survive indoors in pots.

Most agapanthus in the trade are hybrids, experts agree, and the authoritative *Hortus Third* maintains that more are related to *A. orientalis* than other species. *A. orientalis* has about ten leaves and umbels variously described as containing forty to more than one hundred flowers—lots of flowers, however you look at it. This plant grows 2 feet tall or taller. There are white and dark blue flowering, dwarf, and variegated cultivars. A very popular *A. orientalis* dwarf cultivar is 'Peter Pan,' which reaches only 12 to 18 inches in height. *A. orientalis* was recently reclassified *A. praecox* ssp. *orientalis.*

A. africanus is less commonly cultivated, according to *Hortus Third,* although many plants are sold by its name. Most of these are probably hybrids. The species is evergreen, 1½–3½ feet tall, with eight to eighteen leaves ½ inch wide. The flower heads consist of twelve to thirty flowers. This agapanthus is native to the Cape of Good Hope peninsula. It is considered hardy only in Zones 9 and 10, but one gardener reports survival of 14° F by a plant that may be *A. africanus.*

A. campanulatus, a native of the Orange Free State and Lesotho, is deciduous. It grows about 3 feet tall. Like *A. orientalis,* it is somewhat hardier

Lily of the Nile *Agapanthus*

than *A. africanus.* 'Mood Indigo' is a 3-foot June-to-July bloomer derived from it recommended by one Texas gardener.

Agapanthus is properly planted only deep enough to get the rootstock below the frost line, 1 to 3 inches in Texas, depending on the locale. It prefers a spot sheltered from intense sun. Staking is not usually needed. The faded flowers should be removed regularly.

Fertilize annually at the start of the growing season and again after bloom. Slight root constriction reportedly encourages bloom.

In Zone 8 and north and in colder than average winters, mulch agapanthus grown outdoors with 6 to 8 inches of peat moss or straw and cover the foliage with an inverted basket, weighted with a rock or brick. This will usually limit frost damage to the leaf tips. The plants produce larger flowers after mild winters or when well protected.

If you choose to bring plants indoors, deciduous ones will probably winter over dormant, infrequently watered in a cool but not freezing porch or garage. Evergreen ones can grow in a bright but indirectly lit window indoors, if the room is not kept overheated and dry.

৯৯ *Allium*
Allium
AMARYLLIDACEAE

BLOOM: 2–4″ umbels or globular flower heads of tiny white or lilac star-shaped flowers, some sweet-smelling.

PLANT FORM: Narrow foliage, bloom stalks 10–18″ tall, depending on species.

BLOOM SEASON: Spring, spring to summer, or spring to fall, depending on species.

REGIONS: All, depending on species; hardiness varies. *A. tuberosum* grows in all.

LIGHT: Full sun to partial or light shade.

SOIL: Light, rich, moist but well-drained alkaline soil preferred. Tolerates most.

MOISTURE: All ranges. Tolerates drought but thrives with regular watering during growth period.

PROPAGATION: *A. neapolitanum,* division or seed in fall; first refrigerate seed for 4 weeks in moist, sterile medium, *A. subhirsutum,* offsets. *A. schoenoprasum,* offsets in spring or fall, 1 year to mature from seeds. *A. tuberosum,* division, seed, or offsets; can self-sow.

The alliums are a large, diverse group that includes onions, garlics, and chives as well as ornamental types. Many Eurasian species—including some of the largest and showiest of the genus—are not persistent in San Antonio, according to bulb specialist and hybridizer Thaddeus M. Howard. For San Antonio horticulturist Raydon Alexander, "The uglier they are, the better they grow." I have, however, seen unidentified beautiful tall alliums with 5-inch lilac heads that appear to have naturalized on sites with red sandy soil in Dallas County and in the town of Cranfills Gap in Bosque County.

The small alliums that come back year after year are really not ugly, just modest. Two of these, *Allium schoenoprasum* and *A. tuberosum,* are culinary chives that also happen to be pretty. The airy, dainty flowers are effective in large drifts in lawn, woodland, or rock gardens or in the front of the border, as well as in fresh or dried arrangements. The plants naturalize well and are easy to grow. Most perform successfully in Zones 4 to 10.

A. neapolitanum, native to southern Italy, is somewhat more frost-tender than others. It takes a freeze, but loses foliage below 20° F. Bulb experts in San Antonio say it is not considered reliably persistent north of Central Texas. Ten to 18 inches tall, it puts out sweet-scented white flowers in spring or early summer. They are excellent as cut flowers. The cultivar 'Grandiflorum' is the largest-flowered and showiest of the alliums hardy here.

A. schoenoprasum, onion chives, puts out small globelike lilac flower heads in spring. The flowers make attractive garnishes for foods seasoned with the minced fresh leaves. North and East Texas gardeners also praise onion chives for use in low borders. Bonnie Thurber, a Dallas-area herb grower, likens the scent of the flowers to violets. Established plantings are divided every three years or so. Frequent cutting back promotes dense growth.

A. subhirsutum blooms from March to May. Its white bloom umbels are more open and less symmetrical than those of A. neapolitanum. This allium is native to the Mediterranean area from Spain to Greece, where it grows in rocky and sandy places.

Garlic chives *Allium tuberosum*

Chinese ground orchid *Bletilla striata*

A. tuberosum, commonly called Chinese chives or garlic chives, is widely cultivated in eastern Asia. Its leaves are flat, while those of A. schoenoprasum are round. A. tuberosum leaves are garlic-flavored and hotter than onion. This plant thrives in containers and blooms successfully indoors. It can self-sow and become invasive in the garden. It has both a spring form and a summer form; I have seen the latter bloom well into fall.

When garlic and onion chives are grown solely for the leaves, the flower stalks are pinched back to promote leaf growth.

Amarcrinum
See *Crinum* and *Amarcrinum*

Bletilla striata
Chinese Ground Orchid
ORCHIDACEAE

BLOOM: Lilac-magenta or white blooms resemble small cattleya orchids on 10–24″ spikes.
PLANT FORM: Up to 24″ tall with leaf blades shaped like iris foliage but with lengthwise ridges or "pleats."
BLOOM SEASON: Late spring, 2–3 weeks.
REGIONS: All but Trans-Pecos and Plains Country to Zone 8b (20° F). To colder temperatures if mulched.
LIGHT: Full sun, afternoon shade, filtered light.
SOIL: Loose, well-drained. Prefers acid to neutral, tolerates alkaline.
MOISTURE: High annual moisture. Regular watering during the growing season is recommended.
PROPAGATION: Division. Plant new rhizomes in early spring, covered with 1″ soil. Transplant only during winter dormancy.

"Very easy, very pretty, very available," one gardener sums up *Bletilla striata*. The longer it is established, the better it blooms. Eventually the plants form large clumps; one south Texas gardener has a clump that has doubled its original size. This plant naturalizes readily. Its only pests are snails and slugs.

❧ *Cooperia*
See *Zephyranthes*

❧ *Crinum* **and** *Amarcrinum*
AMARYLLIDACEAE

Southern gardener Elizabeth Lawrence wrote of
crinums, "The tropical splendor of their lush foliage
and large flowers is unbelievable in a garden where
the temperature sometimes approaches zero."
Crinums are native to tropical and warm-tempera-
ture zones of both hemispheres. Sometimes called
"crinum-lilies," they are, in fact, a genus of thick- or
bulbous-rooted herbs. Although outdoor culture is
largely restricted to the southernmost states, two or
three species are said to be hardy as far north as New
York City.

Outdoors in the South, crinums left undisturbed
form large clumps. The large, showy flowers appear
in late spring or summer, with the foliage or after it
is well grown. Blooms range from tubular shapes to
trumpet and spider forms. In most varieties the
blooms look up and outward when they open but
start to bow around midday.

Crinums are generally easier to grow and less
exacting than true lilies. Some are somewhat coarser,
particularly as blooms fade, but gorgeous in their
own right and, in the South, far more durable.

Depending on where one lives, crinums can be
permanent heirlooms. "Landscape plants equal to a
shrub," Thaddeus M. Howard of San Antonio, an
expert in the genus and a respected hybridizer, calls
them. He has a crinum that has been in his family
for over one hundred years.

Crinums not only offer deceptively tropical
beauty, late and long bloom, and bold stature; they
also thrive in moist soil and light shade. Heavy
feeders, they do best in rich garden soil with plenty
of water. The soil should be kept moist and fertilized well, particularly in the early part of the growing season. Evergreen types in pots need to be kept
partially dry and under reduced heat for a dormant
rest period in winter.

Amarcrinum
× *Amarcrinum howardii*

❧ × *Amarcrinum howardii*
Amarcrinum

BLOOM: Shell-pink, white throat with green tinge.
Recurved petals to 3″ long; 16 or 17 blooms on
stalk 24–48″ tall. Fragrant.
PLANT FORM: Large clump of strap-shaped leaves
to 24″ long. Evergreen to Zone 8. Freezes to ground
in Plains Country.
BLOOM SEASON: Summer, for several months.
REGIONS: All but Trans-Pecos and possibly
Edwards Plateau. Hardy outdoors to Zone 8. Can
be grown to Zone 7 if mulched in winter.
LIGHT: Full sun, half-day shade, or filtered light.
SOIL: Rich garden soil, acid to alkaline. Tolerates
clay.
MOISTURE: Ample, especially during growing
season.
PROPAGATION: Offsets; division, infrequently.

The amarcrinum was produced by crossing *Amaryllis belladonna* and *Crinum moorei,* both large, handsome flowers. This cross was made simultaneously
by hybridizers in California and in northern Italy,
without each other's knowledge. × *Crinodonna* was
the first registered botanical name for the new
offspring, in Italy, and is used interchangeably with
× *Amarcrinum.* The amaryllis parentage produced
pink flowers, and the crinum side yielded foliage
that is normally evergreen, to make an admirable
garden "lily" for the Deep South and tropical zones.
Its fragrant trumpets open over several months. Like
crinums, amarcrinums do not need division. The
very large bulbous roots should be divided only
when increase is preferred over bloom.

Crinums that produce small offsets from the base of the bulblike roots should be propagated by the offsets. Lifting the plants to divide or move them may interrupt bloom for two or three seasons.

The crinums discussed here are among the most attractive species and hybrids. They are available mainly from breeder catalogs. While crinums are associated with the South and tropical origins, some are cold-hardy by Texas standards. *Crinum bulbispermum, C. herbertii,* and *C. × powelli* are recommended by Texas experts as withstanding zero temperatures with winter protection; northern sources credit them with cold-hardiness to -20° F. Nationally *C. americanum* ranks next in cold-hardiness, but not in Texas, from survey results. Respondents rank *C. americanum* hardy to Zone 9 and, if mulched in winter, to Zone 7b. 'Ellen Bosanquet,' *C. × digweedi,* 'J. C. Harvey,' and *C. moorei* were reported hardier. So, if mulched, were four others (see Chart 2). I cannot account for the difference from national findings on this point. Further, some Texans attribute *C. americanum* with resistance to -10° F temperatures, as northerners do. Perhaps the discrepancy as to minimum survivable temperature is explained by the fact that Texas' typical alternation of freeze and thaw is more stressful to plants than greater absolute, uninterrupted cold. In any case, mulch is very helpful in winter survival.

"Milk-and-wine lily" is a convenient old-fashioned name for crinums with white flowers striped with pink, purple, or red. *C. zeylanicum, C. × digweedi* hybrids, and some *C. × herbertii* hybrids are milk-and-wine types.

The amarcrinums are cultivated hybrids produced from crosses of the *Amaryllis* and *Crinum* genera. They combine the most striking features of both.

A point of terminology: a bloom said to have a contrasting "keel" displays a stripe of color down the outside of its lengthwise ribs. "Midribs" appear inside the blooms.

Specialists in the genus say that catalogs are rife with misidentifications.

Some notable new Texas-raised hybrids are 'Carnival,' 'Stars and Stripes,' and 'William Herbert.'

Crinum americanum
Southern Swamp Lily

BLOOM: Umbels of 2 to 6 fragrant white flowers with long, narrow segments and rose stamens; 3½″ wide with tubes to 4″ long.
PLANT FORM: Leaves few, long, and narrow. Flower stalk 18–24″ tall.
BLOOM SEASON: Late spring to summer or even frost.
REGIONS: All but Plains Country and Trans-Pecos. Hardiness given as Zone 9, but known to have weathered 6° F in Texas. Native to Texas' southern Piney Woods and Lower Gulf Coast and east to Georgia and Florida. Hardy to 5° F (Zone 7b) with winter protection, according to some.
LIGHT: Full sun to partial light or shade.
SOIL: Garden soil, acid to neutral, rich preferred. Tolerates clay.
MOISTURE: Ample; must be kept wet all year long. Grows in low, swampy places.
PROPAGATION: Division, infrequently. Offsets.

The flowers are starlike. Best grown as an aquatic plant or in tubs with no drainage.

Crinum asiaticum
Poison Bulb

BLOOM: White, waxy flowers with narrow, pointed petals, greenish tube, purple-red inside; 20–50 blooms per stalk. Resembles *C. americanum* but with a split corolla. Fragrant.
PLANT FORM: Showy, large rosette of broad, swordlike leaves 3–5″ wide, 36–48″ long. Evergreen. To 36″ tall.
BLOOM SEASON: Summer to late fall.
REGIONS: Gulf Coast, Lower Rio Grande Valley, southern Piney Woods, South Texas, Zones 9–10. With protection, hardy to -10° F (Zone 6) per northern sources.

LIGHT: Full sun to partial or light shade.
SOIL: Well-drained, deep, organic, acid to slightly alkaline.
MOISTURE: Water generously during growth and flowering; reduce watering when leaves begin to yellow.
PROPAGATION: Offsets.

This crinum is native to tropical southern Asia and Melanesia. Some of the flowers have a pinkish cast. The plant is decorative for its leaves alone. No published sources found at the time of publication tell whether the common name indicates actual toxicity.

✿ *Crinum bulbispermum*

BLOOM: Pink, deep rose, or white, with darker wine or rose keel. Flowers to 1″ wide, the tube 3–4″ long and curved. Blooms appear in umbels of 6 to 12.
PLANT FORM: Long, narrow leaves. Plant to 36″ tall.
BLOOM SEASON: Late spring.
REGIONS: All. Considered the hardiest of crinums used in gardens. Hardy to Zones 8 and 9 in Texas and, with winter protection, to Zone 7. Common in Central and South Texas.
LIGHT: Full sun to partial or light shade.
SOIL: Clay, garden soil, or sand. Rich, well-drained preferred. Acid to alkaline.
MOISTURE: Ample, especially during early growing season.
PROPAGATION: Seeds, offsets, infrequent division.

This very attractive, rosy bicolor crinum is native to South Africa. It is one of the species that vie for the title "most popular." "Probably the hardiest [but Texas sources differ] and most commonly cultivated species in the United States," says *Hortus Third*. It is also sold by botanical names *C. longifolium* and *C. capensis*.

✿ *Crinum* × *digweedi*
Digweedi Hybrids

BLOOM: White, striped with pink (sometimes nearly imperceptibly) or red, with showy pink or red stamens. Long, narrow petals form a flaring star.

PLANT FORM: Strap-shaped, arching leaves. Height to 36″.
BLOOM SEASON: Summer.
REGIONS: Gulf Coast, Lower Rio Grande Valley, southern Piney Woods, southern Prairies & Cross Timbers, South Texas. Hardy to Zone 8b.
LIGHT: Full sun to partial light or shade.
SOIL: Clay, garden soil, sand. Rich, well-drained, acid to slightly alkaline.
MOISTURE: Ample in growing season, scant after flowering.
PROPAGATION: Division.

'Royal White' crinum *Crinum* × *digweedi* 'Royal White'

Crinum × *digweedi* includes four hybrids of *C. americanum* and *C. scabrum*. A very common white one is found over much of Texas from south of Dallas to Brownsville. It was reportedly distributed by Henderson Nursery of Fresno, California, as 'Royal White' in 1930.

✿ *Crinum* × 'Ellen Bosanquet'

BLOOM: Widely flaring deep rose-pink trumpets of broad petals with gracefully curved tips. Fragrant.
PLANT FORM: Stocky. Broad, fleshy, spreading leaves. About 24–48″ high.
BLOOM SEASON: Early summer.
REGIONS: Gulf Coast, Lower Rio Grande Valley, Piney Woods, South Texas. Hardy in Zones 7–9.
LIGHT: Full sun to partial light or shade.

SOIL: Rich, well-drained. Deep and organic preferred. Acid to slightly alkaline.
MOISTURE: Ample during active growing season.
PROPAGATION: Abundant offsets.

'Ellen Bosanquet' is considered by many to be one of the best hybrid crinums in existence. One breeder considers it the product of a cross between *Crinum scabrum* and *C.* × 'J. C. Harvey.' It can be grown in pots.

❧ *Crinum* × *herbertii*
Milk-and-Wine Lilies

BLOOM: White with midribs pink to red; 3–4″ wide.
PLANT FORM: 36″ tall.
BLOOM SEASON: Late spring to fall.
REGIONS: All but Plains Country and Trans-Pecos. Hardy to Zone 7 with protection.
LIGHT: Full sun to partial shade.
SOIL: Rich, well-drained. Deep and organic preferred, any tolerated.
MOISTURE: Ample during active growth.
PROPAGATION: Division.

Five hybrids in this group are listed by southern specialty bulb growers. They are from *C. bulbispermum* × *C. scabrum.* The *C.* × *herbertii* clones are among the most common crinums grown in Texas. Many forms are found in the southern half of the state. They are among the "milk-and-wine lilies" of old days.

❧ *Crinum* × 'J. C. Harvey'

BLOOM: Coral pink, chalice-shaped. Fragrant and long-lasting.
PLANT FORM: 5′ tall.
BLOOM SEASON: Summer to fall.
REGIONS: Gulf Coast, Lower Rio Grande Valley, southern Piney Woods, South Texas. Hardy Zones 8b–9.
LIGHT: Full sun, partial shade, filtered light.
SOIL: Rich, well-drained. Deep and organic preferred.

MOISTURE: Ample during active growing season.
PROPAGATION: Offsets.

A very old hybrid of *Crinum zeylanicum* and *C. moorei,* 'J. C. Harvey' has large bulbs that may form ten or more offsets in a year.

❧ *Crinum moorei*

BLOOM: Flowers to 4″ wide, rose-red. Flower stalk to 5′ tall. White and pink cultivars also.
PLANT FORM: Leaves at least 3″ wide, straplike. Height to 5′.
BLOOM SEASON: Early to midsummer.
REGIONS: Gulf Coast, Lower Rio Grande Valley, southern Piney Woods, South Texas. Hardy to Zone 8b.
LIGHT: Partial shade or filtered light.
SOIL: Rich preferred. Well-drained.
MOISTURE: Ample, especially in early growing season.
PROPAGATION: Division, infrequently.

This is one of the most attractive of the crinum lilies. The flowers of one common pastel cultivar of *Crinum moorei,* for example, are broadly flaring like a classic daylily, rather than long and tubular, and the white petals are suffused with soft pink. Native to South Africa.

❧ *Crinum* × *powelli, C.* × *powelli* 'Album,' 'Cecil Houdyshel'

BLOOM: Pink, white.
PLANT FORM: Green, straplike leaves, to 36″ tall.
BLOOM SEASON: Spring to fall.
REGIONS: All but Trans-Pecos. To Zone 7 with winter protection.
LIGHT: Full sun or afternoon shade; 'Cecil Houdyshel' also accepts filtered light.
SOIL: Rich preferred, any tolerated.
MOISTURE: Ample while in active growth.
PROPAGATION: Division.

Crinum × *powelli* 'Album' may be the most commonly grown crinum in Texas, according to Thad

Howard, and is found in the United States wherever crinums are grown. Both color forms make good background plants. The original is a cross of *C. bulbispermum* and *C. moorei*.

'Cecil Houdyshel' is coral pink, a widely flaring, narrow-petaled star that blooms from spring to frost. It is 36″ tall. One of the first pink crinums, it is still highly valued.

℘ *Crinum zeylanicum*
Milk-and-Wine Lily

BLOOM: White trumpets with pink or purple lengthwise midribs and keels. Curved tube to 4″ long, spreading lobes to 8″ wide. Clusters of 10 to 20 blooms. "Milk-and-wine" form has purple keels.
PLANT FORM: Leaves about 4″ wide and 36″ long. To 24″ tall.
BLOOM SEASON: Late spring, early summer.
REGIONS: All but Plains Country and Trans-Pecos. Hardy to Zone 9, 8b with protection.
LIGHT: Full sun to partial light or shade.
SOIL: Rich preferred.
MOISTURE: Ample, especially in early growing season.
PROPAGATION: Division.

These fragrant, extremely lovely crinums are native to tropical Asia.

Montbretia
Crocosmia crocosmiflora

℘ *Crocosmia* × *crocosmiflora*
Montbretia
IRIDACEAE

BLOOM: Red-orange, tube to 1″ long, opening to 2″. Hybrids red-orange to yellow.
PLANT FORM: Long, narrow, swordlike green leaves, ¼–1″ wide, 24–48″ tall, arranged fanwise like gladioli.
BLOOM SEASON: Summer, for several months.
REGIONS: Edwards Plateau, Gulf Coast, Piney Woods, Prairies & Cross Timbers.
LIGHT: Full sun to partial shade. Must have several hours of sun a day to bloom well.
SOIL: Any well-drained, deeply prepared soil. Good drainage is a must, particularly on the Gulf Coast.
MOISTURE: Medium and high ranges. Tolerates drought but needs water during growing season to bloom.
PROPAGATION: Corms, offsets. Division in spring or fall. Spreads by stolons.

Crocosmia is named from the Greek *krokos,* "saffron," and *osme,* "a smell," for the saffron smell the dried flowers give off when soaked in warm water. This striking, slender garden plant is from South Africa. It originated in a cross of *C. aurea* and *C. potsii* that was made in 1800. 'Lucifer' is a fine fiery red variety.

Culture is the same as for gladioli. Corms can be planted at any time. Any that have a varnishlike coating of bacterial scab should be discarded. Plant healthy corms in a trench about 4 inches deep, adding a low-nitrogen fertilizer to the soil at the bottom. Cover the corms with 2 inches of soil, spacing them 3 to 6 inches apart. In areas that tend to be droughty in spring, soil on the poor side is best, because the ample water needed then to promote bloom may cause plants in rich soil to grow lax and weak.

Water well during the growing period, as soon as the bloom spike emerges from the ground. If the season is dry, soak the soil every third day until the first flowers open. Apply a complete fertilizer after the foliage appears. Crocosmia spreads quickly and multiplies rapidly, blocking weeds. It can be invasive in light soils but is easy to pull. The plants grow taller and bloom later in partial shade.

To control thrips, gardeners recommend any of three treatments. Dust the corms with Diazinon or a systemic insecticide before planting or soak them for three hours in a solution of 1¼ tablespoons of household disinfectant to a gallon of water. Follow up by spraying or dusting Diazinon on the plants, especially early in the growing season. In humid areas, gray mold may spot the leaves. Apply fungicide to control it.

African iris *Dietes vegeta*

✣ *Dietes vegeta*
African Iris, Fortnight Lily
IRIDACEAE

BLOOM: Creamy-colored irislike flowers with orange blotches on petals and purple-crested styles (styles are the slender stalks within the flowers that transmit pollen to the ovaries). 3″ wide on 48″ stalk.
PLANT FORM: Leaves basal, sword-shaped or narrow blades, like iris. 30–48″ tall. Evergreen in temperatures not below 20° F.
BLOOM SEASON: In Zone 9b, cycles of 2 weeks of bloom followed by 2 weeks of rest, for most of the year.
REGIONS: Gulf Coast, Lower Rio Grande Valley, southern Piney Woods, South Texas. Hardy only in Zone 9.
HEAT TOLERANCE: High, medium ranges.
LIGHT: Full sun to partial or light shade.
SOIL: Well-drained garden soil preferred.
MOISTURE: Performs best in low and medium ranges. Tolerates both drought, once established, and regular watering.
PROPAGATION: Division and seed, at any time.

African iris is one of the few irises that thrive in the Lower Rio Grande Valley and other Zone 9 regions. In Zone 9, accepts almost any growing situation but dense shade. In Zone 9b, it blooms almost all year, in cycles alternating two weeks' bloom with two weeks' rest, winning it the name "fortnight lily,"

although frost sometimes eliminates blooms in San Antonio. On the Gulf Coast, fall bloom is usual.

The taxonomy of genera *Dietes* and *Moraea* is confused. *Dietes vegeta,* once grouped in the genus *Moraea,* is sometimes found in the trade under the earlier name *M. iriodes.* Some published descriptions describe it as having yellow-and-blue markings, but, in fact, *D. vegeta* has orange blotches on the petals and purple-crested styles.

This plant is easily propagated. Fall and spring are the best planting times. Place the roots 1 inch deep. There is no dormancy. Do not remove the bloom stalks, as new blooms will rise on them. Divide plants when they become crowded.

✣ *Endymion hispanicus*
Spanish Bluebell
LILIACEAE

BLOOM: A spray of lavender-blue or white bells clustered along upright stems. Also mauve and pink forms.
PLANT FORM: Height 12–18″; narrow, straplike leaves.
BLOOM SEASON: Spring for several weeks.
REGIONS: Considered cold-hardy in Zones 4–10. Adapted to Edwards Plateau, Plains Country, southern Prairies & Cross Timbers, probably other Texas regions.

Spanish bluebell *Endymion hispanicus*

HEAT TOLERANCE: Low range preferred.
LIGHT: Half-day sun, filtered sun; full sun only in areas cooler than Texas.
SOIL: Well-drained, organic, acid to neutral preferred; accepts mildly alkaline.
MOISTURE: Water regularly beginning in fall, when growth starts, and continue during flowering. Reduce or stop watering in summer.
PROPAGATION: From bulblets that form around mother bulb, planted in fall. Cover with 1″ or more soil.

Spanish bluebell is lovely in informal drifts in the dappled shade of deciduous trees and of the edges of woods. A hyacinth relative, it resembles Dutch hyacinth but with a spray of bells rather than a tight head of blooms. Endymion is a true bulb native to the woodlands of western Europe and northern Africa. Bulbs can be left in the ground for years without division. High Plains and Edwards Plateau gardeners grow this hardy flower with ease and much pleasure.

Gladiolus byzantinus
Old-Fashioned Gladiolus, Baby Glad
IRIDACEAE

BLOOM: Magenta, white.
PLANT FORM: Typical gladiolus leaves, but smaller; height 12–36″.
BLOOM SEASON: Mid- or late spring to summer for about 3 weeks.
REGIONS: All but Edwards Plateau and Lower Rio Grande Valley.
LIGHT: Full sun to partial or light shade.
SOIL: Any well-drained. Will not tolerate wet clay.
MOISTURE: All ranges. Tolerates both drought and regular watering.
PROPAGATION: Corms, cormels produced around parent plant, division in fall.

This old garden flower repeats faithfully year after year. "Tops among the dainty and charming contingent (of gladioli)," one gardener calls it. Another says it is pretty in wild gardens or open woods or standing proudly in dark green shrubbery. It is a good mixer with other garden plants. "The best glad for the southern Blacklands," yet another gardener says. However, a South Plains grower considers it short-lived.

The stalks of rose-magenta bloom are smaller and more graceful than the florists' gladioli that fall over unless they are staked, and their form blends better in a mixed border. "Baby glads" may lean if they are

Baby glad *Gladiolus byzantinus* with yellow bearded irises

not staked, but those who grow them say that, nevertheless, it is better not to stake them. They naturalize along the Gulf Coast, in East Texas, and even in the black clays of parts of San Antonio. Like their gaudier cousins, they make excellent cut flowers.

These gladioli are propagated by carefully dividing the corms in fall. The swordlike foliage yellows after a freeze and may be cut back. For further details on culture, see *Crocosmia.*

The white form is reported to be somewhat less hardy than the magenta one. A single plant can multiply to thirty or forty by the end of the bloom season.

Many plants offered by this name are reportedly *Gladiolus illyricus,* hardy only in Zones 9–10. Others, in striking shades and combinations of white, pink, and red, are old bigeneric hybrids, *G.* × *colvillei,* often sold by the made-up name *G. nanus.* Gardeners who want perennials and live north of Zone 9 should avoid *G. illyricus* in favor of *G. byzantinus.* For fancy colors and bicolors, *G.* × *colvillei* varieties are advertised as hardy to -30° F. Stick to the solid magenta species, not the fancy bicolors in catalogs. Bloom spikes cut with one flower open have a vase life of a week or two.

❧ Habranthus

See *Zephyranthes*

❧ Hippeastrum

Amaryllis

AMARYLLIDACEAE

BLOOM: Trumpet-shaped. Red, red-and-white, pink, white, orange, yellow. Floral tube to 6″ long (hybrids to 9″), and trumpet as widely flared. Borne in umbels of 2–4 flowers.
PLANT FORM: Strap-shaped basal leaves to 36″ tall (hybrids to 48″). Clump-forming. Deciduous.
BLOOM SEASON: Mid- to late spring, for about 3 weeks.
REGIONS: All but Trans-Pecos. Most types need

Amaryllis
*Hippeastrum
johnsonii*

winter protection or deep planting in zones colder than 9.
LIGHT: Full sun to afternoon shade or light shade.
SOIL: Mixed fibrous loam, leaf mold, and sand best. Alkaline to slightly acid.
MOISTURE: Water frequently during growing season, from winter until foliage withers. Do not overwater. Do not water after foliage withers.
PROPAGATION: Seed; plants reach blooming size in about 2 years. Bulb offsets in fall.

The hippeastrums are native mostly to tropical America; one species comes from West Africa. Nearly all the amaryllis in the trade these days are complex hybrids of six or more species that are produced in Holland. Hundreds of thousands are sold in fall each year, potted up and ready to bloom indoors during the winter holidays. The amaryllis that come up in yards in Texas are smaller, older, and simpler hybrids that are much hardier than the windowsill beauties.

One well-known old garden amaryllis is bright-red *Hippeastrum* × *johnsonii,* a hybrid of the species *H. vittatum* and *H. reginae.* Red-and-white striped *H. vittatum* is still occasionally found in gardens. These old amaryllis are most likely to come to you as gifts from old-time gardeners or from specialty mail-order houses. Although the blooms are smaller, they are produced much more prolifically than those of the newer hybrids.

These amaryllis should be planted in fall, at a depth below the frost line. A Lubbock gardener reports reliable May or June bloom from both species and from hybrid amaryllises planted 9–10 inches deep (note that Lubbock's sandy soil is better aerated than other soil types). The plants are best grown as summer-dormant bulbs in beds mounded higher than the surrounding soil. Water them during the growing season, starting in winter, when the roots begin to grow. Let the plants dry out in summer. When the blooms are spent, cut off the bloom stalk. Winter gift plants can be planted in the garden for a possible second bloom season. Apply snail bait when needed and watch out for mealybugs, thrips, and mites.

Spider lily
Hymenocallis liriosme.
Photo by Thad Howard.

❧ *Hymenocallis*
Spider Lilies
AMARYLLIDACEAE

BLOOM: White or yellow; large, with long, narrow, recurved petals. Fragrant.
PLANT FORM: 12–48″ tall, depending on species. Green, strap-shaped leaves. Evergreen and deciduous types.
BLOOM SEASON: Late spring or summer.
REGIONS: Varies with species; most are reliably hardy only in Zone 9.
LIGHT: Full sun, half-day shade, partial shade.
SOIL: Well-drained, except for *H. liriosme*. Rich, acid to neutral generally preferred. *H. galvestonensis* must have acid soil.
MOISTURE: Medium and high ranges, generally. Moderate to heavy watering during growing season. In Texas, *H. liriosme* is best grown as an aquatic plant.
PROPAGATION: Bulbs, offsets, seeds, depending on species. Offsets need not be separated from the mother plant.

There are many species of *Hymenocallis,* fifteen to twenty in the southeastern United States alone. Two are native to Texas. *H. liriosme* is a swamp-dweller that is best for aquatic culture in most of Texas. It is hardy statewide, to 0° F. "Common as pig tracks," one gardener calls it. *H. galvestonensis* is an uncommon native woodland plant, lovely and difficult to grow. It must have acid soil and is "not for beginners, and not for casual gardeners, except for those who live in East Texas," says an expert, in defense of both its rarity and its difficulty.

Several other spider lilies are more popular and easily grown. *H. × festalis* is a beautiful flower with a large white central crown with frilled edges and long, thin cream-colored outer petals that curve backward. The blooms are borne several to a stem.

H. narcissiflora and *H. n.* 'Sulphur Queen' are called Peruvian daffodil for their narcissus-like crowns. The large, fragrant flowers with funnel-shaped crowns and fringed lobes appear in umbels. 'Sulphur Queen' is yellow with a green throat. 'Advance' is a widely sold variety reportedly to be avoided because it often aborts its buds.

"The best for Texas," bulb specialist Thad Howard calls *H. × festalis* and *H. narcissiflora*. "They thrive with us and are permanent . . . everyone ought to grow both." Both are widely available.

The spectacular 'Tropical Giant' is perhaps the most commonly grown spider lily in the Gulf states. It is large-flowered, with leaves that sometimes reach 4 feet in height. 'Tropical Giant' is a botanical enigma whose identity was yet to be unraveled at the time of writing.

The true bulbs of hymenocallis are best planted 4 to 6 inches deep, according to Texas gardeners.

Ipheion uniflorum
Spring Starflower
AMARYLLIDACEAE

BLOOM: Solitary star-shaped flowers, 1″. Species pale blue or white tinged with blue, with bright orange stamens. Cultivar 'Wisley Blue' is dark blue.
PLANT FORM: Bluish-green grasslike leaves that appear in fall, 5–8″ tall.
BLOOM SEASON: Spring for a long period.
REGIONS: All.
LIGHT: Half-day sun to light shade.
SOIL: Garden loam or sandy soil preferred. Tolerates any well-drained soil, accepts alkalinity well.
MOISTURE: All ranges. Water during the active growing season; withhold water during summer dormancy. Drought-tolerant.
PROPAGATION: Seeds and offsets. Plant 4–5″ deep or below frost level.

Spring starflower *Ipheion uniflorum*

The dainty appearance of this South American native belies its toughness. Its summer dormant period makes it adaptable to hot, dry southwestern summers. It spreads, where adapted. The flowers appear on 5–8-inch stems above the grassy foliage, which has an onionlike odor when crushed. The bulbs should be planted close together for the best effect when the flowers are in bloom.

Ipheion reportedly tends to die out in the Blacklands if it gets summer rain. Raised beds help. It is excellent for growing in containers brought indoors in winter; containerized plants bloom about a month before those planted in the ground. It is well suited to rock gardens, between stepstones, and as edging.

'Wisley Blue' is a dark-blue selection discovered growing among paler *Ipheion* in the National Trust gardens at Wisley outside London.

Iris
Irises
IRIDACEAE

There is something regal about irises, familiar though the common kinds may be. They are mostly tall and stately, with swordlike foliage and elegant flowers held high on straight, strong stalks. The iris was the *fleur de lys* of French heraldry, adopted by King Louis VII as his emblem during the Crusades, and later to become the symbol of the French monarchy. The blooms are crisp and precisely shaped, while at the same time as translucent and delicately veined as a butterfly's wing. The familiar "bearded iris" displays three petals arched upward like a coronet (the "standards") and three gracefully sweeping downward (the "falls"). Other irises bloom in shapes from spidery and slender to flat cartwheels the size of salad plates. They are as elegant as orchids, and their colors, with this century's popularization of the many-hued Louisiana iris hybrids, are as various as a rainbow.

Experimentation with the many iris groups in different locales continues. There are irises for the varied regions of Texas, New Mexico, Oklahoma, Arkansas, and Louisiana and the other Gulf Coast states—for the entire United States, in fact. Various types have been grown sufficiently widely in eight regions of the above-mentioned states to indicate at least one iris group that succeeds in each.

Irises include two hundred or more species of hardy perennials. They fall into two main divisions, those with rhizomatous root stalks and those that grow from bulbs. For perennializing in the Deep and Mid-South and the Southwest, those that grow from rhizomes are of primary concern.

Of the rhizomatous irises, there are two main groups. The first is "bearded" irises, named for the line of short hairs down the center of each fall, often in a contrasting color. They are native to the Old World, from Portugal and Morocco across southern and central Europe all the way to western China. Among the bearded irises are the arilbreds, hybrids obtained from crossing other bearded irises with the aril iris native to arid Eurasia.

The second group is the beardless irises, which include a great number of species in a wide variety of forms. There are subgroups of interest, as well.

All are striking, dramatic plants, many attractive for their foliage as well as their blooms. They are effective in mass plantings, in clumps among flowers of similar culture, and, depending on the species, as water garden and rock garden plants.

The best bearded irises for Texas are "German" bearded and arilbred, depending on the locale. Of the beardless irises, Louisianas and spurias are the best rhizomatous ones, and Dutch iris are the best grown from true bulbs. Gardeners who seek a challenge may also want to try two species of beardless iris that are not well adapted here but may be grown if certain varieties or special techniques are used: the Siberian iris, *I. sibirica,* and the Japanese iris, *I. kaempferi.* Many others available commercially are not at all suited for Texas; *I. cristata, I. ensata,* and *I. tectorum* are a few. Those presented are the irises that are successfully grown in Texas and available.

❧ Arilbred Iris (Persian Iris)

BLOOM: Very large upright petals. Unusual markings and colors, such as blues, purples, greens.
PLANT FORM: 12–16″.
BLOOM SEASON: Mid-spring; earlier than tall bearded iris.
REGIONS: Edwards Plateau, South Texas, Trans-Pecos. Hardy to Zone 8.
LIGHT: Full sun.
SOIL: Well-drained, light, rich. Neutral to alkaline.
MOISTURE: Low, medium annual moisture. Moderate watering; reduce or withhold water during the midsummer dormant period.
PROPAGATION: Division in late summer or early fall.

Arilbred irises are the result of crosses between aril iris, native to eastern Europe and Asia, and other bearded irises. Arilbreds have great tolerance for summer heat and drought, promising success in gardens in the hot, dry regions of Texas and parts of New Mexico. Limited reports from the Edwards Plateau, Trans-Pecos, and South Texas rate their performance there as good to excellent. One Dallas gardener has grown them in raised beds of pure sand by covering them with plastic to keep summer rain off.

❧ "German" Bearded Iris

BLOOM: Every color but true red.
PLANT FORM: Clumps of sword-shaped blades. Grouped in classes ranging from 6″ to 48″ in height.
BLOOM SEASON: 2–3 weeks per variety, during period from late February through May. Some rebloom in fall.
REGIONS: Edwards Plateau, Piney Woods, Plains Country, Prairies & Cross Timbers, Trans-Pecos. Not the Gulf Coast, except with special culture, nor the Lower Rio Grande Valley and most of South Texas. Zones 6 to northern 8b.
LIGHT: Full sun.
SOIL: Well-drained. Neutral to slightly alkaline best; tolerates pH range 6–9. Well-tilled with ample humus and fertilizer preferred, but tolerates poor soil.

Bearded iris

MOISTURE: Low, medium ranges. Prefers moderate soil moisture; drought-tolerant. Low humidity best.
PROPAGATION: Rhizomes take 2 years after planting to bloom well. Divide every 3 years for best continued bloom.

Tall bearded irises are sometimes called "German bearded iris," due to their superficial resemblance to the oldest known iris in cultivation, *Iris × germanica*. In fact, tall bearded irises have a complex hybrid ancestry and no recognized Latin name. "Bearded iris" is an even more common appellation for this group, even though other irises with beards are in cultivation. The true *I. germanica* has a white variant called *I. florentina*, whose dried roots have for centuries been ground to provide a violet-scented powder used in perfumery.

Even today, two of the earliest common bearded irises survive untended in old cemeteries and abandoned homesites, as they did for centuries in Europe. The earlier, which blooms as early as March or even late February after a warm winter, is often called "cemetery white." It is pure white and scented, like the fragrant Florentine iris of yore, but whether the two are truly the same is difficult to say. The deep purple iris that blooms soon afterward is called "early purple."

"Bearded" irises are divided into six classes, by height. Those 27 inches tall and taller are "tall bearded." The "median" irises include the classes "miniature tall," "border," "intermediate," "standard dwarf," and "miniature dwarf," which range in height from 26 to 6 inches. ("Dwarf" refers to the plant height, and "miniature" to the flower size. Thus it is possible to have a tall, small-bloomed iris, or a short, comparatively large-bloomed one.) There is a bearded iris of the proper scale and color for almost any situation.

These irises require some frost. They don't "do" in the semi-tropical Lower Rio Grande Valley, with its almost year-round growth season. There, *Dietes vegeta* or African iris is the iris of choice. Arilbred irises also have potential there, although they are little known at present.

Bearded irises are not recommended for the humid Gulf Coast area, although they are sometimes seen growing abandoned in old fencerows, where they stay dry. For the Gulf Coast, Louisiana irises are far easier and more rewarding to grow.

Culture for all "German bearded" irises is the same. Recommended planting time is July through October; October is best where late summer is very hot. Rhizomes dug in midsummer can be held in a cool, dry place for weeks before planting. These irises like their rhizomes barely covered with soil or even exposed. By forming a mound of soil in the center of the planting hole, one can situate the rhizome high and spread the roots over the mound and downward. The roots should be planted as deep as they will reach. Well-tilled, composted soil is then filled in, watered, and allowed to settle. One or two feet is a good compromise spacing for both growing space and dense color. The leaves of transplanted irises should be trimmed to about 6–8 inches; those left undivided in the beds should not be cut back.

Bearded irises will survive without summer watering, but those watered faithfully will brown only on the leaf tips, rather than yellowing all over. Cutting back the foliage, which produces the plant's food for the next year's growth, is to be avoided.

Every two or three years, the clumps should be dug and the old, center rhizomes disposed of. Healthier outer rhizomes are then replanted.

Irises do well with other perennials that have similar cultural requirements and in beds of their own.

Bearded irises have big appetites. Besides low-nitrogen fertilizer tilled into new beds, a side-dressing of superphosphate in late February or early March will encourage continued growth and bloom. For established plantings, an application of 6-10-6 after bloom or in early fall is recommended.

The common disease of irises in Texas is bacterial soft rot. Recommended treatment is to dig the affected plants, remove the soft spots, and expose the rhizomes to the sun for several days. Some gardeners find an application of sulfur powder or household cleaning powder with chlorine, prior to sun exposure, is helpful. Scorch is another disease. There is no known cure; affected irises should be destroyed. Snail bait will control slugs and snails. Good cultural practices, as follow, will prevent most diseases:

(1) Keep dead foliage removed.

(2) Clean beds of weeds and leaves.

(3) Water on the soil rather than aerially.

(4) Discard old or diseased rhizomes.

Median iris dwarf types begin bloom as early as February in North Central Texas, followed by the intermediates and border bearded (next in height to the tall bearded). These are followed by the tall and miniature-flowered tall bearded iris in about mid-April. A selection of types and varieties can provide two months of bloom.

Reblooming irises are found mostly among the tall bearded irises. These are special varieties that complete two growth cycles in one year. They require more fertilizer and water to rebloom.

✤ *Iris kaempferi*
Japanese Iris

BLOOM: White, blue, lavender, purple, pink, some bicolored and veined; flat and up to 10″ in diameter.
PLANT FORM: Green, swordlike leaves. Bloom stalks to 24″.
BLOOM SEASON: Very late spring.
REGIONS: To date, grown well in Texas only in seasonal aquaculture in northern Prairies & Cross Timbers; also grown with limited success in the Gulf Coast, Piney Woods, and Trans-Pecos. For collectors.
HEAT TOLERANCE: All ranges with special culture; prefers low.
LIGHT: Half-day to filtered sun.
SOIL: Garden loam, sandy soils. Acid. Clay substratum helpful to retain water.
MOISTURE: Grows in all ranges with ample irrigation or immersion in spring and summer, moderate to dry conditions in fall and winter.
PROPAGATION: Rhizomes. Resents division.

Despite the frustrations of growing this plant not well suited to the Southwest, gardeners here try Japanese iris because of its gorgeous flat blooms, some as big as pie pans. Japanese irises require culture similar to that for Siberian and Louisiana irises. They will grow in shallow ponds filled with water in spring and summer and drained in fall and winter. As with Siberian iris, division is not recommended. Japanese iris should be accepted from mail-order suppliers only in the fall, gardeners caution, because spring arrivals will die from the heat of their first summer. It can take several years for a planting to bloom. Winter cold may burn the leaves, but does not seem to affect flowering.

The names *Iris kaempferi* and *I. ensata* are often used interchangeably, but are in fact distinct. *I. kaempferi* is the true Japanese iris native to that country only; the broader range of *I. ensata* includes Japan, Korea, China, and central Asia.

✿ Louisiana Iris

BLOOM: Every color, including pinks and rust reds.
PLANT FORM: Green, swordlike leaves. Height 1–6′.
BLOOM SEASON: A range of early- and late-blooming varieties can provide 2–4 weeks of spring bloom in March to May, depending upon the region.
REGIONS: All, with regionally specific culture.
LIGHT: Full sun. Filtered light or afternoon shade preferred in hot areas in summer.
SOIL: Fertile, moist to wet. Acid; pH 6.5 or lower preferred. Tolerates high-lime alkaline soil if it is amended. Clay base is helpful to retain water.
MOISTURE: High annual rainfall and/or watering. Grows well in shallow water. Tolerates drought after bloom cycle, but this impairs subsequent season's growth and bloom.
PROPAGATION: Division, seed.

The Louisiana irises derive from five species of beardless irises native to the swamps of South Louisiana, where they spread and interbred for centuries unknown to the outside world. The early French trappers and traders there called them "*les gles de marais*," or "the glads of the marsh." Some of these irises occur far north up the Mississippi Valley, and others extend their range along the Gulf Coast. Only in Louisiana are all the species found growing wild. *Iris hexagona,* discovered by the European botanical world in 1788, is deep ultramarine blue to violet-purple. *I. fulva* brought tawny red into the iris world. Dwarf, pale-to-deep-blue *I. brevicaulis* was described in 1817 and proved to be the most cold-hardy and latest-blooming of the species. *I. giganticaerulea,* the immense sky blue iris of the coastal marshes, was put on record only in 1929. The bright reds, purples, and rare yellow-browns admired as "Abbeville reds" and "Abbeville yellows" since the 1930s were identified in 1966 as the fifth Louisiana iris species, *I. nelsonii.*

Louisiana iris hybrids

Interbreeding in nature and controlled hybridization have produced from this natural diversity a seemingly limitless range of colors and flowers as large as 7 inches in diameter. The flower forms of the hybrids range from the spidery, elongated petals of blue-black 'Black Widow' to the almost circular shape of irises such as 'Creole Raspberry.'

Louisiana irises need acid soil, fertilizer, and water. However, they are not so sensitive to alkali that they cannot be grown in areas such as El Paso, if the soil is amended with humus and agricultural sulfur. They have been grown successfully—in shallow water— even in lime soils as alkaline as pH 7.9, and they are quite cheerful in the black clay of the Blacklands.

Although sunlight is necessary for bloom, in really hot areas the blossoms of most varieties hold up better where they get afternoon shade.

Louisianas are heavy feeders and need regular fertilizing in amounts sufficient to maintain an abundance of foliage.

Planting is best done in fall; most dealers will not ship before September because shipping during spring and summer heat stresses the rhizomes. Bare rhizomes must be kept wet while out of the soil. Shipped rhizomes must be planted at once or removed from their plastic wrappings and kept in water until planting.

A well-tilled, compost-rich soil is best for Louisiana irises; a clay substratum helps hold in adequate moisture. If the soil is alkaline, addition of soil sulfur and an acidifying fertilizer when preparing the bed is recommended. Compost or peat moss and manure or commercial fertilizer should be added, also. Plant the rhizome just under or level with the top of the soil, as for bearded irises.

In addition to soil amendment at planting time, old plantings should be fertilized in fall. All plantings benefit from an application of azalea-camellia fertilizer or water-soluble fertilizer in early March and just after bloom.

Mulch in summer protects the rhizome from sun scorch, which can prevent bloom the following season and even kill plants.

Table 4. Marie Caillet's Louisiana Iris Sampler

'Acadian Miss'	Ruffled white, very vigorous.
'Ann Chowning'	Bright red-orange with yellow markings.
'Colorific'	White and lavender-pink bicolor.
'Crisp Lime'	Tall, ruffled white with lime flush.
'Delta Star'	Tall, blue-purple cartwheel blooms with yellow markings.
'Dixie Deb'	Tall, early-blooming small-flowered yellow. Graceful cut flower. Vigorous.
'Freddie Boy'	Large-flowered American Beauty red.
'Full Eclipse'	Dramatic dark violet, almost black.
'Gulf Shores'	Medium height ruffled blue. Excellent increase.
'Marie Caillet'	Tall, late-blooming blue-violet.
'President Hedley'	Very large-flowered bright gold.
'Professor Ike'	Large red-violet with excellent petal substance.

Removal of the spent bloom stalks prevents growing seedpods from sapping the strength of the plant. Seedpods can be left and collected in July or August, but seedlings will not usually be true to the mother plant.

On the Gulf Coast, Louisiana irises bloom from mid- to late March. Soil pH 6.5 or lower is preferred. Marshy areas are ideal sites.

Texas Panhandle growers warn that Louisiana iris must never be allowed to dry out, especially in summer after the bloom period ends. Bloom there starts in mid-May. Morning sun and afternoon shade are recommended. A windbreak is also desirable to protect the stalks and blooms. Prepare an acid bed at least two weeks before planting, by removing sub-surface clay and adding superphosphate, soil sulfur, and cottonseed hulls and meal to the topsoil.

North Central Texas gardeners water Louisiana irises faithfully, especially from July to late September or October and before freezes in dry winters and in earliest spring. Some afternoon shade in summer is recommended. Typical bloom season is late March or early April, one or two weeks after the tall bearded irises. With a range of varieties, a bloom season of a month can be obtained. Summer mulch can remain throughout the year.

Experimentation with water culture in alkaline soils of Central Texas, as reported by Kirk Strawn of College Station, has shown that aquatic culture of Louisiana irises is successful in high lime soils as alkaline as pH 7.6 to 7.9. The optimal water level appears to be 1 inch; water as deep as 3 inches re-tards increase of the plants. Water culture in alkaline soils with minerals other than limestone has yet to be tested. Incorporation of acid bed materials such as manure, leaf mold, peat moss, and grass clippings prior to planting and flooding the beds is desirable. Strawn hazards that success at higher pH than 7.0 will be highly variable according to variety. Late March to the end of May is the usual bloom season in this region, with a range of early-, mid-, and late-season varieties. Some bloom again in November or December.

Louisiana irises grown in the Trans-Pecos around El Paso must never dry out, gardeners say. They require deep watering each week of the growing season and twice weekly in summer. An open, shaded location facing north is best, preferably with a half-day of morning sun. Disyston applied once a year in February or early March controls aphids. The usual bloom season is mid- to late April or early May.

Louisiana irises are happy in beds of their own. They can also be used in perennial borders, wood-land gardens, water gardens, and rock gardens. Day-lilies, with their preference for acid soil and ade-quate moisture and their longer bloom season, are good companion plants for Louisiana irises in all

Table 5. Carl Schoenfeld's Pick of Louisiana Irises for Near the Gulf Coast

'Crisp Lime'	Cool white with lime, blooming after Siberian irises, 24″ tall, sun-proof.
'Bajazzo'	Near-black red-purple, cartwheel form, 30–36″, shade-loving.
'Delta Dude'	Fuchsia with yellow, blooms after Siberian iris, 24–30″, needs afternoon shade or colors fade.
'Rue Royale'	Yellow, blooms after Siberian iris, 30–36″. Takes full sun without fading.

situations but water gardens. Their foliage comfort-ably shades the iris rhizomes, as well. Native *Phlox divaricata* is a good companion plant for spring. So are coreopsis and annual *Papaver rhoeas,* the Shirley poppy, which blooms from the middle of April to May. In midsummer, airy, shallow-rooted annuals such as cosmos can fill in.

Table 4 lists a few choice Louisiana iris hybrids recommended by iris aficionado Marie Caillet for heavy bloom, prolific multiplication, and a range of heights and colors. They withstand the high sum-mer heat and 10° F average winter lows of her North Central Texas home. A longtime grower and hybrid-izer of Louisiana irises, Caillet co-edited *The Louisiana Iris.* Since the 1930s she has helped preserve the wild Louisiana irises in their native marshes. She is a founding member of the Society for Louisiana Irises.

Table 5 is a short list of gardener Carl Schoen-feld's personal favorites, chosen for their beauty, unusual colorations, and ability to withstand the heat and humidity inland from the Gulf in the southern Post Oak country. One of these, 'Crisp Lime,' also appears on Marie Caillet's list.

Iris pseudacorus
Yellow Flag, Water Iris

BLOOM: Cream to yellow.
PLANT FORM: Strap-shaped evergreen leaves; height 4–6′. Double form 'Flora-Plena.'
BLOOM SEASON: Spring.
REGIONS: Native to Gulf Coast and boggy sections of Piney Woods. Also grown in Edwards Plateau, Prairies & Cross Timbers, and South Texas.
LIGHT: Full sun to half-day shade or filtered light; the drier the air and stronger the sunlight, the more shade in less humid areas with stronger sunlight.
SOIL: Acid; pH 6.5 or lower. Fertile. Clay base helpful to retain water.
MOISTURE: Grows in high moisture areas, adaptable to moderate and dry with ample watering. Grows well in shallow water. Tolerates drought after bloom cycle, but subsequent growth and bloom are reduced.
PROPAGATION: Division.

This bog plant of the British Isles and Europe is the iris that became the *fleur de lys,* the national symbol of France. During the Crusades, King Louis VII adopted the flower as his personal emblem; its French name meant the "flower of Louis." In time it came to represent the French monarchy. This beardless iris is closely related to, but not one of, the five species referred to as "Louisiana irises." Naturalized in the southern United States, it frequently fills moist ditches along Gulf Coast roads and in the Piney Woods. Favorite sites are bogs and the sides of rivers and canals. The foliage is tall and very handsome. Unfortunately, "95 percent foliage and 5 percent bloom" is the description many gardeners give it. Its very vigorous growth and freedom from known pests or diseases make it too invasive for small areas; it should be segregated from other plants. For a lake shore or bog, it is useful—but Louisiana irises will grow in the same situation and produce more blooms.

Cultivars are widely grown in Germany, and these flower more profusely than the species. They are not widely available in the United States, although one variety, 'Flora-Plena,' is in the U.S.

trade. This is a double form, described as long-blooming, much showier than the species, and only 3 feet tall.

The yellow iris often offered with Japanese iris as a yellow *I. kaempferi* is in fact a hybrid *I. pseudacorus* that is more compact and floriferous than the species and easier to grow than *I. kaempferi.*

Culture for *Iris pseudacorus* is identical to that for Louisiana iris.

Iris sibirica
Siberian Iris

BLOOM: Many; cultivars adapted here are deep purple 'Caesar's Brother' and light blue, white, and yellow 'Summer Skies.' Many blooms, up to 4″ across, with multiple flowering stalks per plant and several blooms on each stalk.
PLANT FORM: Clump-forming, 24–42″ tall, with narrow leaves.
BLOOM SEASON: Early or late spring, depending on variety, for about 3 weeks.
REGIONS: Piney Woods, Prairies & Cross Timbers, northern South Texas. 'Caesar's Brother' grows in the High Plains as well.
HEAT TOLERANCE: All ranges, but best in low heat, cold winters.
LIGHT: Filtered light to full shade; full sun in cool climates with low humidity.
SOIL: Loose, well-drained, acid to neutral. Accepts slightly alkaline soil, if amended.
MOISTURE: Moist. Water during dry spells.
PROPAGATION: Infrequent division; 'Caesar's Brother' also from seed.

Noted North Carolina gardener Elizabeth Lawrence wrote that *Iris sibirica* 'Caesar's Brother' "endures and increases" and praised it for its deep violet color. This late spring bloomer and another old garden cultivar, early-blooming pale blue, white, and yellow 'Summer Skies,' are so far the only Siberian irises reported to thrive in Texas. Despite the species' general distaste for humidity, 'Summer Skies' does thrive 60 miles inland from the upper Gulf, in shade.

Understandably, irises native to Siberia are accustomed to conditions rather different from those in the Southwest. In the Midwest and northern United States, they are reportedly the easiest irises to grow. There, they prefer sun, cool weather, well-drained, slightly acid soils, and low humidity. They can succeed in parts of Texas if planted 2 inches deep in acid beds, mulched summer, and watered during dry spells. Some, such as 'Summer Skies,' resent being divided. Culture is similar to that for Louisiana irises, but Siberians, like Japanese irises, can take several years to become established here.

Dallas gardener Bob Wilson says that his clump of 'Caesar's Brother' put out eighteen bloom spikes with five flowers on each in its third year. It then followed this display with showy seedpods that were bronzy-brown by the end of summer and red in fall and winter. The seedpods did not sap the strength of the plant, as is the case with many species. 'Caesar's Brother' is reported to be the only *I. sibirica* hybrid that succeeds in the southern Blacklands.

✿ *Iris spuria*
Spuria Iris

BLOOM: All common iris hues, plus browns and tans.

PLANT FORM: 3–6′.

BLOOM SEASON: Late spring, 3 weeks to a month, beginning after bearded irises.

REGIONS: All but Plains Country and Lower Rio Grande Valley.

LIGHT: Full sun to light shade.

SOIL: Accepts any, according to some gardeners; others insist on neutral to slightly alkaline, well-drained.

MOISTURE: All ranges. Water regularly in winter, during active growth. Reduce or stop watering during summer dormancy, say some gardeners; others, in southern Blacklands, say needs summer moisture. Can be allowed to dry out between waterings in fall and spring.

PROPAGATION: Division in fall.

Spuria iris *Iris spuria* 'Barbara's Kiss.' Photo © Carl Schoenfeld.

Spuria irises are excellent for most of Texas. They are lime lovers, like bearded irises, but will thrive in moist and often acid Gulf Coast soils where bearded irises do poorly. Reportedly, they tolerate salt. They like considerable heat and sun, then avoid the worst of both by going dormant in summer. A Dallas gardener considers spurias the best irises for North Texas, for their heat tolerance and because they "like to be left alone." Spurias are also considered among the best irises for cutting, because their blooms remain two or three days and because buds showing color when picked will open. Their foliage remains green all winter. Another advantage of spurias is their ability to withstand high winds.

Their main cultural requirements are full sun to light shade, good drainage, and little or no moisture in late summer, as noted. Water applied in the late-summer dormant period rots the rhizomes. Poor drainage or too much moisture at any time may result in rotting of the rhizomes, caused by mustard-seed fungus. Spurias should be planted in fall, with care to keep the hairy roots on their rhizomes damp when they are dug and divided. The rhizomes are placed 1–2 inches under the soil and kept well watered until growth begins.

Spuria irises, like most irises, are heavy feeders. Fertilizer in fall when the new growth begins is very beneficial.

The foliage of spurias may be cut back. Another attractive feature of this plant is its enthusiastic response to neglect; division is not necessary for as many as ten to fifteen years.

There are few disease and insect problems with spurias. Aphids may be attracted by the sticky nectar in the flowers. Mustard-seed fungus can be deterred by improved drainage and application of fungicide when preparing the bed.

Var. *ochroleuca* is a natural variety of *I. spuria* that is often used to hybridize modern spurias. Its white flowers with a large yellow spot on each fall are often seen growing in abandoned farmyards. During years of neglect, they simply continue to multiply and bloom—although not as well as they would with fertilizer and water.

Burgundy, mauve, and yellow 'Barbara's Kiss' and 'Dress Circle,' blue-violet with gold falls, are two beautiful spuria varieties.

Dutch iris
Iris × xiphium hybrid

❦ *Iris × xiphium*
Dutch iris

BLOOM: Blue, yellow, white, gold, purple, violet, bronze, and bicolor, to 4″ across.
PLANT FORM: Bloom stalks 16–20″ with slightly shorter, slender green leaves.
BLOOM SEASON: Mid- to late spring for 2–3 weeks, generally, but some varieties bloom with the early daffodils.
REGIONS: All, to -10° F (Zone 6a).
LIGHT: Full sun during growth season.
SOIL: Loose, well-drained garden soil. Wide pH range.
MOISTURE: Ample during active growth; stop or reduce watering after foliage withers.
PROPAGATION: Separation of bulbs.

"Dutch irises" were hybridized in Holland from species of North Africa, Spain, and southern France. *Iris xiphium,* the Spanish iris native to southern Europe and Morocco, was important in their parentage.

"*The* iris for Texas," one bulb expert calls them. They are true bulbs. As is characteristic of bulbous plants from arid regions, they go dormant in summer, and their foliage dies back. The blooms resemble bearded iris somewhat, but with narrower standards that are more widely spread and shorter falls with no "beard."

Dutch irises are most effective planted in a group. They disappear from sight in late summer when the foliage dies back. Containers are also good places for Dutch iris.

❦ *Leucojum*
Snowflake
AMARYLLIDACEAE

BLOOM: White pendant 1–1½″ bells, singly or in pairs or clusters.
PLANT FORM: Low, grassy foliage, clump-forming, 6–15″ tall, depending on species. Leaves disappear completely in winter.
BLOOM SEASON: Early or mid-spring, depending on species.
REGIONS: Edwards Plateau, Piney Woods, Plains Country, Prairies & Cross Timbers; *L. aestivum,* also Gulf Coast, northern South Texas, Trans-Pecos.
HEAT TOLERANCE: All ranges. *L. vernum* prefers a cool situation.
LIGHT: Full sun, with moisture, to full shade.
SOIL: Well-drained, sandy, humus-rich best for *L. aestivum;* tolerates any. Moist preferred for *L. vernum.*

MOISTURE: Grows in all ranges. Moist preferred, but *L. aestivum* tolerates drought in shade.
PROPAGATION: By separating offsets once the leaves wither, indicating dormancy. Division.

Spring snowflake, *Leucojum vernum,* was no stranger to old-time southern gardens. It put up its little white bells in earliest spring, from late January to early March, depending on the temperatures, and it lasted until early April. Then its larger cousin, summer snowflake, or *L. aestivum,* began. Elizabeth Lawrence, the well-known chronicler of Southern gardening who gardened for many years in Charlotte, North Carolina, called summer snowflake "much handsomer" for its longer, thicker leaves and clusters of three to seven flowers on each stem, rather than only two. She noted, however, that one would want both types for a longer season of bloom, and that one way to get both would be to order *L. vernum* from several sources. Few nurseries then listed *L. aestivum,* but they often supplied it by the name of the rarer *L. vernum.* Now it appears that *L. vernum* is mostly gone from the trade, and that whatever you order, *L. aestivum* is what you are likely to get. Some horticulturists report that *L. vernum* grows in the Houston and Baton Rouge areas; others say it is not for areas south of Dallas. I have photographed it in Minnie Colquitt's woodland garden outside Shreveport. I suspect that reports of it from the Edwards Plateau and the Plains Country may in fact pertain to *L. aestivum.* Since it is hard to come by and unsuited for the really hot parts of the state, it may be of little present interest west of the Piney Woods.

The little white bells, with a dot of green at each petal tip, are the essence of freshness. The slender, arching green foliage slightly resembles that of lilyturf or grass. *L. aestivum* 'Gravetye Giant' reportedly has flowers twice as large as the species and does well even in San Antonio.

L. aestivum prefers humus-rich, sandy, moist but well-drained soil to perform at its best, but will grow "anywhere," judging from Lawrence's reports and from personal observation. It grows in shade,

Spring snowflake
Leucojum vernum

semi-shade, or full sun, as long as the soil is moist. This preference for moisture makes snowflakes ideal for modern sprinklered beds in which most spring bulbs would rot.

The small bulbs are planted in fall, 4 to 5 inches deep and 4 inches apart. They are rapid increasers and can be propagated by separating the offsets that develop around the bulbs once the leaves wither and the plants are dormant. In winter they disappear completely.

The botanical name·*Leucojum* comes from the Greek for "white violet," and they do indeed have a sweet violet scent.

Lilium
Lilies
LILIACEAE

See Chart 2 for summary of regions, zones, and cultural conditions.

Lilies are among the oldest known cultivated flowers. White *Lilium candidum* appears on Cretan frescoes of 2000 B.C. Among the first flowers cherished in European gardens, the white lily was the only flower as celebrated as the rose; in

Shakespeare's writings it appears sixty-eight times. The Madonna lily, *L. candidum,* is the white lily to which he is believed to have referred. It is traditionally held to have been brought into England from the Middle East in the 1100s, during the Crusades. However, representations of it in English art date back as early as the tenth century. A symbol of purity, it became an emblem for the Virgin Mary. The Madonna lily came to be a standby of the cottage garden.

Many lilies are fragrant. Many are long-lived as cut flowers. Tall and stately in the garden, they provide color in late spring, summer, and fall when the early profusion of spring bloom has subsided.

Why, then, are true lilies so little used in southwestern gardens? Only the "daylily"—a misnomer for this flower with an enlarged root that is not a true lily at all—is widespread in Texas and adjoining states. This is probably because daylilies are more forgiving than the exacting true lilies. However, with attention to excellent drainage and to each species' individual preference for acid or alkaline soil and light requirements, lilies can be a part of most gardens. The necessary care is well rewarded because nothing is more elegant in the garden or in bouquets.

The most problematic areas of Texas for lilies are the hot, humid Gulf Coast, scorching South Texas (including the Valley), and the desert regions of the Trans-Pecos.

Because lily bulbs have no outer covering and, unlike other bulbs, store no food, rich, moist, cool soil is essential. Without excellent drainage, there is no point in attempting to grow lilies, because the soil must be moist during the growing season but never soggy. Heavy soils should be lightened by the addition of well-rotted compost, leaf mold, peat moss, pine-bark mulch, or other organic materials a season or more before planting. Beds should be worked deeply for lilies, as deep as 2 feet for some varieties. This improves drainage and allows space for roots to grow—growing room is necessary because most lilies don't need to be divided for some years and continue to multiply. Organic matter is essential for the high fertility that most lilies prefer, as well as for soil porosity.

In most parts of the South and Southwest, where summers are hot, lilies are best planted where they will receive afternoon shade. Morning sun is needed to dry the leaves of morning dew; left damp on successive days, the plants may eventually succumb to Botrytis rot. In summer temperatures consistently over 90° F, lilies should be mulched well to cool the soil around their bulbs and roots. Small, slow-growing shrubs, such as barberries, and noninvasive ground covers such as *Vinca minor,* are good companion plants to shade the roots. They also provide interest when the deciduous lilies have gone underground for winter. In blooming seasons when it is dry, the soil should be kept moist but not wet by watering it thoroughly as frequently as necessary until the plants flower. After they flower, the soil should be allowed to dry between waterings.

Mulch plants well after the first mild freeze to protect them from alternating freezes and thaws.

Given the proper site, many good garden lilies last a lifetime with minimal care. Most should be lifted and separated every three or four years to avoid crowding, but several species lilies need only infrequent lifting or none at all. The time to lift most lilies is after the bloom stem has browned and begun to die back—early fall for most described here, earlier for Madonna lily.

Fertilizing may be done as seldom as twice a year, with a tablespoon of 5-10-10 fertilizer per bulb in spring when the stems emerge, and another tablespoon just as flowering begins. Some gardeners fertilize monthly.

Spraying for aphids is necessary during the growing season, to keep these virus-spreading pests under control.

A succession of lily varieties can provide bloom from late spring to fall. Most hybrid and species lilies flower for at least three weeks in warm regions. In general, bulbs should be planted as soon as possible after purchase, regardless of the season; exceptions are *L. martagon,* which must be planted in fall, growers say, and Madonna lily, which must be planted early enough in fall to form a basal rosette of leaves before winter. If other varieties can be obtained in time for fall planting, that is preferable but not as critical as getting them in the ground whenever they arrive. Since lilies are never fully dormant, the bulbs must be handled with care; stem roots must be left intact. All but *L. candidum* and its hybrids should be planted two to three times as deep as the bulb is tall, because they root from the stem as well as from the base of the bulb. *L. candidum* bulbs grow only basal roots, so they go just under the soil surface.

Mosaic virus is a common disease of lilies and other bulbs. It appears as a checkerboard pattern of light and dark squares, like a mosaic, hence the name. Some species, when infected, neither display the symptoms nor suffer any loss of vigor. Virus-tolerant species must not be combined with susceptible species, because the virus-tolerant ones may become infected and spread the virus without showing any symptoms themselves.

The first three species lilies described here present mixed blessings to Texas gardeners with patience. They either like or tolerate lime soils—a boon in most of Texas and the Southwest—but may take a year or more to bloom the first time. This laggardly behavior is made up for by their independence thereafter; they require lifting infrequently or not at all.

L. candidum, the fragrant white Madonna lily, celebrated in medieval and renaissance Europe, has a perfume likened to honey. It was common in Elizabethan cottage gardens. This species lily is native to "southern Yugoslavia and Greece south to Lebanon, growing in scrub and on cliffs and rocky slopes at up to 600 meters, flowering in May," according to botanist Martyn Rix.

Madonna lily grows 4–6 feet in height, its white, trumpet-shaped blooms facing outward. Twelve to twenty blooms appear on each stem in May and June. (Its hybrids are more compact.) This lily grows best in well-drained, chalky soil with high fertility. It is fairly virus-tolerant. Madonna lily should be

Madonna lily
Lilium candidum.
Photo © 1986 by
Mark Hayes,
Heron Bulb Farm.

covered with no more than 1 inch of soil. It needs to be lifted only every six to eight years, just as soon as the flowering stem dies back. Basal leaves usually appear soon after flowering stops, or after transplanting, and remain through the winter.

The *L. candidum* hybrids grow 18–48 inches tall with lance-shaped leaves like their parent. The pure white, fragrant flowers are 4–5 inches wide. 'Cascade' is a popular named cultivar.

L. martagon and *L. henryi* are reportedly not so easily grown as the other six lilies described here, but their beauty well rewards the gardener who likes a challenge. Like the Madonna lily, they require patience until the long-awaited first bloom season.

"Indestructible," bulb grower Bob Davis of Port Townsend, Washington, dubs *L. henryi*. While perhaps not so easily grown as some other lilies, it is resistant to problems to which others are susceptible. *L. henryi* tolerates mosaic virus and resists wilt disease. Edwards Plateau gardeners report that it grows well in chalky soils if it has adequate moisture and if the soil is worked to a depth of 2 feet before it is planted.

L. henryi grows 4–6 or, rarely, 7–9 feet tall, good for placement at the back of a border with its feet shaded by other plants. It needs staking. The flowers open 3 inches wide, facing downward, and are apricot-colored with brown spots and recurved petals. Each stem may carry forty or more blooms, which appear in summer. This lily is native to central China. It requires no lifting at all.

The Turk's-cap lily, *L. martagon,* was another favorite cottage garden lily. Neutral or alkaline calcareous soils are said to be its preference, an important trait for survival in much of Texas and the Southwest. Turk's-cap lily is also long-lived and very virus-tolerant, and it does not need to be lifted. These assets are balanced by its tendency to sulk for the first year after planting, which should be done only in fall. In areas it likes, it self-sows heavily and establishes colonies. Native to Europe from France and Portugal eastward to Turkey, the Caucasus, and Siberia, it grows in subalpine meadows, woods, and scrub, flowering there in May to July. In Texas it generally blooms in July.

Martagon lily has a delicate, airy "Tinkerbell" effect, as San Antonio gardener Raydon Alexander puts it. The bloom stalks grow 4 to 6 feet tall, bearing pendant 2-inch blooms of white or dusty pink. The dangling flowers have strongly recurved petals and prominent stamens. They appear in "chandelier-like racemes of twenty or more" blooms, as described by venerable English garden writer Roy Genders. The pink form has showy magenta stamens; the white form, golden ones.

L. martagon prefers sun or partial shade, good drainage and plenty of moisture.

Regal lily, *L. regale,* should grow very easily in many parts of Texas. It is a summer-blooming, fragrant lily, native to western China. Long-lived and very virus-tolerant, this plant ranges from 30 inches to 6 feet in height, with blooms 6 inches long. The blossoms are horizontal and funnel-shaped and number thirty or more per plant. Pure white inside with a yellow-gold throat, they are pink-keeled and have showy orange stamens, a lovely combination. Typical lily conditions of dappled sun or afternoon shade and rich, well-drained, deep soil are *L. regale*'s preference in Texas.

Regal lily typically sets seed its first year and blooms from the seed the next year. Its bulbs multiply, as well.

Japanese lily, *L. speciosum,* is another lily easy to grow in parts of Texas. It is an old garden favorite, frequently referred to as "Rubrum lily," after one of its popular hybrids. Mid- or late July to early August is its bloom time. Three to 5 feet tall, it bears twenty to twenty-five fragrant, drooping blooms on each established plant. Their petals open so widely as to make the blooms almost flat. They are white, so heavily suffused and speckled with pink or red that they appear rosy.

L. speciosum 'Rubrum' is the name of several carmine-red cultivars, marked similarly to their parent and 30–36 inches tall. They are susceptible to

Tiger lily *Lilium lancifolium.* Photo © Carl Schoenfeld.

mosaic virus. These lilies bloom from summer to autumn. 'Rubrum' #10 is a highly recommended variety. "Nearly foolproof," this gem is described by veteran gardeners.

Tiger lily, *L. lancifolium* (previously *L. tigrinum*), is one of the easiest lilies to grow in the South and Southwest. "You cannot kill this one unless you really try," says Bob Davis. It is a saucy thing, with orange blooms heavily freckled with wine-purple. There are also red, pink, yellow, and white hybrids. An essential flower of later English cottage gardens, it reached that country in the beginning of the nineteenth century.

Tiger lilies grow 2½ to 6 feet tall, with as many as twelve blooms on each stalk. They bloom from August to October. Downward-facing blooms with strongly recurved petals are similar to those of Turk's-cap lily. This lily is very prolific, producing bulbils in its leaf axils as well as bulblets at the base of the mother bulb.

Tiger lily's preferred soil is described as "any soil with some humus and shade." The bulbs should be planted 6 to 8 inches deep. The longer tiger lilies are allowed to keep their foliage, the better they will bloom the succeeding year. Unfortunately, gardeners must choose between tiger lilies and many other lilies, because *L. lancifolium* carries mosaic virus; although not affected by it, it spreads this fatal disease to other plants.

L. × 'Enchantment' is a popular florist's lily that also does well in the garden. One of its merits as a cut flower is that even the tight buds bloom long after it is brought indoors. 'Enchantment' is one of the Asiatic hybrids developed by Oregonian Jan de Graaf in the mid-1900s, hence dubbed "Mid-Century Hybrids." It is widely considered the finest product of de Graaf's efforts to produce lilies easy for amateurs to grow; by some, the best twentieth-century lily. Compact in habit, its 2–3-foot height enables it to occupy a middle space in a flower garden, for which most lilies are too tall. The blooms are orange, lightly speckled, and upright, 6 inches wide. This lily prefers full sun or partial

'Enchantment' lily

'Pink Perfection' lily

shade and blooms in summer. It is one of the very few forcers that also hold up in the garden.

Other recommended hybrid lilies are the trumpets derived from Asiatic species, 'Black Dragon,' 'Pink Perfection,' and 'Lady Ann.'

Another species lily grown in Texas is *L. formosanum,* the Philippine lily, often called Easter lily here. (True Easter lily is *L. longiflorum,* which is reportedly short-lived in gardens here.)

Propagation is by separating bulblets from the parent bulb.

ஜ *Lycoris*
Spider Lilies
AMARYLLIDACEAE

BLOOM: White, gold, pink, or red in various species; 1½–3″ long, in umbels.
PLANT FORM: Leaves to ¾″ wide, disappearing before flowers develop. Flower stalk 12–30″ tall.
BLOOM SEASON: 2 weeks in August to September.
REGIONS: Vary with species. See Chart 2.
LIGHT: Full sun, partial or light shade, or full shade, depending on region. (See Light, p. 305.)
SOIL: Rich, well-drained best. Poor tolerated.
MOISTURE: All ranges. Moist winters, dry summers preferred. Drought tolerated. Water amply during active growth; let dry out after foliage dies down watering infrequently. Resume regular watering in fall, and blooms will appear.
PROPAGATION: Bulbs. Bulblets; lycoris increases rapidly. *L. traubii* also from seed.

Toward the middle of September every garden in the South is filled with the flame-like flowers of red spider-lilies, Lycoris radiata. On the first days of the month . . . the season for flowers seems to have passed. Then the naked scapes of the red lilies spring up from bare ground and flower almost overnight, lighting all of the dark corners and even the waste places . . . there cannot be too many of them.

—Elizabeth Lawrence

There are many varieties of lycoris, and their hardiness varies. Root-hardy ones may fail to bloom if the winter foliage is lost. The best for the South are listed here. They are among the few shade-tolerant bulbs, and they perform well under deciduous trees if the soil is good.

Lycoris africana, golden spider lily or golden hurricane lily, is also—more accurately—called *L. aurea.* The accepted name *africana* reflects the one-time belief that it originated in Africa; but actually all lycorises are native to Asia. This one's foliage is often covered with a waxy, whitish bloom. It must be watered generously in winter in arid locales and grown in well-drained soils able to absorb the water

Golden spider lily *Lycoris africana*

without becoming soggy. Some published sources call it hardy to -10° F, but Texas gardeners find it winters over reliably only to Zone 8b (to 15° F). It is lovely, but not as reliable as red *L. radiata.*

L. incarnata, a native of China, is variously described as solid salmon to rose or white with a red stripe. Miss Jo N. Evans, a veteran gardener of Catahoula Parish, in a Zone 8 area of east central Louisiana, grows the striped one and says it "never fails." Because *L. incarnata* needs winter cold, it is a prospect for the High Plains, but as yet no trials of it there are reported. It must be watered in winter in arid regions.

White spider lily *Lycoris radiata* var. *albiflora*

L. radiata, red spider lily, is also from China. It is hardy in Zones 7–9, with the northern limit of its range at Baltimore, Maryland, in Zone 7a. This is the easiest lycoris, widely naturalized in the South. It performs better when grown with ground covers than in lawn grass, but it does come up in lawns, year after year.

L. radiata 'Alba,' white spider lily, is slightly less hardy than the red and particularly should be mulched in winter.

L. squamigera, pink spider lily or magic lily, is shell pink, resembling the tender *Amaryllis belladonna.* It is the most cold-hardy lycoris, to Zone 6. In the South, says Jo Evans, "put it in as cold a spot as you can find and leave it alone." Probably Zone 8 is the furthest south in Texas that it can withstand the summer.

L. traubii is saffron-yellow. It resembles *L. africana* but has glossy, dark green leaves and is hardier. It easily sets seed. Native to Taiwan, it is likely to be adapted far more widely in Texas than it is currently grown.

All lycorises are planted in July to August. Set the bulbs 3–4 inches deep. In cold-winter climates, protect them with a mulch. They should not be disturbed for several years. Mature plantings may be divided after the foliage dies down in the spring.

The first lycoris specimen came into North America from Japan over one hundred years ago, brought back by an officer under Commodore Perry on the historic expedition that opened the port of Japan to western trade.

✿ *Muscari*
Grape Hyacinth
LILIACEAE

BLOOM: Dark blue-violet, ¼″ long, in dense terminal racemes. Some species are fragrant.
PLANT FORM: Narrow leaves in grassy clumps 4–12″ tall.
BLOOM SEASON: Early spring for 2–3 weeks. Plants disappear after blooming.

Grape hyacinth *Muscari neglectum*

REGIONS: All but Piney Woods and western Trans-Pecos.
LIGHT: Full sun to full shade.
SOIL: Deep, rich, porous preferred but poor tolerated.
MOISTURE: Moderate. Drought-tolerant.
PROPAGATION: Seed, bulbs, division.

Grape hyacinth is a little ground-covering bulb with small urn-shaped blue-violet flowers that cluster like grapes on 4–12-inch stems. The thin, grassy foliage resembles dwarf ophiopogon or mondo grass. *Muscari neglectum,* the species most persistent in Texas, has a musky fragrance and small white markings on each floret. It was previously known as *M. racemosum;* that species is now made synonymous with *M. neglectum.* It is considered the only "permanent" muscari in the alkaline Central Texas blacklands. There are many other species and hybrids of grape hyacinth, including white forms. *M. armeniacum* bears slightly larger flowers than *M. neglectum* and performs fairly well in parts of Texas with a cold winter to induce bloom. *M. botryoides,* widely sold by mail order, is said to persist only two years in Zone 8b.

Grape hyacinths bloom for two to three weeks starting between mid-February and mid-March. Their low height and vivid color are inviting at the front of a flower bed or in a rock garden. The foliage turns yellow and unsightly after they bloom, and it must be left on until it turns brown to produce food for growth the following year. To disguise the dead foliage, muscari is often interplanted with low-growing spring flowers such as white candytuft, *Iberis sempervirens*. Another good use of grape hyacinth is in open space under deciduous trees, where it makes a blanket of blue.

Muscari generally likes well-drained, somewhat sandy garden soil in full sun or partial shade. However, it is subject to nematodes in sandy soils. Eliminate them by growing cereal rye the winter before you plant, or by "solarizing" the soil under clear plastic for several warm, sunny days; details are available from Texas' certified nursery professionals or extension agents.

While muscari prefers rich, humusy soil, it tolerates poor. Fertilizer is not necessary. The bulbs should be planted 1–3 inches deep and 3–4 inches apart in fall. They can also be grown from seed and from the offsets that form around the parent bulb. They need water during the growing season, from planting time until after they bloom. These inexpensive bulbs offer the bonus of rapid increase.

✌ *Narcissus*
Narcissi, Daffodils, Jonquils
AMARYLLIDACEAE

See Chart 2 for summary of regions, zones, and cultural conditions.

Louisianans have pet names for the old species narcissi that have surrounded their farmhouses and filled their town gardens for ages. The tiny common daffodil with its golden trumpets is dubbed "gold dollah." The even smaller fragrant cluster-flowering jonquil is "li'l sweetie." In early spring, these and other sunny blooms crowd old dooryards and back roads in much of Louisiana and northeastern Texas. These old-time narcissi are known to have come back in the same spots for fifty years and more. While they naturalize most widely in these regions, many are adapted to other parts of Texas, and every

Species and old narcissus hybrids fill a ceramic vase. Clockwise from lower left: 'Sir Francis Drake,' *Narcissus × odorus*, *N. jonquilla*, *N. triandrus*, 'Mount Hood,' 'Trevithian,' 'Mrs. R. O. Backhouse,' 'Laurens Koster,' 'Actaea.'

region can easily grow at least a few. The longevity, ease of care, and excellence as cut flowers of old-fashioned narcissi make them ideal garden flowers.

There is a narcissus for every situation, from damp stream banks to dry hillsides. They originated in the countries bordering the Mediterranean and they have been used in gardens for centuries. Various members of this large genus bloom from earliest spring, and even winter, to late spring. The sight of their yellow trumpets dancing in the breeze announces the season as surely as if they played a fanfare. Many are fragrant. Some can be potted in winter to bloom indoors.

Daffodils and Jonquils

A frequently asked question about narcissi is, "What's the difference between a daffodil and a jonquil?" Both are common names loosely applied to two different species of the genus *Narcissus* and to their hybrids and other species with the same flower forms. The species daffodil is *N. pseudonarcissus.* Like its descendants, the common large daffodils, the yellow, trumpet-crowned bloom has outward flaring petals, called the "perianth," that make a halo at the base of the cup, or "corona." This wild daffodil, the "gold dollah" of Louisiana, thrives in East Texas, too.

Jonquil blooms are generally much smaller in proportion to the plant as a whole than are daffodils', and they appear two to three on a stem. Strictly speaking, "jonquil" is the common name for the species *N. jonquilla,* but it is applied to *N. jonquilla*'s descendants and others of its type, especially in the South. *N. jonquilla,* Louisiana's "li'l sweetie," is deep yellow and richly scented.

A further difference: daffodils have sword-shaped leaves; the leaves of many jonquils resemble rushes.

"Narcissus" is, of course, the Latin name for not only these species but also twenty-four more. The color range of the genus includes white, ivory, shades of yellow and gold, and bi- and tricolor combinations of white, orange, yellow, red, salmon pink, and green. Species besides *N. jonquilla* flower in clusters of several blooms per stem.

San Antonian Raydon Alexander offers this interesting tidbit on the origin of the name "daffodil": "The long-standing British folk etymology for 'daffodil' is 'David's Flower' . . . This is the narcissus that blooms on the first of March, the Feast of St. David, the patron of Wales. David is pronounced 'Daffy' in Welsh. 'Dil' was 'borrowed' from 'asfodil' (*Asphodelus*)." Alexander further notes that the popular Welsh narcissus is a large yellow trumpet 'King Alfred' type.

The narcissi discussed here are ones known to have come back for three or more years in Texas. More varieties whose longevity is yet to be reported probably also act as perennials. Species often require a year's growth in the garden before they bloom. Early-flowering types are likely to bloom longer, in the cooler weather of early spring. Narcissi like well-aerated, neutral to acid soil, mild winters, and high rainfall. Except as indicated, they prefer full sun, at least from fall to spring, and well-drained soil. General bulb culture applies, particularly as to maintaining dry soil in summer. For further details, see "Growing Narcissi" below.

Not all old-time narcissi are small-flowered. But the glory of the older large-flowered narcissi has been stolen by showy modern large-cupped and trumpet hybrids for most of this century. However, only a few of these modern hybrids repeat reliably in the South. Recommended older repeaters include yellow 'Carlton' and 'Unsurpassable,' bicolor 'Duke of Windsor' and 'Fortune,' and white 'Ice Follies' and 'Mount Hood.' A few color subtleties deserve mention: 'Duke of Windsor' is white with an orange cup that turns yellow; 'Fortune' is deep yellow with shaded orange; 'Ice Follies' is pure white with a cup that begins pale lemon and pales to either ivory or icy white; descriptions and perhaps hues vary. In the cultivar 'Mount Hood,' the ivory trumpet flushed with yellow fades to ivory, in my eye, against its pure white perianth. 'Professor Einstein' is white with a large orange-red cup, and 'Mrs. R. O. Backhouse' is a large-cupped pink-and-white. 'Thalia' is an older large-flowered hybrid of the pure white *triandrus* narcissus that also comes back well. 'King Alfred,' a byword with the general gardening public, is judged less than reliable by many serious gardeners, despite its long-standing reputation; the name has been applied to many different strains of varying longevity over the near-century since its introduction. All the other large, showy varieties mentioned stand a good chance of repeating for several years if planted in well-drained soil and left unwatered in Texas' summer heat, and if their foliage is allowed to wilt naturally for about six weeks—standard practices for narcissi and true bulbs in general. Several large-flowering hybrids have been known to naturalize on a rocky slope of the San Antonio Botanical Center in Zone 8b of the Blacklands with scant summer water and in black clay. In the Plains Country, a nurseryman recommends planting them 9–10 inches deep.

'Yellow Hoop Petticoat' narcissus

Species and older cultivars are longer-lived yet and are well worth considering.

The "yellow hoop petticoat," *N. bulbocodium* var. *conspicuus,* looks like a tiny, old-fashioned hoop-skirt. It is native to Portugal and Spain. "Worth a try," veteran bulb-gardeners say. In a situation it likes, it increases rapidly. Otherwise, it disappears. The "hoop" portion of this bright yellow small flower is much larger than the small, starlike perianth. This daffodil's leaves grow 4 to 18 inches tall and resemble grass. It blooms early to midseason. Zones 6 to 8 are its hardiness range. It is fairly drought-resistant.

The cyclamen-flowered narcissi are remarkable for the upswept lilt of their petals, with the look of a cyclamen flower. They appear about to take flight. One bloom appears on each stem. Considered temperamental by some, particularly in clay in Zone 8, both the species and hybrids are worth a try for their distinctive traits. Diminutive *N. cyclamineus,* the species, is unusual, almost cylindrical, with backswept petals and slender corolla like two tubes fused together end to end. A bright yellow miniature narcissus of 6-inch height, it is among the earliest to bloom. Riverbanks and damp meadows are its natural habitat, as it prefers dampish soil and some shade, unusual in bulbs. This narcissus usually needs a year's growth in the garden before it begins blooming. Zones 6 to 9 are its hardiness range.

'February Gold' and 'February Silver' are two lovely hybrids of the cyclamen narcissus. They bear classic small daffodil-shaped trumpets, framed by upswept petals. The plants are 8 to 12 inches tall. 'February Gold' is bright yellow and blooms in early spring. 'February Silver' blooms slightly later, opening white petals around a yellow crown that quickly fades to pure white. Other *N. cyclamineus* hybrids worth trying are tiny 'Tête à Tête,' considered reliable, and long-nosed 'Peeping Tom.'

N. jonquilla, the species jonquil, self-sows vigorously in spots it likes, once established. It is considered an excellent rock garden plant. It has yielded several striking hybrids. 'Trevithian' is a beautiful clear yellow, about 12 inches tall, fairly large-cupped, and classically daffodil-like in appearance. It is considered one of the best in warm climates and is said to respond well to fertilizing, producing more blooms per stem. 'Suzy' bears pert, scented yellow flowers centered by shallow, deep-orange cups on stems 12 to 16 inches tall. 'Sundial' is a related hybrid. 'Quail' is an excellent new midseason yellow. These narcissi are adapted to Zones 4 to 9a.

Wild jonquil

"Single campernelle" is an old, highly scented narcissus from Spain. It is a hybrid of species daffodil and species jonquil. The Latin name, *N. × odorus,* announces its perfume. Campernelle does well in even the heavy clay soils of the Blacklands. The starlike, golden yellow blooms cluster on 8–12-inch stems in early spring. They have rounded petals and narrow, rushlike leaves. This narcissus is a rapid increaser. Zones 5 to 9 are its cold-hardiness range.

N. poeticus is the "poet's narcissus" much admired in the Romantic period and at one time lauded as the only "true" daffodil by such aesthetes as Shelley and Keats. It is distinguished by pure white petals that are broad and large in comparison to the small, shallow cup. "Pheasant's eye" is another epithet for this narcissus, for its shallow yellow cup edged in red. The poeticus narcissi winter over as far north as Zone 5.

'Actaea' is the poet's narcissus hybridized to an even greater beauty—considered whiter than any other narcissus, long-stemmed, with the striking, vivid bicolor cup. Gardeners report mixed results with it; the only solution is to try it and see if one's garden suits it. The attempt may be well rewarded. Shreveport gardeners Minnie Colquitt and Cleo Barnwell report that garden show attendees regularly vote it most beautiful of show over an array of large modern hybrids. 'Actaea' naturalizes well in grass. It is fragrant and grows 18 inches tall. It flowers in mid- to late season, and Zone 5 is its hardiness limit.

The tazettas are the oldest known and most widely distributed species of narcissi. The "paper-white," *N. tazetta* 'Paper-white,' is as white and translucent as parchment and sweet-scented, almost cloying in a closed room. In its Mediterranean homelands, it grows on hills and in grassy places. This is one of the few narcissi suitable for all of South Texas; it also does well in Central and North Texas. Its hardiness range is Zones 8 to 10. 'Galilee' is the most popular of its hybrids, new 'Grandiflora,' the largest. 'Pearl' is a delightful, very-early-flowering fragrant white tazetta with a citron cup, an old Southern favorite. This early-bloomer usually opens in late December; when the cold comes early and lingers, the flowers still bloom very early in spring. Sixteen to 18 inches tall, the plants bear clusters of up to a dozen tiny, white and citron—pale butter yellow—shallow-cupped flowers with golden stamens. 'Pearl' is ideal for forcing. Another narcissus suited to the Valley and to South Texas is the Chinese sacred lily, or *N. tazetta* var. *orientalis;* much of it is said to be virused, however. Covet the long-lived, healthy-foliaged ones that you find; they are virus-free.

The tazetta hybrids are all cluster-flowering and offer a variety of vibrant color combinations of white, yellow, gold, orange, and red. 'Grand Monarque' is a very old garden hybrid with dark green broad leaves and broad, rounded petals. Its pale citron cups fade to white as the blooms mature. 'Grand Primo' is similar but sterile, and its cups keep their color. 'Golden Dome' has been called the best solid yellow tazetta. 'Cragford' is an excellent white with a shallow, frilled red-orange cup that stands 14 to 18 inches tall, blooming early. 'Geranium,' its descendant, is a striking, very fragrant flower with even broader white petals and an orange-red cup that blooms in mid- to late spring. It ranges from 12 to 14 inches in height. 'Silver Chimes' combines a silver-white perianth with a pale yellow cup in late season. In early spring, 'Soleil d'Or' bears small golden flowers with rounded orange cups on 12–16-inch stems. Much of it in the trade is reportedly virused, however, and thus short-lived. 'Laurens Koster' is a beautiful orange-cupped white tazetta that flowers in mid-spring. These tazettas are hardy to Zone 7.

N. × 'Hawera' is a New Zealand hybrid of the 1930s. Its pendant, clustered yellow blooms and upswept petals make this tiny narcissus very lovely, poised gracefully nodding above the flower bed. It is about 8 inches tall and accepts sun to partial shade. *N. triandrus ×* 'Thalia' is related to 'Hawera.' Also called "the orchid narcissus," it is quite beautiful. Two or more graceful, purest white, medium-sized flowers appear on each 16-inch stem. The petals are

Tazetta narcissus 'Laurens Koster'

The orchid narcissus *N. triandrus* 'Thalia'

'Trevithian' jonquil

gracefully reflexed slightly backward. 'Hawera' is hardy in Zones 4–7 and 'Thalia' in Zones 4–8. Both bloom in mid- to late spring.

Narcissi excellent for forcing include 'Unsurpassable'; paper-whites and Chinese sacred lily; *jonquilla* hybrids 'Trevithian,' 'Suzy,' and 'Sundial'; 'February Gold' and 'February Silver'; 'Hawera'; and 'Soleil d'Or.'

Growing Narcissi

Plant bulbs early enough to allow at least a month for root development before a hard freeze. Good drainage is generally a necessity. Plant so that the bulb is covered by soil at least 1½ times as deep as the bulb is tall; plant deeper in light soil, or in heavy soil if you can successfully withhold water in summer. Conventional advice to fertilize with superphosphate or bone meal in the bottom of the planting hole is valid only in phosphate-deficient soils; elsewhere, a dose of a high-nitrogen product, such as lawn fertilizer, at planting and again during active growth, is helpful.

Some narcissi are infected with mosaic virus, a disease that causes yellow streaks or mottling on leaves, sometimes in a checkerboard pattern. Stocks of some varieties of narcissi are said to be entirely virused today, such as the *N. jonquilla* hybrid 'Baby Moon.' Only some strains of others, such as 'Soleil d'Or,' are virused. Others, such as old 'Grand Monarque,' are disease-resistant. Virus could be eliminated from commercial stock of species by growing from unvirused seeds and, in hybrids, by propagating them vegetatively, but these methods are reportedly prohibitively expensive and time-consuming. Experts say breeding for virus-resistant hybrids is a more practical solution. In the meantime, avoiding varieties commonly known to be virused is recommended. Unvirused plants are generally much more vigorous, floriferous, and longer-lived.

In most gardens, narcissi should be divided every fourth year. Dig them after the leaves wilt and turn yellow (about six weeks or less after bloom time), and dry them in the shade. Use a sharp, clean knife to cut them apart; breaking the bulbs apart can cause serious basal damage. Replant bulbs at once or store them in a cool, dark, airy place until fall, placing them with air space around each bulb to prevent rot.

'Sir Francis Drake' daffodil

❧ *Oxalis*

Oxalis

OXALIDACEAE

BLOOM: White, pink, rose, purple, yellow; 1–1½″.
PLANT FORM: Mounded clumps of "shamrock" foliage, usually low, 4–18″ tall.
BLOOM SEASON: Early or mid-spring to frost.
REGIONS: Edwards Plateau, Gulf Coast, Lower Rio Grande Valley, Piney Woods, Plains Country, Prairies & Cross Timbers, South Texas. Limited success with *O. rosea* in Trans-Pecos. Hardiness varies with species within Zones 6–9.
LIGHT: Half-day or dappled sun or full shade preferred. Survives afternoon summer sun unattractively.
SOIL: Well-drained, sandy; pH preferences vary among species. Poor soil tolerated.
MOISTURE: All ranges. Water regularly for best performance. Tolerates drought.
PROPAGATION: Seed, bulbs, division of roots in early autumn.

Oxalis

Oxalis is an easy-care, mound-forming low plant that is good for edging in much of the state. Spider mites can make the foliage mottled and unattractive if the plants are not treated, particularly in hot weather. There are no other serious pests. Attractive species for this region include the following:

Oxalis adenophylla, hardy to -20° F, Zones 5–10, with showy grass-green foliage and pink flowers with maroon eyes.

O. bowiei, a showy, fall-blooming, tender perennial.

O. crassipes, hardy in Zones 4 through at least 9. Tough, common, and long-flowering, chalk pink or white. It is sometimes identified in books as

O. rubra. Although scarce in the trade, it is easily propagated by division. According to *Hortus Third,* its place of origin is not definitely known but may be South America.

O. pes-caprae, Bermuda buttercup, is hardy in Zone 9b, or to Zone 8 with winter protection. It is a reliable, widely naturalized spreader with 1½-inch lemon yellow flowers, excellent in South Texas. The form 'Flore Pleno' is double.

O. rosea, a handsome pink oxalis from Chile, widely available in the trade, is grown as low border edging through most of Texas, although it performs only fairly well in the Trans-Pecos. Hardy in Zones 7–9, it blooms the entire season. It naturalizes well;

"nothing easier," one gardener says. This oxalis grows near trees where grass won't. It tolerates drought but stays greener with moisture. Although it accepts shade, it is more compact with at least 4 to 5 hours' sun. In full sun in August it may scorch or become chlorotic.

❧ *Rhodophiala bifida*
Oxblood Lily
AMARYLLIDACEAE

BLOOM: Clear, deep red or pink with touch of green in throat. To 2″ long in umbels of 3–6 flowers.
PLANT FORM: Jade green leaves last all winter, go away in spring. To 18″ tall.
BLOOM SEASON: August to September. May bloom several times in a season.
REGIONS: All but Plains Country and Trans-Pecos. Hardy in at least Zones 8–9. May be hardy in colder climates.
LIGHT: Full sun to full shade. Tolerates shade well.
SOIL: Heavy best, neutral to alkaline.
MOISTURE: All ranges. Moderate preferred; tolerates drought. Water during growing season.
PROPAGATION: Common form, by offsets. Wild, by seed. Division in early summer.

These amaryllids are sprightly, vibrant little flowers that naturalize well in grass. Reliable bloomers, they are native to Argentina and Uruguay. *Amaryllis bifida* is another name under which they may be found. Collecting and trading may be the best means of supply, because they are not widely sold. Gardeners who have oxblood lily will likely be happy to share, however, because it increases rapidly. Bulbs moved in early summer, just as they have gone dormant, will bloom again the next season. Fall is a good time to plant new bulbs. The bulbs should be planted about 6 inches deep. There is a fertile form and a sterile one; the only way to identify the fertile one is to watch for seed heads.

This lily is lovely combined with small white flowers that set off its crimson or rarer pink hue.

Oxblood lily *Rhodophiala bifida*

White verbena is an excellent choice, particularly if you shear it in late summer to encourage a fall flush of bloom. Oxblood lily often naturalizes and persists for generations.

❧ *Sprekelia formosissima*
Aztec Lily
AMARYLLIDACEAE

BLOOM: Bright crimson red, 4–6″ across. Exotic, orchidlike bloom. 'Orient Red' has cream stripes.
PLANT FORM: Strap-shaped leaves, dark green and narrow, 10–15″ tall. Evergreen in mild climates.
BLOOM SEASON: Late spring. Species, once or more in spring and summer. Popular cultivars, spring and fall.
REGIONS: To Zone 8b in all but Edwards Plateau and Plains Country.
LIGHT: Full sun or afternoon shade; high shade where sun is intense.
SOIL: Well-drained, rich, organic garden soil.
MOISTURE: All ranges. Allow a dry period after blooming, then resume regular watering.
PROPAGATION: Bulblets.

Aztec lily
Sprekelia formosissima.
Photo © Thad Howard.

Society garlic *Tulbaghia violacea*

Sprekelia is an exotic, striking plant that everyone should try once, in a windowsill pot if the climate doesn't allow wintering it over in the ground. Culture is the same as for *Hippeastrum*. It is native to Mexico, hence the name Aztec lily.

Some sources say that this bulbous plant is hardy to 20° F, others say to 10° F. Winter mulch is recommended to protect against colder-than-average weather in Zone 8b and if one attempts to test its advertised 10° F rating (Zone 8a).

Written sources advise planting Aztec lily with the bulb neck at the soil surface. However, experienced Texas bulb gardeners recommend planting bulbs 4 to 6 inches deep, to get them below the frost line in the most severe winters, which generally occur once or twice per decade. In locales where the ground freezes deeper than 6 inches, tender bulbs should be planted deeper. Of course, this makes well-drained, porous, well-aerated soil essential; planting deep in clay soils results in rot.

Watch for snails, slugs, and mealybugs at the base of the leaves.

𝒢 *Tulbaghia violacea*
Society Garlic
AMARYLLIDACEAE

BLOOM: Bright lilac ¾″ blooms in umbels of 7–20 flowers.
PLANT FORM: Arching clump of dark green blades about 12–30″ tall. Evergreen to Zone 8b.
BLOOM SEASON: Late spring or early summer to frost.
REGIONS: All but Plains Country and Trans-Pecos, Zones 8b–9.
LIGHT: Full sun, partial or light shade.
SOIL: Rich, well-drained preferred; heavy tolerated.
MOISTURE: All ranges. Prefers moderate moisture but tolerates drought.
PROPAGATION: By division or seeds.

This flower gives a modest but consistent display of color almost the whole growing season, even in late summer, when few tuberous plants do. It is most effective planted in masses. The slender foliage and tall bloom stalks with their little crowns of flowers have an airy, cool effect. You can generally plant it and forget it. There is a variegated form that is less hardy. The common name is in part for its slight onionlike odor; whether the reference to the upper crust is for the flavor more subtle than common garlic's or for its understated blooms is anybody's guess. The leaves can be minced and eaten like chives. Society garlic is native to South Africa.

Lady tulip *Tulipa clusiana*

🌺 *Tulipa clusiana*
Lady Tulip
LILIACEAE

BLOOM: Pink to rose-red and yellow or white bicolors.
PLANT FORM: Height range 6–12″. Foliage narrow or strap-shaped.
BLOOM SEASON: Early to late spring for 2 weeks. Disappears after blooms fade.
REGIONS: Hardy to Zone 4. Adapted to Edwards Plateau, Piney Woods, Plains Country, Prairies & Cross Timbers, Trans-Pecos, Zones 6–8.
LIGHT: Full sun to few hours' shade or filtered light.
SOIL: Well-drained, sandy, humus-rich best, but tolerates poor soil well. Neutral to slightly alkaline preferred.
MOISTURE: All ranges. Moderate in growing season; keep dry in summer. Drought-tolerant.
PROPAGATION: Bulbs and division.

There are two wild tulips that are proven repeaters in northern regions of Texas. These are among the species and their hybrids referred to as "botanical tulips."

Tulipa clusiana, the Lady tulip or candy-stick tulip, is a dainty, fragrant flower, peppermint-striped deep rose and white. Its small pointed buds are about thumb-sized and open into little stars on 6–12-inch stems. They bloom in March or April for about two weeks. This tulip is ideal for rock gardens, free-form drifts in grass, or the fronts of raised beds or flower borders that can be left dry in the summer. The spent foliage can either be mowed in midsummer or masked by shallow-rooted, thin-foliaged summer annuals such as cosmos. After the foliage disappears, the tulips remain underground until the following spring.

Lady tulip spreads rapidly, although new bulbs can take several years to become established before they bloom. There are two forms of this flower that differ only in means of propagation. One spreads by stolons; the other produces basally attached offsets.

This tulip is native to Iran and Afghanistan and naturalized in southern Europe. It looks pretty planted with red and white English daisies, *Bellis perennis.* Winter-hardy here, the English daisies can be planted at the same time as the tulip bulbs for color in mild winter weather and in spring.

T. clusiana var. *chrysantha* is native to Iran and northwestern India and sports yellow inner petals and red-striped outer ones. The culture of this form is the same as that of the species. It blooms a few weeks later. It is sometimes sold by the name 'Cynthia' and is difficult to find but worth the search.

Tulip 'Cynthia' *Tulipa clusiana* var. *chrysantha*

T. clusiana requires a very warm, sunny position. It prefers full sun, or at least six hours of sun. The bulbs should be planted in late fall or winter, 4–8 inches deep in well-drained, sandy, humus-rich soil. Bulbs planted 8 inches deep in very well-drained soil will reportedly bloom better for more years but multiply less than shallowly planted ones.

Lady tulip is available at some retail nurseries. Its form *T. clusiana* var. *chrysantha,* or 'Cynthia,' is more often offered by mail-order bulb houses.

Botanical hybrids also may naturalize in sandy soil if left dry in summer. 'Red Riding Hood,' an excellent fancy-leafed, bright red, is an example.

White rain lily *Zephyranthes candida*

🐚 *Zephyranthes, Cooperia, Habranthus*
Rain Lilies
AMARYLLIDACEAE

BLOOM: Rose, pink, yellow, white.
PLANT FORM: Foliage low, arching, grasslike, 5–18″.
BLOOM SEASON: Spring, summer, or late summer to frost.
REGIONS: All (but only a few species in Plains Country and Trans-Pecos). Hardiness varies; some species Zones 8b–9, others hardy to Zone 7.
LIGHT: Full sun to few hours' shade or filtered light.
SOIL: Clay, garden soil, or sandy soil. Humus-rich is best, but poor soil is accepted.
MOISTURE: Moderate in growing season. Drought-tolerant.
PROPAGATION: Seed, offsets.

Our native Texas copper lily is one of life's ephemeral delights. Criticizing its brief bloom, I was rebuffed by someone older and wiser. "One week? That's long enough to feed your soul!" retorted Minnie Colquitt, a gardener for some fifty years in Louisiana. Not all the dainty rain lilies bloom this briefly, but now I take them all as reminders to look close and not let the moment pass me by.

In the wild, the white rain lily, *Zephyranthes candida,* fills meadows with drifts of tiny lilies after the first fall rains. Its dark green, grasslike foliage at first glance resembles the low, arching clumps of monkey grass. There are many other species of rain lilies in a range of colors. *Habranthus* and *Cooperia* are genera related to *Zephyranthes; Cooperia* species readily interbreed with *Zephyranthes.* In an ongoing controversy, botanists disagree whether these two are separate. At present, the "lumpers" are winning against the "splitters," and some sources now list flowers long known as *Cooperia* as *Zephyranthes.* For convenience, both names are given in the plant chart.

Many rain lilies eagerly adapt to garden use, multiplying rapidly. After a freeze, most die back and disappear, to return the following summer; *Z. atamasco* is semi-evergreen, however.

Rain lilies prefer full sun, a few hours' shade, or filtered light and have been known to grow in poor, heavy soils. Vigorous spreaders, they can be kept in bounds by digging up the excess plants, which come up easily. They are useful in groups in a perennial border, to prolong its bloom period through fall, or in difficult areas under trees. They can be combined with ground cover in the same way as narcissi and grape hyacinths. When they are mingled in grass, mowing must be stopped in August to save the fall bloom stalks. Then, combined with grasses in a meadow garden, as in nature, they spring up one morning, a sea of little stars seeming to float an inch or two above the grass.

Z. atamasco, Atamasco lily or wild Easter lily, has a white flower, up to 3 inches across, slightly larger than *Z. candida.* It blooms in spring and summer. The Piney Woods is its preferred Texas region. Native from southeastern Virginia to Florida and Alabama, it prefers acid soil in Zones 7–9. It does not lose its foliage in mild winters.

Z. brazosensis (*Cooperia drummondii*) is a night-blooming, fragrant white rain lily, up to 18 inches tall, with 3–7-inch blooms in late summer and fall. Narrow gray-green leaves appear after the blooms. It is native to Texas, New Mexico, and Mexico.

Z. candida, rain lily or zephyr lily, has 2-inch white blooms in summer and autumn, until frost. It is native to the La Plata region of South America.

Z. citrina, yellow rain lily, blooms all summer. It has narrow, dark green, sprawling foliage 6–8 inches tall. Hardy in Zones 7–9, this bulb is readily available and inexpensive. It self-sows. It is native to the Yucatan Peninsula and the West Indies.

Z. drummondii (*Cooperia pedunculata*) is a mid- to late spring bloomer adapted to Zones 8–9. Its fragrant red-tinged white blooms are 1¼ inches long, 1½ inches wide. The broad blue-green foliage tops out at 5–8 inches and is semi-evergreen. This species resembles *Z. brazosensis* but is showier.

Z. grandiflora, zephyr lily or pink rain lily, has rose or pink blooms to 4 inches across in spring and summer and leaves to 12 inches long. A very showy flower, it is often confused with *Z. rosea,* which is somewhat smaller and very tender. *Z. grandiflora* is native to Mexico and Guatemala.

Z. rosea has rose flowers to 1 inch across and flat, spreading leaves. It blooms in autumn and is hardy only to Zone 9. It is native to Cuba. Flowers sold by this name are likely to be *Z. grandiflora.*

Habranthus robustus has rose-red or pink 3-inch flowers with a short tube and greenish throat. Nine-inch recurved leaves appear after the flowers. *H. robustus* is native to Argentina.

H. tubispathus var. *texanus,* copper lily, has gold flowers with a coppery stripe outside, to 4 inches. It blooms in late summer for a week. The leaves are linear, 6–12 inches long. It grows in sun in Zones 7–9 and naturalizes well in grass.

How to Prepare a Spring Bulb Bed for Fall Planting

Spring-flowering bulbs do best in beds prepared as for perennials. The soil should be dug to the depth of 12 inches if at all possible. Digging in a 6- to 12-inch layer of organic material improves soil aeration, plant nutrition, and drainage, especially needed in heavy clay soils. This will also raise the bed surface

Pink rain lily *Zephyranthes grandiflora*

Copper lily *Habranthus tubispathus* var. *texana*

slightly, further improving drainage. Addition of coarse builder's sand is also recommended by some gardeners but this is repudiated by Texas A&M tests reported by the Texas Agricultural Extension Service. If thorough soil preparation is not done, at least a low-nitrogen, high-calcium and -phosphorus fertilizer such as bone meal should be used, placed in the bottom of each planting hole and topped by an inch of soil, below where the bulb will sit.

For most species, the bulb is covered with at least twice its height in soil. The bed should be watered both after planting and regularly during the winter and the bloom period.

SPECIAL TECHNIQUES TO ENCOURAGE LONGER BULB LIFE

Special planting techniques improve the chances of perennial bulbs and even large hybrid Holland bulbs coming back a second season or more.

(1) Locate summer-dormant bulbs (most spring bulbs) in very well-drained beds that can be left unwatered in summer. (Clay soil and/or watering during their summer dormancy may rot the bulbs in their first season.)

or: (2) Plant bulbs 10 inches deep in almost pure sand, if your soil is light, or if the bed is situated at a height sufficient to drain despite its being surrounded by heavier soil. (Sand beds built in clay soil generally cause a "bucket" effect.) Again, withhold irrigation in summer. Planting deeply in sand is said to put the bulbs below the level that summer rain is likely to reach and thus protect them from rot.

With these regimes, horticulturist Raydon Alexander of Milberger Nursery in San Antonio has successfully induced Darwin tulips not only to repeat, but to multiply.

For Daffodils: (3) Plant bulbs under Bermuda or buffalo grass sod in an area that can be watered only lightly in summer drought and left unmowed for six weeks after the daffodils stop blooming.

For Tulips: (4) Try interplanting tulips and bearded iris. In England, tulips are sometimes planted deep in well-drained beds, with shallow-rooted bearded iris planted above. Both plants accept summer drought and prefer good drainage, so it's a successful combination—one that may work in Texas, too.

BULB BED PREPARATION AT A GLANCE

(1) Dig the bed 12 inches deep. Amend heavy soils with organic matter.

(2) Dig the planting hole at least as deep as three times the height of the bulb, unless otherwise directed. Add a spoonful of bone meal or other low-nitrogen, slow-release fertilizer to the bottom of the planting hole, beneath where the bulb will go. Cover the bulb with at least twice its height in soil. Water in the new planting.

(3) Continue to water deeply every week or two during winter and spring—when there is no rainfall—and during blooming.

(4) Do not cut back the foliage until six weeks after bloom, for daffodils, or until it turns brown, for other species.

The greens and bronzes of Indian hawthorn shrubs, bright russets of nandina, and silver of dusty miller and lamb's-ears provide interest in this garden almost year round. Here, they make effective foils for lavish early spring flowers, ajuga, and a 'White Cloud' dogwood tree. Garden of Lorine and David Gibson, Dallas.

CHAPTER FIFTEEN

Foliage Plants for the Flower Garden

Further delights of a garden in winter are the grey of lavender, the frosted green of santolina, and the dull olive of rosemary.

—*Elizabeth Lawrence*

Flower gardens without ornamental foliage plants are only half as beautiful as they might be. Like the drape behind a painting, beautiful foliage sets off flowers to their best advantage. And foliage plants can provide striking landscape effects on their own. Gardens made of prairie grasses, for example, are now attaining a popularity in the United States that they have long held in Europe. A fern dell of shade-loving plants is another example.

Using foliage plants effectively takes attention to texture and color harmony. Gertrude Jekyll, the famous English gardener of the turn of the century, was a painter first. In planting her "living pictures," as she called them, she made wide use of foliage: "hardy Ferns in bold drifts," "grey *Stachys* and milk-white Tulips," "great groups of Yucca standing up against the sky," as she later wrote. Leaf shapes, textures, and plant forms all enter in. Interest can be created solely by contrasts in texture or form—for example, the contrast of spiky yucca leaves and soft billows of herbs.

Decorative Foliage for Sunny Sites

Gray and silver foliage plants are among the most useful in the garden. They complement a whole range of color schemes. Silver-gray lavender and artemisia make plantings of mauve, lavender, pink, and blue flowers appear positively misty. They soften the wallop of the strong reds and golds or modern roses, zinnias, black-eyed Susans, and sunflowers. English gardener Maggie Guitar, lately of Amarillo, Texas, praises the use of grays in the white garden. "There's a famous white garden at Sissinghurst, created by Vita Sackville-West," she says. "It's all silver and gray foliage and white flowers. You feel cool, just looking at it." Excellent plants for creating that soft effect are artemisia, santolina, dusty miller, and woolly lamb's-ears.

Wormwood and
Mexican petunia
*Artemisia
ludoviciana* and
Ruellia

feet tall and has a feathery effect. Its running roots can be invasive in warm locations with sandy soil. In heavy soil, regular lifting and replanting will control its expansion. Planting in old buckets or cans with the bottoms knocked out also helps. 'Silver Mound,' very fine-leaved, creates soft mounds of misty, cloud-like foliage. It is not usually invasive. Seldom over a foot in height, it makes an excellent border or rock garden plant. The selection 'Nana' is only 3–6 inches tall. The middle of the clump tends to die out, but well-drained soil, allowing ample room for each plant, and trimming plants back before they bloom help prevent this.

Artemisias are not set back by the heat of late summer except in high humidity; the combination makes them prone to rot.

❧ *Artemisia*
Wormwood
COMPOSITAE

COLOR: Silvery gray or green foliage. Grayish-white or yellow inconspicuous flower heads.
FORM: Varies with selection; 3–42″ tall.
SEASON: Dies back in winter but root-hardy. Flowers in midsummer.
REGIONS: Hardy to Zone 4 or 5. Rot-prone in areas with high humidity. See Chart 3 in Chapter 12 for specific regions.
LIGHT: Full sun. *A. abrotanum* and 'Silver King' tolerate afternoon shade.
SOIL: Well-drained. Better in poor, sandy soils than rich ones.
MOISTURE: Moderate. Drought-tolerant. Will not tolerate much winter moisture.
PROPAGATION: Easily increased by root division or from cuttings.

The artemisias, or wormwoods, include many species and hybrids. *Artemisia abrotanum,* or southern-wood, is a cloud of green in the garden and, with its astringent scent, a traditional moth repellent. Two of the best gray-foliaged garden varieties are *A. ludoviciana* var. *albula,* or 'Silver King,' and *A. schmidtiana* 'Silver Mound.' 'Silver King' grows up to 3½

❧ *Rosmarinus officinalis*
Rosemary
LABIATAE

COLOR: Dark gray-green, needlelike foliage. Pale lavender-blue flowers; bright blue in variety 'Tuscan Blue.'
FORM: Species type is upright; some varieties to 6′. Prostrate form mounds to 2′ by as much as 6′ across.
SEASON: Evergreen. Blooms off and on all season.
REGIONS: All to Zone 8; to Zone 7b with winter protection. However, can be damaged by sudden freeze after warm spell. In cold climates, pot it and put it in a sunny window near a humidifier for the winter. Very heat-tolerant.
LIGHT: Full to reflected sun or partial shade.
SOIL: Very tolerant but must have good drainage.
MOISTURE: Moderate to little. Drought-tolerant once established.
PROPAGATION: By division.

Rosemary is one of the oldest garden herbs. It can be sheared if desired to form a low hedge, as it has been used in formal gardens since medieval times. Rosemary can also be grown in clumps or as a trailing ground cover. It lends itself to transitional, desert, or wild garden effects.

Rosemary
*Rosmarinus
officinalis*

A semi-shrub, rosemary can become too woody. In poorly drained soil it may get fungus.

The aromatic foliage is pleasant to brush against in the garden and for seasoning lamb or chicken. Rabbits and deer won't eat it.

'Arp' is the most cold-hardy variety.

❧ *Ruta graveolens*
Rue
RUTACEAE

COLOR: Blue-green foliage; ½" yellow flowers in terminal clusters.
FORM: Mounding, 24–36" tall.
SEASON: Evergreen. Blooms in summer.
REGIONS: All. Hardy to Zone 5. It naturalizes in the Trans-Pecos.
LIGHT: Full sun to partial shade.
SOIL: Light, well-drained, alkaline to neutral preferred.
MOISTURE: Moderate. Drought-tolerant.
PROPAGATION: Division.

Rue is a bitter-tasting herb native to southern Europe that likes the sunny, arid conditions preferred by other Mediterranean herbs. Plants of great size are seen growing wild in the Trans-Pecos region of

Texas. The foliage, when moist, is a skin irritant to some people.

The scallop-edged, alternate leaves form a low mound of blue-green that is a perfect foil to white and pale yellow flowers and ones in the magenta, pink, and rose range. The cultivar 'Jackman's Blue' is intensely blue-green.

Pruning rue to old wood in early spring will keep it bushy. Mulch it in severe winters. Deer don't eat it.

❧ *Santolina*
Lavender Cotton
COMPOSITAE

COLOR: Gray or green. Yellow button flowers, if left unclipped.
PLANT FORM: Mounding, billowy, 12–24" high and 30" wide.
SEASON: Year-round.
REGIONS: Edwards Plateau, Plains Country, Prairies & Cross Timbers, South Texas, Trans-Pecos. Hardy to Zone 6. Tolerates heat and high wind.
LIGHT: Full, part, or reflected sun.
SOIL: Any well-drained. Accepts poor soil.
MOISTURE: Drought-tolerant.
PROPAGATION: Cuttings in moist sand.

Santolina chamaecyparissus is the age-old lavender cotton used in English gardens since medieval times. It was grown in low, clipped hedges as a border for knot gardens. *Chamaecyparissus* comes from Greek

Rue
Ruta graveolens

Gray and green santolina
Santolina chamaecyparissus and *S. virescens*

SOIL: Well-drained, preferably sandy.
MOISTURE: Moderate. Drought-tolerant.
PROPAGATION: Seed. Selected forms by cuttings.

Dusty miller is an excellent foil to blue, lavender, pink, white, and yellow flowers. It also tones down reds and bronzes in red gardens and softens the contrast between bright colors and white. It often dies back in the summer, probably from rot promoted by the combination of heat and excessive irrigation or poor drainage.

roots meaning "ground-hugging cypress"; the gray foliage resembles that of cypress trees.

S. virens is the green form. It is slightly smaller and takes the same culture. The two santolinas are attractive grown together. The aromatic foliage is a pleasure to brush against along a path.

These plants are native to Spain and South America. They should be clipped to remove the bloom; otherwise the plants lose their dense, compact form. Shear them annually as the flowers appear. After a few years, santolina becomes woody and should be replaced.

❧ *Senecio cineraria*
Dusty Miller
COMPOSITAE

COLOR: Felted, silver-gray foliage. Small dark yellow daisy flowers.
FORM: Upright, deeply lobed leaves to 24″ tall.
SEASON: Reliably evergray in Zones 8–9 and portions of southern Zone 7b in West Texas; see Chart 3. Hardiness varies among selections.
REGIONS: Edwards Plateaus, Lower Rio Grande Valley, Piney Woods, Prairies & Cross Timbers, South Texas, southern (Zone 7b) portions of Plains Country and Davis Mountains of Trans-Pecos. Susceptible to rot in humid areas.
LIGHT: Full sun, high shade.

❧ *Stachys byzantina*
Lamb's-ears
LABIATAE

COLOR: Felted, silver-gray leaves. Purple-and-gray bloom stalks.
FORM: Dense mat of leaves 3″ high. Blooms to 18″ tall.
SEASON: Dies back in winter but root-hardy. Blooms in midsummer.
REGIONS: Edwards Plateau, Plains Country, Prairies & Cross Timbers, South Texas, Trans-Pecos.
LIGHT: Full sun to partial shade. Up to 70% shade in South Plains.
SOIL: Well-drained. Accepts poor soil well.
MOISTURE: Moderate. Drought-tolerant.
PROPAGATION: Seed in early spring or division in early spring or fall.

Dusty miller (left rear), daffodil, English primrose, pansies, lamb's-ears

Lamb's ears
Stachys byzantina

ᔎ Ferns

COLOR: Green. Some have bronze tints in new leaves or in winter foliage.
FORM: 18″ to 5′. Clump of basal leaves.
SEASON: Summer through fall or year-round.
REGIONS: Hardiness varies with species. Not adapted to drought or extreme heat.
LIGHT: Morning sun, filtered light, or deep shade. Avoid southern exposure except in shade. Avoid extreme temperature variations.
SOIL: Well-drained but moisture-retentive. Humus. Avoid heavy clay.
MOISTURE: Moderate to moist. Avoid standing water and extreme variations in moisture.
PROPAGATION: Spores or division.

Lamb's-ears form a dense, low mat of felted, silvery leaves from which purple-and-gray bloom stalks rise in midsummer. "At its best where it can overflow onto a path," garden writer Pamela Harper says. Children are delighted to stroke the velvety leaves of this unusual plant. "A crowd-pleaser," Midlander Burr Williams calls it. It is propagated from seeds or by division in early spring or fall.

'Silver Carpet' is a non-flowering English cultivar recently introduced to the Texas trade.

Another name by which lamb's-ears is sometimes listed is *Stachys lanata.*

Both stachys and artemisia do best in full sun and relatively dry, poor soil—a boon for much of Texas. In wet soil, the roots may rot. In high humidity, the foliage may rot. Raised beds and organic matter added to the soil will help with both problems in damper regions.

Greens for the Shade

There is more to color in the shade than impatiens and caladiums. Consider the rainbow of greens, golds, white and near-black available in the ferns, hostas, and lilyturfs.

There are many ferns suited for subtropical and southern temperate regions of the United States. They are soft, soothing plants that conjure up cool, shady glades and forests. Some form soft ground covers and others make striking specimen plants. They combine well with moisture-loving, shade-tolerant flowers, especially as a backdrop or a repeating element. Good companions include violets, columbines, *Phlox divaricata,* and Atamasco lily (*Zephyranthes atamasco*). Ferns' finely cut foliage contrasts well with more common ground covers such as liriope and mondo grass. In the shade of deciduous trees, they make great companions for early spring bulbs; the ferns mask the bulb foliage as it fades. And they are naturals for a woodland garden. Ferns work, whether in a formal or an informal setting. They're easy, to boot.

Ferns generally enjoy extra humus, moderate moisture while they are actively growing, and some shade.

Generally, the light level in high shade under tall trees is ideal for ferns. It's a standard to judge by in choosing other sites. If you don't have large trees, make use of patio covers and the north and east sides of houses and fences. In regions with intense sunlight and high round-the-clock summer heat, shade is a must. Some ferns will accept morning sun, however. Some, such as wood fern, survive full sun, but by July they burn or yellow. On the other hand, dark, deep shade produces weak plants.

Well-drained sites with soil that can be kept evenly moist are ideal for most ferns. They are native to soil full of crumbly, decomposed leaf mulch, but even black gumbo clay will support the ferns recommended for Texas if you add organic matter. Coarse peat moss, compost, and slow-acting fertilizers such as bone meal or coated urea are good additions to the soil at planting time. Woodland ferns may go into dormancy during summer drought if the soil dries out; few survive boggy soil, however.

Avoid windy spots such as house corners or between buildings.

Plant ferns in early fall or just as they go into active growth in spring. Make sure that the crown is at soil level. Mulch is helpful for winter survival and moisture retention in summer. All ferns drop aging fronds as new ones form. Pruning of faded or damaged growth is advised.

While no ferns are truly evergreen in the sense that evergreen shrubs are, some species normally retain their leaves through winter in mild climates.

In general, these attractive ferns take two to three years to reach the mature sizes given. All thrive in moist (not soggy) soil and high shade and accept other conditions as noted.

Adiantum capillus-veneris, southern maidenhair fern or Venus'-hair fern, grows 18–24 inches high in shade or filtered light in Zones 1–9. It needs even moisture and rich soil and is deciduous.

Athyrium niponicum 'Pictum,' Japanese painted fern, is gray-green washed with silver and burgundy. It grows to 12 inches in bright shade and rich, moist-to-wet soil. Deciduous.

Cyrtomium falcatum, Japanese holly fern, is hardy to Zone 8b. This 24–36-inch-tall dark green, leathery fern is evergreen where hardy. It prefers bright to medium shade and moist to dry soil.

Dryopteris erythrosora, autumn fern or Japanese shield fern, grows 18–30 inches high. The young fronds are a beautiful copper color. This fern is evergreen through Zone 8, although susceptible to leaf

Wood fern *Thelypteris normalis*

burn, and hardy to Zone 3. It accepts lower light. Single stemmed.

Osmunda cinnamomea, cinnamon fern, is green with cinnamon-colored spores, 3–5 feet tall. It grows in shade to partial sun and even low light in moist to wet soil. Deciduous, with yellow-orange fall color, it is hardy to Zone 4. Offsets form readily.

Polystichum acrostichoides, Christmas fern, is 24–36 inches tall with evergreen, leathery fronds often used in floristry. This native of eastern North America prefers shade but tolerates filtered light or lower light. It prefers moist, rich soil. Humus is required.

Thelypteris normalis, a commonly available wood fern, or river fern, is a deciduous green fern native to the coastal and southern United States. It grows in shade, filtered light, or morning sun. It accepts poor drainage. Spreading from rhizomes, it quickly forms a mass of soft, knee-deep fronds.

❧ *Hosta*
Plantain Lily
LILIACEAE

COLOR: Shades of green from blue-green to chartreuse, solid and variegated with white or yellow. White to lavender-blue bloom spikes.
FORM: Clump-forming, 8–48″ tall, depending on variety.

SEASON: Root-hardy, but leaves die back in winter. Flowers bloom in midsummer.

REGIONS: Hardy Zones 4–8. Not adapted to High Plains, Lower Rio Grande Valley, South Texas, or Trans-Pecos.

LIGHT: Light to deep shade or less than three hours morning sun, in summer.

SOIL: Rich, well-prepared, moist in summer, but well-drained. Even moisture is preferred; survives serious drought-damage but loses top growth and regrows from roots.

MOISTURE: Moderate to ample.

Hostas, the perennial "plantain lilies," have broad, very shiny, strongly ribbed leaves that are heart-shaped, oval, or lanceolate. Large drifts of two or three contrasting varieties on a shady slope can be very showy. A single large plant offers a bold accent in low light. Among *Hosta fortunei, H. lancifolia, H. sieboldiana,* and their many hybrids are varieties that are solid green, gray-blue, pale yellow, pale green edged with white, yellow-edged, and gold with green. *Sieboldianas* are the best-known blues. Other interesting hostas are species *H. decorata, ventricosa, venusta,* and *albomarginata.* Don't overlook their textures, from smooth, to seersucker, to ruffle-edged.

Hostas like rich soil that is moist in summer. In Texas, where temperatures often exceed 90° F, light shade is preferable, and deep shade will do. Lilylike

Hosta

white to lavender-blue flowers that rise up above the foliage in midsummer are an added bonus.

Hostas can easily be increased by fall or spring division, and the plants last for years. An annual feeding and three or four applications of snail bait per year keep them in prime condition.

It generally takes two years for the top of a new rootstock to start to fill out and three years before it begins to become a large, stately clump. Hostas can live for years without being divided. Because hostas are deciduous, a hosta planting becomes bare ground in winter unless it includes evergreens such as hollies, boxwoods, or yaupons or perennials with persistent foliage.

Liriope, Ophiopogon
Lilyturfs
LILIACEAE

COLOR: Dark green, green and white, green and yellow, near-black. Lilac-blue flower spikes.

FORM: Arching, low, and grassy. 4–36″, depending on variety.

SEASON: Evergreen.

REGIONS: All.

LIGHT: Anywhere but the Gulf Coast, filtered sun, partial shade, or full shade is best. Except near the Gulf, solid greens tip burn in full sun; in the Trans-Pecos and far South Texas, they don't survive it.

SOIL: Average well-drained garden soil is best. Tolerates clay, sandy, or poor soil.

MOISTURE: Moderate. Drought-tolerant. Occasional deep soaking is best.

PROPAGATION: By division in early spring.

These members of the lily family are native to Japan and China. They are excellent as ground covers and in masses or clumps. The liriopes are commonly called "monkey grass," the ophiopogons, "mondo grass."

Two less commonly used mondo grasses are attractive additions to the garden. *Ophiopogon jaburan,* or giant lilyturf, grows up to 3 feet tall. It makes a striking specimen plant in the ground or a container. Giant lilyturf spreads by runners, tolerates

Monkey grass *Liriope muscari*

west sun, and is cold-hardy at least to Zone 8. Sometimes this plant is sold by the name *Liriope gigantea.* Black mondo grass, *O. planiscapus* 'Arabicus,' is a striking accent to pastel plants and surfaces. Its dwarf form, only 3–5 inches tall, is an effective but slow-growing ground cover for small areas. Indirect sunlight is best for black mondo grasses.

Broader-leaved, shorter liriopes are the "monkey grasses" commonly used in Texas. 'Big Blue' and 'Majestic' are good green-leaved *L. muscari* selections. 'Silver Dragon' and 'Silvery Sunproof' are attractive white-variegated liriopes. In controlled plantings, avoid *L. spicata,* which spreads aggressively by underground stolons.

Although evergreen, lilyturfs may get frost-burned in the winter. Clean them up in early spring, before the flush of new leaves comes on, by shearing; sheep shears or long-bladed garden shears are ideal tools. String-trimmers will shred leaves and leave them ragged; new growth soon covers the ragged edges, however. The accumulated soil salts that burn leaves can be removed by an occasional deep soaking.

Perennial Grasses

Ornamental grasses have won a place in American gardens in recent years. Their striking forms and showy seed heads make them attractive year-round, even when dried in winter. They have few pests or diseases and require little maintenance. Most are drought-tolerant. Their color changes from green to shades of gold, rose, and beige in fall add interest to the garden. These perennial grasses range in height from 1 foot to head-high and taller. Their long leaves typically fan out in a vase or fountain shape. In time, the roots grow to form large clumps. These plants can create a meadow effect or blanket small areas as ground covers. In flower borders, the grasses' sculptural forms and long, arching leaves are perfect foils for the textures and shapes of flowers. Individual plants or small groupings can add emphasis to gates or doorways or provide a focal point in a lawn. Grasses serve in a wide range of landscape styles, adding a fresh note of wilderness or stately shapes appropriate to a formal garden. Their popularity continues to grow.

❧ *Andropogon gerardii*
Big Bluestem
GRAMINEAE

COLOR: Blue-green; ruddy gold in fall. Tawny seed tufts.
FORM: Narrow clump 3–6′ tall, slowly spreading to form a wide colony up to 30′ across.
SEASON: Fall foliage and stem color. Silvery seeds in fall.
REGIONS: All; rare in nature in extreme West Texas. Hardy to Zone 4.
LIGHT: Full sun.
SOIL: Sands, loams, and clays, including calcareous soils.
MOISTURE: Keep moist but not wet to germinate. Once plants are established, available rainfall suffices except in dry Panhandle and Trans-Pecos, where additional moisture is required. Tolerates seasonally wet soil.
PROPAGATION: Seed, root division in winter.

Big bluestem is the tall, strong-textured grass topped with bristly clusters of seed heads one now sees mostly in roadside ditches and fencerows. It was a dominant grass in the North American Tallgrass Prairies of a hundred years ago. In Texas, it appears

Big bluestem
Andropogon gerardii

Northern sea oats
Chasmanthium latifolium

in low prairies and in seeps at the bases of hills and other low places where moisture collects. If you look at the seed heads, you will see the three-pronged shape that prompted early settlers to call it "turkey-foot." The Greek-derived word "andropogon" means "man's beard." This grass appears in all the Plains states.

Big bluestem's foliage and stalks are blue-green or blue-gray during the growing season. They turn a warm ruddy gold in fall when the plant's sugars are withdrawn from the top growth to the roots and photosynthesis stops. In landscapes, big bluestem makes an attractive tall accent plant among shorter grasses and flowers.

🐚 *Chasmanthium latifolium*
Northern Sea Oats
GRAMINEAE

COLOR: Green; bronze to pale yellow winter color. Tawny seed heads.
FORM: 2–5′ tall with thin, arching seedstalks.
SEASON: Sets seed in summer and fall. Winter-dormant.
REGIONS: All but Trans-Pecos in moist, shady sites. Hardy to Zone 5.

LIGHT: Full sun to full shade.
SOIL: Prefers moist, loamy soil, neutral to alkaline. Accepts poor drainage. Salt-tolerant.
MOISTURE: Ample.
PROPAGATION: Seed. Root division in fall or early spring.

Northern sea oats is loved for its showy seed heads that hang like pendants from the arching stems. They appear in summer. A woodland plant native to Central and East Texas stream banks, sea oats tolerates shade, an uncommon trait in grasses. It makes this one very useful in the garden. Moist, loamy soil is preferred. The dried seed heads are attractive in winter, outdoors or in dried arrangements.

🐚 *Festuca ovina* var. *glauca*
Blue Fescue
GRAMINEAE

COLOR: Blue-gray. Blooms insignificant.
FORM: 6–12″ tall with very fine, slender stems and threadlike leaves. No stolons.
SEASON: Winter-dormant.
REGIONS: Edwards Plateau, Gulf Coast, Prairies & Cross Timbers, South Texas. Hardy to Zone 4. Poor results so far in West Texas.

Blue fescue *Festuca ovina* var. *glauca*

Maidengrass *Miscanthus sinensis*

LIGHT: Full to half-day sun.
SOIL: Well-drained garden or sandy soil preferred.
MOISTURE: Drought-tolerant.
PROPAGATION: Division.

Blue fescue is a low, tufted, slender-leaved grass in a whispery silver-blue shade that is striking in low mixed borders or foliage plantings. Although Midwestern sources describe this European native as tolerant of heat and drought, gardeners in Texas' High Plains and Trans-Pecos find that it isn't heat- and drought-tolerant enough for them. Nevertheless, it is an attractive, gray-blue ground cover for less trying locales. Clumps that die out in the center can be renovated by dividing the roots and replanting the viable portions, cutting back the top growth.

Miscanthus sinensis
Maidengrass, Eulalia Grass
GRAMINEAE

COLOR: Green; green and cream, green and yellow striped and banded leaves in some varieties. Pale pink blooms, ivory to buff seed tassels.
FORM: 5–8′ seedstalks over 4–6′ clumps of leaves.
SEASON: Blooms in fall; attractive year-round.
REGIONS: Edwards Plateau, Gulf Coast, Piney Woods, Prairies & Cross Timbers.
LIGHT: Full sun to partial shade or filtered light.
SOIL: Tolerant as to soil texture; prefers acid but accepts neutral, alkaline.

MOISTURE: 'Gracillimus' is drought-tolerant; other cultivars reportedly accept moist soil.
PROPAGATION: Seed, division.

Maidengrass offers several striking leaf colors and patterns. *Miscanthus sinensis* 'Gracillimus,' 'Variegatus,' and 'Zebrinus' all send up 5–8-foot seedstalks above 4–6-foot clumps of leaves. 'Gracillimus' is solid green with ivory seed tassels. 'Variegatus' has sage green leaves with lengthwise cream or whitish stripes and cream-colored seed tufts. The leaves of 'Zebrinus' are barred with gold or off-white, and the seed heads are buff-colored. These maidengrasses are native to east Asia.

All are striking, stand-alone specimen plants on a scale almost as tall as popular Argentine pampas grass but more refined and without its sharp leaf edges. They can be used at the rear of a border, much as shrubs are. When sunlight shines through the seed tassels, they sparkle like crystal. Only at the end of the winter does the dried growth need to be cut down to make way for new leaves.

Muhlenbergia lindheimeri
Lindheimer's Muhly Grass
GRAMINEAE

COLOR: Pale green, turning off-white after frost. Tawny seed plumes.
FORM: Broad, fountainlike clumps, 2–5′ tall.

SEASON: Late summer to winter bloom; attractive year-round.
REGIONS: Edwards Plateau, Gulf Coast, Plains Country, Prairies & Cross Timbers, South Texas, Trans-Pecos.
LIGHT: Full sun to partial shade or filtered light.
SOIL: Native to rocky limestone soils; prefers well-drained, alkaline.
MOISTURE: Tolerates drought.
PROPAGATION: Seed, division.

Lindheimer's muhly is a native Texas grass with a special airy beauty. It is endemic to the Edwards Plateau, where it grows on limestone uplands, usually near creeks. Two to 5 feet tall, it bears long, featherlike seed plumes that appear primarily in fall. This grass, like little bluestem and big bluestem, is best suited to limestone soils and full sun. It is drought-tolerant. Lindheimer's muhly grass makes a somewhat smaller substitute for Argentine pampas grass that is not troublesome to cut back at winter's end like the sharp-edged pampas grass. It forms a large, round clump tipped with light-catching feathers of seed.

✇ *Nolina texana*
Bear grass, *sacahuista*
AGAVACEAE

COLOR: Gray-green, wiry leaves with large stalks of creamy flowers.
FORM: Clumps to 30″ tall.
SEASON: Evergreen.
REGIONS: Edwards Plateau, Gulf Coast, Lower Rio Grande Valley, Plains Country, South Texas, Trans-Pecos to Zone 7b.
LIGHT: Full sun to partial shade or filtered light, depending on the light intensity in the region.
SOIL: Any well-drained, neutral to alkaline.
MOISTURE: Drought-tolerant.
PROPAGATION: Seeds in fall or winter, root division.

Bear grass is really in the agave family, not among the true grasses. Its 18–30-inch clumps of evergreen, grasslike leaves are attractive and useful in dry, western locales.

Bear grass *Nolina texana.* Photo © 1990 by Barton H. Warnock.

Nolina texana is the most cold-hardy of the nolinas. Large stalks of small creamy white flowers open inside the plant clump, giving an intriguing glimpse of delicate blooms through the foliage. The nolinas are toxic to livestock, particularly sheep.

✇ *Pennisetum*
Fountain Grass
GRAMINEAE

COLOR: Green, wine-red, or mink-black leaves, depending on variety, that turn straw-colored after frost. Cream, copper, rose, brown-black, or ivory seed plumes in fall.
FORM: Clumps 1–6′ tall, depending on variety, and as wide. Narrow leaves, fuzzy and bristly seed plumes.
SEASON: Attractive all season, including dry foliage in dormant period.
REGIONS: All but Piney Woods, for one species or the other. *P. alopecuroides* and hybrids are hardy in Zones 6–9. *P. setaceum* and cultivar 'Rubrum' are hardy to Zone 8b.
LIGHT: Full to reflected. Tolerates partial shade.
SOIL: Tolerant.
MOISTURE: Little to moderate. Survives and multiplies with 6–12″ annual rainfall and some runoff.
PROPAGATION: By division. Species, from seed in porous soil.

The fountain grasses are a popular group widely hybridized for garden use. Green fountain grass,

Burgundy fountain grass *Pennisetum setaceum rubrum* (behind *Plumbago*)

Pennisetum alopecuroides, forms a 30-inch clump. With its mink-black bottlebrush seed heads in fall, it is beautiful paired with the large rust-red flower clusters of 'Autumn Joy' sedum. Dwarf fountain grass 'Hameln' is a foot-high green fountain topped with ivory tassels, perfect for a small border.

Burgundy fountain grass, *P. setaceum* 'Rubrum,' forms large, burgundy foliage clumps with rose-to-buff plumes in summer and fall. It is reliably winter-hardy only through southern Zone 8, but it is used widely as an annual further north for its looks and low water and maintenance requirements. Massed against tall, purple-flowering Mexican bush sage with red-orange *Hamelia patens,* or firebush, at its feet, burgundy fountain grass dominates a striking border at the Dallas Civic Garden Center.

The fountain grasses lend themselves to desert, waterside, and Oriental effects. They control soil erosion, and the taller ones make effective low windbreaks.

Fall pruning will clean up dried foliage, if desired, but the dried winter plumes can be very attractive.

Schizachyrium scoparium
Little Bluestem
GRAMINEAE

COLOR: Blue-green in summer, copper-red in winter.
FORM: 12–24″ tall, occasionally 48″.
SEASON: Fall-blooming. Winter-dormant.
REGIONS: Throughout Texas except the Piney Woods, where another species occurs.
LIGHT: Full sun to partial shade.
SOIL: Any well-drained.
MOISTURE: Drought-tolerant.
PROPAGATION: Seed.

Little bluestem is one of the four grasses that dominated the central North American Tallgrass Prairie, once the second-largest expanse of native grassland in the world. The others are big bluestem, switchgrass, and Indiangrass. Different naturally occurring varieties of little bluestem grow from Massachusetts west to Ontario and south to Florida and New Mexico, including distinct varieties across the regions of Texas, but with rarity in the extreme west of the state.

The beauties of this grass are its knee-high, upright shocks of richly colored foliage, blue-green in summer and copper-red in winter, flecked with feathery, shining seed tufts. Like big bluestem, it is

Little bluestem
Schizachyrium scoparium

a bunchgrass that gradually becomes a very drought-resistant large clump to 5 feet wide. The bluestems are attractive combined with wildflowers, their companions in nature.

While we will never again know what it is to stand surrounded by endless miles of Texas tallgrass prairie, we can still relish the color and form of the plants that composed it in smaller expanses. We can know we are keeping such genetic treasures alive—and share the benefits of their perfect adaptation to their native terrain.

Meadow of little bluegrass and Indiangrass, Lampasas County

✤ *Sorghastrum nutans*
Indiangrass
GRAMINEAE

COLOR: Green, blue-green, to blue. Off-white in winter.
FORM: Leaves 2–3′ tall, seedstalks 3–5′, occasionally to 7′.
SEASON: Blooms in fall.
REGIONS: All. In the Trans-Pecos it is found only occasionally in protected draws.
LIGHT: Full sun to partial shade.
SOIL: Sandy loams, clays.
MOISTURE: Drought-tolerant.
PROPAGATION: Seed or division.

Indiangrass is native to Texas and the Great Plains. It is a major component of the tallgrass and mid-grass prairies, and highly desirable livestock forage. It is frequently called golden Indiangrass, for the color of the maturing seed heads in the fall. These are strikingly beautiful in the light of the setting sun.

For some two hundred years, the nomenclature of this plant had been confused, various authors listing specimens by *Sorghastrum avenaceum* and other names. The 1990 update of *The Manual of the Vascular Plants of Texas* adopts *S. nutans* as correct, naturalists will like to know (and gardeners will care little).

Indiangrass spreads slowly by underground stems to form a clump that enlarges, so it should be given ample room in the garden. The fairly stiff foliage

Closeup of Indiangrass *Sorghastrum nutans*

contrasts well with fall wildflowers. In spring, the leaves are softer and mound over. The variety 'Lometa' is considered the best adapted for Texas conditions. Another strain, 'Mauldin,' is also well adapted.

Trailing roses for a pergola, robust shrubs, and low border roses fill all the roles in this Central Texas garden. Antique Rose Emporium.

An Old Rose Sampler

Rich they were, rich as a fig broken open, soft as a ripened peach, freckled as an apricot, coral as a pomegranate, bloomy as a bunch of grapes. It is of these that the old roses remind me.

—*Vita Sackville-West*

Few gardens of the turn of the century were without the sweet perfume and gentle color of old-fashioned roses. They twined picket fences, shaded arbors, and formed stout, blossom-covered hedges. Some bore dainty four- or five-petaled flowers. Others nodded with heavy blooms so many-petaled and fat that they were called "cabbage roses."

Generations passed, and these early roses were almost forgotten. Beginning in 1867, the tapering buds and large, boldly colored modern Hybrid Tea roses won such popularity that they soon became the criterion for show roses and the standard of the nursery industry. For much of the twentieth century, they were all that the public knew by the name of "rose." The excitement caused by the new roses' charms overshadowed their weaknesses as landscape plants. Bred for gorgeous blooms and long stems, they are admirable for the show ring and as florist flowers but spindly as landscape shrubs and short-lived. Despite the customary grafting of their weaker bloom stock onto the roots of hardier rose species, Hybrid Tea plants generally thrive in full vigor for only a few years.

At length, the trustier virtues of antique roses have regained favor. Their hardiness, individuality, fragrance, diversity as landscape plants, and easy care are invaluable in modern gardens. Some survive many human lifetimes. Their blooms are seemingly infinite in form. Their many aromas from lemon to true "rose" to soft musk and even peppery foliage scents render the term "rose-scented" as inadequate for rose fragrances as the word "love" for the many shades of human affection. Antique roses comprise vigorous climbers, hearty hedge plants, tough ground covers, and compact small shrubs. Susceptibility to mildew and blackspot that makes frequent treatment a necessity for modern roses is insignificant in most of the old types. And the romance of their names and histories appeals to many people, as well.

Introduction to Old Roses

The fossil record indicates that the genus *Rosa* has occupied the planet since the Tertiary periods 60 million to 3 million years ago. Roses originated in the northern hemisphere in Europe, America, Asia, and the Middle East. They have been involved in the turnings of human history for millennia. The tender shoots and fruits, or "hips," were eaten in prehistory. They were first cultivated in China as long as five thousand years ago. Roses were used medicinally and in perfumes and scattered indoors as fragrant "strews" in ancient Asia, the Roman Empire, and medieval Europe.

The movements of both war and trade brought roses in their wake. A Gallica rose was brought from Damascus to France by soldiers returning from the Crusades. Yellow roses native to the Middle East mingled their color strain with the European lines that had previously been only white, pink, or red and thereby introduced yellow coloration to European and American roses for all time—and the disease of blackspot, as well. In the late eighteenth and early nineteenth centuries, the tea trade brought to England four Chinese roses possessed of *remontancy,* or recurring bloom, another quality absent in the original European once-blooming species. Most modern roses are repeat-blooming, thanks to those early predecessors.

By the time of Napoleon, conditions were ripe for a "rose revolution." The Empress Josephine's famous rose garden at Malmaison, and the attention attracted by the publication of Pierre Joseph Redouté's paintings of it, conspired to launch this flowery tumult. Roses attained a new fame. Soon the Industrial Revolution extended the luxury of ornamental gardens to the middle class. Rose catalogs of Queen Victoria's days showed a new generation of hybrids every year. And so it goes today.

Old roses were passed down from generation to generation as rooted cuttings. Many were named for a person or place familiar to their originator: 'Duchesse de Brabant,' 'Souvenir de la Malmaison,' 'La Marne.' They are reproduced by cuttings and grown on their own roots, rather than grafted onto other rootstock as modern Hybrid Teas are. Texas rose grower Michael Shoup points out that the antique rose that one grows today contains cells of an actual plant that may have grown in the garden of Empress Josephine, arrived from the Chinese imperial court via English clipper ship, or been carried West by an American pioneer woman.

Today, "old roses" are defined by the internationally authoritative American Rose Society as those species roses and cultivars in existence before 1867, the debut of the first modern Hybrid Tea rose, 'La France.' Some rosarians include not only bona fide pre-1867 old roses but also roses of old-fashioned heredity or character.

CLASSIFICATION

Botanists have divided genus *Rosa* into thirteen different subgenera and sections. The *Rosaceae* are further classified by ancestry, individual characteristics, and range of adaptation into numerous "classes." Seven of the classes of old roses are particularly well suited to the Deep South and southwestern United States. They are the Bourbons, Chinas, Hybrid Musks, Hybrid Perpetuals, Noisettes, Polyanthas, and Teas. In addition, Hybrid Perpetuals are especially useful in subtropical Zone 10 and mild coastal ranges in Zone 9.

Of further note are two new groups of roses in the old-rose vein, David Austin's English Roses and the Meidiland roses from southern France. These are described briefly at the end of this section. English Roses (a commercial trademark) are notable for combining both the bloodlines and the virtues of old and modern roses. The Meidilands, although modern, are own-root roses with the durability, disease-resistance, and landscape character of old roses. Both types reflect the growing interest in antique and antique-style varieties and ongoing experimentation.

Early roses offer a diversity of landscape uses unknown with modern Hybrid Teas. They include dwarf varieties ideal for containers and small gardens, vigorous climbers, ground covers, and sturdy shrubs. They can be espaliered, trained into garlands, pillars, and fountain shapes, grown in old trees, and used to shade pergolas and arbors.

Although old roses are not carefree, as sometimes described, most old rose varieties do require only about the same amount of maintenance given to common evergreen landscape shrubs like pittosporum and boxwood. As evidenced by their decades of survival untended in old cemeteries and abandoned homesites, old roses survive neglect that would quickly kill a Hybrid Tea.

Conventional notions of what a rose looks like are exploded by antique roses. No two varieties are alike, even within the same class. It hardly needs to be said that there are hundreds of old rose varieties. Those featured here are just a sampling of the feast that is currently on hand. This variety and surprise make old roses a special treat to grow, as can be judged from this rose sampler of twenty-six choice varieties excellent for the South and Southwest.

Care of Old Roses

SITE SELECTION

In general, antique roses like rich, well-drained beds. They need at least six hours of sunlight a day, preferably in the morning, and perform best with more. In cool, frequently cloudy locales, more than six hours of sun is a must. Hybrid Musk roses are said to be the most shade-tolerant, accepting up to a half-day's shade. Avoid planting roses near large trees, whose roots will rob them of moisture and nutrients. Be sure that the soil is well-drained. Rosarian Mitzi Van Sant of Austin checks drainage by a simple method:

Drainage Check for Rose Gardens

Dig a hole 18 to 24 inches deep. Fill it with water and let it drain. Then refill the hole with water—if it does not drain the second time within an hour, roses will not do well there.

PEST AND DISEASE CONTROL

Old-fashioned roses are more resistant to insects and diseases than modern roses. Blackspot and mildew that can seriously weaken Hybrid Teas are minor problems to most older roses. This means that a missed spraying won't spell disaster. Survival is not the same as peak beauty and health, however; treatment may be necessary for roses to look their best and to quell bad cases. In summer, watch for signs of thrips and spider mites and treat accordingly. Blackspot and mildew can be combated by spraying and by removing and destroying spotted foliage. See Chapter 18 for details on pest controls.

SOIL AMENDMENT

Slightly acid soil with a pH of 6.5 to 6.9 is best for roses. Alkaline soils may be acidified gradually by the addition of acidic organic material such as composted pine bark or rapidly with ground sulfur or quick-acting ferrous sulfate (copperas). Organic amendment is beneficial over the long term and in addition to mineral acidifiers, because it improves the soil structure. Residents of areas with very acid soils add hydrated lime or ordinary ground limestone (calcium carbonate) to make it more neutral. Roses like humus-rich soils best.

Start fertilizing established rose plants lightly when they first leaf out. Newly planted roses should not be fertilized for sixty days or until the first bloom flush, to avoid burning tender roots. Fertilize every month or two thereafter, more heavily for established plants, until two months before frost. Chemical fertilizers should be applied either in slow-release form or in more frequent applications than organic fertilizers because they are used up more rapidly. Stop fertilizing at least two months before your area's usual first frost date to avoid inducing a flush of tender new growth right before freezing weather.

RATE OF GROWTH

Gardeners should be aware that different types of roses grow at different rates, says horticulturist Liz Druitt. Chinas and Polyanthas are fastest to grow and bloom. Teas can be a little slow the first year, then catch up in a rush. Climbing varieties often don't perform well until the third year; so the first and second years of bloom should be overlooked if they're not up to peak.

PRUNING AND TRAINING

Pruning of old roses is directed toward eliminating weak wood, maintaining good shrub form, and promoting bloom. In practice, this is very different from the severe pruning required to maintain Hybrid Teas in the desired open, vase shape. For many antique varieties, maintaining robust form can be left to the plant itself. Deadheading, the removal of spent blooms, encourages prolific bloom and is recommended for most. With old roses, pruning practice varies from class to class and, to some extent, among individual varieties within classes, according to growth habit. In the first year, however, pruning for most varieties is much the same, although species and some Hybrid Musks and Teas seem to be exceptions to general pruning practice. Even in the first year, merely tip-pruning Hybrid Musks and species while in active growth can cause them to throw stout new canes at awkward angles. The variety 'Penelope' deforms badly. Teas resent trimming by more than one-third. "They will sulk for a year without blooming," according to Pamela Puryear, a long-time rosarian who resides in Navasota, Texas.

First-year pruning of classes other than Hybrid Musks and Teas is outlined below. Pruning in subsequent years is discussed in the descriptions of the individual classes that follow.

First-year Pruning of Old Roses Other than Hybrid Musks and Teas

(1) When planting bare-root roses, remove only coarse and damaged roots and damaged shoots.

(2) After spring flowering, remove thin, weak growth.

(3) Prune regularly to remove spent flowers, if possible, unless the fruits are desired. Pruning for outward growth as for modern roses, rather than simply removing the dead flower head, is optional. Make a slantwise cut across the stem ¼ inch above an outward-facing bud, angled away from the bud so as to direct rainfall away from rather than into the bud joint, where accumulated moisture can cause rot.

(4) For shrub roses but not most climbers, a second light pruning in early September, combined with deep, regular watering, monthly fertilizing, and mulch to cool roots, will stimulate new growth and abundant fall bloom about six weeks later.

(5) In winter, when the rose is dormant, tip back all vigorous shoots by a few inches to encourage flowering secondary, or lateral, branches the next spring.

Training

Most old garden roses grow larger and require wider spacing than modern roses. Refer to the dimensions given in rose catalogs and allow room for the plants' mature sizes. To create a full-looking planting, it is preferable to plant annuals among new roses rather than planting the roses too close together.

Those described as having lax canes are best grown with the support of a column, trellis, or fence, or "pegged" with branches spread horizontally in an arched position and fastened to the ground at the ends with stakes or metal pins. Lateral training of canes increases bloom; new growth and buds sprout readily from the horizontal canes.

When training a rose on a pillar, *spiral* the plant around it rather than training it straight up; this also increases bloom. Old garden books, such as *Roses for English Gardens* by Gertrude Jekyll and Edward Mawley, give detailed instructions for elaborate effects with roses, including training them on pergolas and on chains hung between posts to form garlands. Illustrations of training on pillars and pegging appear here; for "fountain" form, see photo of 'Ballerina,' page 263.

STARTING ROSES FROM CUTTINGS

Veteran rose growers say that no variety of rose is impossible to root from cuttings. Moss roses are considered more difficult than other types. Most species roses are easily rooted. Chinas are "as easy to root as a sweet potato," according to one Austin gardener. Roses easily propagated from cuttings are individually noted in the descriptions herein. This knack is especially rewarding when a desired rose is not available commercially.

In Texas, the highest success rate is obtained with cuttings taken in April, May, October, and November, says Dallas rosarian Joe M. Woodard, based on systematic tests in his garden. Roses can be rooted at any time, however. Pamela Puryear roots hers in December so as to have them ready to set out in early spring. In her Grimes County (Zone 8b) location, "June to early September is just too stressful for setting out [new transplants]. If one starts in winter, they should be ready [by early spring] and good big plants by early fall."

Cuttings are taken from recently bloomed stems, referred to as "softwood cuttings." Non-bloomed or "blind" wood grows less floriferous rose plants, reportedly. Cut 7–9-inch stem portions with blooms attached (as short as 4 inches for some types of roses). Take three or four cuttings, as not all will root. Remove the bloom just above a compound leaf of five leaflets, leaving a 5–6-inch cutting. Strip the lower leaves, leaving two sets of compound leaves at the top. Soak cuttings in willow water, as described below, or simply dip the lower stem end in a rooting hormone. Then insert it halfway into a moist rooting medium, such as equal parts peat and sand, in a rooting bed (see below) or a 4–6-inch pot. A stick can be used to open a small hole in the rooting medium. Gently tap the cutting to knock off excess rooting compound that could burn it. The soil

Pegging a rose. Photo © 1988 by G. Michael Shoup.

around the cutting should be well firmed to eliminate air pockets. A plastic bag placed over the pot and tucked under it will preserve humidity. Put the potted slip in bright, indirect light with a northern exposure and keep it from drying out. Rooting generally takes three to five weeks. As new growth appears, gradually loosen the bag. If the cutting has rooted by winter, the new plant may be set out in the garden, if it can be protected. If not, winter it over in a cold frame.

Puryear roots roses in plastic cold-drink cups, which are either sunk in the vegetable garden in full shade or put in a mister. The rooting medium is equal parts of washed sand, peat moss, and compost.

Veteran rose-growers who use rooting beds rather than pots recommend 1- or 2-liter green plastic cold-drink bottles, tops cut off, inverted over the planted cuttings. Seated securely over each cutting in indirect light, not full sun, they act as miniature greenhouses. The cutting bed must be kept moist but not wet. A gentle tug on a cutting will show whether it has rooted; if it resists, roots have started. Then the cover can be removed. Well-rooted cuttings can be transplanted to pots, with care to preserve the root ball.

Rooting with Willow Water

Before they are inserted in the rooting medium, cuttings may be soaked in willow water, a reported growth stimulant which has tested effective in trials conducted by Professor Makoto Kawase at the Ohio Agricultural Research and Development Center in Wooster, Ohio. Willow water is made by steeping 1-inch cut stems of any *Salix* species right side up in a half-inch of water heated to boiling. Willow water can be refrigerated and lasts up to three months, according to Puryear. New cuttings are soaked for twenty-four hours in this solution and then planted in the rooting medium. At least the base of each rose cutting must be in darkness for rooting to occur. Use of a rooting hormone after soaking in willow water further increases the success rate.

Bourbon Roses

One might think that Bourbon roses were named for some contribution to Kentucky sour mash. But they and their birthplace, the Ile de Bourbon (now Réunion), reflect the fame of the French royal house in power at their birth. On the Ile de Bourbon, roses were grown as partition hedges (no doubt a makeshift before the invention of barbed wire). The parents of the new rose were the China rose 'Old Blush' and the Autumn Damask *Rosa × damascena* 'Quatre Saisons.' Seeds of the rose resulting from this union were sent to the head gardener of the Duc d'Orléans in France, according to one account. He politically dubbed this first rose of its kind 'Bourbon Rose.' The ensuing race of very double, perfumed roses dominated the nursery trade well into the nineteenth century. Some of these excellent repeat-flowering shrub roses are still favorites today.

The blooms of Bourbons are composed of layers upon layers of petals. Some display a form described as "quartered": the petals repeat their pattern of ruffling in four quadrants of the bloom like wedges of a pie or sectors in a kaleidoscope; the rose appears to be made of four identical quarters. Blooms of some varieties are deeply cupped; others are so shallow as to be almost flat.

CULTURE

Bourbon roses do best where the temperature rarely drops below 0° F (Zone 6b). They are somewhat more susceptible to blackspot than most old varieties. For this reason, they may not do well in humid areas where mildew and blackspot become severe, such as the Gulf Coast and the Piney Woods. Yet true old rose lovers say the luxuriant, fragrant blooms and vigorous, bushy shrubs are well worth the extra effort needed to keep them healthy there.

PRUNING OF BOURBON AND CHINA ROSES

These detailed pruning practices are from gardeners of the National Trust gardens in England. They are ideal guidelines for optimum shape and bloom;

many Texas gardeners don't bother to prune laterals, although this does promote bloom. Some do not prune Bourbons at all.

First-year pruning: see page 256.

In second and following years, Bourbons and most China roses are pruned as follows:

(1) In very early spring (after the last expected hard freeze), cut back very long *new* basal shoots and near basal *year-old* shoots by up to one-third. Cut back laterals on shoots that flowered last year to two or three eyes. Cut out weak or badly placed shoots.

(2) Cut dead and diseased wood out of established plants.

(3) In spring, remove weak growth after the first flowering, and in spring and summer tip-prune to remove spent blooms as in the first year.

(4) In winter, tip back all vigorous shoots by a few inches.

Other wonderful Bourbons besides those described below are 'Zephirine Drouhin' and 'Honorine de Brabant.'

❦ 'Madame Isaac Pereire'
1881

BLOOM: Deep mauve pink 3½–5″, globular. Usually quartered; sometimes muddled. Very double. Intense fragrance.
PLANT FORM: Vigorous, leggy 5–8′ shrub. Best on a fence or trellis, with long new canes pruned back, or pegged.
BLOOM SEASON: Spring with occasional fall repeat; sometimes several bloom cycles from early summer until late autumn.
REGIONS: Hardy to Zone 7. Not recommended for Gulf Coast or Piney Woods because of severe mildew and blackspot.
SPRAYING: Occasionally for mildew and blackspot.

'Madame Isaac Pereire' is considered the most fra-

Bourbon rose 'Madame Isaac Pereire.' Photo © 1988 by G. Michael Shoup.

grant Bourbon, perhaps the most fragrant of all roses. Its intense scent, likened to that of fresh raspberries, is heady and lingering. The plant requires a little more spraying than 'Souvenir de la Malmaison.' English gardener and author Graham Stuart Thomas says of this rose, "When it is well grown, on good deep soil, it has no peer in flower, foliage, or stance." "Big and billowy," it is often described. It is said to propagate easily from cuttings.

❦ 'Madame Ernst Calvat'
1888

'Madame Ernst Calvat' is a lighter pink sport, or natural mutation, of 'Madame Isaac Pereire' that is said to perform better on the Gulf Coast. Rose gardeners say it repeats regularly there. As with its parent, fungus susceptibility necessitates weekly sprayings in the humid coastal air.

❦ 'Souvenir de la Malmaison'
1843

BLOOM: Pale pink, 4½″, flat. Well-quartered, very double. Strong spicy fragrance.
PLANT FORM: Vigorous, compact 3′ shrub or 6–12′ climber. Shrub form needs no support. Suitable for container growing.
BLOOM SEASON: Spring bloom with fall repeat in the northern third of Texas. Continuous bloom

Bourbon rose 'Souvenir de la Malmaison'

flush on the Lower Gulf and even in summer's heat in the middle Blacklands, where fall bloom may continue until Christmas.

REGIONS: Hardy to Zone 7, but tender until well established. Not recommended for Gulf Coast or Piney Woods due to mildew and severe blackspot. Mildew- and blackspot-free in central Blacklands.

SPRAYING: In the Gulf Coast and Piney Woods, requires weekly spraying as for Hybrid Teas because of mildew and severe blackspot. Climber is said to be less susceptible than rest of Bourbons.

'Souvenir de la Malmaison' is considered by many rose growers to be the best Bourbon rose for Texas. The flowers are large, quartered, and extremely fragrant. In recent years, this rose has been honored as best old garden rose of show at national and regional competitions, as well as at numerous local competitions. So popular is 'Souvenir' that 1,000 separate entries were made in one event, says Joe M. Woodard, a Dallas rose aficionado. It was named after Malmaison, the splendid residence of the Empress Josephine just outside Paris. Not part of her fine collection there, it was named in her honor after her death. The large, leathery leaves are medium green and semi-glossy.

A pink climbing sport of 'Souvenir de la Malmaison' was introduced in 1893.

'Kronprinzessin Viktoria'
1888

'Kronprinzessin Viktoria' is a white sport of 'Souvenir de la Malmaison.' Its flowers are loose half-cups, white with lemon tints in the center and a pale pink flush at the edges. The rose is excellent as a low border or in a pot.

China Roses

A dwarf China rose that has been cultivated in its homeland for centuries transferred the genes for continuous flowering to once-blooming Western garden roses in the early 1800s. They were transformed forever. As a result of receiving genes that cause a continuous sprouting of new flowering shoots, the rose classes developed since the infusion of the China strains are repeat bloomers. These include both roses that we now consider old roses and the modern Hybrid Teas. Chinese gardeners had evidently discovered this mutation for perennial bloom cycles among ancient wild roses and begun cultivating those roses that displayed it.

There is evidence that China roses came into Europe as early as the 1500s. They were depicted in Italian paintings of the 1500s and identified by Linnaeus in the mid-1700s. It was not these early introductions that contributed to the development of modern roses, however, but rather four Chinas brought into England in the late eighteenth and early nineteenth centuries, sometimes called the "stud" Chinas. Two of these, 'Slater's Crimson China' and 'Parsons' Pink China,' or 'Old Blush,' are still excellent garden shrubs. They may live a hundred years or more. In Central and South Texas, 'Old Blush' may bloom twelve months of the year. Although its rather loose, double blooms are not blue-ribbon show specimens, the sturdy shrub provides almost nonstop color.

In general, Chinas are adapted to areas where the temperature rarely drops below 10° F (Zone 8), but those included here are hardy to Zone 7. They are considered more tolerant of alkaline soils than most roses. They are pruned in the same manner as Bourbon roses. Bloom color is usually deeper in the milder sunlight of fall.

Pamela Puryear of Navasota in East Central Texas finds Chinas much more resistant to blackspot than Teas. On the Gulf Coast, where such problems are frequent, a sunny location and good air circulation help.

"If a person can grow only one rose, Chinas are closest to fail-proof for Texas," says Liz Druitt of Washington County.

In addition to those Chinas described in detail here, 'Martha Gonzales,' a Texas "found" rose, is a delightful bright-red single on a small, fine-leaved shrub. Corpus Christi gardeners say that pale pink 'Hermosa,' white 'Ducher,' and rose crimson 'Louis Philippe' do well in their gardens. In fact, they are traditional all over the South.

❧ 'Archduke Charles'
Before 1837

BLOOM: Cupped 2½–3″. Deep rose-red outer petals enclose smaller petals that are palest pink. Rose color gradually suffuses entire bloom. Sweet-pea scented.
PLANT FORM: Fairly vigorous, 3–4′ shrub, slowly growing to 5–6′. Compact, dense. Needs no support. Good in pots, for foundation plantings, and as a hedge rose or moderate-sized specimen plant.
BLOOM SEASON: 10–12 months, starting in early spring.
REGIONS: Hardy to Zone 7. Adapted to humid regions.
SPRAYING: For mildew, only in very humid weather. Disease-resistant.
PRUNING: See page 256.

'Archduke Charles' is an excellent medium-sized shrub rose that combines very attractively with lavender, blue salvias, and pink and white dianthuses. In the Lower Rio Grande Valley, Spanish-speaking residents know it as 'Rosa Confederada,' Brownsville nurseryman Morris Clint notes.

❧ 'Cramoisi Supérieur'
1832

'Cramoisi Supérieur' is a rose-red China rose similar to 'Archduke Charles' in growth habit and appearance and equal in quality. The velvety crimson petals reverse to silver, in contrast to the light center and red outer petals of 'Archduke Charles.' 'Cramoisi Supérieur' is also long-blooming and disease-resistant. It is said to resemble *Rosa chinensis* 'Semperflorens,' the original China rose introduced to England in 1792 as 'Slater's Crimson China.' 'Agrippina' is another name by which 'Cramoisi Supérieur' is known.

Rosa chinensis 'Mutabilis'

❧ *Rosa chinensis* 'Mutabilis'
Introduced to Europe before 1894

BLOOM: Single 2½″ blooms that open yellow and turn to apricot, pink, and finally crimson.
PLANT FORM: Vigorous, typically 5–6′ shrub. Grows slowly to 10′. Somewhat twiggy. Healthy. Benefits from support of a wall. Grand as a large specimen.
BLOOM SEASON: Ever-blooming, 8–12 months of the year.
REGIONS: Hardy to Zone 7.
SPRAYING: Fairly disease-free. On the Gulf Coast, spray occasionally for mildew and blackspot.
PRUNING: Lightly to shape.

'Mutabilis' is sometimes called "the butterfly rose" for the delicate, fluttering petals that cover it. Its gradual deepening of color is characteristic of the wild China rose. Often, four colors of flowers will adorn the bush at the same time. The young foliage is an attractive bronze.

This unusual rose first came to the notice of botanists in 1896, when it was given to a Genevan gentleman by Prince Ghilberto Borromeo.

China rose 'Old Blush'

✌ 'Old Blush'
Introduced to Europe in 1752

BLOOM: Double 3″ blooms, medium pink, often with darker flush on outer edge. Form loose, cupped. Vaguely sweet fragrance.
PLANT FORM: Upright, moderately vigorous, slow-growing shrub to over 5′. Good hedge or foundation plant. Climbing form reaches 8–10′. Few thorns.
BLOOM SEASON: Ever-blooming throughout the growing season.
REGIONS: Hardy to Zone 7.
SPRAYING: Rarely, in very humid weather.
PRUNING: Lightly to shape.

The descendants of 'Old Blush' are legion, numbering among them the Noisettes, the French Bourbon rose, and, via the Bourbons, the Teas. "Always the first to bloom and the last to go dormant," Mitzi Van Sant, lately of Austin, says of 'Old Blush.' Both bush and climbing forms are dependable in the Deep South and excellent, easy landscape plants.

Graham Stuart Thomas notes that China roses similar to the four original "stud" Chinas that revolutionized European garden roses are still cultivated in Chinese gardens. The cousins of 'Old Blush' are among them.

Hybrid Musk Roses

An important development in shrub roses occurred in England in the early twentieth century. A class of roses eventually known as Hybrid Musks came into existence. The Reverend Joseph Pemberton, a clergyman living in rural Essex, bred this distinct strain of long-flowering shrub roses with abundant clusters of deliciously fragrant, pastel flowers. As the foundation for these first varieties, he used two German roses of *Rosa moschata* and *R. multiflora* parentage, 'Aglaia' and 'Trier.' By crossing these with selected Teas, Hybrid Teas, and Hybrid Perpetuals, he came up with the unique strain first called "Pemberton roses." They are among the very best garden roses. Hardy to Zone 7 and disease-resistant, they make excellent large arching shrubs, climbers, pillars, and broad informal hedges. These aren't roses for tight corners. Hybrid musks reportedly sometimes bloom sparsely the first year after planting but improve each year thereafter. They require only minimal pruning and will accept more shade than other roses. Several of Pemberton's first creations are among the best-loved Hybrid Musks today.

Pruning of Hybrid Musks in their *third and following* years is as follows: .

(1) In winter, thin (remove) one or two sparsely flowering canes at base.

(2) If you want to try the Royal Horticultural Society's recommended winter trimming, tip back vigorous shoots by a few inches—*in winter only*—to encourage flowering laterals for next season.

(3) After flowering, remove weak growth. Cut out diseased and dead wood.

(4) Do not deadhead.

❦ 'Ballerina'

1937

BLOOM: Single 2″ blooms. Light pink with white eyes, borne in huge clusters. Slight musk fragrance. Followed by fall foliage color and a profusion of small red hips in winter.
PLANT FORM: Dense, healthy, and vigorous arching shrub, 3–4′, slowly growing to 6′ in diameter. Requires cage or low fence for support initially. Leaves light green, semi-glossy. Few thorns.
BLOOM SEASON: Mid-spring with good repeat. Profuse in spring and fall, scattered in summer.
REGIONS: Hardy to 0° F. Adapted to humid regions.
SPRAYING: Rarely needed. Disease-resistant.
PRUNING: Minimal, as outlined in introduction to Hybrid Musks. Tip pruning during bloom season is not advised.

The name 'Ballerina' perfectly captures the arching shrub's resemblance to a ballerina's skirt. In spring and fall, 'Ballerina' almost foams with flowers.

Thought to have been one of Pemberton's seedlings, this rose was introduced after his death by his successor J. A. Bentall. It lends itself well to a grouping or mass planting. The draping habit makes it effective behind retaining walls or next to water.

Hybrid Musk rose 'Ballerina'

Hybrid Musk rose 'Cornelia'

❦ 'Cornelia'

1925

BLOOM: Semi-double 2″ rosettes in profuse clusters. Coral and gold buds open medium pink and fade to blush. Subtle musk scent. Bronze foliage color.
PLANT FORM: Dense, healthy, and vigorous arching shrub, 3–4′ slowly growing to 5′ diameter. To perfect the "fountain" shape that is its tendency, requires cage or low fence for support initially. Good trained as pillar or on trellis, arbor, or pergola. Few thorns.
BLOOM SEASON: Midseason with good repeat. Profuse in spring and fall, scattered in summer.
REGIONS: Hardy to 0° F. Adapted to humid regions.
SPRAYING: Rarely. Disease-resistant.
PRUNING: Minimal, as outlined in introduction to this class. Deadheading is not advised.

'Cornelia' is a name a nineteenth-century father might have given to his daughter. In fact, this rose of Pemberton's and his 'Penelope' both seem sweet and girlish, with their sweet fragrance and soft hues that change from day to day. Given room to expand, they gradually become large, arching shrubs that resemble hoopskirts—grand and stately. I have noticed that the petals close up in the cool of evening and reopen in the morning.

Rosarians say that today's 'Cornelia' may not be the same as the rose Pemberton introduced. Its beauty and usefulness make this ambiguity seem unimportant, however.

Hybrid Musk rose 'Penelope'

🌹 'Penelope'

1924

BLOOM: Semi-double 2–3″ rosettes in profuse clusters. Coral-pink and gold buds open apricot and fade to pale peach-pink and then to white. Strong musk fragrance. Large orange hips in winter.
PLANT FORM: Dense, healthy, vigorous arching shrub, 3–4′, slowly grows to 5′ by 6′ or more. Requires cage or low fence for support initially. Twiggy. Trainable as pillar or any type of *treillage*. Large leaves, few thorns.
BLOOM SEASON: Mid-spring with good repeat all season. Most profuse bloom in spring and fall.
REGIONS: Hardy to 0° F. Adapted to humid regions.
SPRAYING: Rarely needed. Disease-resistant.
PRUNING: Not during the growing season; even tip-pruning faded flowers causes this rose to throw stout new canes at awkward angles. Minimal dormant-season thinning, as for other Hybrid Musks, is discouraged by some, advised by others.

'Penelope' is the most popular Pemberton rose. My two-year-old 'Penelope' that had been six months in the garden put out six new stalks with foot-long corymbs of bloom in August. When it flowers, the progression of bloom color lures me out to take a look first thing every morning. The coral-and-gold

buds pale to apricot when half-open and finally to pink-flushed white open blooms. Their sweet musk fragrance fills the air. The flowers close at night.

A well-prepared bed, spring composting, and regular waterings are about the only exertions 'Penelope' demands. Position it near a window to admire, because cutting the tempting clusters of blooms at the branch tips promotes large, gawky new canes in odd positions, disfiguring the entire shrub. Your restraint will be rewarded by a pretty display of cherry-tomato-sized orange hips in winter.

🌹 'Skyrocket'

1934

BLOOM: Semi-double 2″ open flowers, true red with white center and gold stamens, in small clusters (larger in fall). Light musk fragrance. Bright orange-red hips in winter.
PLANT FORM: Dense, healthy, vigorous arching shrub, 5′ or broader. Early support of cage or low fence improves its natural form. Can be grown as pillar or on any form of *treillage*. Twiggy. Foliage dark green, healthy.
BLOOM SEASON: Flushes starting mid-spring with good repeat and large clusters of bloom in fall.
REGIONS: Hardy to 0° F (Zone 7). Adapted to humid regions.
SPRAYING: Rarely needed. Disease-resistant.
PRUNING: Minimal. Remove weak and diseased growth after flowering. Regular removal of spent blooms to encourage repeat flowering is recommended for this Hybrid Musk. Tip back in winter, when plant is fully dormant.

Hybrid Musk rose 'Skyrocket'

'Skyrocket' is the American name for 'Wilhelm,' for Wilhelm Kordes of Germany, who raised it there in 1934. "Rose rustlers" report having found this plant growing in many places in Texas and the Deep South. It is a true red, rare among the Hybrid Musks.

❧ 'Will Scarlet'

1947

'Will Scarlet' is a 1947 sport of 'Skyrocket.' It is also an excellent garden rose, with blooms a slightly more scarlet red.

Hybrid Perpetual Roses

Hybrid Perpetuals claim among their parentage almost all classes of roses grown in the early nineteenth century. Their sometimes ungainly long canes are more than made up for by the very large, full, wonderfully scented blooms. Both heat- and cold-tolerant, they can be grown nationwide and are of particular benefit on the Gulf Coast.

❧ 'Baronne Prévost'

1842

BLOOM: Large, flat, very double blooms of rich, soft pink. Very fragrant.
PLANT FORM: Upright shrub, 4–5′ tall, erect, but somewhat leggy.
BLOOM SEASON: Heavy bloom in mid-spring, repeat sparse in summer, good in fall.
REGIONS: Hardy to Zone 4. Recommended by Lower Gulf Coast gardeners.
SPRAYING: Rarely.
PRUNING: Pruning as for Bourbons corrects the lanky appearance of long canes not in full leaf. Or plant them in a mixed flower border to hide their bare ankles.

'Baronne Prévost' and 'Marquise Boccella' are considered two of the easiest Hybrid Perpetual roses. They are hardy throughout Texas and, indeed, the entire United States. Lower Gulf Coast gardeners recommend 'Baronne Prévost,' finding it proof

Hybrid Perpetual 'Baronne Prévost.' Photo © 1990 by G. Michael Shoup.

against their long, hot summers. While Hybrid Perpetuals in general may not have the best shrub form among old garden roses, they do offer very large, full flowers with heavy rose fragrance. 'Baronne Prévost' is considered to be a better-shaped plant than many in its class.

Noisette Roses

The Noisettes are the first truly American class of roses. The original 'Champneys' Pink Cluster' and its offspring 'Blush Noisette' are, as English rosarian Peter Beales says, "well worth garden space." 'Champneys' Pink Cluster,' writes horticulturist Graham Stuart Thomas, "combined the climbing habit, large open clusters of flowers and odor of the Musk with the semi-double pink flowers of the China and the handsome foliage of both."

Striking characteristics of all the early Noisettes include large flower clusters, musky scent, and vigorous growth. They vary in size and plant form. Most bloom later than the Bourbons, and many bloom virtually continuously through the growing season. They are fairly cold-tender and therefore suited to climates where the temperature rarely drops below 10° F. They have been extremely popular in the South since their origination.

The Noisettes came into existence as a result of plant-swapping among a Charleston rice planter and gardener, John Champneys, and two brothers, Philippe and Louis Noisette, nurserymen in Charleston and Paris, respectively. Philippe Noisette gave Champneys an 'Old Blush' rose. Champneys crossed it with a white Musk and gave some of the offspring back to his neighbor as a thank-you. Noisette then produced more hybrids, which he sent to his brother in Paris. The delighted Louis dubbed the first seedling 'Rosier de Philippe Noisette,' later shortened to 'Noisette' and applied to all the offspring roses. In America, Noisette's first rose came to be known as 'Blush Noisette.'

Noisette climber 'Lamarque'

℘ 'Lamarque'

1830

BLOOM: Double 2″ ivory blooms with yellow centers. Borne in clusters on long stems. Nodding. Fragrant.
PLANT FORM: Climber to 10′. Abundant light green foliage. Few thorns.
BLOOM SEASON: Mid-spring with good repeat to late in the year.
REGIONS: Cold-tender below 10° F (Zone 8). Adapted to humid regions.
SPRAYING: Rarely needed. Disease-resistant.
PRUNING: Minimal, as for Hybrid Musks, with the difference that regular removal of spent blooms is advised. Remove weak and diseased growth after flowering. Tip back in winter. Because of its twiggy growth, requires more pruning to keep "clean" than other Noisettes.

'Lamarque' is a child of 'Blush Noisette.' It was raised in France by Maréchal. The other parent was 'Parks' Yellow Tea-Scented China,' brought into England in 1824 and the last of the four "stud" China introductions. Thus yellow was added to the spectrum of climbing and rambling roses. 'Lamarque' was the first of the yellow descendants of 'Parks' Yellow Tea-Scented China.'

'Lamarque' has a tendency to nod which is attractive in climbing roses. "There's something special about having roses hanging down over you," as Michael Shoup of Independence says.

℘ 'Nastarana'

Introduced to Europe in 1879

BLOOM: Single white 2½″ flowers open from pink buds. Fragrant.
PLANT FORM: Upright, 3–4′. Slender dark-green leaves with a slight blue tinge. Very vigorous.
BLOOM SEASON: Mid-spring; thereafter almost continuous through the growing season.
REGIONS: Generally cold-hardy to 0° F; hardier than most other Noisettes.
SPRAYING: Spray for blackspot on the Gulf Coast.
PRUNING: Lightly. See page 271.

'Nastarana' is thought to be the offspring of an early cross between the species Musk, *Rosa moschata,* and *R. chinensis.* Brought to Europe in 1879, it is believed to have been grown in Persia long before.

R. moschata, the Musk rose, originated in the Middle East and in southern Europe. It was introduced to northern Europe probably during the reign of Henry VIII. Its descendant, 'Nastarana,' was once called the "Persian Musk rose." It is still an excellent

Noisette 'Nastarana'

garden shrub today, as its forebear was in ancient Persia, and is more cold-hardy than other Noisettes. The dainty, soft blooms, tender coloration, and perfume are very pleasing.

Polyantha Roses

The Polyantha class was created in 1875 by the crossing of a now-unknown hybrid China with a low-growing form of the Japanese *Rosa multiflora*. The continuous-blooming characteristic and shrub shape of the Chinas was carried over to some of the Polyanthas. Naturally occurring Asian hybrids of the two parent roses were imported into France in 1865 and bred there, also.

Described as "happy-go-lucky little flowers," the Polyanthas produce clusters of small, slightly cupped semi-double blooms all season. Polyanthas are generally hardy and disease-resistant, except in the Valley, where some nurserypeople say that many varieties are prone to mildew. Several are dwarf, compact plants ideal for patios, containers, and ground-cover plantings. Although the popularity of Polyanthas declined after World War II, it is on an upswing. Their revival is natural, because Polyanthas are compact, reliable, easily maintained plants ideal for small modern homesites.

✿ 'Cécile Brunner'
1881

BLOOM: Double 1½″ pale pink flowers. Borne in clusters. Slightly fragrant.
PLANT FORM: Shrub form 3–4′. Vigorous climber 10–20′. Abundant dark green foliage. Few thorns.
BLOOM SEASON: Heavy late spring bloom followed by continuous flowering until freezing weather.
REGIONS: Cold-tender below 10° F (Zone 8).
SPRAYING: Rarely, in very humid weather. Generally disease-resistant, except for powdery-mildew susceptibility in South Texas and Lower Rio Grande Valley.
PRUNING: Minimal. Remove weak and diseased growth after flowering. Regular removal of spent blooms encourages repeat flowering. Tip back in winter.

'Cécile Brunner,' better known as "the Sweetheart Rose," is the most popular Polyantha. It is famous as a boutonniere. The perfect little pointed pink buds are the image of a tiny Hybrid Tea. 'Cécile Brunner' was created in France from the cross of an earlier French Polyantha, 'Mignonette,' and the Tea rose 'Madame de Tartas.' Although the bush form is small, the climber is vigorous and large. The shrub form is ideal for pots, patio plantings, and small beds.

Based on its excellent performance in the Lower Rio Grande Valley, aside from slight powdery-mildew problems, 'Cécile Brunner' should also do well on the Lower Gulf Coast and in South Texas.

✿ 'Perle d'Or'
1884

'Perle d'Or' is another Polyantha remarkably similar to 'Cécile Brunner' but yellow-apricot in color. It may in fact be a sport of 'Cécile Brunner,' and its uses are the same.

❧ 'The Fairy'

1932

BLOOM: Double 1–1½" rose pink flowers. Borne in sprays.
PLANT FORM: Shrub form 2–4′. Sometimes upright, sometimes trailing. Abundant, tiny light-to-medium-green leaves. Moderately thorny.
BLOOM SEASON: Heavy spring bloom followed by continuous flowering until freezing weather.
REGIONS: Cold-tender below 10° F.
SPRAYING: In Central and North Central Texas, rarely, in very humid weather. Mildew-prone in South Texas but otherwise "a very fine rose" there.
PRUNING: Minimal. Remove weak and diseased growth after flowering. Regular removal of spent blooms encourages repeat flowering. Tip back in winter.

'The Fairy' is perfect for mass plantings and in containers. It can be maintained as a low hedge by pruning. The blooms turn nearly white in summer's heat but continue to appear as long as moisture is provided. It is valuable for the blanket of bright pink it creates in the spring and its almost continuous blooming thereafter. While the open flowers are loosely formed, their overall effect is lovely and reliable.

Polyantha 'La Marne'

❧ 'La Marne'

1915

'La Marne' is a popular, prolific Polyantha that blows "cleanly," shedding its spent petals before they turn brown.

Tea Roses

The Tea rose is another long-blooming rose that originated in the Orient. It found its way into the hands of European rose breeders at about the same time as the China rose. Either it had been developed earlier by the Chinese or it arose as a result of chance alliances between the wild Tea rose, *Rosa gigantea*, and *R. chinensis*. The advent of the Teas to England, like that of the Chinas, was in the holds of ships of the East India Tea Company. One of the roses that made the trip to England was 'Parks' Yellow Tea-Scented China,' classified variously as Tea and China. The epithet "Tea-Scented" somehow stuck, whether inspired by the flowers' own unusual scent or by some aroma that lingered from the cargo. The early Teas, like Chinas, brought remontancy; they also passed their valuable yellow coloring into some of the many Teas bred in the early twentieth century. The Tea roses rapidly became very popular, particularly in southern Europe.

Polyantha 'The Fairy'

Tea roses are considered by some to be more mildew-resistant than most other classes of roses (when they have six hours' sun and free air circulation). They are somewhat cold-tender and do best in climates where the mercury rarely drops below 10° F. This makes them ideal for Zone 8 and warmer regions of the American South. The varieties listed here all are particularly easy to propagate from cuttings.

The tapering buds and high-centered, many-petaled blooms of Tea roses became the rose breeders' ideal. This flower form was pursued and eventually standardized in the modern Hybrid Tea roses—which are nonetheless mostly scentless and rather predictable compared to the original Teas.

Tea rose 'Duchesse de Brabant'

🌺 'Duchesse de Brabant'

1857

BLOOM: Double, clear pink to rose, 3–4". Cupped, free-flowering. Fragrant. There is also a white form.
PLANT FORM: Spreading shrub, 3–5' tall. Thickly foliaged.
BLOOM SEASON: Almost continuous throughout the growing season.
REGIONS: Somewhat cold-hardier than its class as a whole, which is hardy to 10° F. One of the best Teas for the Lower Gulf Coast.
SPRAYING: Rarely needed. Fairly disease-resistant.
PRUNING: Resents it. Clear dead wood and shape lightly in very early spring only. Remove spent blooms.

'Duchesse de Brabant' is fragrant, free-flowering, and disease-resistant. It is leafy almost to the ground rather than bare at the base like most roses, which makes it a particularly attractive shrub. The rose long known among South Texans by the traditional Spanish name 'Aurelia' has recently been tentatively identified by horticulturist Scott Ogden as the famous 'Duchesse.' Nurseryman Morris Clint calls it "the finest antique rose you can find for Corpus to Brownsville.

🌺 'Lady Hillingdon'

1910

BLOOM: Classic Tea shape in rich apricot-yellow buds, opening to loose and blousy apricot-flushed ivory flowers. Very fragrant.
PLANT FORM: Upright, 4–6'. Purplish new shoots and dark green leaves. Almost thornless. A climbing form reaches 15' by 8' in size.
BLOOM SEASON: Almost continuous during the growing season. Prolific.

Tea rose 'Lady Hillingdon'

REGIONS: Cold-tender below 10° F.
SPRAYING: Rarely needed.
PRUNING: Only to remove spent blooms and weak and diseased growth and to lightly shape in very early spring.

The deliciously colored blooms of this rose are beautifully set off by the dark green leaves and purplish new shoots. The open flowers are considered loose by some rose enthusiasts, pleasantly informal by others. Some afternoon shade preserves the flower color.

❦ 'Maman Cochet'

1893

BLOOM: Soft rose color with deeper flush and lemon center, 3″. Classic long-budded Hybrid Tea form. Fragrant.
PLANT FORM: Upright 4′ plant. Strong stems. Dark green, leathery foliage.
BLOOM SEASON: Almost continuous.
REGIONS: Cold-tender below 10° F. Blooms may "ball" in humid climates.
SPRAYING: Spray for blackspot on the Gulf Coast.
PRUNING: Lightly, as for other Tea roses.

Mother Cochet must have been pleased to have been memorialized in this rose. Its blooms as well as the shrub itself have a strong, rounded, ample form.

❦ 'Sombreuil'

1850

BLOOM: Large, flat, very double rose to 3½″. Buds have a citron tinge. Open blooms are pure white with pale flesh or ivory tints at the heart. Sometimes quartered. Fragrant.
PLANT FORM: Climber, to 10–15′. Ample, lush green foliage. Vigorous. Ideal as a pillar or on a wall, fence, or trellis.
BLOOM SEASON: Spring flush, scattered summer bloom, and fall flush. Good repeat for a climber.
REGIONS: Considered the hardiest of the Teas, to Zone 7b at least.
SPRAYING: Reportedly mildew-free.
PRUNING: Lightly, as for other Tea roses.

Tea rose 'Maman Cochet'

Climbing Tea 'Sombreuil.' Photo © 1987 by G. Michael Shoup.

A lovely white climbing rose. The plump buds have a hint of lemon yellow deep inside as they open. This turns to a tinge of flesh-pink in the center of the fully opened rose. The fragrance is fresh and lemony, to my nose. A French friend mistook the name 'Sombreuil' for "Sans Bruit," meaning "No Noise" or "Without a Sound," and that is how observers are likely to be when they see it in first, full bloom.

Lady Banks rose
Rosa banksiae 'Lutea'

Species Roses and Near-Species Hybrids

Species roses are the original wild roses as found in nature. There are also many hybrids very closely related to the species forms and similar in character. They are vigorous and, for the most part, disease-resistant. Properly planted and well cared for in their first year or so, they will often thrive untended from then on.

Pruning of climbing species and near-species hybrids is specialized. It is intended to establish a strong framework and keep the plant healthy and free-flowering. When such climbers are grown unrestricted in old trees, it is impractical to prune or train them at all, except for removing dead, diseased, and weak wood when possible. In other situations, a strong, evenly spaced framework of branches should be trained early on. Horizontal or angled training of new leader shoots will prevent bareness at the bottom of the plant. *Do not prune back the tops of newly planted roses in this group.* Trim damaged roots before planting and remove very weak top growth and damaged or diseased wood. Tie in new shoots as they develop. In winter, prune back flowered lateral shoots very lightly and tie in leading shoots.

✤ *Rosa Banksiae* 'Lady Banks Rose'
1824

BLOOM: Three forms: double 1″ pale yellow, double white, and single yellow. Borne in clusters.
PLANT FORM: Climber 10–30′. Very vigorous with very long canes. Leaves small, light green, profuse. Almost thornless.
BLOOM SEASON: Very early spring. No repeat.
REGIONS: Generally cold-tender below 15° F. Adapted to humidity and to subtropical climates.
SPRAYING: None. No serious insect or disease problems.
PRUNING: See instructions for pruning of species and near-species climbers above.

The Banksia roses were brought back from China in the days of the English tea trade. They are old stand-bys of the South, often living for many generations. The "largest rose in the world," in Tombstone, Arizona, is a double white 'Lady Banks,' *R. banksiae* var. *banksiae* 'Alba Plena.' Brought from Scotland in 1885, it now covers a 7,000-square-foot arbor from one trunk. It has a sweet fragrance likened to violets. *R. banksiae* 'Lutea,' the yellow double, is more widely seen in the South. There is also a yellow single form, *R. banksiae* 'Lutescens.'

The Banksias' only apparent enemy is severe freezing weather. Planted in a sheltered spot, they may live indefinitely. They have one massive flowering in very early spring, producing large cascading trusses of small flowers at tulip time. 'Lutea' is the variety readily available in nurseries. Ample space is needed for all three forms. A gazebo is an ideal situation.

× *Rosa bracteata* 'Mermaid'

✿ × *Rosa bracteata* 'Mermaid'
1918

BLOOM: Single 4½–5½″ yellow bloom with prominent golden stamens. Fades to pale yellow. Fragrant.
PLANT FORM: Canes trailing to 15′ and beyond. Vigorous, very lax canes that can be trained up. Can be supported or allowed to spread as an enormous ground cover. Very thorny. Large, rich dark green leaves and dark brownish maroon wood. Almost evergreen.
BLOOM SEASON: Long, bountiful mid-spring bloom and occasional bloom thereafter.
REGIONS: Cold-tender below 10° F. Mildew-free.
SPRAYING: None. Very disease-resistant.
PRUNING: To remove weak and diseased growth, to train first- and second-year plants, and to remove at their base canes that reach out of bounds. Early training is the best chance to direct the growth of a 'Mermaid.' If the plant is grown spreading outward from its trunk rather than trained close to a wall or trellis, you'll need a pole pruner after a year or two to remove canes at the base.

'Mermaid' is the offspring of an unnamed double yellow Tea and the wild Chinese *Rosa bracteata* that is naturalized in the southeastern United States. In 1917, it won the Royal National Rose Society Gold Medal. In Texas it has been known to cover 20 feet of fence in a season. With its long purple thorns, there is little better burglar-proofing. Pruning can be hazardous to your health and usually does not improve the exuberant form of the plant. This rose must be planted where it can ramble—just try to stop it.

The large, sulfur-flushed flowers with their halo of gold stamens, against the dark, rich foliage, are captivating. Many a casual observer has become an old-rose lover upon sight of 'Mermaid.' My neighbors responded to its first bloom season in my garden by demanding "What *is* that?!"

✿ *Rosa wichuraiana* 'Poteriifolia'
1879

BLOOM: Single, white 1½–2″ flowers with showy golden stamens.
PLANT FORM: Creeping, 1–3′ tall. Shiny near-evergreen foliage. Red hips in winter.
BLOOM SEASON: Spring and summer.
REGIONS: Cold-hardy throughout the United States.
SPRAYING: Not needed; disease-free.
PRUNING: Cut back to 3–4″ above ground in late winter or very early spring. Well-established (three- or four-year-old) plants can be mowed annually with mower at highest setting.

Rosa wichuraiana 'Poteriifolia' is recommended by the National Arboretum in Washington, D.C., as a ground cover. The species, native to Japan, is known as "the Memorial Rose" for its extensive use as a ground cover on grave sites. The hybrid is vigorous, but not so aggressive that it can't be used in home landscapes. "It's as hardy as Asian jasmine," says Michael Shoup, owner of the Antique Rose Emporium in Independence. "For any place where you can't mow—ditches, banks, rocky areas—or in big

Memorial rose *Rosa wichuraiana* 'Poterifolia.'
Photo © Glenn M. Austin.

planters, it's ideal." This unusual rose grows only
1 to 3 feet tall. It cascades with small white flowers
periodically from spring through summer, with
red oval hips in winter. It is virtually evergreen and
hardy way below zero. It looks best when it gets
consistent moisture, but even unwatered plants
survive.

A rose you can prune with a lawnmower? That's
how many old-time gardeners treat Wichuraiana
roses. "These roses are used by country gardeners
who take the attitude, 'If it doesn't live and grow,
who needs it?'" says Shoup. "In February, when
most roses look like a stick anyway, they get out
the mower and mow them to the ground." The
Wichuraianas and certain thicket-forming China
and Polyantha roses have strong underground roots
that send up new shoots. Cutting them back
severely once a year keeps them "clean." Of course,
they shouldn't be cut to the ground until they are
well established. For the first year or two, they
shouldn't be cut lower than 2 or 3 inches.

New English Roses in the Old Manner

ENGLISH ROSES

"English Roses" are the product of more than thirty
years of work by English grower David Austin,
cross-breeding old roses such as Gallicas and
Damasks with Hybrid Teas and Floribundas. One
goal was the cupped, many-petaled "cabbage"
bloom found in some old roses, along with their
other virtues, in an ever-blooming plant.

Reports from San Antonio and Dallas a couple of
years after English roses' introduction to Texas indicate that Austin's prodigies do perform here largely
as advertised. They combine the vigorous shrub
forms, disease-resistance, soft colors, rich perfumes,
and varied old-rose flower forms with the repeat-
flowering and wider color range of modern roses.
Particularly welcome in the South were the fully
double, hundred-petaled flower varieties. These are
most numerous among the antique Gallicas, Damasks, and Centifolias, classes that are mildew-prone
here and once-flowering. English roses offer this
classic bloom form without the accompanying
drawbacks.

Dallas gardeners report no blackspot and note
powdery mildew only on the variety 'Fisherman's
Friend.'

Heat-resistance is another asset. Despite their
origin in cool, damp England, heat doesn't seem to
bother them at all, at least not in North Texas. In
late summer, when Hybrid Tea roses are not at
their best, English roses 'Warwick' and 'William
Shakespeare' "bloomed their heads off."

While blooms of many are cupped and very
double, some are semi-doubles like peonies or simple wild roses. The shrubs range in height from 2 to
8 feet, upright to arching.

The more unusual hues include salmons, apricots,
blends of yellow and pink, and deep, unfading reds
in the bluish range.

Many are said to be excellent cut flowers that last
for five or six days in bouquets.

The following varieties have been grown with excellent results in the Dallas area. Supply is limited and the breed is largely untried locally, so any you can get are worth trying.

'The Squire.' Blooms deep crimson, very double, to 5 inches across. To 4 feet.

'Belle Story.' Pale pink with prominent gold stamens, like a single peony, 4 inches across. Perfumed. To 5 feet.

'Windrush.' Pale yellow, peony form with double row of petals, gold stamens. Fragrant. To 5 feet.

'Othello.' Dark crimson, very large and double. Fragrant. To 5 feet.

'Mary Rose.' Rose pink, large, very double. Longest-blooming. To 5 feet.

'Winchester Cathedral.' White form of 'Mary Rose.' To 5 feet.

'Heritage.' Shell-pink, cupped, lemon scent. To 4 feet.

'Fisherman's Friend.' Garnet-red, flat, very double, large flowers. Fragrant. To 7 feet first year. Somewhat mildew-prone.

'English Garden.' Soft apricot-yellow, full-petaled flat rosettes, lightly fragrant. To 3 feet.

'Fair Bianca.' White, very double. Myrrh scent. To 3 feet.

'Bredon.' Small, numerous, buff-yellow rosettes. To 5 feet.

'Graham Thomas.' Most popular of the group. Golden yellow, cupped, Tea Rose scent. To 6 feet.

'Abraham Darby.' Peach-pink shading to pale yellow. Fragrant. To 5 feet; climbs with support to 8–10 feet.

Meidiland roses come from the Meilland family of southern France, longtime rose growers. Francis Meilland developed the rose 'Peace,' possibly the most famous rose in the world.

The Meidilands are billed as landscape roses. They offer dense, vigorous arching shrubs and ground covers. Mass-flowering, they offer season-long color that persists even through the heat of August in North Texas. (Further south, they reportedly take a dog-day breather.) Several also produce heavy displays of showy, orange-red hips in late fall and winter.

What sets these apart from modern roses is that they grow on their own roots, not grafted onto a different rootstock as are the less-hardy Hybrid Teas. As true shrub roses, like old rose varieties, they are devoid of the "suckers" that sprout from below the graft on grafted roses, and they grow and spread true to type.

The best known of the group and the first introduced was pink 'Bonica,' the 1987 All-America Rose Selection and the first shrub rose awarded that honor.

A San Antonio horticulturist says that licensed grower Park Seed is overselling a little when they call the Meidilands "a gardener's 'dream shrub' . . . bone hardy, versatile and care-free." But Dallasites agree, based on two years' experience. Both 2-foot, trailing 'White Meidiland' and upright, 4-foot 'Pink Meidiland,' a bright pink with a white eye, thrived in clay pots—a trying summer situation for most roses.

Meidiland roses were found disease-free and thriving in the Tyler Municipal Rose Garden in June, when the Hybrid Teas often look as if they are struggling.

Meidilands are recommended for practical uses in the landscape, as ground covers, hedges, or erosion-controlling slope covers. Cascading tree roses are a romantic, innovative use of the trailing varieties. The hips may also be a colorful asset in winter, compared to those of heavy-fruiting species roses that are once-bloomers.

The Meidiland roses that are commercially available include: mounding ground covers 'White,' 'Pearl,' 'Red,' and 'Scarlet Meidiland' and upright shrubs 'Bonica,' 'Pink Meidiland,' 'Scarlet Meidiland,' crimson 'Sevillana,' and coral 'Ferdy.'

HOW TO GROW THE NEW ROSES

Plant like any roses, in well-drained, fertile soil to the same depth as the rose was originally grown. February is ideal planting time for bare-root plants; containerized ones may be planted at any time. Full sun is preferred; late-afternoon shade is acceptable. Addition of organic material is particularly beneficial in alkaline and/or heavy soils.

Water when the top inch of soil becomes dry.

Fertilize periodically during the growing season.

A 3-inch layer of mulch conserves moisture and reduces stress from summer heat and winter cold.

With English roses, expect somewhat spindly growth the first year; shrubs start filling in the second year. Mature heights in Texas are somewhat taller than given in eastern catalogs.

The first year, prune only to remove damaged growth. In general, prune in subsequent years only to remove damaged growth and lightly to shape. However, tall English Rose varieties can be maintained at a shorter height by pruning, if desired.

Deadheading greatly increases flowering.

Disease problems are minimal to nonexistent; treat as for other roses.

Old-fashioned reseeding petunias and annual standing cypress, or scarlet gillia, mingle with mealy blue sage and white penstemon. Antique Rose Emporium, Independence.

CHAPTER SEVENTEEN

Companion Plants for Perennial Gardens

The beauty and variety of the broad-leaved evergreens is most apparent in winter . . . Buds of many of the spring-flowering shrubs begin to expand on summer-seeming winter days . . . I am making . . . a shaded path bordered by ferns and other woodsy things . . . Flowering vines that are native to us . . . add to the profusion of scent and color . . .

—Elizabeth Lawrence

Dooryard gardens of many cultures combined fruit trees, vines, flowers, and herbs—whatever was useful or caught the cottager's eye. This cottage mixture was revived in the late 1800s in the English perennial garden style perfected by Gertrude Jekyll, in part from nostalgia for the earlier tradition. Miss Jekyll also undoubtedly recognized in these diverse plant materials the new qualities they brought to perennial garden design. Variety of form, texture and scale, seasonal display, and year-round interest all were gained by the addition of other types of plants to the strictly herbaceous borders of Jekyll's early predecessors. They afford the same visual variety and longevity in perennial gardens today.

Evergreen shrubs formed the background of the traditional perennial border. This green curtain defined the space, set off flower and foliage colors, and gave a sense of solidity and permanence particularly needed in winter. Low evergreen shrubs served as edging. In the French classical and Tudor periods, flower beds were outlined with low clipped hedges of boxwood or shrubby semi-deciduous herbs and subshrubs such as lavender and santolina.

Flowering and fruiting trees provide vertical elements in a garden's design. They may be used singly, in a naturalistic clump, or in formal rows. Used formally, such deciduous trees and flowering shrubs may serve as a tall tier of color between taller evergreen shrubs in the background and low flowers that fill the foreground. They may punctuate the end of a bed or anchor an accent planting of smaller plants. The shrubs may form masses of seasonal color within a border, much as tall perennials do. Dwarf flowering shrubs serve the same purposes in smaller areas.

Flowering vines give more than bloom. They also serve as backdrops, much as tall shrubbery does. They cover unsightly structures and other flaws. Their foliage makes light-colored walls appear to recede, creating a sense of spaciousness in small areas. They can camouflage utilitarian fences and define an inviting private space. Finally, there is a special charm to plants twining up columns or trailing overhead on arches and arbors. Vines may either complement elaborate floral plantings or so fully furnish a green space that only a clump of iris or a potted rose is necessary to complete it.

Annuals fill in the spaces that inevitably occur in a perennial garden, either from newness, evolution, or seasonal change. They provide variety. Bought as nursery transplants, they can be an instantaneous source of color. Started from seed indoors or in a cold frame or greenhouse, they are economical and fun to grow. Reseeding varieties both give seed to save for later planting and, let ripen naturally, scatter seed that gives a natural look by coming up where it may.

Following are lists of selected old-fashioned and other less-usual—but available—annuals, vines, shrubs, and small trees for backgrounds and bed-mates in perennial gardens. The most obvious basic landscape selections are omitted, in the interest of presenting plants one may not know from simply looking around the neighborhood or walking through a nursery. Special attributes and regional limitations are noted.

Reseeding Annuals

Table 6. Annuals and Biennials for Fall Planting from Seed

Black-eyed Susan	*Rudbeckia hirta*
Common hollyhock (B)	*Alcea rosea*
Cornflower or bachelor's button	*Centaurea cyanus*
Johnny-jump-up	*Viola tricolor*
Larkspur	*Consolida orientalis, C. ambigua (Delphinium consolida, D. ajacis)*
Phlox, Drummond's	*Phlox drummondii*
Plains coreopsis	*Coreopsis tinctoria*
Poppy, California	*Eschscholzia californica*
Poppy, Mexican	*E. californica var. mexicana*
Standing cypress (B)	*Ipomopsis rubra*
Tahoka daisy	*Machaeranthera tanacetifolia*

B   Biennial.

Table 7. Warm-Season Annuals to Start in Spring

Cleome (WS)	*Cleome hasslerana*
Cockscomb (WS)	*Celosia cristata, C. plumosa*
Four o'clock (AF)	*Mirabilis jalapa*
Globe amaranth (AF)	*Gomphrena globosa*
Petunia, old-fashioned (AF)	*Petunia × hybrida*
Touch-me-not (WS)	*Impatiens balsamina*
Wishbone flower (AF)	*Torenia fournieri*
Zinnia 'Rose Pinwheel' (WS)	*Zinnia elegans × Z. angustifolia*

AF After Frost: Seed outdoors after last frost or indoors 6–8 weeks before last frost (10 weeks for petunia, wishbone flower).

WS Warm Season: Doesn't grow well until soil warms. Plant seed indoors 6–8 weeks before average last frost date, seed or starter plants outdoors in mid-spring.

Vines

Table 8. Flowering Vines

Carolina jessamine (P, EV)	*Gelsemium sempervirens*
Cat's-claw creeper (P, EV)	*Macfadyena unguis-cati*
Clematis (P, EV)	(Many; see Chapter 13, Perennials)
Coral honeysuckle (P, SEV)	*Lonicera sempervirens*
Coral vine, queen's wreath (A)	*Antigonon leptopus*
Crossvine (P, EV)	*Bignonia capreolata*
Moonvine (A)	*Ipomoea alba*
Morning glory (A)	*I. purpurea*
Silverlace vine (A)	*Polygonum aubertii*
Trumpet vine 'Madame Galen' (P)	*Campsis radicans* 'Madame Galen'

A   Annual
P   Perennial
EV   Evergreen
SEV Semi-evergreen

Shrubs and Small Trees

EVERGREEN SHRUBS

Table 9. Selected Tall and Medium-height Evergreen Shrubs Suitable for Backgrounds

Chinese photinia (*, +)	*Photinia serrulata*
Carolina cherry laurel (*, +, –)	*Prunus caroliniana*
Eleagnus (**, *, +)	*Elaeagnus macrophylla, E. pungens*
Holly, Burford (+)	*Ilex cornuta* 'Burfordi'
dwarf Burford (+)	*I. cornuta* 'Burfordi Nana'
'Blue Princess' (+)	*I.* × *meservae*
'China Girl'(+)	*I.* × *meservae*
'Nellie R. Stevens' (+)	*I.* × 'Nellie R. Stevens'
'Sizzler' (+)	*I.* × 'Sizzler'
yaupon (+)	*I. vomitoria*
Juniper, Chinese	*Juniperus chinensis* 'Blue Point,' 'Spartan' ('Spearmint')
eastern red cedar (+)	*J. virginiana* 'Burkii,' 'Manhattan Blue'
Rocky Mountain	*J. scopulorum* 'Gray Gleam,' 'Welchi'
Privet, Japanese	*Ligustrum japonicum* 'Texanum'
variegated Chinese (S)	*L. sinense* 'Variegatum'
Yucca	*Yucca thompsoniana, Y. filamentosa, Y. glauca*

  **   Flowers. Eleagnus' late-winter blooms are inconspicuous but very fragrant.
   *   Fall foliage color.
   +   Winter berries.
   –   Acid soils preferred.
   S   Semi-evergreen in Zone 8 and north.

Table 10. Low-growing Evergreen Shrubs for Low Backgrounds and Edging and in the Border

Abelia, dwarf (**)	*Abelia grandiflora* 'Sherwoodi'
'Edward Goucher' (**)	*A. grandiflora* 'Edward Goucher'
prostrate (**)	*A. grandiflora* 'Prostrata'
Boxwood, common English (PC)	*Buxus sempervirens*
Japanese	*B. microphylla*
Cenizo, dwarf (*, S)	*Leucophyllum laevigatum*
Creeping juniper	*Juniperus horizontalis* and cultivars ('Bar Harbor,' 'Blue Rug,' 'Wiltoni')
Red yucca	*Hesperaloe parviflora*
Yaupon holly, dwarf	*Ilex vomitoria nana*
Yucca	*Yucca arkansana, Y. pallida*

**	Flowers.
*	Foliage color.
S	Semi-evergreen.
PC	Preferred species in Plains Country.

DECIDUOUS FLOWERING, FRUITING, OR COLORFUL-LEAVED SHRUBS AND SMALL TREES

Table 11. Small Trees

Crabapple	*Malus* spp.
Dogwood (*, +, −)	*Cornus* spp.
Flowering plum	*Prunus blireana, P. mexicana*
Flowering quince	*Chaenomeles* spp.
Mexican buckeye (*, +)	*Ungnadia speciosa*
Scarlet buckeye	*Aesculus pavia*
Silverbells (−)	*Halesia* spp.
Snowbells	*Styrax grandiflora*
Texas mountain laurel (+, ×)	*Sophora secundiflora*
Texas redbud, whitebud	*Cercis canadensis* var. *texensis*

*	Fall foliage color.	−	Acid soils preferred.
+	Berries or showy seedpods or capsules.	×	Zones 8b–9; late freezes take blooms further north.

Table 12. Spring-flowering Large and Medium-sized Shrubs

Barberry, redleaf Japanese	*Berberis thunbergii* 'Atropurpurea'
Beautyberry, French mulberry	*Callicarpa americana*
Cenizo, Texas sage (**, S)	*Leucophyllum frutescens*
Firebush (A)	*Hamelia patens*
Flowering quince (+)	*Chaenomeles japonica*
Forsythia (+)	*Forsythia* spp.
Mock orange	*Philadelphus* spp.
Oak-leaf hydrangea (–)	*Hydrangea quercifolia*
Privet, golden vicary	*Ligustrum* × *vicaryi*
Spiraea, early-flowering (+)	*Spiraea reevesiana, S. vanhouttei*
Snowball viburnum (+)	*Viburnum opulus* 'Sterile'
Winter jasmine (+)	*Jasminum nudiflorum*

**	Flowers intermittently all season.
+	Blooms in late winter or early spring.
–	Acid soils preferred.
S	Semi-evergreen.
A	Tender perennial used as annual north of Zone 9.

Table 13. Spring-flowering or Fruiting Small Shrubs

Cenizo, Texas sage (**)	*Leucophyllum laevigatum, L. frutescens* 'Green Cloud'
Hydrangea (–)	*Hydrangea macrophylla*
Coralberry (+)	*Symphoricarpos orbiculata*

**	Flowers intermittently all season.
–	Acid soils preferred.
+	Berries or fruits.

Table 14. Summer-flowering Small Trees and Large Shrubs

Althea (**)	*Hibiscus syriacus*
Buddleia	*Buddleia davidii, B. marrubifolia*
Candlestick tree, senna (**, A)	*Cassia alata*
Cenizo, Texas sage (**)	*Leucophyllum frutescens*
Clerodendrum (**, ×)	*Clerodendrum speciosissimum*
Crape myrtle (**)	*Lagerstroemia indica*
Desert willow (**)	*Chilopsis linearis*
Pomegranate, standard (+)	*Punica granatum*
Vitex, lavender chaste tree (**)	*Vitex agnus-castus*

**	Flowers intermittently all season.
+	Berries or fruits.
×	Hardy to Zone 8b.
A	Tender perennial used as annual where frost occurs.

Table 15. Summer-flowering Small Shrubs

Abelia, dwarf (**)	*Abelia grandiflora* 'Sherwoodi'
'Edward Goucher' (**)	*A. grandiflora* 'Edward Goucher'
prostrate (**)	*A. grandiflora* 'Prostrata'
Cenizo, Texas sage (**)	*Leucophyllum laevigatum, L. frutescens* 'Green Cloud'
Pomegranate, dwarf	*Punica granatum* 'Nana'
Spiraea, summer-flowering	*Spiraea bumalda* 'Anthony Waterer,' 'Little Princess'

**	Flowers intermittently all season.

The hues of pale salmon cockscomb, ginger, crayon-gold cosmos, and pink summer phlox compete with the neighbors' laundry in this homey back yard garden. Garden of Jack and Cora Gamblin, San Antonio.

CHAPTER EIGHTEEN

Techniques:
Smart "Dirt-Gardening"

The key to happy gardening is mastery of the central techniques.

—The Encyclopedia of Gardening Techniques

"In real estate, it's 'location, location, location!' In gardening, it's 'bed prep, bed prep, bed prep!'" Dallas gardener Nick Brock sums up the conviction of countless green-thumbed gardeners. There's really nothing more important to plants' health and beauty than good soil. In good soil, plants thrive and multiply. In poor soil, a new garden soon declines.

Bed Preparation

The ideal "good garden soil" referred to in gardening manuals is dark and crumbly with the fresh smell of rain-moistened earth. It is neutral to slightly acid in chemical reaction, fluffy, friable, and absorbent. Most garden plants love it. Unfortunately, such garden soil is scarce in the Southwest. All kinds of difficult soils abound here: sugar sand, caliche, and black gumbo. Of course, they aren't difficult to plants native to them. If you happen to have soil that is near to its native condition, the indigenous plants will thrive in it. This is a large "if." Much soil has been subjected to erosion, compaction, grading, filling with a different type soil, or nutrient depletion from long use without replenishment. And to grow a wider range of plants than local natives, even relatively undisturbed native soil must be improved and adapted. All this makes it important to accurately assess soil and improve it to gardenable quality, or all subsequent labor may be lost.

SOIL BASICS

Soil texture, pH, and nutrient levels fundamentally affect plants. These characteristics can all be learned from soil tests. Agricultural extension specialists say that inadequate understanding and misuse of soil are among novice gardeners' most common mistakes.

Soil Texture

Soil is composed of three different types of particles: from the coarsest to the finest, sand, silt, and clay. Taking a pinch of soil and rubbing it between your fingers gives some idea of these particles' textures. "Sand feels gritty. Silt is powdery, like talcum powder. Clay is hard when dry, slippery when wet, and rubbery when moist," the *Encyclopedia of Organic Gardening* sums them up.

Sand and silt are the primary determinants of soil texture. Both are chemically stable, retaining the chemical composition of the rock from which they came.

Sand is well aerated, easily warmed, and fast-draining. It tends to dryness and infertility because water passes through it quickly and leaches away minerals.

Silt is water-borne soil matter that is deposited as sediment. It is smooth and floury when dry; when wet, it feels smooth but not slick or sticky. Silt is fairly heavy and needs large amounts of added organic matter to be cultivated easily.

Because clay is made of extremely fine particles, spaces for water and air among them are small. Thus clay soils are often poorly drained, poorly aerated, and slow to warm. But because these particles are very reactive chemically, they serve as a storehouse of soil nutrients.

The terms "loam," "sandy loam," and "clay loam" refer to soils of specific percentages of sand, silt, and clay. Contrary to popular impression, these descriptions do not imply high fertility levels or any general notion of soil quality.

Organic Content

As you may know, the term "organic" refers to all living and once-living things and substances derived from them, such as plants, animals, and coal. Inorganic substances are nonliving. Chemically, what distinguishes organic from inorganic substances is the presence of carbon compounds; carbon is a molecular building block of all known life forms. Organic content of soil is involved in its texture and chemical processes. While 5 to 6 percent organic matter is desirable, soils in urban areas often contain as little as 0.5 percent.

The Term "Organic"

Of course, the word "organic" is loosely used in several senses. With regard to fertilizers and pesticides, it is often but inaccurately used to mean "derived from naturally occurring substances, not synthetic." A better term for such materials is "botanically derived" or "botanical." Contrary to common misconceptions, "organic" does not mean "non-toxic." (See "'Organic' versus Conventional Horticulture.") "Organically grown" with regard to plants is generally used to mean raised without synthetic fertilizers or pesticides.

Soil Chemistry

Minerals. Sixteen minerals are essential to plants; they are obtained from soil, air, and water. Most of these nutrients are present in soil in sufficient supply that none need be added. However, the three "major" nutrients that research indicates are used in the largest amounts by plants—nitrogen, phosphorus, and potassium (N, P, and K)—may be inadequate, particularly in urban soils, to maintain the green color and rapid growth most people expect. They are the primary active ingredients in general-purpose fertilizers, both synthetic and "organic." It is easy to get the impression from the prominence of N-P-K ratios on fertilizer bags and in advertising that soil is just an inert medium to which water and N, P, and K are added, but that is far from true.

pH. Relative acidity or alkalinity of soil and water determines the availability of mineral nutrients to plants. The degree of acidity or alkalinity is expressed in terms of pH, a measure of free hydrogen ions. These ions are involved in the chemical transfer of nutrients to plant cells. A pH of 7.0 is neutral; higher pH levels are alkaline, and lower levels are acidic. The scale is logarithmic; that is, pH 8 is ten times more alkaline than pH 7.

Some types of plant growth occur anywhere in the pH range from 3.5 to 10. However, at a pH of 6.5, more nutrients are available in greater percentages to be absorbed by plants than at higher or lower pH levels. At extremes of pH, nutrient uptake stops. Extremes in pH seriously affect plant nutrition by impeding both the transmission of needed minerals to plant cells and the bacterial action that breaks down organic matter to nutrients usable by plants.

Optimal pH is not required for healthy growth of most plants, if other factors are favorable. Slightly alkaline soils (pH levels of 7.6 to 7.8), if amended with organic material and fertilized, can successfully grow almost any plants other than acid-insistent ones such as rhododendrons. Acid-loving plants are enabled to grow in slightly alkaline soils by use of acidifying minerals and acid organic matter such as composted pine-bark mulch. Of equal if not greater importance are improvements in drainage and aeration. This is generally economically feasible for small areas, such as shrub borders or flower beds, but not for lawns or large expanses of ground covers. For details on adjusting pH, see "Altering pH."

Fertility

In horticulture, fertility means availability of nutrients for plant use. Adding organic matter to soil is beneficial. However, in point of fact, the nutrients it contains are taken up only when the organic matter is broken down to *inorganic* form. Earthworms, microorganisms including bacteria, and weathering make this transformation.

When chemical fertilizers are applied, organic matter should always be present to avoid a deficit of carbon. Carbon is another vital food for the soil organisms that feed plants.

HOW TO SOLVE SOIL AND DRAINAGE PROBLEMS

Soil Testing

In preparing new planting areas or when you are assessing the results of past treatment for soil deficiency, try having a soil test done. Texas A&M University and agricultural colleges in other states perform basic soil tests for nominal fees. In Texas, kits to package and submit samples for testing are available at county extension offices at no charge at the time of writing.

Soil is dynamic, so results vary with rainfall and other conditions. Keep in mind that soil tests simply measure certain vital chemicals isolated from your soil and the living community of bugs, bacteria, roots, and wrigglers it houses. News, but not the whole story. Read on.

Drainage

Avoid low spots where water collects after rains unless you plan to use specially suited plants or to raise the soil level. Changing the grade or making raised beds may be helpful. Be careful not to divert the water somewhere else that you don't want it, however. Minor low spots can easily be filled with excess soil from another spot in the yard, but a major grade change is a job for a professional or a motivated and methodical do-it-yourselfer who is willing to research and follow proper techniques. Do not add soil of a type other than that of the existing soil, as this may cause drainage problems in moisture dispersal.

Raising bed levels improves drainage, and proper grading improves runoff.

Check the soil's internal drainage or percolation—the passage of air and water through the soil. One method is to dig a hole 2 feet deep and fill it with water. Let it drain and refill it. If it drains within an hour the second time, it is well-drained and suitable for roses and many other plants that insist on good drainage. If it drains within six hours, it is suitable for plants that accept heavy soil. If it doesn't, the options are to use bog plants, to raise the bed surface, or to install a gravel layer and a subsurface drain.

Low raised beds can be made with steel edging or simply by mounding and leveling soil, with the bed sides slanted and a small trench around the edges to collect runoff. Contain deeper beds with landscape timbers, brick, stone, or landscape blocks. Some gardeners avoid railroad ties, because the creosote with which they are treated is toxic to plants. There is also concern that "pressure-treated" landscape timbers may leach arsenic into the soil.

Just a 2-to-3-inch layer of gravel below the cultivated bed soil may help. If surrounding soil is very dense, however, the gravel layer may collect too much runoff under the bed and may promote moisture-dependent harmful microorganisms and cause root rot. One remedy is a "French drain," made by laying perforated PVC pipe in a deeper gravel layer, with one end of the pipe slightly lower than the other to carry water away. The pipe should be wrapped and covered at both ends with fiberglass landscape cloth to keep soil from filling it up. The pipe should be placed so as to drain where the run-off won't cause a problem.

Long-standing advice is to add sand to loosen clay soil. While this is theoretically possible, it is not usually practical. The volume of sand needed can be exorbitantly expensive and almost impossible to mix in. In fact, when small amounts of sand are added, the microscopically fine clay particles fill in the spaces among the coarse sand grains and can produce an even tighter mixture. (Adobe building brick is an example.) Or the sand may wash down through the clay over time and form a sand layer, impeding even water permeation throughout the soil. (See the next paragraph.) Organic matter is a much better additive than sand to open up air passages in dense clay.

Planting areas should not be filled with a type of soil foreign to the site. Because water does not move well from one type of soil to another, it tends to flood one soil layer until that is saturated before penetrating to the layer below. Thus, moisture may not penetrate to plant roots where it is needed. It is generally better to simply add a layer of soil of the same type that is in your yard on top of existing soil, rather than to try to *change* the soil texture by mixing in a different type of soil particle.

This means that "pocket-planting" is not a solution for bad drainage in clay soils, notwithstanding use of this method by some landscape companies. Planting holes are dug in clay and filled with a light soil mix that is then mounded above the surrounding grade. A light rain runs off, but in heavy rain, the hole acts as a bucket, collecting all the water that pours in from the less permeable surrounding soil—a sure recipe for root rot.

Gypsum, often recommended to improve drainage, works only in high-sodium soils, according to Texas Agricultural Extension Service sources.

Common watering mistakes contribute to moisture-related garden problems. Soil watered beyond its saturation point can hold no oxygen, which is vital to plant life. (Puddles indicate saturation.) Watering in brief heavy spurts, such as fifteen minutes a day, a typical sprinkler system setting, can cause soil to become saturated close to the surface. Oxygen then fails to penetrate below the saturated soil to dry soil below where the roots are.

Compaction and Poor Aeration

Because plant roots require oxygen to absorb nutrients and water, plants won't thrive in waterlogged or dense, compacted soils. In beds, aeration (air space among soil particles) is improved by addition of organic matter and by tilling. However, after clay soil is thoroughly soaked, wait a few days to till. Tilling wet clay compacts the fine soil particles to near-impenetrability and can ruin soil texture for the entire season.

Compaction can be avoided by keeping foot and vehicle traffic off planting areas and can be remedied by aeration. Proper mechanical aerators cut and remove soil plugs rather than simply punching holes in the sod, which packs the soil in the sides of the holes.

Altering pH

High alkalinity is a common problem in much of Texas. Soil sulfur is used by experienced gardeners to acidify soil, a process accomplished by the sulfur's conversion to sulfuric acid. Overdoses can be harmful. Apply no more than 1 pound of ground sulfur per 100 square feet, twice a year, starting six months before planting. The lead time is necessary because sulfur is slow-acting, and amounts sufficient to boost pH quickly are toxic. Calcium sulfate, iron sulfate, and aluminum sulfate are also used by some gardeners. Continued high-dosage applications of acid fertilizers are said to have the potential to make soil too acid, but I have not yet observed this in the areas of Texas with which I am most familiar. Organic matter that is very acid, such as peat moss, composted pine-bark mulch, and composted oak leaves, both acidifies soil and improves its structure and fertility long-term. If you must grow acid-dependent plants in alkaline conditions, to convert beds, the latest university findings recommend a 40:60 mixture of chunky-coarse grade Lambert Canadian peat moss and fine-grain composted pine-bark mulch (particles ½ inch and smaller). This tested as the best easily moistened acid planting mix for ideal drainage, aeration, and moisture retention.

The addition of composted organic material of any kind helps compensate for extreme pH. If enough organic matter is added to the soil, it modifies pH to some extent and improves the soil's fertility, aeration, and drainage to the extent that pH is not so critical a factor, extension specialists and experienced landscapers reported. Some experts recommend that home gardeners rely on composted organic matter alone in high-pH soils and leave sulfur treatments to professionals.

The pH of highly acid soils can be raised by addition of some form of lime, such as ground agricultural limestone or dolomitic limestone. They should not be applied within several weeks of chemical fertilizers, or manures, which they counteract. (Lime reacts with manure and other fertilizers and releases valuable nitrogen into the air.)

Nutrient Deficiency

Homeowners should follow a garden care program based on good soil and sound general horticulture practices, rather than focusing on plant symptoms and attempting to diagnose specific deficiencies and treat for them, experts say. This can hardly be over-emphasized; too many homeowners douse sickly plants with expensive preparations while neglecting soil and basic care.

Well-drained, well-aerated soil of pH between 4.5 and 8.0 with 5 or 6 percent organic matter will generally have no serious nutrient deficiencies, according to William Knoop, Ph.D. Knoop is a turf grass specialist for the Texas Agricultural Experiment Station (TAES) with national sports fields expertise; he teaches extension soils seminars for landscape professionals. With soils that have low organic content—one sign is a pale color—a soil test will identify deficiencies. When submitting soil samples, state what the area sampled will grow (flowers, shrubs, vegetables, or trees). Test reports include treatment recommendations; but, again, there's more to the story.

Addition of composted organic matter (compost, composted cottonseed hulls from defoliant-free cotton, composted pine-bark mulch), as well as specific fertilizers, is always recommended.

Chlorosis, seen in yellowed new leaves with green veins, is a sign of iron deficiency, common at both extremely high and extremely low pH levels. Iron, as well as other minerals, becomes chemically bound—in calcareous alkaline soils, calcium carbonate is the culprit—and is not available to plants. Foliar (leaf) application of the missing element in a balanced water-soluble fertilizer gives the quickest response.

Plants that display iron chlorosis in alkaline soils can be grown successfully by applying chelated iron sulfate to the soil. Soil applications are longer-lasting.

Salinity

Avoid "salting" your soil by overfertilizing. Overuse of chemical salts or manure may salinize soil, and prolonged overuse can even sterilize it. Salt deposits are removed by running water through the soil, difficult to do in heavy soils and potentially harmful downstream, or by removing and replacing soil. Dry gardens of drought-tolerant plants are an option in areas with intrinsically salty soil and water. In these areas, reduced watering also means reduced salt application.

"Organic" versus Conventional Horticulture

A CROSSROADS

American gardens and the "green" industry are often depicted in the news media and special-interest magazines as being at a crossroads between conventional chemical-based horticulture, which has dominated the United States since the 1950s, and an alternative, commonly called organic gardening. One, it is said, dramatically combats plant problems with test-tube solutions; the other starts from traditional agricultural practices that prevailed before the development of the modern chemical industry and innovates on them.

It is painted as a stark controversy—falsely so, in some respects. Good gardening never meant abandoning sound cultural practices when garden chemicals were adopted. And alternative horticulture is not merely a return to primitive methods; many technological innovations are coming from this new approach.

Misconceptions proliferate. Common ones were mine, too. As a child in the fifties, exposed to conventional lawn care and television commercials but with only casual involvement in gardening and farming, I grew up with a skewed view. Working in nurseries later, I discovered I thought that any soil plus fertilizer equaled gardenable soil. Pesticides and herbicides appeared to be a pharmacy of cures for all plant problems. And, thinking that fertilizers and "cides" were all you needed to garden successfully, I missed the whole living system of the garden.

Misconceptions also abound among casual proponents of organic gardening. One such misconception is equating "natural" with "nontoxic." Among botanically derived pesticides, there are all degrees of toxicity, as with synthetic ones. For example, nicotine sulfate, a botanical pesticide, is among the most toxic pesticides for home use. The minerals that organic fertilizers supply to plants are no different from those in synthetic fertilizers; however, some offer the added benefit of organic matter that improves soil texture. Some knowledgeable horticulturists supplement synthetic fertilizers with compost, for this reason.

Long-time agents of the nationwide cooperative agricultural extension service, who channel information among researchers, urban gardeners, ranchers, and farmers, say that sound gardening practice has always incorporated standbys of organic gardening, such as mulching and composting. Conversely, many experienced organic gardeners add nitrogen fertilizer along with fresh organic material, because they know nitrogen will be taken from the soil in the decomposition process. I don't know any trained horticulturists who propound wholesale "spray and slay" or the overuse of fertilizers so often deplored by organics proponents. These are errors an overzealous public and slipshod professionals fall into, on the theory that "if a little is good, a lot is better," or out of ignorance or carelessness. Excess isn't intrinsic to chemical use.

When you get down to it, the source of the dispute does not seem to be disagreement on the nature of soil, plants, microorganisms, or how they interact—at least not among those with basic science background and practical gardening experience. It's philosophical. When you filter out emotionality, romance, and misinformation, the differences in world view seem wider than the differences in the actual growing of plants. Although some people are vehemently pro- or anti-chemical, I follow the lead of many knowledgeable researchers and gardeners whom I respect and judge each product and practice on its own merits.

THE NEW GARDENING

Advances are being made not only at agricultural universities and large corporations, but also at non-profit foundations and small companies. State-of-the-art agriculture and horticulture are rapidly synthesizing the best of new technology and traditional practices. The old dichotomy of "natural" and "chemical" doesn't really hold. There are thousands of synthetic and botanical products on the market, each with distinct mechanisms, toxicities, residual life, and shelf life.

An example of the synergy of chemical-based and organic techniques is "integrated pest management," or IPM. This approach combines sound cultural practices, natural predators, and, as a last resort, the least toxic, most specific pesticide to combat weeds and diseases.

Another example of adaptive horticulture is water-conserving "xeriscape" gardening.

Organic gardening promotes understanding nature and incorporating its processes. Conventional horticulture is good at combating acute symptoms and problems with no present non-chemical remedy. In my own garden, I try to use the best of both approaches, based on personal experience and the advice of reliable organic gardeners and horticulturists.

The basic premises of modern organic practice are paraphrased here from "Six Organic Rules" in Malcolm C. Beck's booklet *The Garden-Ville Method*. They concur with horticultural advice from conventional sources, such as extension services. Beck's tips, among the most cogent and soundly researched in Texas organic gardening, are summarized here with his kind permission.

Six Organic Rules

(1) Use adapted plant varieties.

(2) Plant in the preferred season.

(3) Establish balanced mineral content in the soil.

(4) Enrich soil with organic matter.

(5) Establish rich beneficial soil life. (This is done by following rules 3 and 4 and avoiding pesticides harmful to earthworms and other soil organisms.)

(6) Recognize troublesome insects and diseases as symptoms of deeper problems.

Digging the Bed and Improving the Soil

DIGGING TIME

The following garden practices are offered as a common-sense blend of conventional and alternative techniques, both age-old and new.

Whenever you dig, try to allow a season, preferably, or at least a few weeks before planting, for the soil level to settle. Planting in the season opposite a plant's blooming/fruiting time is ideal. Fall and winter are the best seasons to start new beds, to give the elements a chance to break down the fresh-dug clods and, say organic gardeners, to allow microbial activity encouraged by added compost and minerals to "get cooking" before spring.

Cultivating 1 to 2 feet deep is desirable to give deep-rooted perennials room to grow. When the soil is not that deep, add topsoil from the same site or at least of the same type sufficient to build the bed higher, and till in organic material—ideally, well-rotted compost.

WEED AND GRASS REMOVAL AND DIGGING

The Lazy Way

This takes time and working well in advance but almost no labor. In fall, cover proposed spring beds with at least a 6-inch layer of dry leaves. Let the elements, aided by an occasional watering, decompose the leaves and soften the soil underneath. The heavy mulch will kill existing weeds and suppress new sprouts. In very early spring, dig the area; shake soil off roots of remaining perennial grasses and weeds before discarding them. If annual weeds occupied the space and these are dead, simply till. Let the soil sit a couple of weeks to allow newly exposed weed seeds to sprout, till again, and then plant.

Single-Digging

This is an old and widely used method that quells weeds. Begin by taking out a trench one spade deep and about a foot wide at one end of the plot. Pile the soil to one side. Add compost or manure in the bottom of the trench. Dig the next trench, turning the soil upside down into the first trench, so that annual weeds are buried head-down. Carefully remove perennial weeds such as Dallis grass, Johnson grass, nutgrass and dandelions and lawn grasses such as Bermuda that would regrow. (Bermuda regrows from rhizomes.) Continue this process down the bed. When the end of the bed is reached, fill the last trench with the soil set aside from the first.

Scalp and Till

Remove grass top-growth and stolons or runners with a spade and dig out weeds, shaking soil from roots to retain as much topsoil as possible. Add additional topsoil to within 2 inches of the adjacent grade. Put a 6-inch layer of compost or pine-bark mulch on top and till it in.

This method doesn't remove weeds as effectively as single-digging, but if the grass roots are not too thick or you have enough muscle or tiller-power to penetrate them, it is quicker.

If you have a cultivator or tiller with specially designed sharp tines, it will cut through and chop turf and weeds without a preliminary scalping. Rake them off and make repeated passes with the tiller to the desired depth.

Once the bed is prepared, water it *before* planting seed. Watering twenty-four hours or more in advance of planting seed is advised; watering newly planted seed is reported to foster harmful moisture-borne microorganisms. With transplants, I water after planting, for neatness' sake. Young plants are rapidly dehydrated by dry soil. After planting them, I cover the soil with a 2-inch layer of mulch, preferably fine-textured, partly composted bark mulch, to suppress weeds and conserve moisture.

EDGING

Edging is important as a barrier against lawn grasses. Steel edging, brick, stone, synthetic pavers, and landscape timbers are all workable. Some gardeners avoid true railroad ties, which contain creosote toxic to plants, and treated landscape timbers. Ties and timbers, because of their width, seem to slow down Bermuda grass runners more than steel edging does, by making them creep under. Cut into the sod deep enough to lay the first timber or bottom row of bricks below turf level. Brick laid so that the top of the edging is just above soil level will allow mower tires to run on the edging when you are mowing adjacent grass, without the mower blades hitting the brick.

COMPOST

Compost is an article of faith among veteran gardeners, who consider it the best soil conditioner and general fertilizer to be had. People who haven't used compost, on the other hand, often associate it with the slimy vegetable goo that accumulates in the bottom of two-day-old salads or the vegetable crisper between refrigerator cleanings. That stuff is the product of vegetable decomposition in the absence of oxygen. It is totally unlike ripe compost, which is dark brown, crumbly, and fresh-smelling like the forest floor.

Malcolm Beck succinctly states benefits from organic matter such as compost:

Benefits of Organic Matter in the Top 4 Inches of Soil

(1) Growth-promoting hormones.

(2) Toxins and antibiotics that help control diseases, root rot, and damping-off fungi.

(3) Development of beneficial microorganisms. Certain root fungi aid in nutrient absorption; other microorganisms make soil particles adhere, producing better soil structure.

(4) Unlocks soil minerals.

(5) Provides nitrogen-fixing microorganisms.

(6) Increases moisture retention.

(7) Improves drainage and aeration.

(8) Buffers chemicals and soil pH.

(9) Releases nutrients long-term.

(10) Improves soil tilth, making it easy to work wet or dry.

(11) Recycles waste products.

(12) Reduces erosion.

Compost is made from any organic matter except meat or animal fat: leaves, branches, twigs, bark, grass clippings, kitchen vegetable scraps. Meat products encourage nematodes. Twenty percent manure is recommended. A compost pile needs some sunlight to warm it, a ventilated container if it is containerized, and preferably air space between it and the ground, provided either by a base such as a platform of crisscrossed evergreen branches or a wooden packing pallet, or just by a layer of small twigs or chopped cornstalks. The container can be as simple as a fence-wire enclosure or as elaborate as a $300 rotating steel-drum compost-maker. Plant and kitchen waste piled in a sunny spot and layered with a little soil if the material contained none, that is watered or rained on and turned periodically with a fork, produces well-decomposed compost in as little as a couple of months. The heat of decomposition will sterilize grass seeds if temperatures are boosted by covering only the top of the pile—not the sides as well—with black plastic. A temperature of 140° F is sufficient to kill disease organisms but not helpful bacteria. The plastic covering also speeds decomposition. The result is excellent fertilizer and soil conditioner—free.

Grass clippings mat together, so they should be mixed with other, coarser materials to admit air. It is generally not recommended to compost weeds or weedy grass.

Compost can also be bought, either bagged or in bulk.

Propagation

Plants reproduce by seed and vegetatively. There are several types of vegetative reproduction. Plants may form new "plantlets" on shoots either from their roots or from creeping stems called stolons. They may form new bulblets at the sides of the mother bulb.

There are several ways to start and to increase plants in the garden. Recommended techniques are listed for each plant in the book. The following are some common propagation methods.

SEED

Some cold-hardy perennials are sown directly in beds or, as nurserypeople say, "direct-seeded," in the fall. Less hardy early-season ones must be started indoors in the fall. Many early-season ones must be started indoors in flats before frost ends and transplanted as small seedlings to a second flat or small pots and then, when danger of frost is past, to the ground. Some require stratification, or chilling for a few weeks, to germinate. This can be done in the lower part of the refrigerator. Put sand or vermiculite in a clay pot to 1 inch from the top. Place the seeds on top of the medium and cover another ½ inch deep. Wet the pot and allow it to drain. Place the pot and all in a plastic bag and tie it closed. Refrigerate 10 to 12 weeks, checking moisture periodically. Thereafter, set the pot in a warm place indoors, watering often enough to maintain moistness. When emerging seedlings grow 3 inches tall, pot them up.

Warm-season plants are direct-seeded after frost and thinned to the proper spacing. However, most hybrids do not breed true from seed and must be started from nursery plants propagated vegetatively. Some gardeners prefer the convenience and quick results of buying nursery-grown plants rather than starting their own from seed. Others enjoy planting seed and saving seed from their plants for the next season.

DIVISION

Root or crown division is an easy way to get new plants. The crown is where the roots and the top growth of an herbaceous perennial join. Perennials with fibrous roots and a fairly loose crown can be propagated by pulling the crown into pieces, cutting through tough spots with a sharp knife, and planting the new pieces. Over two or three years the center of the crown may have become woody and unproductive, so it is discarded.

For plants with compact, fleshy crowns, such as hostas, wash the roots, cut the crown into pieces with well-developed shoots, dust the cut surfaces with fungicide, and replant immediately. This is best done at the end of the dormant season when new growth appears.

Stolons or runners are creeping stems that take root at joints and form new plants. These can be separated and planted.

Bulblets and bulbils. Bulblets form underground on some bulbs. Bulbils are tiny bulbs that form in the leaf axils on the stem of some bulbous plants, such as lilies. They can be removed and grown to blooming size in a few seasons. Bulbil production is encouraged by removing flower buds just before they open, if you can bear to do this.

Rhizomes are swollen underground stems, like those of bearded irises, with roots and eyes from which new plants grow. These are divided, with at least one eye in each new section. They differ from stolons in that energy storage is one of their primary functions.

CUTTINGS

Cuttings are taken from soft wood, hard wood, or roots.

Stem cuttings can be from soft or woody stems. Hardwood cuttings are made from about 3-inch pieces cut from the end of a stalk. Pull off all but the top leaves, dip the cutting in a rooting hormone, and put it upright in a bed of sand. Keep it well watered and shaded until roots form and then move it to a loamy bed. A young side shoot can be stripped away with a "heel," a thin sliver of bark and wood from the main stem that tears off when you pull down sharply. Heel cuttings are rot-resistant and root-productive.

Soft-wood cuttings are best taken in early spring from fast-growing tips of plants. Cut them below a leaf joint, remove the leaves from the bottom third, dip the cut in rooting hormone, and plant the cutting in compost up to the remaining leaves. Keep it in a brightly lit protected area at room temperature. Liquid fungicide spray weekly is recommended. Harden off rooted cuttings gradually to outdoor conditions and then repot them to grow to transplanting size.

Root cuttings. The difference between root cuttings and root divisions is the cutting's absence of top growth. One-inch-long pieces of root from a plant such as plumbago produce new plants if they are planted in a flat of good soil and watered and shaded until they put out new root fibers.

LAYERING

Layering is a simple, reliable way to reproduce the original plant. A part of the plant is rooted without detaching it until roots form. This method works well with pinks (*Dianthus*). Fasten a young shoot to the earth near an eye or joint and cover it with earth. A callus will form from which roots will grow. The new plant is then separated and planted.

Care

WATERING

Grouping plants of like moisture requirements is basic to proper watering. Water use can be further reduced through a broad approach dubbed "Xeriscape," based on the Greek word *xeros*, meaning dry. The Xeriscape concept, developed at the University of Colorado, involves zoning the garden for differing plant moisture needs, watering with drip irrigation, and using mulches to conserve water.

Water according to plant needs and weather, not by a set schedule. Observe your plants and check the soil. Wilting indicates root damage from either lack of water or overwatering. Excess water on the roots can cause fungal diseases that wilt plants. Dig below the soil surface a few inches and see if it's dry, or try the screwdriver test. Push a long screwdriver into the soil; it will penetrate moist soil easily, bringing up mud on the blade, and dry soil with difficulty, unless the soil is quite light.

Morning is the best time to water, but water when plants need it, regardless of time of day. Evening watering may encourage mildew and fungus, especially if done by the overhead method, because water evaporates more slowly from damp plants in the cool of evening.

Water shrubs and deep-rooted plants deeply. For them, less-frequent deep soakings are better than sprinkling, which causes roots to stay near the surface, where they are more vulnerable to heat, drought, and frost. Seedlings and other shallow-rooted plants need more frequent light waterings.

Be sensitive to seasonal variations. A rule of thumb in Texas, adjustable to plants' specific requirements, is to water sufficiently to provide (from rainfall and irrigation combined) 1 to 2 inches of water per week in summer, per two weeks in fall, and per month in winter. Water output can be roughly gauged by setting cans around your lawn in the path of the sprinkler and measuring the water that collects. This exercise brings home the length of time it takes to deliver just 1 inch of water. It should give a general feel for the watering time at the same rate of flow through your soaker hose.

In winter, both overwatering and underwatering are common problems. People fail to take into account the great change out of doors and either continue a heavy summer watering program or forget to water altogether. Plants need less water, and evaporation is slower in cooler temperatures, so irrigation should be decreased. Transpiration rates from winter winds can be high, however, so regular watering is still needed. Checking the soil is the best guide. Watering before a freeze will fill air-pockets in the soil and insulate plant roots from freeze damage.

Porous soaker hoses, sprinkler hoses used upside down, and drip-irrigation systems are the easiest, most efficient tools for deep watering. Subsurface drip irrigation, which emits drops of water through submerged small-gauge rubber water lines, does not work in heavy compact soil. A similar system for clay soils uses half-inch perforated rubber hose laid on the soil surface and concealed with mulch. Such systems are more durable than soaker and especially sprinkler hoses commonly available from hardware and lawn and garden stores.

MULCH

Mulch ranks almost as high among gardeners' wonder-workers as compost. They are not the same thing, although compost is considered an excellent mulch. Mulch is simply dried plant, animal, or inorganic matter used to blanket soil and cover plant roots, thereby reducing water loss, weed germination, and exposure of roots to high heat and frost. Common organic mulches are pine-bark mulch (composted is best), pine needles, and ground hardwood or pine-bark chips. These and almost any other organic materials can be turned into compost.

Organic mulch has several benefits:

(1) Increases plants' root zones.

(2) Maintains even soil temperature.

(3) Conserves moisture.

(4) Prevents soil crusting, increasing absorption of water and aeration.

(5) Stops erosion.

(6) Controls weeds, eliminating need for cultivating.

(7) Increases both number and activity of beneficial soil organisms.

Dry leaves and grass clippings are not recommended as mulch unless they have been composted. Grass clippings "plate," that is, stick together in layers impermeable to water and air. Both leaves and grass clippings, uncomposted, consume nitrogen as they decompose and rob it from the soil. Grass clippings should be composted in a very sunny, hot, frequently turned compost pile to kill seeds that would sprout in flower beds. While weed seeds can theoretically be killed in the same way, I never compost weeds, just to be on the safe side.

PEST AND DISEASE CONTROL

In combating weeds, animals, and diseases, cultural and mechanical methods are used, as well as the last resort, pesticides. Low-toxicity alternatives are preferred, to disrupt the garden's own ecology less and

avoid thereby opening the way for worse pests. Environmental preservation and the user's health are also important considerations.

Weeds

Weeds are nature's method of erosion control. Bare soil must be planted or mulched, or weeds will step in to perform their service of soil-saving. I am continually amazed at zealots who wage war on attractive wildflowers that volunteer in alleys and other waste spaces—thereby ensuring that the bare ground will be covered by less sightly encroachers such as Johnson grass and crabgrass.

If weeds are not removed from flower beds, they compete with garden plants for light and nutrients. This is especially important for young seedlings that are easily shaded or crowded out. Weeds also harbor insect pests.

Two great aids to controlling weeds are good bed preparation and mulch. Weeds pull out of fluffy, well-worked soil with a satisfying flick of the wrist, especially after a rain. Tight soil traps their roots and makes weeding an ordeal. Mulch reduces weed seed germination by preventing seeds from touching soil. A heavy layer will also kill weeds that sprout underneath it by cutting off air and light.

Old, reliable removal techniques are hand weeding, hoeing, and timely cultivating. Watering the day before weeding will soften the soil and ease weed extraction. When you must cultivate around roses and other shallow-rooted plants, use a fork lightly so as not to damage fragile feeder roots.

Once a planting is well grown, mature perennials, shrubs, and roses reduce weeds greatly by shading them out.

Antigerminants such as Treflan are applied by some commercial maintenance companies to deter weed germination. They also exterminate fallen flower seeds, eliminating reseeding, and they may have undesirable environmental effects.

Herbicides can drift on the breeze and damage

garden plants. Some remain in the soil for months. Some, such as Vapan, a soil fumigant, kill beneficial as well as detrimental soil organisms. These are best used, if at all, only in initial bed preparation. Tenacious invaders such as Bermuda grass can be killed with herbicides containing glyphosate, a nonspecific herbicide that is most effective on grassy weeds. Broadleaf weeds can be eliminated with MSMA, a selective herbicide. Or, as has been said, these unwanted plants can simply be dug out, although they hang on more tightly with live roots.

Pests and Diseases

Intelligent, informed scientists and agriculturists of both organic and chemical care schools of thought agree that overuse and misuse of chemical pesticides and herbicides pose a serious environmental problem. Homeowners are among the worst offenders. We don't read labels, we think if a little is good a lot is better, and we pour poisons down the sink. We have become a nation of quick-fix, "what spray do I use?" kill-all-bugs people who sometimes seem to have no more understanding of the natural world than would lifelong residents of a shopping mall.

Such mistakes are easily avoided, if people are informed of their potentially disastrous effects. In the same spirit, both conventional and alternative options for pest and disease control are presented here, with preference for the least toxic. Some organic methods are well tested; others need more study. Some pests as yet have no adequate organic control. You may prefer an effective chemical specific against a heavy infestation, such as Kelthane for spider mites, to losing your feverfew while waiting for a milder remedy to help nature restore balance. (Or you may not.)

It is only sensible gardening to use mechanical and cultural controls when possible, and then the least toxic controls specific to the pest or disease. This avoids killing beneficial insects, not to mention the beneficial soil microbes and earthworms essential to soil fertility to grow healthy plants.

Destructive insects prey on unhealthy and stressed plants. (They also prey on healthy ones, as in the case of thrips on my roses in summer.) Elimination of the sickly specimens results in more space, light, and nutrients for the rest of the population. The best protection for garden plants, therefore, appears to be general good health; healthy, well-nourished, vigorous plants are resistant to disease and less vulnerable to harmful insects and other pests, such as slugs and snails. An organic gardener I know reports having grown thriving, insect-free plants with compost and natural fertilizers while plants of the same kind but in poor soil nearby were devoured by bugs. The contention of organics proponent Malcolm Beck is that "the bad bugs may really be . . . trying to tell you all is not well with your ways of growing things." The chief checks against harmful insects are the predatory and parasitic insects that feed on them—the "good bugs."

Planting many varieties rather than just one species reduces problems, because a bout with a disease or insect associated with a single species will not wipe out the entire garden as it would a "monoculture" planting.

Keeping fungus-spotted leaves and other diseased material picked up helps. As has been mentioned, eliminating standing water by means of drainage improvements and proper watering reduces moisture-dependent organisms.

Good bed preparation and plenty of well-decomposed organic material are fundamental to fertile, well-aerated soil. In these conditions, plants experience less stress from drought and other adverse weather conditions.

But despite all precautions, diseases and insects do appear. There are well-established chemical and organic remedies. One is use of beneficial insects: ladybugs, lacewings, praying mantises, ant lions or "doodlebugs," damsel bugs, pirate bugs, assassin bugs, and fireflies. Wise gardeners encourage the natural predators of destructive insects by refraining from using general pesticides when possible.

Non-specific pesticides that kill beneficial insects as well as destructive ones, in ascending order of toxicity to mammals, are: methoxychlor (synthetic); pyrethrum (botanical); Malathion and carbaryl, or Sevin (both synthetic); rotenone (botanical); and Diazinon (synthetic).

Keep in mind that over the years insects often develop a resistance to the substance used to control them. You may need to change pesticides occasionally.

Many more bugs and blights exist than can be discussed here, but only a few cause the majority of problems.

Aphids are tiny sucking insects that commonly appear on tender new growth in spring and sap plants' vitality. They can cause serious damage and should be combated before the infestation becomes severe. Forceful sprayings with water, daily, or with insecticidal soap repeatedly at 4- or 5-day intervals, can be effective. So can ladybugs and green lacewings, available from some nurseries and catalogs. Lacewing larvae feed on not only aphids, but also spider mites, leafhoppers, thrips, moth eggs, and smaller larvae. Adult lacewings feed on honeydew, nectar, and pollen, which must be in ready supply, or they will leave. With ladybugs, only part of your supply should be put out at a time, straight from the refrigerator in the evening, when they are unlikely to fly away. The best way to encourage beneficial predators in your garden is to avoid using general pesticides. Bear in mind that, since the population of "good" bugs increases only with the number of "bad" bugs on which they feed, you are unlikely to ever entirely wipe out a pest population by using beneficial insects. However, they do help in the battle.

When aphid numbers are beyond control with milder methods, use products containing the following pesticides, in ascending order of toxicity: synergized pyrethrins, Malathion, acephate (Orthene), carbaryl (Sevin), rotenone, Cygon, Diazinon, Meta-systox-R, nicotine sulfate, or Di-Syston. (Synergized pyrethrins, rotenone, and nicotine sulfate are botanicals that dissipate rapidly after use. Meta-systox-R and Di-Syston are systemics that must be applied to the soil.)

Spider mites hop into action as weather warms up. So tiny they are almost invisible, they are often first detected by the lighter-colored mottling or dotted pattern they make on leaves. Left alone, they will reduce leaves to a mere web. In early stages, insecticidal soap or forceful water spray can be effective if it is thorough, covering undersides as well as the tops of leaves, and repeated, as for aphids. Kelthane is the most effective chemical specific for spider mites. Other pesticides for use against spider mites, in ascending order of toxicity to humans include: horticultural oils (dormant and summer), synergized pyrethrins, chlorpyrifos (Dursban), Meta-systox-R, di-sulfoton (Di-Syston).

Leaf rollers, webworms, bagworms, leafhoppers, loopers, and various other worms are controlled by *Bacillus thuringiensis.* This bacterium kills these pests without affecting beneficial insects.

Slugs, snails, and pillbugs chew plants, gathering wherever there is moisture. Slugs and pillbugs can be trapped under boards placed on the ground. Other controls are Sevin, Dylox, and Mesurol. Slugs and snails can be attracted by small dishes of beer placed at soil level in the ground, in which they drown. Other controls for snails and slugs are metaldehyde, which is toxic to children and pets, and Mesurol. Pyrethrum, a botanical poison made from ground-up flowers of painted daisy, also combats pillbugs.

Thrips are invisible, but their damage is evident in blooms that discolor, fade prematurely, and even blacken around the edges. Thrips drain plant sap. Commonly recommended organic controls include thrips' natural predator, the green lacewing; insecticidal soap spray on the whole plant (the mechanism of which is unclear, since thrips are inside the plant tissue); diatomaceous earth, also unclear; and synergized pyrethrins. A recommended, fairly mild chemical control of thrips on roses is Orthene spray on blooms two or three times a week. Di-Syston is a systemic applied as a soil drench. It may kill beneficial soil organisms in the root area where it is poured but has a short residual effect. Since it is a systemic, it won't affect beneficial insects, other than leaf chewers, that land on the plants. Other controls, intermediate in toxicity between Orthene and Di-Syston, are: Sevin, Diazinon, Cygon, Malathion, methoxychlor, and nicotine sulfate.

Powdery mildew appears as a white dust on plant leaves. Unlike other mildew, it is not caused by wet conditions but by ambient humidity when cool nights follow warm days. Flowable sulfur is the least toxic control. Other controls in ascending order of toxicity are: benomyl (Benlate), folpet (Phaltan), Acti-dione PM, and dinocap (Karathane). Karathane is not cleared for use on phlox. Refer to labels for ornamentals treatable with Acti-dione.

Downy mildew appears as white downy patches in wet weather. Sulfur can also be effective against it. Benomyl at seven-to-ten-day intervals is a common remedy that doesn't always work.

Fungal leaf spots are caused by various fungi, controlled organically with Bordeaux mix or liquid copper spray; alternatively, depending on the specific disease, treat with benomyl, captan, mancozeb (Manzate 20, Dithane M-45), or zineb (Dithane Z-78).

Damping off is a common fungus problem evidenced in plants that suddenly wilt and die with no shortage of water. It is caused by a microorganism called *Phytophthora*. Annual periwinkles are particularly prone to it. Infected plants should be removed and destroyed and replaced with less susceptible varieties. In extreme cases, soil must be removed and replaced.

DEADHEADING AND PINCHING

These nefarious-sounding practices are really quite innocent. "Deadheading" refers to removing dead flower heads. This is done to encourage production of new blooms rather than seed, which continues to develop after flowers fade. Regular deadheading can prolong a plant's bloom season greatly.

Pinching off the terminal, or topmost, bud of a flower stalk will encourage side-branching and greater flower production. Pinching side-buds, as is done with chrysanthemums, produces larger terminal flowers.

Shearing is cutting back the plant lightly all over. This stimulates new growth. Some plants, such as the larger perennial salvias, hardy blue aster, and lythrum, benefit from cutting back by one-third to one-half at midseason to keep them dense and encourage strong late-season bloom.

STAKING

Staking may be necessary for tall, weak-stemmed perennials. It is often unattractive, but saving your favorite top-heavy phlox may be worth the unnatural effect. Stakes of natural materials, such as bamboo and dead plant stalks, are fairly unobtrusive. The dried stalks of last season's plants make good supports. The dried branches and stem of a bush plant like aster can be kept and thrust among the stems of a growing plant and into the ground for an almost invisible support.

WINTER PROTECTION

General good care and proper watering are basic to winter survival. Heavy mulch, put on after declining temperatures and light frost "harden off" the plant, is helpful. Applied too early, however, mulch holds in the soil's warmth and may promote tender plant growth that is susceptible to a sudden hard freeze. A fall mulch of compost has the added benefit of promoting winter root growth. High-nitrogen fertilizers should not be applied in fall, because they encourage frost-vulnerable top growth rather than energy storage in roots.

Prune woody perennials back after light frosts have hardened off the growth. This reduces the tissue exposed to frost.

Water deeply when a hard freeze is expected. This protects roots otherwise exposed to pockets of cold air in the soil and helps prevent plant dehydration by cold, dry winds.

Cloches are bell-shaped individual covers long used in Europe. Bushel or half-bushel baskets weighted with a rock are also excellent plant protectors. Even an inverted paper bag weighted with rocks provides some protection. A shingle pushed into the soil on the windward side of the plant will help. Plastic milk jugs with the bottom cut out, tied to a stake to hold them down, are effective, if peculiar-looking.

TRANSPLANTING

Transplanting of large established plants is best done in the season opposite when they bloom, that is, spring for fall-blooming plants and vice versa. Overcast or cool days are best. In hot weather, I find transplanting in the cool of evening is best. In summer, transplanted seedlings may need the shade of an old sheet on stakes or shade-cloth. First water the plant and the soil into which you are transplanting. Dig around the plant well before attempting to lift it, like loosening the edges of a cake from a baking pan. Keep as much of the soil in the roots as possible and replant the plant immediately. Water it. This is the time to divide the plant or remove woody root portions, as described in Propagation.

PART FOUR

Plant Charts

Dusty miller, daffodil, English primroses, pansies, and lamb's-ears.

Chart Legend

The following charts are the first such compilation of statewide information on perennials in gardens. Annuals have been tested fairly widely by the Texas Agricultural Extension Service, but at the time of this writing, few area trials, either public or commercial, have been made with perennials. The information offered here is from the long-term observations of experienced gardeners in eight regions of Texas and northern Louisiana, growing the plants in residential, public, and commercial display gardens. It is presented as a helpful first—by no means last—word.

Items in the chart for which no solid information could be found by the time of writing were left blank; ongoing work will hopefully soon fill them in. This approach will, it is hoped, provide a more helpful contribution to continuing experimentation and public information than would a less detailed summary in which gaps were glossed over.

In the charts, the first two columns after the plant names give the plants' regions of use and the minimum temperature ranges to which they are adapted. The next two columns pertain to factors more easily influenced by the gardener: soil characteristics and exposure to light. Useful information for garden planning—bloom season, flower and foliage color, and plant height—appear next.

In the plant profiles in Chapters 13–15 the above information is detailed further, along with heat tolerance, moisture needs, propagation methods, and pest and disease problems.

REGIONS

The charts give results with perennials in eight regions of Texas, shown in Map 4 in Part Two. They are somewhat simplified from widely accepted vegetational regions defined by Frank W. Gould in *Texas Plants: A Checklist and Ecological Survey.*

If you live in Texas, you can identify your bioregion by this map. Readers outside Texas can learn from the region descriptions in Part Two and local climate data which Texas region is most like their own and thus judge which plants are likely to thrive for them. Regional conditions other than the obvious ones of temperature and moisture greatly affect plant viability. Variations in sun intensity (not just hours of sunlight) and humidity, for example, can make a plant thrive 300 miles away and fail where you live.

Gardeners should determine *local* seasonal average high and low temperatures, first and last frost dates, and humidity levels and, in addition, the soil types on their sites. Local publications, extension agents, and nursery horticulturists will be helpful. A specific site may vary from the surrounding region, a fact easy to observe. Within each locality, even within one site, may exist "microclimates" that are more humid or more arid, more acid or more alkaline, hotter or cooler than the larger system of which they are a part. For example, a south-facing wall with a sunny exposure may create a warm microclimate where plants outside their normal cold-hardiness range will grow.

Texas regions in the chart are as follows (see Map 4):

Piney Woods (PW)
Prairies and Cross Timbers (PCT)
Edwards Plateau (EP)
Plains Country (PC)
Trans-Pecos (TP)
Gulf Coast (GC)
South Texas (ST)
Lower Rio Grande Valley (LRGV)

Symbols in the region columns of the chart rate each plant's viability there:

* Well-adapted. This region's conditions are ideal for this plant.

\+ Usable.

– Not suited.

A Treated as an annual in this region.

Plants may be used in a region for which they are not naturally suited if the soil, exposure, and other conditions can be modified to approximate the plant's preferences. This isn't always practical or worthwhile.

In a given region, a plant may be adapted to one locale and not another. In such instances, a footnote appears on the chart to alert readers to exceptions to the rating given.

USDA ZONES (COLD-HARDINESS)

As you may know, the U.S. Department of Agriculture has compiled average minimum temperatures throughout the United States and developed a system of numbered "hardiness zones." The zones correspond to 10° ranges of average low temperatures. If a plant is said to be "hardy to Zone 9," that means it can withstand the average minimum temperatures of Zone 9 (30–20° F). Cold-hardiness of plants is commonly given in books and on nursery tags in these zone ratings.

For a few plants, the chart also lists zone ratings divided further into *a* and *b* portions that cover only 5° ranges. When a plant's hardiness limit is given on the chart as Zone 9b, for example, it is hardy only through the southern half of Zone 9, that is, to 30–25° F, not all the way to 20° F. For some plants, this 5° difference in winter cold can be important.

For plants listed, the charts give the zones in the South and Southwest in which each plant is *root-hardy*. Persistence of top-growth depends on the habit of the plant species (deciduous versus evergreen) as well as on temperature.

In addition, the plant's absolute minimum hardiness zone (which may not occur in the regions covered in this book) is shown in parentheses, when known.

The new USDA map published in 1990 redraws the zones and makes them more accurate, based on new, more detailed climate data gathered since the map's previous revision in 1965. Readers familiar with the old map should consult the new map for more exact average minimum temperatures for their locales, particularly if they live on the edge of a zone; they may find that their area is in fact colder than the old map indicated and is now included in another zone. In general, the new map shows drastically redrawn boundaries between zones 7a and 7b and 9a and 9b and movement southward of all the other zones, as well as some changed boundary delineations. South Texas' Zone 9a area has shrunk greatly, taken in by a much larger zone 8b. The Texas portion of the new map is included in this book as Map 1.

Even with such good information, selecting plants with appropriate zone ratings isn't all there is to cold-hardiness. Below-average lows, sudden freezes without a preceding cool period to "harden off" plants, soggy soil, and winter drought can cause losses. Good care can prevent almost all of these casualties, however. Sheltered sites, mulch, and other aids discussed in Chapter 18 improve winter survival. With experimentation, they may enable plants to grow outside their normal range.

SOIL

The charts present two characteristics of soil that figure in evaluating planting sites and selecting appropriate plants: soil structure and pH, or relative acidity or alkalinity. Preferences as to soil structure and soil pH are noted for each plant.

LIGHT

The continuum from sun to shade is represented by the following symbols on the charts:

⁂ *Reflected sun.* Light reflected from walls or pavement. The accompanying heat is detrimental to many plants, so plants that accept reflected sun are a boon for such situations.

○ *Full sun.* Unobstructed sun all day. In the South in summer, even most full-sun plants benefit from a couple hours' afternoon shade.

◐ *Three-quarters sun.* Shade for not more than a quarter of the day.

◑ *Half-day sun/shade.* The infinitely preferable combination is morning sun and afternoon shade. The reverse—hot afternoon sun after the comparative cool of morning shade—is a shock to plants, particularly in summer. The most difficult half-day shade exposure is with sun only at midday. Heat-loving tropical plants that accept some shade withstand it best.

◍ *Partial shade/filtered sun.* The term "partial shade" is used somewhat loosely among gardeners to mean either shade part of the day or dappled shade. Here it is used to mean dappled shade, such as is made by a lattice or a thin foliage cover. This is bright shade, the kind of light found beneath tall, high-branching trees ("high shade") and in areas open to light from the sky but not touched by direct sunlight ("open shade").

◕ *Three-quarters shade.* Direct sun for not more than a quarter of the day.

● *Full shade.* No direct sun or reflected light. This does not mean deep shade like that found in dark corners and under shrubs and low-branching, dense trees. Such deep, dark shade is accepted by only a few plants, such as some ferns, blue ginger, and the common foliage plants aspidistra and rohdea. Deep shade poses problems not only from inadequate light but also from poor air circulation. Such areas may be brightened and ventilated by thinning dense growth.

Humidity, heat, and light intensity directly influence recommended light levels for a given plant. Thus, in areas where high humidity, heat, and/or intense sunlight prevail, the sun exposures on the shadier end of the range indicated on the charts are advised.

Full sun in El Paso provides more light than full

sun in East Texas, to say nothing of Boston or Portland. The closer to the equator, the higher in elevation, and the farther from large bodies of water a location is, the more intense is the sunlight received at ground level. Closer to the equator, the sun's angle to the earth is more direct, and therefore its light passes through less shielding atmosphere. At higher elevations, the thinner air transmits more light. Air containing little water vapor also conveys light at greater intensity. In Texas, those circumstances are found in the southern and western parts of the state, where there is also less sun-screening air pollution. "You wear more sunscreen in El Paso than in Longview—your plants may need more shade," as a native puts it.

BLOOM SEASON

Bloom seasons indicated in the charts are general. With the great variations in weather from year to year in these regions, in a given locale a plant may bloom as much as two months earlier or later from year to year. "Spring" means "spring, whenever it comes," although the average frost-free date is a general guideline. Obviously, bloom times vary from north to south, also. Within the various regions of Texas, the average frost-free date is as early as February 9 or as late as April 20, a nearly ten-week difference. Growth and bloom cycles vary accordingly. One can usually count on different flower species blooming in the same order year after year, despite weather variations, if rarely at the same time. Occasionally, though, one species will get nipped by a late freeze at a critical time and will then rebud and bloom out of its usual sequence, with the roses rather than the daffodils, for instance.

BLOOM AND FOLIAGE COLOR

Many species and varieties appear in several colors. These are indicated. Flower colors often vary from plant to plant in wildflowers that haven't had the genetic diversity bred out of them. Colors of all flowers tend to fade in hot sun and appear more intense on milder days and at cooler times of year.

PLANT HEIGHT

The charts and text give the size range of mature plants. This varies according to moisture supply, nutrition, and light levels. (Plants grow taller reaching for sun in insufficient light, as you have probably noticed.)

Care should be taken in planting new plants or thinning seedlings to allow space for their mature size, particularly with plants with deep taproots that do not transplant well, such as butterfly weed (*Asclepias tuberosa*). The resulting open bed space presents the need to mulch heavily or interplant seasonal annuals, or else to pull the weeds that will inevitably sprout there.

HEAT TOLERANCE

The regions studied fall into three zones based on average summer day and night temperatures, as shown in Table 16. The heat ranges in which each plant is known to grow are indicated in the plant profiles (Chapters 13–15). Where no heat range is given, the plant can be grown in all three ranges.

These zones were arrived at by averaging together the average July and August highs and lows from 1951 to 1980 for representative towns in each vegetational region, as compiled by George W. Bomar in his book *Texas Weather*. With 93° F average highs, the comparatively coolest zone was labeled "moderate" rather than "low." (See Chapter 12 for more information.)

Table 16. Heat Tolerance Zones

AVERAGE SUMMER TEMPERATURES ($^{\circ}$F)

ZONE	DAY	NIGHT	AVERAGE	REGIONS
High	97	74	85.5	Prairies & Cross Timbers Lower Rio Grande Valley South Texas
Medium	94 (High humidity)	73	83.3	Piney Woods Upper & Lower Gulf Coast
Moderate	93 (Low humidity)	69	81.5	Edwards Plateau Plains Country Trans-Pecos

Summary of Abbreviations and Symbols Used in Charts 1–3

REGIONS

PW	Piney Woods
PCT	Prairies and Cross Timbers
EP	Edwards Plateau
PC	Plains Country
TP	Trans-Pecos
GC	Gulf Coast
ST	South Texas
LRGV	Lower Rio Grande Valley

LIGHT

- ✷ Reflected sun
- ○ Full sun
- ◑ Three-quarters sun
- ◐ Half-day sun/shade
- ◍ Partial shade
- ◕ Three-quarters shade
- ● Full shade

- * Well adapted to the region
- + Usable in the region
- − Not suited to the region
- A Treated as an annual in the region

SOIL

A	Adobe
C	Clay
G	Garden loam
S	Sand

wd	Well-drained
mr	Moisture-retentive

Ac	Acid
N	Neutral
Al	Alkaline

SEASONS

E	Early
M	Mid
L	Late

Sp	Spring
Su	Summer
F	Fall
W	Winter

Herbaceous Perennials

	REGIONS								USDA
	PW	PCT	EP	PC	TP	GC	ST	LRGV	ZONES
Achillea millefolium Common yarrow	*	*	*	*	+	*	*	*	(3)6–9
'Cerise Queen,' 'Rosea,' 'Rose Beauty'	*	+	+	*	+	*	*	−	(3)6–9
'Fire King'	*	+	+	*	+	*	*	−	(3)6–9
'Red Beauty'	*	+	+			*			6–9
A. filipendulina Fern-leaf yarrow	+	+	*	*	*	−	−	−	(4)6–8
× 'Coronation Gold'	+	+	*	*	*	−	*	−	(4)6–9
A. taygetea	+	+	*	*	*	−	−	−	(4)6–8
× 'Moonshine'	+	*	*	*	*	−	*	−	(4)6–8
A. tomentosa Woolly yarrow	*	+		+	+				(4)6–8
Adenophora liliifolia Lilyleaf ladybells	*	*	+	+	−		−	−	(4)6–9
Alcea rosea Hollyhock	−	*	*	*	*	−	+	*	(2)6–9(10)
× 'Indian Spring,' × 'Indian Summer'	*	+	*	*	*	+	*	+	(4)6–9
'Powder Puff'	+	+	*	*	*	−	−	−	(4)6–8
Anisacanthus quadrifidus var. *wrightii* Flame acanthus	+	*	*	*	*	+	*	*	7–9(10)
Aquilegia canadensis Columbine	*	*	*	*	+	*	+	+	(4)6–9(10)

†Foliage color is green if not otherwise stated.
¹"Tolerates" other soils well, not merely marginally.
²Sometimes intermittent until frost.
³Pink, crimson, and magenta cultivars also available.

SOIL: PREFERRED (TOLERATED)	LIGHT	BLOOM SEASON	COLOR: BLOOM/FOLIAGE[†]	HEIGHT
S[1](A,C,G); N–Ac(Al); wd	○ ◑ ◍	Sp–F[2]	White	12–24″
S(A,C,G); N–Ac(Al); wd	○ ◑ ◍	Sp–Su	Pink, rose	To 15″
S(A,C,G); N–Ac(Al); wd	○ ◑ ◍	Sp	Rose-red	12–24″
S(A,C,G); N–Ac(Al); wd	◑	Sp–Su	Rose-red/silvery green	To 18″
A,C,G,S; N–Al; wd	○ ◑ ◍ ●	Su	Lemon/gray-green	18–36″
A,C,G,S; N–Al; wd	○ ◑ ◍ ●	Sp–ESu	Yellow/gray-green	12–18″
G,S; N(Ac,Al); wd, mr	○ ◑ ◍	Su	Sulphur[3]/silver gray	12–18″
G,S; N(Ac,Al); wd, mr	○ ◑ ◍	MSp–Su	Lemon/silver gray	12–24″
G,S; N(Ac,Al)	○ ◑ ◍	ESu–MSu	Yellow	6–12″
G; N–Ac	◑ ◍ ●	Sp–LSu	Pale blue	18–48″
G(A,C,S); N–Al (Ac); wd	○ ◑ ◍	LSp–ESu	Red, pink, white, yellow	5–7′
G(A,C,S); N–Al(Ac); wd	○ ◑ ◍	LSp–MSu	White, pink, rose	3–9′
G(A,C,S); N–Al(Ac); wd	○ ◑ ◍	Su	White, pink, red, yellow	4–6′
A,C,G,S; N–Al; wd	○ ◑ ◍	Su–F	Orange	3–5′
A,C,G,S; Al(N–Ac)	○ ◑ ◍	ESp–ESu	Yellow & red	6–30″

| | REGIONS | | | | | | | | USDA |
	PW	PCT	EP	PC	TP	GC	ST	LRGV	ZONES
A. chrysantha	+	*	*	*	*	+	+	+	(4)6–9(10)
A. dichroa	*	*				*			6–9a
A. hinckleyana Hinckley's columbine	*	*	*	*	*	+	+	+	(4)6–9
A. longissima Longspur columbine	+	*	*	*	*	+	+	+	(4)6–9(10)
Asclepias curassavica Tropical milkweed, bloodflower	*[4]	+[4]	+[4]	−	A	*	*	*	8b–9(10)
A. tuberosa Butterfly weed, orange milkweed	*	*	*	*	+[5]	*	*	*	(4)6–9(10)
Aster × frikartii 'Mönch' Frikart aster	*	*	*	*	*	+	*	+	(6)6–9
Aster spp. Hardy blue aster	+	*	*	*	*	+	*	+	(4)6–9(10)
Bouvardia ternifolia Firecracker bush, *trompetilla*					*[6]		*	*	7b–9(10)
Callirhoe involucrata Winecup, poppy mallow	*	*	*	*	*	*	*	*	(3)6–9(10)
Campanula carpatica Carpathian harebell	−	+	+	+[7]	*[8]	−	+[9]	−	(4)6–8
C. persicifolia Peach-leaved bellflower	+	+	*	−[10]	*[11]	+	+		(4)6–9
C. portenschlagiana Dalmatian bellflower	*	+	*	−[10]		*	−	−	(4)6–9a
C. poscharskyana Serbian harebell	*	+	+	−[10]		*	−	−	(3)6–9a
Ceratostigma plumbaginoides Hardy blue plumbago	+	*	*	*[12]	−	+	+	+	(6)[13]7b–9(10)

[†]Foliage color is green if not otherwise stated.
[4]Ratings are for the warmer (b) portion of Zone 8.
[5]Native in the Davis and Guadalupe Mountains' specialized climate.
[6]Native to Davis and Chisos Mountains, mostly above 4,000 feet.
[7]Rated + for Lubbock and north; − for South Plains.
[8]Rating for El Paso.

SOIL: PREFERRED (TOLERATED)	LIGHT	BLOOM SEASON	COLOR: BLOOM/FOLIAGE[†]	HEIGHT
A,C,G,S; Al(N–Ac)	○ ◐ ◍	Sp–F	Golden yellow	12–36″
G,S; N–Ac	◐ ◍	Sp–ESu	Blue-violet/blue-green	To 24″
A,C,G,S; Al(Ac); wd	○ ◐ ◍ ●	Sp–F	Deep yellow/blue-green	12–24″
A,C,G,S; Al(Ac)	◐ ◍ ●	Sp–Su	Lemon yellow/clear green	18–36″
S; Ac–Al	○ ◐ ◍	Sp–F	Yellow & red	3–5′
S(A,C,G); Ac–Al	○ ◐ ◍	Sp–LSu	Orange/gray-green	12–36″
A,C,G,S; Ac–Al	○ ◐	Sp–F	Lavender-blue/dark green	24–36″
A,C,G,S; Al	○ ◐	LSu–F	Lavender-blue/dark green	18–48″
A,S; N–Al; wd	○	LSp–EF	Scarlet	24–48″
A,C,G,S; Ac–Al; wd	○	Sp–Su	Red-purple	12″
G,S; N–Al; wd, mr	◐ ◍ ●	LSu–F	Blue, white	6–12″
G,S; Ac–Al	○ ◐ ◍	Sp–Su	White to violet/bright green, evergreen	24–36″
G,S; N–Al; wd	◐ ◍ ●	Sp–Su	Blue/evergreen	4–6″
G,S; Ac–Al	◐ ◍	Sp, F	Blue/evergreen	12″
G(S,A,C); N(Ac,Al); wd, rich best	○ ◐ ◍	Su–F	Cobalt blue/green, tinged red in fall	To 12″

[9]Rated + for San Antonio; − for more southerly parts of region.
[10]Rated − in southern PC; no rating for northern part.
[11]Rated for western part of region only, based on El Paso results.
[12]Rated * for South Plains; annual in northern PC.
[13]With winter mulch.

	REGIONS								USDA
	PW	PCT	EP	PC	TP	GC	ST	LRGV	ZONES
C. willmottianum Chinese plumbago	*	*	+	+	+	*	*	*	(7)7–9(10)
Chrysanthemum leucanthemum Oxeye daisy, May daisy	*	*	*	*	+	*	*	+	(3)6–9(10)
C. parthenium Feverfew	*	+	+	+	+	+	+	+	(4)6–9(10)
C. × superbum Shasta daisy	*	*	*	*	+	*	*	*	(4)6–9(10)
'Alaska'	*	*	+	*	+	*	+	*	(4)6–9(10)
'Little Miss Muffett'	*	*	*	*	+	*	+	+	(5)6–9(10)
'Snow Lady'	*	*	+	*	+	*	+	+	(4)6–9(10)
'Snow Princess'	*	*[14]	+	*	+	*	+	+	(4)6–9(10)
Clematis armandii	*	*	*	−		*	*		(7)7–9a
C. paniculata Sweet autumn clematis	*	*	*	*	*	*	*[16]		(5)6–9
C. texensis Scarlet leatherflower	*	*	*	+[17]	*	+[17]	*[16]	*	(5)6–9(10)
× 'Duchess of Albany'	*	*	*	+	*	*	*[16]		(3)6–9
× 'Madame Julia Correvon'	*	*		−	*				(3)6–9
C. × (large-flowered hybrids)	+	+	*	−			+[16]		(4)6–8
Coreopsis lanceolata Golden-wave	*	*	*	*	*	*	*	*	(4)6–9(10)
'Baby Sun'	*	*	*	*	*	−	*	−	(4)6–9(10)
'Early Sunrise'	*	*	*	*	*		*		(4)6–9
'Sun Ray'	*	*	*	*	*	*	*	*	(4)6–9(10)

[†]Foliage color is green if not otherwise stated.
[14]Rated − by one Cross Timbers gardener.
[15]Blooms in sun, roots in shade.
[16]Recommended for the northern part of ST on basis of San Antonio results.
[17]Rated * by some gardeners.

SOIL: PREFERRED (TOLERATED)	LIGHT				BLOOM SEASON	COLOR: BLOOM/FOLIAGE[†]	HEIGHT
A,C,G,S; N(Ac,Al)	○	◐	◍		Su	Blue	24–48″
C,G,S; Ac–Al	○	◐	◍		MSp–ESu	White/evergreen	24″
G,S(A,C); Ac(N,Al); wd, mr	○	◐	◍		ESu–LF	White, yellow/pale green	15–36″
G; N–Al; wd, rich	○	◐	◍		ESp–Su	White	8–48″
G; N–Al; wd, rich	○	◐	◍		Sp–ESu	White	20–48″
G; N–Al; wd, rich	○	◐	◍		Sp–ESu	White	12–15″
G; N–Al; wd, rich	○	◐	◍		Sp–LSu	White	10″
G; N–Al; wd, rich	○	◐	◍		LSu	White	12″
G; N–Al	○[15]	◐	◍		Sp	White/evergreen	To 20′
G; Ac–Al	○[15]	◐			LSu–F	White	6–30′
G,S; N–Al(Ac)		◐	◍	●	Sp–Su	Scarlet, rose/blue-green	5–10′
G,S; N–Al(Ac)			◍	●	Su	Pink	To 12′
G; N–Al(Ac)			◍	●	Su	Wine-red	6–8′
G; N–Al		◐			Su	White, purple, pink, rose	varied
C,G,S; Ac–Al; wd	○	◐	◍		Sp–MSu	Yellow	10–36″
C,G,S; Ac–Al; wd	○	◐	◍		MSp–MSu	Gold, red eye	12–18″
C,G,S; Ac–Al; wd	○	◐			LSp–MSu	Yellow	12–15″
C,G,S; Ac–Al; wd	○	◐	◍		MSp–MSu	Golden-orange	12–24″

| | REGIONS | | | | | | | | USDA |
	PW	PCT	EP	PC	TP	GC	ST	LRGV	ZONES
C. verticillata Threadleaf coreopsis	*	*[18]	*	*	*	−	*	*	(4)6–9(10)
'Moonbeam'	*	*[18]	*	*	*	−	*	*	(4)6–9(10)
Cuphea micropetala Cigar plant, hummingbird bush	*	*	*	−	+[19]	*	*	*	8b–9(10)
Dianthus × *allwoodii,* *D. alpinus* 'Allwoodii' Allwood pinks	*	−	*	*	+	−	−	−	(4)6–8
D. caryophyllus Clove pink	+	*	+	*	+	−	−	−	(4)6–9
D. deltoides Maiden pink (e.g., 'Zing Rose')	+	+	*	*	*	−	+[21]	−	(4)6–9a
D. gratianopolitanus Cheddar pink (e.g., 'Tiny Rubies')	*	+	+	*	+		+[21]		(5)6–9a
D. plumarius and cultivars Grass pink	+	+	*	*	+	−	+[21]	−	(4)6–9a
D., unnamed border carnation	+	*	*	*	+	+	−	−	7–8
D., unnamed single pink, magenta	+	*	*	*	+	+	−	−	7–8
D., unnamed single pink, bicolor	+	*	*	*	+	+	−	−	7–8
Dichorisandra thyrsiflora Blue ginger	*	*	−	−	−	*	+	*	8b–9
Echinacea laevigata Smoothleaf coneflower	*	*				*			8–9[22]
E. pallida	*	*							(4b)6–8
E. purpurea Purple coneflower	*	*	*	*	+	*	*	+	(4)6–9(10)
'Bright Star'	*	*	*	*	+	*	*	+	(4)6–9(10)
'White Lustre'	*	*	*	*	+	*	*	+	(4)6–9(10)

[†]Foliage color is green if not otherwise stated.
[18]Poor in Zone 9 Blacklands of San Antonio.
[19]Rated + for Fort Davis area; − for El Paso.
[20]Flowers in spring in frost-free areas.

SOIL: PREFERRED (TOLERATED)	LIGHT	BLOOM SEASON	COLOR: BLOOM/FOLIAGE[†]	HEIGHT
C,G,S; Ac–Al; wd	○ ◐ ◍	Su	Golden yellow	To 36″
C,G,S; Ac–Al; wd	○ ◐ ◍	ESu–MSu	Butter yellow	12–24″
A,C,G,S; Ac–Al; wd	○	LSu–LF[20]	Yellow & red-orange	3–5′
G,S; N–Al	○ ◍	Sp–Su	Rose, pink, white, wine/blue-green	8–18″
G,S; N–Al	○ ◔ ◍	Sp	White, pink, red, purple/blue-gray	8–24″
G,S; Al	○ ◐ ◍	Sp	Pink, white; cultivars also red/green or gray	6–18″
G,S; N–Al	○ ◍	Sp, F	Pink; cultivars also red, rose	4–6″
G,S; N–Al	○ ◍	Sp	Rose, purple, white/gray	8–18″
G,S; N–Al	○ ◍	Sp–F	Red	12–18″
G,S; N–Al	○ ◍	Sp	Magenta	8″
G,S; N–Al	○ ◍	Sp	Pink & rose/gray	8″
G,S; Ac(N–Al); with humus	◍ ●	LSu–LF	Deep blue-violet/dark green	3–5′
A,C,G,S; N–slightly Ac; wd with humus	◐ ◍	Sp–F	Pink, bronze cone	24–36″
G,S(A,C); Al–Ac; with humus	◐ ◍	Sp–ESu	Pale pink/grayish	24″
G(A,C,S); N(Ac,Al); wd	○ ◐ ◍[23] ◑[23]	Sp–LSu	Rose to pink/gray-green	12–16″
G(A,C,S); N(Ac,Al)	○ ◐ ◍[23] ●[23]	MSp–LF	Hot pink, orange cone/gray-green	18–36″
G(A,C,S); N(Ac–Al)	○ ◐ ◍	MSp–LF	White, gold cone/gray-green	24–36″

[21] Usable only in northern part of region (to Zone 9a).
[22] Hardiness zones in which known by author to occur; range may be broader.
[23] Shadier exposures only in strong-sun, high-heat areas.

| | REGIONS | | | | | | | | USDA |
	PW	PCT	EP	PC	TP	GC	ST	LRGV	ZONES
Eustoma grandiflorum Texas bluebell, prairie gentian	+	*	*	*	+	+	+	+	(4)6–9(10)
Gaillardia × *grandiflora* Indian blanket	+	+	*	*	+	+	*	+	(4)6–9
Galphimia glauca (*Thryallis glauca*) Rain-of-gold							*	*	9(10)
Gaura lindheimeri False honeysuckle	*	*	*	*	*	*	*	*	6–9(10)
Gerbera jamesonii Gerber daisy	+	+	+	–	–	*	+	+	8–9(10)
Hedychium gardneranum Ginger		*[24]			–	*	+	*	8b–9(10)
Helenium autumnale 'Crimson Beauty'	*	+[26]	+[26]	+[26]	+		+		(3)6–9
H. flexuosum	*	*			+	*			(3)6–9
H. × 'Sunny Boy'	*	+	*		+				(3)6–9
H. × 'Sunshine Hybrids'	*	*	*[27]	*[27]			+		(3)6–9
Helianthus angustifolius Swamp sunflower	*	+	+	–	–	*	+	+	6–9(10)
H. maximiliani Maximilian sunflower	+	*	*	*	+	+	+	*	6–9(10)
H. × *multiflorus* Perennial sunflower	+	*	*	+	+	+	+	+	(5)6–9(10)
Heliopsis helianthoides var. *scabra* 'Summer Sun' False sunflower	*	*	*	*	+	*	+		(4)6–9
Hemerocallis fulva 'Europa' Tawny daylily	*	*	+	*	+	*	+	+	6–9(10)
H. lilioasphodelus (*H. flava*) Lemon lily	*	*	*	*	+	*	*	+	6–9(10)

†Foliage color is green if not otherwise stated.
[24]Zone 8b portion only.
[25]Must have consistent watering if grown in full sun.

SOIL: PREFERRED (TOLERATED)	LIGHT	BLOOM SEASON	COLOR: BLOOM/FOLIAGE[†]	HEIGHT
C(A,G,S); Al(N,Ac)	○ ◑ ◍	Su–F	Deep blue/blue-green	12–24″
S(A,C,G); Al–Ac; wd	○ ◑	ESu–F	Red and yellow	12–30″
A,C,G,S; Ac–Al; wd	○	ESp–EW	Yellow	3–6′
A,C,G,S; Ac–Al; wd	○	Sp–F	White, pink	18–48″
G; N; wd	◑ ◍ ●	Sp–F	Red	12–24″
G; rich	○[25] ◑ ◍	ESu–LF	Orange	5–8′
A,C,G,S; Ac–Al; mr	○	LSu–EF	Mahogany	24″
S; moist	○	LSp–ES	Yellow	To 36″
A,C,G,S; Ac–Al; rich, mr	○	ESu–EF	Yellow	12–24″
A,C,G,S; Ac–Al; mr	○	Su	Yellow, bronze, red-brown	12–24″
A,C,G,S; Ac–Al; moist	○ ◑	F	Yellow, purple-brown eye	3–7′
A,C,G,S; N–Al	○	LS–F	Yellow, yellow eye	3–7′
A,C,G,S; N–Al	○	Su–F	Yellow	3–5′
A,C,G,S; Ac–Al	○ ◑ ◍	LS; occ. Sp–LF	Yellow/dark green	24–48″
A,C,G,S; Ac–Al; wd	○ ◑ ◍	ESu–MSu	Orange, red eye-zone	30″–6′
G(A,C,S if wd); Ac(N,Al improved)	○ ◑ ◍	ESu–MSu	Lemon yellow	24″

[26]Hybrid rated − to +; species * here in conditions described.
[27]Rated + in some gardens.

	REGIONS								USDA ZONES
	PW	PCT	EP	PC	TP	GC	ST	LRGV	
H., dormant hybrids	*	*	*	*	+	−	−	−	6–9
H., evergreen hybrids	−	−	+	−	+	*[29]	−	*	9(10)
H., semi-evergreen hybrids	*	*	+	−	+	*	*	*	8–9(10)
Hibiscus laevis (*H. militaris*) Halberd-leaf hibiscus	*	+	+	+[30]	+	*			8–9
H. martianus (*H. cardiophyllus*) Heart-leaf hibiscus, *tulipán del monte*	*	*[31]	*[31]	−	*[32]	*	*	*	8–9(10)
H. moscheutos Common rose mallow	*	+	*	*	+	*	*	+	(5)6–9(10)
H. moscheutos hybrids ('Disco Belle,' 'Southern Belle')	*	+	+	*	+	*	+	+	(5)6–9(10)
Kniphofia uvaria (*Tritoma*) Torch lily, red-hot poker		+	+	+	+	−	−	−	6–8[33]
'Earliest of All'	+	+	+	*	+	−	−	−	6–8[33]
Lantana camara	+	*	*	+[34]	*[35]	*	*	*	7b–9(10)
'Confetti'	+	+	*	−	*[35]	*	*	*	8b–9(10)
'New Gold'	+	*	*	−	*[35]	*	*	*	8b–9(10)
'Radiation'	+	+	*	−	*[35]	*	*	*	8b–9(10)
'Silver Mound'	+	+	*	−	*[35]	*	*	*	8b–9(10)

[†]Foliage color is green if not otherwise stated.
[28]May stop in August; some varieties rebloom in fall.
[29]Rated * for Lower GC; + for Upper GC.
[30]Does well by pond or with ample, consistent watering.
[31]Rated for southern part of region only; no reports from northern part.

SOIL: PREFERRED (TOLERATED)	LIGHT	BLOOM SEASON	COLOR: BLOOM/FOLIAGE[†]	HEIGHT
G(A,C,S if wd); Ac(N,Al improved)	○ ◐ ●	ESp–MSu,F[28]	All but blue	8–48″
G(A,C,S if wd); Ac(N,Al improved)	○ ◐ ●	ESp–MSu,F[28]	All but blue	8–48″
G(A,C,S if wd); Ac(N,Al improved)	○ ◐ ●	ESp–MSu,F[28]	All but blue	8–48″
C,G; Ac–slightly Al	○ ◐ ●	ESu–LF	Pink, white	3–8′
A,C,G,S; Ac–Al; wd	○ ◐ ●	ESu–LF	Rose-red	12–36″
C,G; Ac–N	○ ◐ ●	ESu–LSu	White, pink, rose, maroon	To 8′
C,G; Ac–N	○ ◐ ●	ESu–LSu	White, pink, rose, maroon	18–48″
G,S(C); N–Al(Ac); wd, rich, humus	○ ◐ ●	LSp–ESu	Yellow, orange, red/gray-green	24–48″
G,S(C); N–Al(Ac); wd, rich, humus	○ ◐ ●	Sp; repeats	Coral-red/gray-green	30–48″
A,C,G,S; N–Al(Ac); wd, tol. salt	☀ ○ ◐	LSp–LF	Orange & yellow, pink & yellow/dark green	12–36″
A,C,G,S; N–Al(Ac); wd, tol. salt	☀ ○ ◐	Su–LF	Pink & yellow/dark green	To 36″
A,C,G,S; N–Al(Ac); wd, tol. salt	☀ ○ ◐	Su–LF	Yellow/dark green	To 12″
A,C,G,S; N–Al(Ac); wd, tol. salt	☀ ○ ◐	Su–LF	Red/dark green	12–18″
A,C,G,S; N–Al(Ac); wd, tol. salt	☀ ○ ◐	Su–LF	White	12–18″

[32]Rated + in El Paso.
[33]To Zone 9 with good irrigation, drainage, low humidity.
[34]Dies two of four winters in South Plains; annual in northern PC.
[35]Rated + in El Paso.

	REGIONS								USDA
	PW	PCT	EP	PC	TP	GC	ST	LRGV	ZONES
L. horrida Texas lantana, *hierba de cristo*	+	*	*	*[36]	*[35]	*	*	*	7b–9(10)
L. montevidensis (*L. sellowiana*) Trailing lantana	+	+	*	−	*	*	*	*	8b–9(10)
Lathyrus latifolius Perennial sweet pea	*	*	*	*[38]	+[39]	*	*	*	(4)6–9(10)
Lavandula angustifolia English lavender	+	*	*	+	+	+	*		(7)7–9(10)
L. dentata French lavender	+	*	*	−	−	+	*		8b–9(10)
L. stoechas Spanish lavender	+	*	*	−	+	+	*		8–9(10)
Liatris spp. Gayfeather, blazing star	*	*	*	*	*	*	*	*	(4)6–9(10)
L. spicata 'Kobold'	+	*	*	*	*	+	+	+	(4)6–9
Lobelia cardinalis Cardinal flower	*	*[41]	*[42]	*[42]	*[42]	*	*[42]	−	(3)6–9
Lychnis coronaria Rose campion	+	*	*	+[45]	+	−	+	+	(4)6–9(10)
L. viscaria German catchfly	+	+	*	−	+[46]	−	+	+	(4)6–9(10)
'Zulu'	+	+	*	−	+[46]	−	+	+	(4)6–9
Lythrum salicaria Willow-leaf loosestrife	*	+	+	+	−	*	*	−	(4)6–9
'Robert'	*	+	+	+	−	*	*	−	(4)6–8
L. virgatum 'Morden Gleam,' 'Morden Pink'	*	+	+	+	−	*	*	−	(4)6–9

[†]Foliage color is green if not otherwise stated.
[35]Rated + in El Paso.
[36]Rated * for South Plains and east of Cap Rock only. Used as annual farther north and at higher elevations.
[37]With good drainage and air circulation.
[38]Rated * for northern PC; − for South Plains.
[39]Rated * in El Paso.

SOIL: PREFERRED (TOLERATED)	LIGHT	BLOOM SEASON	COLOR: BLOOM/FOLIAGE†	HEIGHT
A,C,G,S; N–Al(Ac); wd, tol. salt	☼ ○ ◐	Sp–LF	Orange & yellow/gray-green	To 3′; rarely, 6′
A,C,G,S; Ac–Al; wd, tol. salt	☼ ○ ◐[37]	Sp–LF	Lavender/sage green	12″
A,C,G,S; Ac–Al; wd	☼ ○ ◐ ●	Sp–Su	Pink, rose, red, purple, white/gray-green	To 9′
G,S; N–Al; wd	☼ ○ ◐	Su–EF	Lavender, white/gray	12–36″
G,S; N–Al; wd	☼ ○ ◐	Su–EF	Lavender/gray	12–24″
G,S; N–Al; wd	☼ ○ ◐	Su–EF	Dark lavender/gray	12″
G,S(C); Ac–Al; wd	○ ◔ ●	LSp–LF[40]	Pinkish-purple, purple, white	12–48″
C,G,S; N–Al; wd	○ ◔ ●	Su–EF	Purple	15–18″
C,G,S; Ac–Al; mr	○[43] ◐ ●	ESu–MF	Red/green, deep red	18–36″[44]
G,S; N–Al; very wd	○	Su	Magenta/gray-white	24–36″
G,S; N–Al; mr	○ ◐ ●	LSp–Su	Magenta, cultivars pink, white	12–15″
G,S; N–Al; mr	○ ●	ESp	Deep salmon	12–15″
A,C,G; Ac–N	○	Sp–Su; repeats	Magenta pink	2–6′
A,C,G; Ac–N	○	Sp–Su; repeats	Rose-pink	18–24″
A,C,G; Ac–N	○	Sp–Su; repeats	Carmine, magenta-pink	3–5′

[40]LSu–LF in wild.
[41]Rated * for northern portion; − for south.
[42]Only in moist soil on margins of ponds or waterfalls.
[43]Tolerates sun in ST if roots stay wet.
[44]Rarely to 6′.
[45]Rated + for southern portion; − north.
[46]Rated − in El Paso.

| | REGIONS | | | | | | | | USDA |
	PW	PCT	EP	PC	TP	GC	ST	LRGV	ZONES
Malva sylvestris 'Zebrina' (*Alcea zebrina*)[47] French hollyhock	*	*	+		*	+	*		(3)7b–9
Malvaviscus arboreus var. *drummondii* Turk's cap, bleeding heart	*	*	*	*[48]	+	*	*	*	(7b)7b–9 (10)
M. arboreus var. *mexicanus* Wax mallow				*[49]		*	*	*	8b[47]–9(10)
Melampodium cinereum, *M. leucanthum* Blackfoot daisy	+	*	*	*	*	−	+	+	6–9(10)
Monarda didyma Bee balm, Bergamot, Oswego tea	+	+	+	*[50]		−	−[51]	−	(4)6–8
'Adam'	+	+	+	−	*[52]	−	−	−	(4)6–8
'Cambridge Scarlet'	+	+	+	−		−	−	−	(4)6–7
'Croftway Pink'	+	+	+	−		−	−	−	(4)6–8
M. fistulosa Wild bergamot	*	*	*	+	−	+			(4)6–9a
Oenothera spp. Evening primroses, sundrops	*	*	*	*	*	*	*	*	6–9(10)
Pavonia lasiopetala Rock rose	*	*	*	*[53]	*	*	*	*	7[54]–9(10)
Penstemon baccharifolius Rock penstemon	+	*	*	*[55]	*	−	*	−	7–9a
P. barbatus Beardlip penstemon	*	+	+	*	−	+	+	−	(5)6–9
P. barbatus var. *torreyi* Beardlip penstemon, *jarritos*				*[56]	*[57]				8–9a

[†]Foliage color is green if not otherwise stated.
[47]Reseeding biennial or short-lived perennial.
[48]Rated * for southern portion; − north.
[49]To Zone 7b in southern PC if mulched after top growth dies back.
[50]Rated as biennial. "No monardas are true perennials in the Plains."
[51]Some success in San Antonio in one garden (+).

SOIL: PREFERRED (TOLERATED)	LIGHT	BLOOM SEASON	COLOR: BLOOM/FOLIAGE[†]	HEIGHT
G(A,C,S); N–Al(Ac); wd	○ ◑ ◉	LSp–MSu	White to pink, striped rose to purple	12–48″
C,G,S; Ac–Al	○ ◑ ◉ ●	LSp–LF	Red/dull green	30–36″
C,G,S; N–Al	○ ◑ ◉	ESu–MF	Red, pink/green, shiny	To 5′
A,C,G; Al; wd	○	Sp–LF	White	6–12″
G,S; Ac–N(Al); mr	○ ◑ ◉	ESu–MSu	White, lilac, red, pink/dark green	24–48″
G,S(C); Ac–N(Al); mr	○ ◑ ◉	Su	Red/dark green	24–36″
G,S; Ac–N; mr	◑ ◉	ESu–LSu	Scarlet/dark green	36″
G,S; Ac–N; mr	◑ ◉	ESu–MSu	Pink/dark green	24–48″
C,G,S; Ac–Al; wd	○ ◑ ◉	MSu–LSu	Lilac, pink, white/gray-green	12–16″
A,C,G,S; Ac–Al; wd, rich to poor	○ ◑	MSp–Su	White, pink, yellow/dark to gray-green	9–30″
A,C,G,S; Al; wd	○ ◑ ◉	LSp–LF	Soft pink	12–36″
G,S; N–Al; wd, gravelly	○	Sp–F	Coral pink to red	6–18″
G,S; N–Al; wd	○ ◑ ◉	LSp–MSu	Red with yellow lip	18–36″
G,S; N–Al; wd	○	ESu–LF	Scarlet/gray-green	24–36″

[52]At high altitudes.
[53]Rated * for South Plains; + in Panhandle.
[54]With winter mulch.
[55]Rated * for New Mexico and Texas' South Plains only; − in northern PC.
[56]Rated * for southern portion; − in north.
[57]Rated * for Chisos and Davis Mountains; + in El Paso.

| | REGIONS | | | | | | | | USDA ZONES |
	PW	PCT	EP	PC	TP	GC	ST	LRGV	
P. cobaea Wild foxglove	*	*	*	*	+	*[58]	*	−	(5)6–9
P. digitalis	*	*	*				*	*	8–9
P. tenuis Gulf Coast penstemon	*	*	*	−[59]	+	*	*		6–9a
Phlox divaricata Wild sweet William, Louisiana phlox	*	*[60]	+	+[61]	+[62]		*		(4)6–9a
P. maculata 'Miss Lingard,' 'Rosalinde'	*	+	+	*[63]	+[64]	+	+	−	(3)6–9a
P. paniculata and hybrids Summer phlox, garden phlox	*	*[60]	+	*	*	−	+	−	(3)6–8
Border hybrids, e.g., 'Mount Fuji'	*	+	+	+	+	+	+	−	(3)6–8
Symons-Jeune hybrids	*	+		*[65]		−	+	−	(3)6–8
P. pilosa Downy phlox, prairie phlox	*	*	*	*[65]			+		(4)6–8
P. subulata Thrift, moss pink	*	*	+	+[66]	+	+	+	−	6–9a
Physostegia virginiana False dragonhead, obedient plant	*	*	*	*	+[67]	*	+	−	(4)6–9
'Rosy Spire'	*	*	+	*	+[67]	*	+	−	(4)6–9
'Summer Snow'	*	*	+	*	+[67]	*	+	−	(4)6–9
'Vivid'	*	*	+	*	+[67]	*	+	−	(4)6–9
Platycodon grandiflorus Balloon flower		*	*	*		−			(4)6–9a

[†]Foliage color is green if not otherwise stated.
[58]Rated * for Upper GC; + for Lower GC.
[59]Rated − for South Plains; not rated for northern PC.
[60]Rated + by some gardeners.
[61]Rated + for northern PC; * for South Plains.
[62]Rated * by some Big Bend gardeners, + by others; + in El Paso.

SOIL: PREFERRED (TOLERATED)	LIGHT	BLOOM SEASON	COLOR: BLOOM/FOLIAGE†	HEIGHT
G,S; N–Al; wd, good to poor	○ ◐ ▦	Sp	White, lavender, pink	12–24″
C,G; N–Al	○ ◐ ▦	MSp–LSp	White	12–36″
C,G,S; Ac–slightly Al; mr	○ ◐ ▦	Sp–EF	Lavender-pink, white, blue, wine-purple	12–36″
G,S; Ac–N; wd, rich, deep	◐ ▦	ESp–LSp	Lavender-blue, lilac-pink	12–15″
G,S; Ac–N; wd	○ ◐ ▦	Sp–Su	White, lilac-pink	24–48″
C,G,S; Ac–Al; wd, mr, rich	○ ◐ ▦	Su	White, pink, rose, lilac, salmon, blue	1–6′
C,G,S; Ac–Al; wd, mr, rich	○ ◐ ▦	LSp, repeats	White, pink, rose, lilac, salmon, blue	36–42″
C,G,S; Ac–Al; wd, mr, rich	○ ◐ ▦	ESu–F	Pink, rose, lilac, red, salmon, blue, white	24–42″
C,G,S; Ac–Al; wd	○ ◐ ▦	Sp	Rose, pink, lavender, white	4–16″, sprawling
A,C,G,S; Ac–Al; wd, deep	○ ◐	Sp	Pink, rose, white, lavender-blue	6–10″
A,C,G,S; Ac–Al; dry	○ ◐ ▦ ●	LSu–F	Purplish-pink/dark green	12–24″
C,G,S; Ac–Al	◐ ▦ ●	LS–F	Red-violet	36″
C,G,S; Ac–Al; wd	◐ ▦ ●	ESu–LF	White	18–30″
C,G,S; Ac–Al	◐ ▦ ●	LSu–LF	Dark red-violet or pink	24–36″
G; slightly Ac(Al); wd	○ ◐	Su	Blue, lilac, white	18–30″

[63]Rated * for South Plains; no northern PC reports.

[64]Rated − by some gardeners; + in El Paso.

[65]Rated * for South Plains; no reports for northern PC.

[66]Rated + for northern PC; − for South Plains.

[67]Rated − by some Big Bend gardeners, + by others; + in El Paso.

	REGIONS								USDA
	PW	PCT	EP	PC	TP	GC	ST	LRGV	ZONES
Plumbago auriculata (*P. capensis*) Tropical plumbago	A	A	A	A	A	*	*	*	8[68]–9
Poliomintha longiflora Mexican oregano	+	*	*	*	*	*[70]	*	*	(7b)7b–9(10)
Ratibida columnifera[71] Mexican hat, prairie coneflower	+[72]	*	*	*	*	+	*	*	(4)6–9(10)
Rudbeckia fulgida var. *sullivantii* 'Goldsturm'	*	*	*	*	+	*	+	+	(3)6–9(10)
R. hirta 'Gloriosa Daisy'	+	*	*	A	+	+	*		(4)6–9(10)
'Goldilocks'	+	*	*	A	+	+	*		(4)6–9(10)
'Marmalade'	+	*	*	A	+	+	*		(4)6–9(10)
R. laciniata 'Goldquelle' Cutleaf coneflower	+	*	*	*	*	+	+	+	(3)6–9(10)
'Hortensia' ('Golden Glow')	+	*	*	*	*	+	+	+	(3)6–9(10)
Ruellia brittoniana Narrowleaf Mexican petunia	*	*	*	*[74]	*	*	*	*	(7b)7b–9(10)
R. malacosperma Mexican petunia	*	*	*	*[74]	*	*	*	*	(7)7b–9(10)
R. nudiflora Common wild petunia	*	*	*	*[74]	+	*	*	*	(7)7b–9(10)
Russelia equisetiformis Firecracker plant	–	–	–	–	–	*	*	*	9(10)
Salvia azurea var. *grandiflora* Pitcher's sage, sky-blue sage	+	*	*	*	+	+	+	+	(4)6–9(10)
S. coccinea Scarlet sage	*	*[75]	*	A[76]	+	*	*	*	(7b)7b–9(10)

[†]Foliage color is green if not otherwise stated.
[68]Winters over in mild Zone 8 winters with mulch.
[69]Reflected heat from walls only, not from below.
[70]According to one nurseryman in Corpus Christi.
[71]Biennial or reseeding annual.

SOIL: PREFERRED (TOLERATED)	LIGHT	BLOOM SEASON	COLOR: BLOOM/FOLIAGE†	HEIGHT
C,G,S; Ac–Al	☼69 ○ ◑ ◉	LSp–LF	White or dark to pale blue	To 36″
A,G,S(C); N–Al(Ac); wd	○ ◑ ◉	LSp–LF	Pale pink to lilac	2–5′
A,C,G,S; N–Al; wd	○ ◑73 ◉73	Sp–F	Red-brown & yellow or all yellow	24–36″
A,C,G,S; N; wd	○ ◑ ◉	MSu–F	Gold, black or brown cone/dark green	24–30″
A,C,G,S; N–Al; wd	○ ◑	MSu–LSu	Yellow, rust, bicolors	16–36″
A,C,G,S; N–Al; wd	○ ◑	MSu–F	Dark yellow	To 24″
A,C,G,S; N–Al; wd	○ ◑	MSu–LSu	Orange, black cone; gray-green	To 24″
C,G; N; wd but mr; fairly infertile	○ ◑ ◉	MSu–MF	Dark yellow/dark green	30–48″
A,C,G,S; N	○ ◑ ◉	ESu–MF	Yellow/dark green	5–8′
A,C,G,S; Ac–Al	○ ◑ ◉ ●	LSp–LF	Blue-violet/dark green, thin	3–5′
A,C,G,S; N–Al(Ac)	○ ◑ ◉ ●	LSp–LF	Blue-violet/dark green, broad	12–36″
A,C,G,S; Ac–Al	○ ◑ ◉	MSp–LF	Lavender, white/dull green	12–24″
A,C,G,S; N–Al; wd; tol. salt; moderately fertile	○ ◑	Sp–Su	Red	To 48″
A,C,G,S; N–Al; wd	○ ◑ ◉ ◐	LSp–F	Blue, white	3–6′
A,C,G,S; Ac–Al; wd, poor	○ ◑ ◉	Sp–F	Scarlet, salmon, white	12–36″

[72]Rated + for all but extreme eastern PW.

[73]In well-drained soil.

[74]Rated for South Plains.

[75]Annual in North Texas. Freeze survival in all regions improved with winter mulch.

[76]Rated ✳ in Midland; reseeding annual in most of PC.

	PW	PCT	EP	PC	TP	GC	ST	LRGV	ZONES
S. farinacea Mealy-cup sage, mealy blue sage	+	*	*	*	*	+	*	*	(6)6–9(10)
'Alba,' 'Victoria'	+	*	*	*	*	+	*	*	(6)6–9(10)
S. forskahlei		*[77]							8b–9(10)
S. greggii Cherry sage, autumn sage	+	*[78]	*	*[79]	*	+	*	*	7b–9(10)
S. leucantha	*	*[80]	*	A	+	*	*	*	8–9(10)
S. moorcroftiana Moorcroft sage	*	*					*		
S. × 'Purple Majesty'	*[81]	*[81]							8–9(10)
S. × *superba* (*S. pratensis*)	+	*	*	*	+	−	−	−	(4)6–8
Sedum × 'Autumn Joy' ('Indian Chief')	+	*	*	*	*	*	*	*	(4)6–9
S. spectabile 'Brilliant,' 'Carmen,' 'Meteor'	+	*	*	*	*	*	*	*	(4)6–9
Solidago spp. Goldenrod	*	*	*	*	*	*	+	+	(3)6–9
Tagetes lucida Mexican mint marigold, *yerba anís*	+	*	*	*	*	*	*	*	(7)7–9(10)
Tecoma stans Yellow-bells, *esperanza*					*[82]	*[82]	*	*	8b–9(10)
Tradescantia spp. and hybrids Spiderwort	*	*	*	*	*	*	*	*	(5)6–9(10)
Verbena bipinnatifida Prairie verbena	*	*	*	*[83]	+[84]	+	*	+	(4)6–9
V. canadensis and cultivars Rose verbena	*	*	*	+	*	+	*	*	(5)6–9(10)

[†]Foliage color is green if not otherwise stated.
[77]Only region reporting at time of publication.
[78]Rated * for southern part; not reported from far North Texas.
[79]Rated * in Midland; + in Lubbock; − in Panhandle.
[80]Rated * for southern portion; annual in north.

SOIL: PREFERRED (TOLERATED)	LIGHT	BLOOM SEASON	COLOR: BLOOM/FOLIAGE[†]	HEIGHT
A,C,G,S; N–Al(Ac); wd	○ ◑	Sp–LF	Blue, white	18–36″
A,C,G,S; N–Al(Ac); wd	○ ◑	Sp–LF	White, deep blue	13–36″
C,G,S; Ac–N; wd	◑	LSp–Msu; repeats	Blue-violet and white/gray-green, felted; evergreen	24–36″
A,G,S(C); N–Al(Ac); wd	○ ◑ ◍	Sp–F	Red, pink, salmon, white/dull green	24–36″
A,C,G,S; Ac–Al; wd	○ ◑ ◍	EF–LF	Violet & white/gray-green	3–6′
G,S; N; moist or dry	○ ◑	MSp–LSp	Violet-blue & white/felted gray-green	36–48″
C,G,S; Ac–Al; wd	○ ◑ ◍	Sp–LF	Cobalt blue	12–48″
G,S; N; wd	○ ◑	Su	Purple/gray-green	24″
A,C,G,S; Ac–Al; wd but mr, rich	☼ ○ ◑ ◍	Su–LF	Brick red to salmon/gray-green	12–30″
A,C,G,S; Ac–Al; wd	☼ ○ ◑ ◍	Su–LF	Red to pink/blue-green to gray-green	12–18″
A,C,G,S; Ac–Al; poor, dry to wet	○ ◑ ◍	LSu–F	Golden yellow	1–6½′
A,G,S(C); N–Al(Ac); wd	○ ◑ ◍	LSu–LF	Yellow-gold	24–48″
A,G,S(C); Ac–Al; wd	○	LSp–MF	Golden yellow	36–48″
A,C,G,S; Ac–Al; mr, poor to rich	◑ ◍	Sp–F	Blue, rose, purple, white	To 36″
A,C,G,S; Al(N,Ac); wd	○ ◑ ◍	Sp–LF	Lavender-blue to lilac/sage green to dark green	4–12″
A,C,G,S; Ac–Al; wd	○ ◑ ◍	Sp–LF	Pink, lilac, white	8–12″

[81]Reliable in southern portion of region; reports lacking elsewhere.
[82]Rated for southern part of region only.
[83]Biennial in South Plains according to one gardener.
[84]Rated + in El Paso; − for rest of TP.

	REGIONS								USDA
	PW	PCT	EP	PC	TP	GC	ST	LRGV	ZONES
V. 'Elegans'	*	*	+	−	+[85]	+	+	+	8–9(10)
V. × *hybrida* (*V. hortensis*) Garden verbena	*[86]	*[86]	+[86]	+[86]	*[86]	+	*	*	9(10)
V. peruviana Peruvian verbena	*	*	*	*[87]	*[88]	+	+	*	(5)7b–9(10)
V. rigida (*V. venosa*) Vervain, tube vervain	*	*	*	*	*	*	*	*	(4)7–9(10)
V. tenuisecta Moss vervain	*	*	*		+	*	+	*	8–9(10)
Viola cornuta and hybrids Horned violet			+	−	+[89]		−	−	(5)6–8
V. hederacea	*	*							8–9
V. odorata and hybrids Sweet violet	*	*	+	*[90]	+	*	*	*	(5)6–9(10)
V. pedata Bird's-foot violet	*		−	−					(5)7b–8
V. sagittata Arrowleaf violet	*								(5)7b–8
V. sororia (*V. priceana*) and hybrids Woolly blue violet	*	*	*			*			(5)6–8
V. walteri	*	*				*			(5)8–9
Zinnia acerosa Dwarf zinnia				*	*			*	7b–9b
Z. angustifolia (*Z. linearis*)		*[92]	*	A	+		*		8–9(10)
Z. grandiflora Prairie zinnia, Rocky Mountain zinnia			+	*	*				(5)6–9

†Foliage color is green if not otherwise stated.
[85]Rating for El Paso.
[86]Ratings north of Zone 9 are for use as annual.
[87]Occasionally freezes out in Zone 7a.
[88]Rated + by some gardeners.

SOIL: PREFERRED (TOLERATED)	LIGHT	BLOOM SEASON	COLOR: BLOOM/FOLIAGE[†]	HEIGHT
G,S; N–Al; wd	○ ◐	Sp–MF	Pink, purple, red	8–12″
G,S; N–Al; wd	○ ◐	Sp–F	Red, pink, white, purple, bicolor	6–12″
A,C,G,S; N–Al	※ ○ ◐ ◉	Sp–F	Red, pink, purple, white, pink & white	2–4′
G,S; Ac–Al; wd	○	Su	Purple, white	12–24″
G,S; Ac–N	○	ESp–LF	Violet-pink, white	4–6″
G,S(A,C); Al; mr, wd, rich	◐ ◉	Sp or Sp–F	Purple; hybrids various colors	6–8″
G,S; Ac–N; with humus	◐ ◉	Sp	Violet	6–8″
G,S(A,C); Ac–N; mr, wd, rich	◐ ◉ ●	ESp[91]	Violet, white; hybrids also rose, purple, bicolor	2½–12″
G,S; Ac; mr, wd, poor, rocky	○ ◐ ◉	ESp–LSp	Lilac, violet, white, pinkish	2–6″
G,S; Ac; mr, rich	◐ ◉	Sp	Deep violet	To 4″
G,S; Ac; mr, rich	◐ ◉ ●	Sp, F	Blue-violet, various	3–6″
G,S; Ac–slightly Al; mr, wd	◐ ◉	LW–ESp	Pale violet	2–6″
G,S; Al; wd	○	Su–F	White/grayish	To 6″
A,G,S; Al; wd	○ ◐	Sp–LF	Gold	6–8″
A,G,S; Al; wd	※ ○	Su–F	Yellow	4–10″

[89]Davis Mountains and El Paso.
[90]Rated * for northern portion; − in South Plains.
[91]Some also MF–LF.
[92]Annual in northern PCT.

Bulbs, Corms, Rhizomes, and Tubers

	REGIONS								USDA
	PW	PCT	EP	PC	TP	GC	ST	LRGV	ZONES
Agapanthus africanus Lily of the Nile	*	*	+	−	−¹	*	*	*	9^2(10)
A. orientalis	*	*	+	−	−¹	*	*	*	8–9(10)
Allium neapolitanum 'Grandiflorum'	*	*	*			*	*	*	9(10)
A. schoenoprasum Onion chive	*	*				*			(3)6–9(10)
A. subhirsutum			*			*	*	*	(4)6–9(10)
A. tuberosum Chinese chive, garlic chive	*	*	*	*	*	*	*	*	(4)6–9(10)
× *Amarcrinum howardii*	*	*		*⁴	−	*	*	*	8^5–9(10)
Bletilla striata Chinese ground orchid	*	*⁶	*		−	*	*	*	8b–9(10)
Crinum americanum Southern swamp lily	*	*⁶	*	−	−	*	*	*	9^7(10)
C. asiaticum Poison bulb	*⁶					*	*	*	9(10)
C. bulbispermum	*	+	+	*	+	*	*	*	8–9
C. × digweedi Digweedi hybrids	*⁶	*⁶				*	*	*	8b–9(10)
C. × 'Ellen Bosanquet'	*					*	*	*	7–9(10)
C. × herbertii Milk-and-wine lilies	*	*	*			*	*	*	7^8–9(10)

†Foliage color is green if not otherwise stated.
¹Rated + by El Paso respondents.
²Zone 8b with winter protection.
³Two forms with different bloom seasons.
⁴Rated * for northern PC; + for South Plains.

SOIL: PREFERRED (TOLERATED)	LIGHT	BLOOM SEASON	COLOR: BLOOM/FOLIAGE[†]	HEIGHT
G,S; Ac–Al; humus	◐ ◍ ●	Su	Blue, white	18–40″
G,S; Ac–Al; humus	◐ ◍ ●	Su	Blue	24+″
G; Al	○ ◐	Sp–Su	White	10–18″
G; Al; mr, light, rich	○ ◐	Sp	Lilac	To 12″
G; Al	○ ◐	Sp–Su	White	10–12″
G(A,C,S); Al	○ ◐	Sp; Su–F[3]	White	15″
G(C); Ac–Al; rich	○ ◐ ◍	Su	Pink	24–48″
C,G,S; Ac–N(Al); wd	○ ◐ ◍	LSp	White, lilac	10–24″
G(C); Ac–N; rich	○ ◐ ◍	LSp–F	White	18–24″
G; Ac–slightly Al; wd	○ ◐ ◍	Su–LF	White	36″
C,G,S; Ac–Al; rich	○ ◐ ◍	LSp	Pink, wine, or white	To 36″
C,G,S; Ac–slightly Al; wd, rich	○ ◐ ◍	Su	White, striped pink or red	To 36″
G,S; Ac–slightly Al; rich, wd	○ ◐ ◍	ESu	Deep rose-pink	24–48″
A,C,G,S; Ac–Al; rich, wd	○ ◐	LSp–F	White, midribs pink to red	36″

[5]Zone 7 with winter protection.
[6]Rated * for southern portion; no rating for north.
[7]Zone 7b with winter protection.
[8]With winter protection.

	REGIONS								USDA ZONES
	PW	PCT	EP	PC	TP	GC	ST	LRGV	
C. × 'J. C. Harvey'	*[9]					*	*	*	8b–9(10)
C. moorei	*[9]					*	*	*	8b–9(10)
C. × powellii	*	*	+	+[9]		*	*	*	7[8]–9(10)
C. × p. 'Album'	*	*	+	+[9]		*	*	*	7[8]–9(10)
C. × p. 'Cecil Houdyshel'	*		+	+[10]	−	*	*	*	7[8]–9(10)
C. zeylanicum Milk-and-wine lily	+[9]	+[9]	+	−	−	*[9]	*	*	9[11](10)
Crocosmia × crocosmiiflora Montbretia	*	*	+			*			7–9
Dietes vegeta African iris, fortnight lily	+	−	−	−	−	+	*	*	9(10)
Endymion hispanicus Spanish bluebell		*[9]	+	*					(4)7–9(10)
Gladiolus byzantinus Old-fashioned gladiolus, baby glad	*	*	−	+	+	*	*		(5)6–9(10)
Habranthus. See Zephyranthes									
Hippeastrum × johnsonii Amaryllis, St. John's lily	*	*	*	+[12]	−	*	*	*	8–9(10)
H. vittatum (Amaryllis vittata) Amaryllis	+	+[13]	*	+[12]	−	*	*	*	9[14](10)
H. fancy hybrids Hybrid amaryllis	+	*	*	+[12]	−	*	*	*	9(10)
Hymenocallis × festalis Spider lily						*	*		9(10)
H. galvestonensis	*	*[15]			−	+			9(10)
H. liriosme[16]	*	*	−	−	−	*	−	−	7–9(10)
H. narcissiflora 'Sulphur Queen' Peruvian daffodil		*			−	*	*	*	9(10)

[†]Foliage color is green if not otherwise stated.
[8]With winter protection.
[9]For southern portion; no rating for north.
[10]Rated + for southern portion; − in north.
[11]Zone 8b with winter protection.

SOIL: PREFERRED (TOLERATED)	LIGHT	BLOOM SEASON	COLOR: BLOOM/FOLIAGE[†]	HEIGHT
G; Ac–Al; wd, rich	○ ◐ ●	Su–F	Coral pink	5′
G; Ac–Al; wd, rich	◐ ●	ESu–MSu	Rose, white, pink	To 5′
A,C,G,S; Ac–Al, rich	○ ◐	LSp–F	Pink	36″
A,C,G,S; Ac–Al, rich	○ ◐	LSp–F	White	36″
G,S; N–Al; rich	○ ◐ ●	Sp–LF	Coral pink	36″
A,C,G,S; Ac–Al; rich	○ ◐ ●	LSp, ESu	White, pink or purple midribs	To 24″
A,C,G,S; Ac–Al; wd	○ ◐	Su	Red-orange	24–48″
G; Ac–Al; wd	○ ◐ ●	F to year-long	Cream, orange blotches	30–48″
G,S; Ac–slightly Al; wd, organic	◐ ●	Sp	Lavender-blue, white, pink	15–18″
A,C,G,S; Ac–Al; wd; not wet clay	○ ◐ ●	MSp, Su	Magenta, white	12–36″
G; Al–slightly Ac; wd, humus	○ ◐ ●	MSp–LSp	Red	12–24″
G; Al–slightly Ac; wd, humus	○ ◐ ●	MSp–LSp	White, red stripes	36″
G; Al–slightly Ac	○ ◐ ●	MSp–LSp	Red, orange, yellow, white, pink	To 48″
G,S; Ac–N; wd	○ ◐ ●	Su	White and cream	To 24″
G,S; Ac	◐ ●	LSu	White/blue-green	24″
G,S; N–Ac; wet	○ ◐ ●	Sp–ESu	White, yellow center	12–36″
N–Ac; wd	○ ◐ ●	Su	Green-white or pale yellow	24–36″

[12]Rated good perennial in Lubbock when planted 9–10″ deep.
[13]Rated + for southern portion; − in north.
[14]Zone 8 with winter protection.
[15]Rated * for southern portion; not rated for north.
[16]Can be grown in all regions as an aquatic.

| | REGIONS | | | | | | | | USDA |
	PW	PCT	EP	PC	TP	GC	ST	LRGV	ZONES
H. × 'Tropical Giant'		*			−	*	*	*	9(10)
Ipheion uniflorum Spring starflower	*	+	*	*	*	*	*	*	(6)6–9(10)
Iris, arilbred hybrids Persian iris	−	−	*		+		+		8–9(10)
I., bearded hybrids	+	*	*	*	+	−	−	−	(4b)6–8b
I. kaempferi Japanese iris	+	+			+	+			8
I., Louisiana hybrids	*	*	+	+	+	*	*	*	6–9(10)
I. pseudacorus Yellow flag, water iris	*	+	+	−	−	*	+		6–8
I. sibirica × 'Caesar's Brother' Siberian iris	+	*	−	*	−	−	*[18]	−	6–8b
× 'Summer Skies'	+	*			−				6–8b
I. spuria Spuria iris	*	*	*		+	+	*		(4)6–9
I. × *xiphium* Dutch iris	*	*	*	*	+	*	*	*	(5)6b–9(10)
Leucojum aestivum Summer snowflake	*	*	*	+	+	*	*[19]		(4)6–9a
L. vernum Spring snowflake	*	*[19]	*	+			−		(4)6–8a
Lilium × 'Black Dragon' (*L. henryi* × *L. speciosum*)		*	*	+[19]	−		*[20]		7–9a
L. candidum & hybrids Madonna lily	*	*	*	*[21]	−	+	−		7–8
L. × 'Enchantment' (Asiatic hybrid) Enchantment lily		*[22]	*	+	−		−	−	7–9a

[†]Foliage color is green if not otherwise stated.
[17]Tolerates alkalinity to pH 7.9 in aquaculture.
[18]Rated * for northern portion only.
[19]For northern portion; − in south.

SOIL: PREFERRED (TOLERATED)	LIGHT	BLOOM SEASON	COLOR: BLOOM/FOLIAGE[†]	HEIGHT
G,S; Ac–N; wd	○ ◐ ◍	Su	White	To 48″
G,S(A,C); Ac–Al; wd	◐ ◍	Sp	White, blue/bluish-green	5–8″
G,S; N–Al; wd, light, rich	○	MSp	Blues, purples, greens	12–16″
G,S(C); N–Al(Ac); wd, humus	○	Sp; some F	All but true red	6–48″
G,S; Ac; seasonally wet	◐ ◍	LSp	Most colors	To 24″
A,C,G,S; Ac–N;[17] mr	○ ◐ ◍	Sp	All colors	1–6′
C,G,S; Ac–slightly Al; wet, fertile	○ ◐ ◍	Sp	Yellow/evergreen	4–6′
C,G,S; Ac–N(slightly Al); wd, humus	○ ◐ ◍ ●	Sp	Deep purple	24″
C,G,S; Ac–N; wd, humus	○ ◐ ◍ ●	Sp	Blue, white, & yellow	24–30″
G,S; slightly Al–N(Ac); wd, rich; tolerates salt	○ ◍	LSp–ESu	Most colors	3–6′
G; Al–Ac	○	Sp	Blue, purple, yellow, white	16–20″
G,S(C); Ac–Al; humus; wd	○ ◐ ◍ ●	ESp–MSp	White	9–15″
G,S(C); Ac–Al; mr, cool	○ ◐ ◍ ●	LW–ESp	White	6–8″
G,S; Ac–Al; wd, mr	○ ◐ ◍	Su	Deep wine-red	2–5′
G,S; Al; wd, fertile	○ ◐ ◍	LSp–ESu	White	1½–6′
G,S; Ac	○ ◐ ◍	Su	Orange	24–36″

[20]Rated ✳ for northern portion; no report in south.
[21]Rated ✳ for northern portion; no report south of Lubbock.
[22]Rated ✳ for southern portion, in sandy soils; + in north.

	REGIONS								USDA ZONES
	PW	PCT	EP	PC	TP	GC	ST	LRGV	
L. henryi	*	*	*	+	−		+[23]		7
L. × 'Lady Ann'		*		+			−		6–8
L. lancifolium (*L. tigrinum*) Tiger lily	*	*	*	*	+	*	−		(4)6–8
L. martagon Turk's-cap lily	*	*[24]		−	−	+	*[23]		8–9a
L. × 'Pink Perfection'		*		+[23]	−		−		6–8
L. regale Regal lily	*	*	*	*	−	*	*		7–9a
L. speciosum Japanese lily	*	*[24]	*	*	−	+	*		7–8
'Rubrum'	*	*[24]	*	*[25]		+	*		7–8
Lycoris africana (*L. aurea*) Golden spider lily	*	*[26]	+[26]	−		*	*	*	8b–9(10)
L. incarnata	−	+				−	−		6–8a
L. radiata Red spider lily	*	*	*	*[27]	+	*	*	*	7–9
'Alba' White spider lily	*	*		−		*	*	*	7–9
L. squamigera Magic lily, pink spider lily	*	*		*	−	−		−	6–8
L. traubii							*[28]		7–9(10)
Muscari armeniacum Grape hyacinth		*		*	+	+	−		6–8
M. neglectum (*M. racemosum*) Grape hyacinth		*	*	*	−[29]	+	*	+	6–9

[†]Foliage color is green if not otherwise stated.
[23]For northern portion; − in south.
[24]Rated * for northern portion; − in southern Blacklands.
[25]Rated * for northern portion; no report in south.

SOIL: PREFERRED (TOLERATED)	LIGHT	BLOOM SEASON	COLOR: BLOOM/FOLIAGE[†]	HEIGHT
G,S; Ac–N(Al); wd, mr, rich	◍ ●	Su	Apricot	4–9′
G,S; Ac–Al; wd, mr	○ ◑ ◍	Su	Pink	2–5′
A,G,S(C); Ac; humus	○ ◑ ◍ ●	Su–F	Orange/dark green	2½–6′
G,S; Ac–Al; wd	○ ◑ ◍	Su	White, pink	4–6′
G,S; Ac–N; wd, rich	○ ◑ ◍	Su	Pink	3–5′
G,S; Ac–N; wd, rich	○ ◑ ◍	Su	White, pink ribs	2½–6′
G,S; Ac–N	○ ◑ ◍	MSu	White, speckled pink	4–5′
G,S; Ac–N	○ ◑ ◍	Su–F	Carmine	30–36″
A,C,G,S; Ac–Al; wd	◑ ◍ ●	LSu–MF	Golden yellow/green, glaucous	12–24″
A,C,G,S; Ac–Al; wd	○ ◑ ◍	F	Salmon to rose; white with red stripe	To 20″
A,C,G,S; Ac–Al; wd	○ ◑ ◍ ●	LSu–F	Coral-red	12–24″
A,C,G,S; Ac–Al; wd	○ ◑ ◍ ●	LSu–F	White	12–24″
A,C,G,S; Ac–Al; mr–wet	○ ◑ ◍ ●	MSu—LSu	Pale pink	16–30″
A,C,G,S; Ac–Al; wd	◑ ◍ ●	F	Yellow/dark green	12–24″
A,C,G,S; Ac–Al; rich (poor)	○ ◑ ◍ ●	Sp	Blue-violet	4–8″
A,C,G,S; Ac–Al; rich (poor)	○ ◑ ◍	ESp	Dark purple & white	6–12″

[26]Southern portion only.

[27]Rated * in southern portion; + in Panhandle, with winter protection.

[28]Reports available only for this region.

[29]Rated − for eastern portion; not rated in El Paso area.

	REGIONS								USDA
	PW	PCT	EP	PC	TP	GC	ST	LRGV	ZONES
Narcissus bulbocodium var. conspicuus Yellow hoop petticoat	*	*[30]					+[31]		6–8
N. cyclamineus Cyclamen-flowered narcissus	*	*							6–9
'February Gold'	*	*				*	*		6–9
'February Silver'	*	*					*		6–9
'Peeping Tom'	*	*		*			*		6–9
'Tête à Tête'	*	*		*		*	*		6–9
N. jonquilla Species jonquil, "li'l sweetie"	*	*		*	+		*		6–9
'Quail'	*	*[32]			+	*	*		(4)6–9a
'Suzy'	*	*			+		*		(4)6–9a
'Trevithian'	*	*[32]			+	*	*		(4)6–9a
N., large-cup hybrid daffodils									
'Carlton'	*	*	*	*	+		*		6–9a
'Duke of Windsor'	*			*					6–9a
'Fortune'	*	+[33]		*		*			6–9a
'Ice Follies'	*	*		*			*		6–9a
'Mount Hood'	*	*[33]		*		*			6–9a
'Unsurpassable'	*	*	*	*			*		6–9a
N. × *odorus* Single campernelle	*	*				*	*	+	(5)6–9
N. poeticus Pheasant-eye, poet's narcissus	*	*[33]		*					(5)6–9a
'Actaea'	*	*[34]				*	–	–	(5)6–9a
N. pseudonarcissus Species daffodil, Lent lily	*	*[33]				*	+	–	6–9

[†]Foliage color is green if not otherwise stated.

[30]Rated * for northern portion; – in south.

[31]Rated + for northern portion; not rated in south.

SOIL: PREFERRED (TOLERATED)	LIGHT	BLOOM SEASON	COLOR: BLOOM/FOLIAGE[†]	HEIGHT
G,S; Ac–N; wd	○ ◐ ●	ESp	Yellow	4–18″
G,S; Ac–N; damp	◐ ●	ESp	Yellow	6″
G,S; Ac–N	○ ◐ ●	ESp	Yellow	8–12″
G,S; Ac–N	○ ◐ ●	ESp	White	8–12″
G,S; Ac–N; damp	○ ●	ESp	Yellow	8–12″
G,S; Ac–N; damp	○ ◐ ●	ESp	Yellow	6–8″
G,S; Ac–N; wd	○ ●	VESp	Deep yellow	6–18″
G,S; Ac–N; wd	○	MSp	Yellow	6–8″
G,S; Ac–N; wd	○	ESp	Yellow & orange	12–16″
G,S; Ac–N; wd	○	MSp	Lemon	12″
G,S; Ac–N; wd	○ ●	ESp	Yellow	15–20″
G,S; Ac–N; wd	○ ●	ESp	White with orange to yellow	12–15″
G,S; Ac–N; wd	○ ●	ESp	Yellow & orange	12–15″
G,S; Ac–N; wd	○ ●	MSp	White	12–15″
G,S; Ac–N; wd	○ ●	MSp	White	12–16″
G,S; Ac–N; wd	○ ●	MSp	Yellow	20″
G,S; Ac–N; wd	○	ESp	Golden yellow	8–16″
G,S; Ac–N; wd	○ ●	MSp–LSp	White, bicolor cup	8–12″
G,S; Ac–N; wd	○	MSp–LSp	White, bicolor cup	15–18″
G,S; Ac–N; wd	○	VESp	Yellow	6–10″

[32]Rated ✳ for southern portion; no reports from north.
[33]For northern portion; no reports from south.
[34]Rated ✳ for northern portion; − in south.

	PW	PCT	EP	PC	TP	GC	ST	LRGV	USDA ZONES
N. tazetta									
'Cheerfulness,' 'Yellow Cheerfulness'		+[35]	*			*	*[35]	−	(5)6–8b
'Cragford'	*	*[36]	+			*	+		7–9a
'Grand Monarque'	*	*				*	*	*	6–9b
'Grand Primo'	*	*				*	*	*	6–9b
'Laurens Koster'	*	*[37]	+			−	+	−	7–8
var. *ochroleucus*	*	*							8–9(10)
var. *orientalis* Chinese sacred lily						*	*	*	9(10)
cv. 'Paper-white' Paper-white narcissus	*	+	*	−		*	*	*	8–9(10)
'Pearl'	*	*					*		7–9a
'Soleil d'Or'	*[38]	*		+		*	*	*	7–9a
N. triandrus × 'Thalia' Orchid narcissus	*	*		+		*	−		(4)6–8
Oxalis adenophylla	*	*[39]				*	*	*	(5)6–9(10)
O. bowiei			*					*	9b[40](10)
O. braziliensis		*				*			8–9(10)
O. crassipes	*	*	*	*		*	*		(4)6–9
O. pes-caprae Bermuda buttercup	*	*[39]				*	*	*	9b[40]
O. rosea	*	*	*	*	+	*	*	*	7–9(10)
Rhodophiala bifida Oxblood lily	*	*	*	−		*	*	*	8–9(10)
Sprekelia formosissima 'Orient Red' Aztec lily	*	*			+	*	*	*	8b–9(10)

[†]Foliage color is green if not otherwise stated.

[35]Rated − by some.

[36]Rated * for northern portion; + to * in south.

[37]Rated * for northern portion; + in south.

SOIL: PREFERRED (TOLERATED)	LIGHT	BLOOM SEASON	COLOR: BLOOM/FOLIAGE[†]	HEIGHT
G,S; Ac–N; wd, humus	○ ◐ ◍	ESp	White & yellow, yellow	12″
G,S; Ac–N; wd	○ ◐ ◍	ESp	White & red-orange	14–18″
G,S; Ac–N; wd	○ ◐ ◍	M–LSp	Yellow-white	12–15″
G,S; Ac–N; wd	○ ◐ ◍	M–LSp	White & citron	12–15″
G,S; Ac–N; wd	○ ◐ ◍	MSp	White & yellow-orange	12″
G,S; Ac–N; wd	○	ESp	White & citron	6–10″
G,S; N–Al; wd	○ ◐ ◍	LSp	White & gold	12″
G,S; Ac–N; wd	○ ◐ ◍	W–ESp	White	16–18″
G,S; Ac–N; wd	○ ◐ ◍	LW	Citron & ivory	16–18″
G,S; Ac–N; wd	○ ◐ ◍	ESp	Golden yellow	12–16″
G,S; Ac–N; wd	○ ◐ ◍	MSp	White	12–16″
C,G,S; Ac–Al	◐ ◍	LSp–Su	Lilac pink/gray-green	To 6″
G,S; N–Al	◐ ◍	F	Pink or purple	To 12″
G,S; N–Al	◍	Su	Deep pink	5–10″
G,S; Ac–Al	○ ◐ ◍	Sp, Su, F	Pink or white	To 6″
C,G,S; Ac–N	○ ◍	ESp	Lemon	To 12″
C,G,S; Ac–Al	○ ◐ ◍	ESp–EW	Pink	6–12″
C(G,S); N–Al	○ ◐ ◍ ●	LSu–EF	Deep red or pink	12–18″
G; Ac–Al; wd, rich	○ ◐ ◍	Sp, Su, F	Red, cream stripe	10–15″

[38]Rated + to * in southern portion; not rated in north.
[39]Rated * for southern portion; + in north.
[40]To Zone 8 with winter protection.

	REGIONS								USDA ZONES
	PW	PCT	EP	PC	TP	GC	ST	LRGV	
Tulbaghia violacea Society garlic	*	*	+	−	−	*	*	*	8b–9(10)
Tulipa clusiana Lady tulip, candystick tulip	*	*[41]	+	*	+	−	−	−	(4)6–8
var. *chrysantha*	*	*[41]	+	*	+	−	−	−	(4)6–8
Zephyranthes atamasco Atamasco lily, wild Easter lily	*	+	+	−	+	*	+	+	7–9(10)
Z. brazosensis (*Cooperia drummondii*)	*	*	*			*	*	*	7–9(10)
Z. candida Rain lily, zephyr lily	*	*[42]	+	+[43]	+	*	*	*	7–9(10)
Z. citrina Yellow rain lily	*	*				*	*	*	7–9(10)
Z. drummondii (*Cooperia pedunculata*)			*	*		*	*	*	8–9(10)
Z. grandiflora Zephyr lily, pink rain lily	*	*	+	−	−	*	*	*	8–9(10)
Z. rosea	*	*	+	−	−	*	*	*	8b[44]–9(10)
Z. smallii (*Cooperia smallii*)						*	*	*	8b–9(10)
Habranthus robustus	*	*	+	−	+	*	*	*	8–9(10)
H. tubispathus var. *texanus* Copper lily	*	*	*	+	+	*	*	*	7–9(10)

[†]Foliage color is green if not otherwise stated.
[41]Rated * for northern portion; − in south.
[42]Rated + by some.
[43]Rated * by some.
[44]Hardy to Zone 8a with winter protection.

SOIL: PREFERRED (TOLERATED)	LIGHT	BLOOM SEASON	COLOR: BLOOM/FOLIAGE[†]	HEIGHT
C,G,S; Ac–Al	○ ◑ ●	Sp–LF	Lavender/dark green	12–30″
G,S(A,C); N–slightly Al; wd	○ ◑ ●	MSp	Rose & white	8″
G,S(A,C); slightly Al; wd	○ ◑ ●	MSp	Rose & yellow	6–10″
C,G,S; Ac–Al; moist	○ ◑ ●	LSp–ESu	White/dark green	7–12″
C,G,S; Ac–Al	○ ◑ ●	LSu–F	White/gray-green	12–18″
C,G,S; Ac–Al	○ ◑ ●	Su–F	White/dark green	To 12″
C,G,S; Ac–Al	○ ◑ ●	Su	Deep yellow/dark green	6–8″
C,G,S; Ac–Al	○ ◑ ●	MSp–F	White, red-tinged/blue-green	5–8″
G,S; Ac–N	○ ◑ ●	Sp, Su	Rose or pink/dark green	To 12″
G,S; Ac–Al	○ ◑ ●	F	Rose-red/dark green	To 12″
C,G,S; Ac–Al	○		Yellow	To 6″
C,G,S; wd; Ac–Al	○ ◑ ●	Su–F	Rose-red/dark green	8–18″
C,G,S; wd; Ac–Al	○ ◑ ●	Su–F	Yellow, coppery stripes/ dark green	6–12″

Foliage Plants and Grasses

	REGIONS								USDA
	PW	PCT	EP	PC	TP	GC	ST	LRGV	ZONES
Adiantum capillus-veneris Southern maidenhair fern, Venus'-hair fern	*	+	*	+[1]	*	*	*	+	(1)6–9
Andropogon gerardii Big bluestem	*	*	+	+	+	*	*	*	(4)6–9
Artemisia abrotanum Southernwood	+	*	*		+	–			6–9(10)
A. ludoviciana 'Silver King'		*[2]	*	*[3]	*[3]			*	(5)6–9(10)
A. schmidtiana 'Silver Mound'		+	*	*	*			*	(4)6–9(10)
Athyrium niponicum 'Pictum' Japanese painted fern	*	*	*			*			(5)6–9(10)
Chasmanthium latifolium Northern sea oats	*	*	*	*		*	*	*	(5)6–9(10)
Cyrtomium falcatum Japanese holly fern	*	*	+	–		*		*	8b–9(10)
Dryopteris erythrosora Autumn fern, Japanese shield fern	*	*		–		*			(3)6[4]–9(10)
Festuca ovina var. *glauca* Blue fescue		*	*	–	–	*	*		(4)7b–9(10)
Hosta spp. Plaintain lily	*	*	*	–	–	*	–	–	(4)6–8
H. fortunei cultivars	*	*	*	–	–	*	–	–	(4)6–8

[1]Rated + in southern portion; − in Panhandle.
[2]Rated * in northern portion; + in south.
[3]Rated + by some.
[4]Evergreen to Zone 8; deciduous farther north.

SOIL: PREFERRED (TOLERATED)	LIGHT	BLOOM SEASON	COLOR: BLOOM/FOLIAGE	HEIGHT
C,G,S; Ac–Al; mr, rich	◍ ●	None	None/clear green; deciduous	18–24″
C,G,S; Ac–Al	○	LSu–F	Tawny seedtufts/blue-green; reddish in F	3–6′
A,C,G,S; N–Al; wd	○ ◐	Su	Yellow-white/green	To 12″
A,C,G,S; N–Al; wd, poor	○ ◐	MSu	Inconspicuous/silver	24–42″
G,S; N–Al; wd, poor, light	○	MSu	Inconspicuous/silver	3–12″
G,S; Ac–Al; mr, rich	◍	None	Green marked with silver, burgundy	12″
C,G,S; N–Al; mr, tol. salt, poor drainage	○ ◐ ◍ ●	LSu–F	Tawny seed heads/green; bronze to yellow in W	2–5′
A,C,G,S; N–Al	◍ ●	None	None/dark green; semi-evergreen	24–36″
G,S; Ac–Al; mr, wd, rich	◍ ●	None	None/copper to green; evergreen	18–30″
G,S; Ac–Al; wd	○ ◐	Insignificant	Insignificant/gray-blue; evergreen	6–12″
G; Ac–N; mr, wd, rich	◐ ◍ ●	Su	Lavender-blue to white/blue-green to chartreuse	4–48″
G; Ac–N, wd, rich	◐ ◍ ●	Su	Pale lilac/blue-green, pale green to yellow; edged white, gray, cream, or green	12–24″

	PW	PCT	EP	PC	TP	GC	ST	LRGV	USDA ZONES
H. lancifolia Lance-leaf hosta	*	*	*	—	—	*	—	—	(4)6–8
H. sieboldiana	*	*	*	—	—	*	—	—	(4)6–8
× 'Elegans'	*	*	*	—	—	*	—	—	(4)6–8
× 'Frances Williams'	*	*	*	—	—	*	—	—	(4)6–8
Liriope muscari 'Big Blue' Big blue lilyturf	*	*	*	*	+	*		*	7–9(10)
'Majestic'	*	*	*	*	+	*	*	*	6–9(10)
'Silver Dragon'	*	*	*	*	+	*		*	7–9(10)
'Silvery Sunproof'	*	*	*	*	+	*		*	6–9(10)
'Variegata'	*	*	*	+	+	*		*	7–9(10)
Miscanthus sinensis Maidengrass, Eulalia grass	*	*	*	—		*			6–9
Muhlenbergia lindheimeri Lindheimer's muhly grass		*	*	*	+		*		8–9
Nolina texana Bear grass, *sacahuista*			*	*[5]	*		*	*	6–9(10)
Ophiopogon jaburan (*Liriope gigantea*) Giant lilyturf	*	*	*	*	+	*	*	*	7–9(10)
O. planiscapus 'Arabicus' Black mondo grass			*	+	+	*			(4)6–9(10)
Osmunda cinnamomea Cinnamon fern	*	*	+	—	—	*			(4)8–9
Pennisetum alopecuroides Green fountain grass		*	*	*	+	*	*		6–9
P. setaceum and cultivars Fountain grass		*	*[6]	*[5]	+	*		*	8b–9(10)

[5]Rated * for South Plains and below Cap Rock; − in Panhandle.
[6]Reliably root-hardy only in southern portion.

SOIL: PREFERRED (TOLERATED)	LIGHT	BLOOM SEASON	COLOR: BLOOM/FOLIAGE	HEIGHT
G; Ac–Al; wd, rich	◑ ◍ ●	Su	Lilac/deep green	12–18″
G; Ac–Al; wd, rich	◑ ◍ ●	Su	Pale lilac/blue-green	To 36″
G; Ac–Al; wd, rich	◑ ◍ ●	Su	Lavender/blue-green	10″
G; Ac–Al; wd, rich	◑ ◍ ●	Su	Lavender/blue-green, gold edge	To 30″
C,G; N–Ac(Al); wd	○ ◑ ◍ ●	Su	Lavender-blue, black fruit/green	12–18″
C,G; N–Ac(Al); wd	○ ◑ ◍ ●	Su	Lavender/green	12–16″
C,G; N–Ac(Al); wd	◑ ◍ ●	Su	Purple/green & white	To 10″
C,G; N–Ac(Al); wd	◑ ◍ ●	Su	Lavender/green & white	15–18″
C,G; N–Ac(Al); wd	◑ ◍ ●	Su	Lavender/yellow & green	10–12″
A,C,G,S; Ac(N,Al); wd	○ ◑ ◍	MF	Pink, ivory, buff/green, green & cream, green & yellow	5–8′
G,S(A,C); Al(Ac,N)	○ ◑	F	Tawny seed plume/green	2–5′
A,C,G,S; N–Al; wd	○ ◑ ◍	Sp	Creamy white/gray-green	18–30″
C,G; N–Ac(Al); wd	○ ◑ ◍ ●	Su	Lavender-blue, blue fruit/dark green	15–36″
C,G; Al–Ac	◑ ◍ ●	None	None/near-black	6″
G; mr to wet	◑ ◍ ●	None	None/green; cinnamon spores; golden-orange in F	3–5′
A,C,G,S; Ac–Al	☼ ○ ◑ ◍	Su; seed plumes F	Brown-black, ivory seed plumes/green	To 30″
A,C,G,S; Ac–Al	☼ ○ ◑ ◍	Su; seed plumes F	Cream, copper, rose seed plumes/green, wine-red	3–6′

	REGIONS								USDA ZONES
	PW	PCT	EP	PC	TP	GC	ST	LRGV	
Polystichum acrostichoides Christmas fern	*	*				*			(4)6[7]–9a
Rosmarinus officinalis Rosemary	+	*	*	*[8]	*	*	*	*	8[9]–9(10)
Ruta graveolens Rue	*	*	*	*[10]	+	*	*	*	(5)6–9(10)
Santolina chamaecyparissus Lavender cotton		*[11]	*	*[11]	*		*		6–9(10)
S. virens Green lavender cotton		*	*	+	*		*		7–9(10)
Schizachyrium scoparium Little bluestem	[12]	*	*	*	*	*	*	*	7–9(10)
Senecio cineraria Dusty miller	+	*	*	A[13]	+[13]		*	*	7b–9(10)
Sorghastrum nutans Indiangrass	*	*	*	*	*	*	*	*	6–9(10)
Stachys byzantina Lamb's-ears	−	+	*	*[14]	*	−	*		(5)7–9(10)
'Silver Carpet'	−	+	*	*[14]	*	−	*		(5)6–9
Thelypteris normalis Wood fern	*	*	*	−	+	*	*	*	(4)6–9(10)

[7]Reliably evergreen only in Zone 8 and south.
[8]Rated * for South Plains, with winter protection; − farther north.
[9]Zone 7b with winter protection.
[10]Rated * for South Plains and below Cap Rock; − in Panhandle.
[11]Rated * for northern portion; − in south.
[12]Another species occurs in the Piney Woods.
[13]Hardy in southern (Zone 7b) portion of PC and Davis Mountains of TP.
[14]Rated * for southern portion; + in north.
[15]50–70% shade recommended in South Plains.

SOIL: PREFERRED (TOLERATED)	LIGHT	BLOOM SEASON	COLOR: BLOOM/FOLIAGE	HEIGHT
G,S; Ac–Al; mr, rich	◐ ●	None	None/green	24–36″
A,C,G,S; Al–Ac; wd	※ ○ ◑ ◐	Intermittent	Pale lavender-blue, white/dark gray-green	To 6′
G,S; Al–N; wd, light	○ ◑	MSu	Yellow/blue-green	24–36″
A,G,S(C); Ac–Al; wd	※ ○ ◑ ◐	Su	Yellow/gray	12–24″
A,G,S(C); Ac–Al; fairly infertile	○ ◑ ◐	Su	Yellow/green	12–24″
A,C,G,S; Al(Ac–N); wd	○ ◑	Su–F	Whitish seed tufts/blue-green; red-gold in W	12–48″
S(A,C,G); Ac–Al; wd; tol. salt	○ ◑ ◐	Su	Dark yellow/silver-gray	12–24″
A,C,G,S; Al; mr, rich	○ ◑	LSu–F	Gold/blue-green	2–7′
A,C,G,S; Ac–Al; wd, poor	○ ◑ ◐[15]	Recurrent	Purple & gray/silver-gray	To 18″; foliage 3″
A,C,G,S; Ac–Al; wd, poor	○ ◑ ◐	None	None/silver-gray	3″
G,S; Al–Ac; mr, tol. poor drainage	◑ ◐ ●	None	None/green	12–36″

Mail-Order Suppliers of Perennials, Bulbs, and Old Roses

Antique Rose Emporium
RR 5, Box 143
Brenham, TX 77833-9204
800/441-0002
FAX 409/836-0928
Own-root roses adapted to the South

Bay View Gardens
Joseph Ghio
1201 Bay St.
Santa Cruz, CA 95060-4790
Louisiana iris rhizomes

Bear Creek Farms
June Stagg
16910 Loch Maree Ln.
Houston, TX 77084-3357
Daylilies and other perennials

Bluestone Perennials
7211 Middle Ridge Rd.
Madison, OH 44057-3096

Bois d'Arc Gardens
Ed and Rusty Ostheimer
P.O. Box 485
Houma, LA 70361-0485
Louisiana iris rhizomes

W. Atlee Burpee Company
300 Park Ave.
Warminster, PA 18974-4818
215/674-4900, 800/888-1447
Seeds, plants, and bulbs

Contemporary Gardens
Perry Dyer
P.O. Box 534
Blanchard, OK 73010-0534
Louisiana iris rhizomes

Cordon Bleu Farms
Brooks & Chesnik
P.O. Box 2017
San Marcos, CA 92079-2017
Louisiana iris rhizomes, spuria iris, daylilies

The Daffodil Mart
RR 3, Box 794
Gloucester, VA 23061
804/693-3966

Davids & Royston Bulb Co., Inc.
550 W. 135th St.
Gardena, CA 90248-1506
Wholesale only

Deep South Garden
Dormon Haymon and Sandy Duhon
1218 Duhon Rd.
Duson, LA 70529-8702
Louisiana iris rhizomes

Albert C. Faggard, Grower, Hybridizer, Distributor
3840 LeBleu St.
Beaumont, TX 77707-2444
Daylilies, own introductions and general listing
Catalog $1, deductible from first order

The Fragrant Path
Ed Rasmussen
P.O. Box 328
Fort Calhoun, NE 68023-0328
Seeds; emphasis on fragrant plants and cottage-garden standards

Fults Garden Shop
Bertha Fults
RR 2, Box 276
Alto, TX 75925-9669
Daylilies, own introductions and general; other perennials
Price list for self-addressed stamped envelope

Glidden Gardens
Anna Rosa Glidden
714 Benbrook Dr.
Houston, TX 77076-1902
Daylilies, own introductions and general
Price list $.50

Green Horizons
Sherry Miller
218 Quinlan St. #571
Kerrville, TX 78028-5314
210/257-5141
Texas native wildflower seed, in-state and out-of-state grown

Peggy Hammel's Garden
804 Koen Ln.
Euless, TX 76040-4730
Daylilies and perennials

Heirloom Old Garden Roses
John and Louise Clements
24062 Riverside Dr. NE
St. Paul, OR 97137-9715
503/538-1576
Own-root roses in 6-inch-deep pots

Heritage Rose Gardens
Virginia Hopper and Joyce Demits
16831 Mitchell Creek Dr.
Fort Bragg, CA 95437-8727

Hortico, Inc.
Robson Rd. RR #1
Waterdown, Ontario
Canada LOR 2H1
416/689-6984
Bare-root roses, own-root and grafted

Hughes Gardens
Tom J. Hughes
2450 N. Main St.
Mansfield, TX 76063-3941
Daylilies, own introductions and general

McClure and Zimmerman
Kenneth McClure and Mark Zimmerman
P.O. Box 368
Friesland, WI 53935-0368
414/326-4220
FAX 414/326-5769
Bulbs, corms, and tubers

Mid-America Iris Gardens
Paul W. Black
3409 Geraldine Ave.
Oklahoma City, OK 73112-2806
405/946-5743
Tall bearded, median, and arilbred irises

Native American Seed
Jan and Bill Neiman
3400 Long Prairie Rd.
Flower Mound, TX 75028-2736
214/539-0534
FAX 817/464-3987
All Texas-grown, Texas native flower and grass seed

Old House Gardens
Scott Kunst
536 Third St.
Ann Arbor, MI 48103
313/995-1486
Old garden and species narcissi and other bulbs

Park Seed Company
Cokesbury Rd.
Greenwood, SC 29647-0001
800/845-3369
Seeds, plants, and bulbs

Pickering Nurseries, Inc.
670 Kingston Rd.
Pickering, Ontario
Canada L1V 1A6
Roses

Plants of the Southwest
Gail Haggard
RR 6, Box 11A, Agua Fria
Santa Fe, NM 87501-9229
505/471-2212, 438-8888
Native flower and grass seed

Pleasure Iris Gardens
Luella Danielson
425 E. Luna Azul Dr.
Chapparal, NM 88021-7934
505/824-4299
Specialty aril and arilbred iris; some Louisianas and Japanese

Pope's Perennials
39 Highland Ave.
Gorham, ME 04038-1701
Siberian iris

Redbud Land Iris Garden
Melody and Jerry Wilhoit
RR 1, Box 141
Kansas, IL 61933-9752
All irises

Roses of Yesterday and Today
Patricia Stemler Wiley
802 Brown's Valley Rd.
Watsonville, CA 95076-0341
408/724-3537, 724-2755
FAX 408/724-1408

John Scheepers, Inc.
Jan S. Ohms
P.O. Box 700
Bantam, CT 06750-0700
203/567-0838
FAX 203/567-5323
Bulbs

Schreiners Gardens
3625 Quinaby Rd. NE
Salem, OR 97303-9720
503/393-3232, 800/525-2367
FAX 503/393-5590
Tall bearded iris

Shepherd's Garden Seeds
Renee Shepherd
30 Irene St.
Torrington, CT 06790
860/482-3638
Seed of heirloom vegetable, flower, and herb varieties

Spring Creek Daylily Garden
Mary and Eddie Gage
25150 Gosling Rd.
Spring, TX 77389-3225
Daylilies

Tarrant Daylily Garden
Inez Tarrant
7135 Highway 36
Freeport, TX 77541-9421
Daylilies, own introductions and general listing
Catalog $2, deductible from first order

Thompson & Morgan
Keith Sangster
P.O. Box 1308
Jackson, NJ 08527-0308
908/363-2225
FAX 908/363-9356
Seed

Turner Seed Company
RR 1, Box 292
Breckenridge, TX 76424-9078
817/559-2065, 800/722-8616
FAX 817/559-8076
Native grass seed

Ty Ty Plantation
P.O. Box 159
Ty Ty, GA 31795
800/972-2101
Southern-adapted bulbs

Mary Walker Bulb Company
P.O. Box 256
Omega, GA 31775-0256
912/386-1919
Crinums, lilies, iris; rarities

Wayside Gardens
1 Garden Ln.
Hodges, SC 29695-0001
800/845-1124
FAX 800/457-9712
Perennials, flowering shrubs, and bulbs

We-Du Nurseries
Dr. Richard Weaver and Rene Duval
RR 5, Box 724
Marion, NC 28752-9338
704/738-8300
Southeastern U.S. native plants

White Flower Farm
P.O. Box 50
Litchfield, CT 06759-0050
800/503-9624, FAX 860/496-1418
Perennials, flowering shrubs, and bulbs

Wildseed Farms
P.O. Box 308
Eagle Lake, TX 77434-0308
409/234-7353, 800/848-0078
FAX 409/234-7407
Seed for U.S. wildflowers and grasses, some Texas-grown

Yucca Do Nursery
John G. Fairey and Carl M. Schoenfeld
P.O. Box 655
Waller, TX 77484-0655
409/826-6363 (10 A.M. to 5 P.M., Central)
Texas and Southern native plants and world equivalents

Organizations and Periodicals

American Daffodil Society
Mary Lou Gripshover
1686 Grey Fox Trails
Milford, OH 45150-1521
513/248-9137

American Hemerocallis Society
Elly Launius, Executive Secretary
1454 Rebel Dr.
Jackson, MS 39211-6334
601/366-4362
A source of source lists

American Horticultural Society
7931 E. Boulevard Dr.
Alexandria, VA 22308-1300
703/768-5700

American Hosta Society
Robyn Duback
7802 NE 63rd St.
Vancouver, WA 98662-4348

American Iris Society
Marilyn Harlow, Membership Secretary
P.O. Box 8455
San Jose, CA 95155-8455
408/971-0444

American Rose Society
Julia Cecil, Sally Allen
P.O. Box 30,000
Shreveport, LA 71130-0030
318/938-5402

Bulletin of American Garden History
Box 397-A, Planetarium Station
New York, NY 10024

Herb Society of America
9019 Kirtland Chardon Rd.
Kirtland, OH 44094-5156
216/256-0514

Heritage Rose Foundation
Charles A. Walker, Jr., Ph.D.
1512 Gorman St.
Raleigh, NC 27606-2919
919/834-2591

Heritage Roses Group
Conrad Tips, South Central Coordinator
1007 Highland Ave.
Houston TX 77009-6514
Send self-addressed stamped envelope

National Wildflower Research Center
4801 La Crosse Ave.
Austin, TX 78739-1702
512/292-4100

Native Plant Society of Texas
Dana Tucker
P.O. Box 891
Georgetown, TX 78627-0891
512/863-9685
Twenty-nine chapters

North American Lily Society, Inc.
Dr. Robert Gilman, Executive Secretary
P.O. Box 272
Owatonna, MN 55060-0272
507/451-2170
gilman@ll.net

Old Texas Rose Newsletter
Texas Rose Rustlers
Mrs. Margaret P. Sharpe
9426 Kerrwood Ln.
Houston, TX 77080-5428
713/464-8607

Perennial Plant Association
Dr. Steven M. Still
3383 Schirtzinger Rd.
Hilliard, OH 43026-2513
614/771-8431

Seed Savers Exchange
3076 N. Winn Rd.
Decorah, IA 52101-7776
319/382-5990
Four-page color brochure available by calling

Society for Louisiana Irises
Elaine Bourque
1812 Broussard Rd. E.
Lafayette, LA 70508-7847

Southern Garden History Society
Old Salem, Inc.
Drawer F., Salem Station
Winston-Salem, NC 27108-0346
910/721-7300

The Yellow Rose
(Journal of the Dallas Historical Rose Society)
Belinda Pavageau
2827 Ava Ln.
Dallas, TX 75227-6710

International

The Royal Horticultural Society
80 Vincent Square
London SW1P 2PE
United Kingdom

Public Gardens with Perennial Plantings

Austin

Austin Nature and Science Center, 301 Nature Center Dr. Native landscape with pond; salvia and herb garden by old trail house; nature walks. Free. 512/327-8180.

Zilker Botanical Garden, Zilker Park, Barton Springs Rd. west of Lamar. Open sunrise to sunset daily. Free. 512/477-8672.

Big Bend

Chihuahuan Desert Research Institute, P.O. Box 1334, Alpine, TX 79831. Three miles south of Fort Davis on Highway 118. Greenhouse and trails. Free. 915/837-8370.

Desert Garden at Lajitas, Highway 170, 13 miles north of Study Butte. Open 9–6, 364 days a year. Free.

Judge Roy Bean Visitor Center, Loop 25 off Texas Highway 90, Langtry, TX 78871. Desert garden of the region. 8–5 daily. Free. 915/291-3340.

Corpus Christi

Corpus Christi Botanical Society, Inc., E545 South Staples, Corpus Christi, TX 78413. Open daily. $2 adults, $1.50 seniors, $1 children, under 5 free. 512/852-7875.

Dallas

Dallas Arboretum and Botanical Garden, 8525 Garland Rd., Dallas, TX 75218-4335. March–October 10–6 daily; November–February 10–5 daily. Admission $6 adults, $5 seniors, $3 children 6–12, children under 6 free. Parking $2. 214/327-8263.

Dallas Horticulture Center, 3601 Martin Luther King Blvd.; P.O. Box 152537, Dallas, TX 75315-2537. Gardens open daily. Visitor Center and Conservatory, Tues.–Sat. 10-5; Sun. 1–5. Free. 214/428-7476.

Fort Worth

Fort Worth Botanic Gardens, 3220 Botanic Garden Blvd., Fort Worth, TX 76107-3496. Open daily. Call for hours and admission fees. 817/871-7686.

Houston

Armand Bayou Nature Center, 8600 Bay Area Boulevard, 7 miles east of IH-45 in Clear Lake; P.O. Box 58828, Houston, TX 77258-8828. Wed.–Sat. 9–5, Sun. 12–dusk. Admission $2.50 adults, $1 seniors and children 5–17. 713/474-2551.

Bayou Bend Collection and Gardens, 1 Westcott St., Houston, TX 77007-77009 (off Memorial Drive). Call for opening times and admission fees. 713/639-7750.

Houston Arboretum and Nature Center, 4501
Woodway Dr., Houston, TX 77024-7774. Open 9–5
daily, grounds open 8:30–6. Free. 713/681-8433.

Mercer Arboretum and Botanical Gardens, 22306
Aldine-Westfield Rd., Humble, TX 77338-1071
(1 mile north of F.M. 1960). Open 364 days a year,
summer hours 8–7. Free. 713/443-8731.

San Antonio

San Antonio Botanical Gardens, 555 Funston Place,
San Antonio, TX 78209-6635 (north of downtown
and west of Fort Sam Houston). Open Tues.–Sun.
9–6; conservatory, 9–5. Adults $3, seniors $2,
children 3–13 $1.50. 210/821-5115.

References to Published Sources

(Quotations not listed here or otherwise identified in the text are from interviews conducted by the author.)

Part One Introduction: In Search of Regional Gardens

Voltaire, *Candide* (1759), Chapter 30.

Chapter 1. Cottage Gardens and Perennial Borders

Gertrude Jekyll, *Colour Schemes for the Flower Garden.*
Roy Genders, *The Cottage Garden and the Old-Fashioned Flowers,* p. 14.
John Feltwell, *The Naturalist's Garden,* p. 128.
William C. Welch, *Perennial Garden Color for Texas and the South,* p. 10.

Chapter 2. A Garden Sampler

Reginald Blomfield, *The Formal Garden in England,* 2d ed.

Part Two Introduction: Regionally Speaking

Elizabeth Lawrence, *A Southern Garden: A Handbook for the Middle South,* pp. xxvi–xxvii.

Chapter 3. The Prairies and Cross Timbers

James Hall, early visitor to North Central Texas, quoted by William Kennedy, *Texas: The Rise, Progress and Prospects of the Republic of Texas,* 2d ed. (Fort Worth: Molyneaux Craftsmen, 1925; reprinted from 2d ed., London, 1841).

Chapter 4. The Edwards Plateau

J. W. Benedict, "Diary of a Campaign against the Comanches," *Southwestern Historical Quarterly* 32, no. 4 (April 1929): 300–310.

Chapter 5. The Plains Country

A. W. Whipple, "Report on the Botany of the Expedition," Part 5 of "Report on the Topographical Features and Character of the Country," in *Reports of Explorations and Surveys to Ascertain the Most Practicable and Economical Route for a Railroad from the Mississippi River to the Pacific Ocean* (Washington, D.C.: War Department, 1855–1860).
Fred Rathjen, "The Physiography of the Texas Panhandle," *Southwestern Historical Quarterly* 64 (January 1961).

Chapter 6. The Trans-Pecos

Julius Froebel, *Seven Years' Travel in Central America, Northern Mexico, and the Far West of the United States* (London: R. Bentley, 1859).
Barton H. Warnock, *Wildflowers of the Big Bend Country, Texas,* p. x.

Chapter 7. The Piney Woods

J. de Córdova, letter of June 29, 1849, to Edward Smith and John Barrow, in "Account of a Journey through North-Eastern Texas as Undertaken in 1849," *East Texas Historical Journal* 8, no. 1 (March 1970): 29–91.

Chapter 8. The Gulf Coast

Francis C. Sheridan, *Galveston Island, or A Few Months off the Coast of Texas: The Journal of Francis C. Sheridan, 1839–1840,* ed. Willis W. Pratt (Austin: University of Texas Press, 1954), p. 19.

Chapter 9. The South Texas Plains

Richard Phelan and Jim Bones, *Texas Wild.*

Chapter 10. The Lower Rio Grande Valley

Phelan and Bones, *Texas Wild.*
Lawrence, *A Southern Garden,* p. 96.

Part Three Introduction: Plants That "Do" and How to Grow Them

Dewey Compton, *Southwest Gardener,* p. iii.
Josephine Von Miklos and Evelyn Fiore, *The Story, the Beauty and the Riches of the Gardener's World,* p. 12.

Chapter 11. Design with Perennials

Lewis Carroll, *Through the Looking-Glass.*

Chapter 12. Plant Selection and Growth Requirements

Allen Lacy, *Farther Afield,* p. 233.
Alfred C. Hottes, *A Little Book of Annuals,* as quoted by Peter Loewer, *The Annual Garden,* p. 4.

Chapter 13. Flowering Perennials

James Shirley Hibberd, *The Amateur's Flower Garden.*

Campanula
Pamela Harper and Frederick McGourty, *Perennials: How to Select, Grow and Enjoy.*

Ceratostigma
Lawrence, *A Southern Garden,* p. 115.

Chrysanthemum leucanthemum
Genders, *The Cottage Garden,* p. 142.

Chrysanthemum parthenium
Thomas Tusser, *A Hundredth Good Pointes of Husbandrie* (London, 1557).

Coreopsis
James Thurber, "The Secret Life of Walter Mitty," in *My World—and Welcome to It* (New York: Harcourt, Brace and Company, 1942), p. 75.

Helenium
Graham Stuart Thomas, as quoted by Emily Brown, "Some Daisies and Sunflowers," *Pacific Horticulture* 47, no. 1 (Spring 1986): 28.

Hibiscus
Lawrence, *A Southern Garden,* p. 109.

Monarda
Lawrence, *A Southern Garden,* p. 109.

Oenothera
Ruth Rogers Clausen and Nicolas H. Ekstrom, *Perennials for American Gardens,* p. 388.

Phlox
Caroline Dormon, *Natives Preferred* (Baton Rouge: Claitor's Book Store, 1965).

Chapter 14. Bulbs

Alfred F. Scheider, *Park's Success with Bulbs.*

Crinums and Amarcrinums
Lawrence, *A Southern Garden,* p. 128.

Siberian Iris
Lawrence, *A Southern Garden,* p. 231.

Leucojum
Lawrence, *A Southern Garden,* pp. 36–37.

Lilium
Martyn Rix and Roger Phillips, *The Bulb Book,* p. 209.
Genders, *The Cottage Garden,* p. 229.

Chapter 15. Foliage Plants for the Flower Garden

Lawrence, *A Southern Garden,* p. 4.
Gertrude Jekyll, *Colour Schemes for the Flower Garden.*

Stachys byzantina
Harper and McGourty, *Perennials.*

Chapter 16. An Old Rose Sampler

Vita Sackville-West, as quoted by Graham Stuart Thomas, *The Old Shrub Roses.*

'Madame Isaac Pereire'
Thomas, *The Old Shrub Roses.*

'Old Blush'
Thomas, *The Old Shrub Roses.*

Noisette Roses
Thomas, *The Old Shrub Roses.*

Chapter 17. Companion Plants for Perennial Gardens

Lawrence, *A Southern Garden,* pp. 4, 22, 40, 86.

Chapter 18. Techniques: Smart "Dirt-Gardening"

Christopher Brickell, ed., *The Encyclopedia of Gardening Techniques* (New York: Exeter Books, 1984).
"Six Organic Rules" paraphrased from Malcolm C. Beck, *The Garden-Ville Method,* p. 3.

Bibliography

Ajilvsgi, Geyata. *Wild Flowers of the Big Thicket, East Texas, and Western Louisiana*. College Station and London: Texas A&M University Press, 1979.

———. *Wildflowers of Texas*. Bryan: Shearer Publishing, 1984.

Anderson, Edgar. *Plants, Man and Life*. Berkeley and Los Angeles: University of California Press, 1967.

Bailey, Liberty Hyde, and Ethel Zoe Bailey. *Hortus Third: A Concise Dictionary of Plants Cultivated in the United States and Canada*. New York: MacMillan Publishing Co., 1976.

Beales, Peter. *Classic Roses: An Illustrated Encyclopedia and Growers' Manual of Old Roses, Shrub Roses and Climbers*. New York: Holt, Rinehart and Winston, 1985.

Beck, Malcolm C. *The Garden-Ville Method*. San Antonio: Garden-Ville (Route 3, Box 210-TA, San Antonio, TX 78128), 1988. 2d ed., 1993.

Berrall, Julia S. *The Garden: An Illustrated History*. New York: Viking Press, 1966.

Blomfield, Reginald. *The Formal Garden in England*. 3d ed. London: Macmillan and Co., 1901.

Bomar, George W. *Texas Weather*. Austin: University of Texas Press, 1983.

Bowles, E. A. *A Handbook of Narcissus*. London: Waterstone and Co., 1985.

Caillet, Marie, and Joseph K. Mertzweiller, eds. *The Louisiana Iris: The History and Culture of Five Native American Species and Their Hybrids*. Waco: Texas Gardener Press, 1988.

Cannatella, Mary Michael, and Rita Emigh Arnold. *Plants of the Texas Shore: A Beachcomber's Guide*. College Station: Texas A&M University Press, 1985.

Clausen, Ruth Rogers, and Nicolas H. Ekstrom. *Perennials for American Gardens*. New York: Random House, 1989.

Compton, Dewey. *Southwest Gardener*. Houston: Gulf Coast Press, 1961.

Coon, Nelson, with Georgianne Giffen. *The Complete Book of Violets*. South Brunswick and New York: A. S. Barnes and Co., 1977.

Correll, Donovan Stewart, and Marshall Conring Johnston. *Manual of the Vascular Plants of Texas*. Contributions from Texas Research Foundation: A Series of Botanical Studies, edited by Cyrus Longworth Lundell, vol. 6. Richardson: University of Texas at Dallas, 1979.

Cox, Paul W., and Patty Leslie. *Texas Trees: A Friendly Guide*. San Antonio: Corona Publishing Co., 1988.

Damrosch, Barbara. *The Garden Primer*. New York: Workman Publishing Co., 1988.

———. *Theme Gardens*. New York: Workman, 1982.

Davis, Ben Arthur. *The Southern Garden*. Philadelphia and New York: J. B. Lippincott Co., 1971.

de Bray, Lys. *Lys de Bray's Manual of Old-Fashioned Shrubs*. Newbury Park, Calif.: Haynes Publications, 1986.

Drew, John K. *Pictorial Guide to Hardy Perennials*. Kalamazoo, Mich.: Merchants Publishing Co., 1984.

Duffield, Mary Rose, and Warren D. Jones. *Plants for Dry Climates: How to Select, Grow and Enjoy*. Tucson: HPBooks, 1981.

The Encyclopedia of Organic Gardening. Emmaus, Pa.: Rodale Press, 1978.

Enquist, Marshall. *Wildflowers of the Texas Hill Country*. Austin: Lone Star Botanical, 1987.

Feltwell, John. *The Naturalist's Garden*. Topfield, Mass.: Salem House Publishers, 1987.

Fisk, Jim. *Clematis, the Queen of Climbers*. London: Cassell, 1989.

Genders, Roy. *The Cottage Garden and the Old-Fashioned Flowers*. New ed. London: Pelham Books, 1983.

————. *Miniature Bulbs*. New York: St. Martin's Press, 1961.

Gould, Frank W. *Texas Plants: A Checklist and Ecological Summary*. Bryan: Texas Agricultural Experiment Station (Publication MP-585 Revised), 1969.

Graf, Alfred B. *Exotica: Pictorial Cyclopedia of Exotic Plants*. Fairfield, N.J.: A. Horowitz and Son, 1976.

Ham, Hal. *South Texas Wildflowers*. Illustrated by Martha Bruce. Kingsville: Texas A&I University, 1984.

Haring, P. A., ed. *Modern Roses 9: The International Checklist of Roses in Cultivation or of Historical or Botanical Importance*. Shreveport: American Rose Society, 1986.

Harper, Pamela, and Frederick McGourty. *Perennials: How to Select, Grow and Enjoy*. Tucson: HPBooks, 1985.

Hatch, Stephen L., Kanchepuram N. Gandhi, and Larry E. Brown. *Checklist of the Vascular Plants of Texas*. Texas A&M University Publication No. 1655. July 1990.

Hazeltine, Cheryl, and Joan Filvaroff. *The Central Texas Gardener*. College Station: Texas A&M University Press, 1980.

Hill, Madalene, and Gwen Barclay with Jean Hardy. *Southern Herb Growing*. Fredericksburg: Shearer Publishing, 1987.

Horan, Anne, Barbara Levitt, and Robert G. Mason, eds. *The Time-Life Gardener's Guide: Perennials*. Alexandria, Va.: Time-Life Books, 1988.

Horton, Alvin, and James McNair. *All about Bulbs*. San Francisco: Ortho Books, 1986.

Hottes, Alfred C. *A Little Book of Annuals*. New York: A. T. De La Mare Co., 1925.

Jekyll, Gertrude. *Colour Schemes for the Flower Garden*. Revised by Graham Stuart Thomas. Salem, N.H.: Ayer Co., 1983.

Jekyll, Gertrude, and Edward Mawley. *Roses for English Gardens*. Revised by Graham Stuart Thomas. Salem, N.H.: Ayer Co., 1983.

Johnston, Marshall C. *The Vascular Plants of Texas: A List, Up-dating the Manual of the Vascular Plants of Texas*. 2d ed. January 1990.

Kawase, Makota. "A Dream Chemical to Aid Propagation of Woody Plants." *The Ohio Report*, January–February 1981, pp. 8–10.

Kowalchik, Claire, and William H. Hylton, eds. *Rodale's Illustrated Encyclopedia of Herbs*. Emmaus, Pa.: Rodale Press, 1987.

Lacy, Allen. *Farther Afield*. New York: Farrar, Straus & Giroux, 1981.

Lawrence, Elizabeth. *A Southern Garden: A Handbook for the Middle South*. Rev. ed. Chapel Hill, N.C.: University of North Carolina Press, 1984.

Loewer, Peter. *The Annual Garden: Flowers, Foliage, Fruits, and Grasses for One Summer Season*. Emmaus, Pa.: Rodale Press, 1988.

Loughmiller, Campbell and Lynn. *Texas Wildflowers: A Field Guide*. Austin: University of Texas Press, 1984.

Mason, Hamilton. *Your Garden in the South*. Princeton, N.J.: D. Van Nostrand Co., 1961.

Meikle, Catherine E., ed. *Modern Roses 8: The International Checklist of Roses*. Harrisburg, Pa.: McFarland Co., 1980.

Monroe, W. E., ed. *Hemerocallis Check List: July 1, 1957, to July 1, 1973*. Baton Rouge: American Hemerocallis Society, 1973.

———. *Hemerocallis Check List: July 1, 1973 to December 31, 1983*. Baton Rouge: American Hemerocallis Society, 1984.

Nokes, Jill. *How to Grow Native Plants of Texas and the Southwest*. Austin: Texas Monthly Press, 1986.

Ortloff, Henry Stuart. *A Garden Bluebook of Annuals and Biennials*. New York: Doubleday, Doran & Co., 1924.

Perrero, Laurie and Louis. *The World of Tropical Flowers*. Miami: Windward Publishing, 1976.

Phelan, Richard. *Texas Wild: The Land, Plants, and Animals of the Lone Star State*. New York: E. P. Dalton and Co., 1976.

Phillips, Roger, and Martyn Rix. *Roses: Over 1400 Roses in Full-Color Photographs*. New York: Random House, 1988.

Rix, Martyn, and Roger Phillips. *The Bulb Book: A Photographic Guide to over 800 Hardy Bulbs*. London: Pan Books, 1981.

Rose, Francis L., and Russell W. Strandtmann. *Wildflowers of the Llano Estacado*. Dallas: Taylor Publishing Co., 1986.

Scheider, Alfred F. *Park's Success with Bulbs*. Greenwood, S.C.: George W. Park Seed Co., 1981.

Scott, George Harmon. *Bulbs: How to Select, Grow and Enjoy*. Tucson: HPBooks, 1982.

Scruggs, Mrs. Gross R., and Margaret All Scruggs, eds. *Gardening in the South and West*. Garden City, N.Y.: Garden City Books, 1947.

Simpson, Benny. *A Field Guide to Texas Trees*. Austin: Texas Monthly Press, 1988.

Sperry, Neil. *Neil Sperry's Complete Guide to Texas Gardening*. Dallas: Taylor Publishing Co., 1982.

Still, Steven M. *Herbaceous Ornamental Plants*. Champaign, Ill.: Stipes Publishing Co., 1988.

Stout, A. B. *Daylilies: The Wild Species and Garden Clones, Both Old and New, of the Genus Hemerocallis*. Updated by Darrell Apps. Millwood, N.Y.: Sagapress, 1986.

Swindells, Philip. *Cottage Gardening in Town and Country*. London: Ward Lock, 1986.

Taylor, Norman. *Taylor's Guide to Annuals*. Revised and edited by Gordon P. De Wolf, Jr. New York: Houghton Mifflin Co., 1986.

———. *Taylor's Guide to Bulbs*. Revised and edited by Gordon P. De Wolf, Jr. New York: Houghton Mifflin Co., 1986.

———. *Taylor's Guide to Ground Covers, Vines and Grasses*. Revised and edited by Gordon P. De Wolf, Jr. New York: Houghton Mifflin Co., 1987.

———. *Taylor's Guide to Perennials*. Revised and edited by Gordon P. De Wolf, Jr. New York: Houghton Mifflin Co., 1986.

———. *Taylor's Guide to Roses.* Revised and edited by Gordon P. De Wolf, Jr. New York: Houghton Mifflin Co., 1986.

———. *Taylor's Guide to Shrubs.* Revised and edited by Gordon P. De Wolf, Jr. New York: Houghton Mifflin Co., 1987.

Terrell, Mrs. Arthur P., ed. *A Garden Book for Houston and the Gulf Coast.* 3d ed. Houston: Pacesetter Press, 1975.

Thomas, Graham Stuart. *The Old Shrub Roses.* Rev. ed. London: J. M. Dent and Sons, 1980.

Verey, Rosemary. *Classic Garden Design.* New York: Congdon and Weed, 1984.

———. *The Garden in Winter.* Boston and Toronto: Little, Brown and Company, 1988.

Von Miklos, Josephine, and Evelyn Fiore. *The Story, the Beauty and the Riches of the Gardener's World.* New York: Random House, 1969.

Warnock, Barton H. *Wildflowers of the Big Bend Country, Texas.* Alpine: Sul Ross State University, 1970.

———. *Wildflowers of the Davis Mountains and the Marathon Basin, Texas.* Alpine: Sul Ross State University, 1977.

———. *Wildflowers of the Guadalupe Mountains and the Sand Dune Country, Texas.* Alpine: Sul Ross State University, 1974.

Wasowski, Sally, and Julie Ryan. *Landscaping with Native Texas Plants.* Austin: Texas Monthly Press, 1985.

Welch, William C. *Perennial Garden Color for Texas and the South.* Dallas: Taylor Publishing Co., 1989.

Whitcomb, Carl E. *Know It and Grow It.* Rev. ed. Stillwater, Okla.: Lacebark Publications, 1985.

Whiteside, Katherine. *Antique Flowers: A Guide to Using Old-Fashioned Species in Contemporary Gardens.* New York: Villard Books, 1989.

Williamson, John. *Perennial Gardens: A Practical Guide to Home Landscaping.* New York: Harper and Row, 1988.

Williamson, Joseph F., ed. *Sunset Western Garden Book.* Menlo Park, Calif.: Lane Magazine and Book Co., 1974.

Index

Boldfaced page numbers refer to major discussions of a plant.

Compost, 292–293

Compton, Dewey, 100

Concan, Tex., 47

Coneflower, 12, 45, 49; cutleaf (*Rudbeckia*), **179**, 326–327; pink or purple (*Echinacea*), 19, 44, 58, 75, 90, III, **141–142**, 314–315; prairie (*Ratibida*), 109, **177–178**, 325–327

Confederate jasmine, 90

Confederate rose, **157**

Consolida. See Larkspur

Container-growing, 103

Cooperia species, **235–236**, 344–345. *See also* Rain lily

Copper lily, **236**, 344–345. *See also* Rain lily

Coralberry, 282

Coral honeysuckle, 90, 279

Coral plant. *See* Firecracker plant

Coral vine, 8, 21, 94, 279. *See also* Queen's wreath

Cordia bossieri, 83, 90

Córdova, J. de, 73

Coreopsis, II–12, 17, 19, 29, 49, 50, 109, 215; *Coreopsis* species and cultivars, 278, **136–137**, 312–315

Corm: definition of, 196

Corn, 8, 23

Cornflower, 9, 29, 109, 278

Corn poppy, 49

Cornus species. *See* Dogwood

Corpus Christi, Tex., 81–85, 261; Corpus Christi Botanical Gardens, 82–83

Correll, Donovan Stewart, 114

Cosmos, 9, 21, 22, 28, 29, 51, 56, 57, 109, III, 151, 215, 284; *Cosmos* species, 151

Cottage gardens: at Antique Rose Emporium, 10–15; English, 5–7, 11, 64, 78–80, 107, 277; history of, 5–7; prairie style, 15–16; urbane, 16–17; with Victorian cottage, 17–18

Cotton plant, 19

Cox, Paul, 29, 30, 124–125

Crabapple, 281

Cranfills Gap, Tex., 4, 198

Crape myrtle, 9, 24, 80, 81, 85, 90, 91, 283

Crassulaceae, 185

Creeping juniper, 281

Creosote bush, 66

× *Crinodonna. See* × *Amarcrinum*

Crinum lily, 9, 17, 18, 19, 21, 53, 108, 109, 196; *Crinum* species and hybrids, **200–204**, 332–335

Crocosmia, 78; *Crocosmia* species and hybrids, 183, **204–205**, 334–335. *See also* Montbretia

Crocus, 51

Cross Timbers. *See* Prairies and Cross Timbers

Crossvine, 279

Croton, 84

Crown division, 294

Cultivar: defined, 114

Cuphea, 12, 29, 31, 45, 47; *Cuphea micropetala*, 21, 109, **138**, 314–315

Curry plant, 18

Cutleaf daisy, 58

Cuttings: of old roses, 257–258; propagation by, 294–295

Cycad, 82, 83

Cyclamen species, 51

Cypress, 54, 55, 56

Cyrtomium falcatum, **244**, 346–347

Daffodil, 78, 89, 109, 195, **226–231**, 237, 301, 340–343. *See also* Narcissus; Peruvian daffodil

Dahlia, 20, 57

Daisy: blackfoot, 109, III, **166–167**, 322–323; cutleaf, 58; Engelmann's, 64; English, 109, 234; Gerber, 85, 94, 106, **145–146**, 316–317; Gloriosa, **178**, 326–327; in Gulf Coast region, 78; lazy, 18; in Lower Rio Grande Valley, 93; Marguerite, 132; May, **131**, 312–313; medallion, III; Michaelmas, 127, 128; oxeye, **131–132**, 312–313; in perennial borders, 20; at San Antonio Botanical Center, 28, 29; Shasta, 10, 17, 56, 57, 78, 85, 106, 131–132, **133–134**, 312–313; Tahoka, III, 278; in Trans-Pecos, 64, 69; wild, 59, 60

Dakota verbena, 190

Dalea, 91; *Dalea greggii*, 27

Dallas, Tex., 15–18, 78, 105, 109, 125, 131, 134, 135, 144, 145, 157, 199, 210, 217, 219, 238, 260, 273, 274, 285; Dallas Arboretum, 8; Dallas Civic Garden Center, 250

Dallas County, 198

Dalmatian bellflower, **130**, 310–311

Damping off, 299

Datura wrightii, 59–60

Davis, Bob, 221, 223

Davis Mountains, 63, 68, 69–71, 177, 191

Davis Mountain sage, 70

Daylily, **149–155**, 316–317; aesthetic concerns in selection of, 151; bareroot, 152; bloom forms of, 151; bloom season of, 153–155; bloom size of, 151; as companion plant for Louisiana irises, 215; companion plants for, 151; in cottage gardens, 17; "diurnal," 151; dormant, 151; evergreen, 151; in Gulf Coast region, 78; hardiness of, 150–151; height of, 151, 153–155; "nocturnal," 151; in North Central Texas, 109; in Plains Country, 56, 57, 59, 61; planting of, 151–152; potted, 152; in Prairies and Cross Timbers, 45, 46; at San Antonio Botanical Center, 28, 29; semi-evergreen, 151; in shade gardens, 24; theme garden of, 108; varieties of, 44, 49, 150, 153–155; widespread use of, 220

Deadheading, 299

Deciduous trees and shrubs, 277, 281–283

De Graaf, Jan, 223

Delphinium, 109; *Delphinium* species, 278

Del Rio, Tex., 87

Desert gardens, 66–71

Desert willow, 30, 283

Design with perennials: balance of perennial and annuals in garden, 105; bloom season, 107; color, 105, 110, III; garden seasons, 108–110; myths about perennials, 106; planning, III; setting and, 107; site

Sweet William, 57, 138, **139**
"Swept yard," 8–9
Symphoricarpos orbiculata, 282

Tagetes species. *See* Marigold
Tahoka daisy, 111, 278
Tall bearded iris, 211
Tallgrass prairie, 41
Tamarisk, 64
Tansy aster, 56, 58
Tasajillo, 67
Tawny daylily, **149**, 150, 154–155, 316–317
Taylor, James, 175
Tazetta narcissus, 51, 89, **229**, 230, 342–343
Tea roses, 254, 256, 267, 268, **269–270**. *See also* Hybrid Tea Roses
Tecoma stans, 59, 94, 96, **187**, 328–329
Terraces, 29–30, 48
Texas A&M University, 13, 44, 134, 287
Texas Agricultural Experiment Station, 97, 289
Texas Agricultural Extension Service, 35, 125, 288, 303
Texas ash, 65
Texas bluebell, 21, 56, 57, 58, 101, **142–143**, 316–317
Texas lantana, **159**, 320–321. *See also* Lantana
Texas mountain laurel, 24, 281
Texas Natural Heritage Program, 41, 102
Texas pistachio, 16, 65
Texas redbud, 281
Texas sage. *See* Cenizo
"Texas star" hibiscus, 19
Texas Tech University, 130
"Texas virgin's bower," 135
Texas whitebud, 24, 281
Thelesperma filiofolium, 137
Thelypteris normalis. *See* river fern; wood fern
Thomas, Graham Stuart, 259, 262, 265
Threadleaf coreopsis, 314–315
Threeleaf barberry, 26
Thrift, 18, 19, 20, 24, 109, 112, **173–174**, 324–325

Thrips, 255, 298–299
Thryallis glauca. *See* *Galphimia glauca*
Thurber, Bonnie, 198
Thurber, James, 136
Thyme, 16, 51
Tickseed. *See* Coreopsis
Tiger lily, 44, 46, **223**, 338–339
Tofanari, Sirio, 24
Tomato, 8, 23
Tomball, Tex., 27
Tombstone, Ariz., 271
Torch lily. *See* Red-hot poker
Torenia, 22; *Torenia fournieri*, 279
Torrey yucca, 67
Touch-me-not, 22, 23, 279
Tracy, Tex., 9
Tradescant, John (the Younger), 188
Tradescantia species, 22, **188**, 328–329. *See also* Spiderwort
Trailing lantana, **159**, 320–321. *See also* Lantana
Trans-Pecos: description of, 63–64; Glass Mountains shrub garden in, 64–66; irrigation in, 68; Lajitas Museum and Desert Garden in, 66–68; Quinta Pintada desert mountain garden in, 64, 69–71; rainfall in, 63, 70; soils of, 63, 68, 70–71, 116; vegetational areas map, 39
Transplanting, 300
Trees: as companion plants for perennial gardens, 277, 281, 283; ornamental, 15, 16, 19, 53; small, 281. *See also specific trees*
Treflan, 296
Trellised roses, 78, 79
Trillium, 103
Tritoma. See *Kniphofia*
Trompetilla. *See* Firecracker bush
Tropical gingers, 21, 22, 23
Tropical hibiscus, 80, 81, 93, 94
Tropical milkweed. *See* Bloodflower
Tropical plants, 75, 81–82, 83, 85, 89, 90, 93, 94, 96, 106
Tropical plumbago, 89, 91, 94, 96, **176**, 326–327
Trumpet vine, 22, 84, 90, 279

Tuberous roots: definition of, 196
Tubers, 196, 332–345
Tube vervain, 190, 330–331
Tulbaghia violacea, **233**, 344–345. *See also* Society garlic
Tulip, 16, 17, 53, 101, 195, 196; *Tulipa* species and cultivar, **234–235**, 344–345
Tulipán del monte, 156–157, 318–319
"Turkey-foot," 247
Turk's cap, 16, 57, 59, 60, 90, 93, 106, 114, **165–166**, 322–323
Turk's cap lily, **222**, 338–339
Turner, Elaine and Ted, 83–84
Tusser, Thomas, 132
Tweedy, Malcolm, 64
Tyler Municipal Rose Garden, 274

Ungnadia speciosa, 281
University of British Columbia Botanical Garden, 45
University of Illinois at Urbana-Champaign, 127; Herbarium, 53
University Park, Dallas, 16–17
Upright, A. C. and Janice, 74–75
USDA hardiness zones, xii, 36–39, 304–305

Van Sant, Mitzi, 7, 255, 262
Vaquelinia angustifolia, 58–59
Variegated Chinese privet, 280
Variegated privet, 80, 81
Variety names, 114
Vegetational areas map, 39
Venus'-hair fern, **244**, 346–347
Verbena, 9, 10, 13, 17, 19, 29, 31, 80, 81, 85, 89, 109, 111; *Verbena* species and cultivars, 19, 26, 56, 58, 90, 94, **189–190**, 328–331. *See also* Sand verbena
Verbenaceae, 158–159, 189–190
Verey, Rosemary, 7
Veronica, 29; *Veronica repens*, 53
Versailles gardens, 107
Vervain, 190, 330–331. *See also* Verbena
Viburnum opulus, 282
Victoria, Queen, 253
Victoria, Tex., 87